THE CHRONIC
CRISIS IN
PSYCHOLOGICAL
MEASUREMENT
AND ASSESSMENT

THE CHRONIC CRISIS IN PSYCHOLOGICAL MEASUREMENT AND ASSESSMENT

A HISTORICAL SURVEY

Scott T. Meier
SUNY Buffalo

Academic Press
San Diego   New York   Boston   London   Sydney   Tokyo   Toronto

This book is printed on acid-free paper.

Copyright © 1994 by ACADEMIC PRESS, INC.
All Rights Reserved.

Academic Press, Inc.
A Division of Harcourt Brace & Company
525 B Street, Suite 1900, San Diego, California 92101-4495

United Kingdom Edition published by
Academic Press Limited
24-28 Oval Road, London NW1 7DX

Library of Congress Cataloging-in-Publication Data

Meier, Scott T., [DATE]
    The chronic crisis in psychological measurement and assessment : a historical survey / by Scott T. Meier.
        p.   cm.
    Includes bibliographical references and indexes.
    ISBN 0-12-488440-7
    1. Psychological tests.   2. Behavioral assessment.
    3. Psychological tests--History.   4. Behavioral assessment-History.
    I. Title.
    BF176.M45   1994
    150'.28'7--dc20   94-14626
                                                            CIP

PRINTED IN THE UNITED STATES OF AMERICA
94   95   96   97   98   99   QW   9   8   7   6   5   4   3   2   1

To Katherine Beauty

CONTENTS

PREFACE

Discussions about the adequacy of psychological measurement and assessment can quickly become controversial. When I have presented portions of this manuscript to other psychologists, I have been surprised at their strong reactions. An anonymous reviewer had this to say after reading an earlier version:

> So much for what the paper says. I am even more concerned about what it implies; namely, that we should cease and desist because applied psychological measurement has flaws. But then how shall we choose pilots, nuclear power plant operators, CIA agents, and air traffic controllers? This is persistently ignored by academic critics such as Mischel, Kagan, and the author. Applied measurement is the primary contribution that psychology has made to society. The author is right that . . . more progress is desirable and necessary; but many academics who are hostile, in principle, to the concept of individual differences will use this paper as an excuse to throw the baby out with the dirty bath water.

Debates about the usefulness of criticism of psychological testing are longstanding: Even early psychologists such as Cattell and Jastrow disagreed on this issue (Cronbach, 1992). Let me make it clear that I do not believe that use of contemporary tests should cease. On the contrary, I share the view that "psychological tests often provide the fairest and most accurate method of making important decisions" (K. R. Murphy & Davidshofer, 1988, p. xii).

My first purpose, then, is to provide a historical survey of relevant measurement and assessment concepts. I do not delve into intimate details and complexities, but trace measurement and assessment controversies over time and across psychological domains. This approach produced an overview, a broad picture of how psychological measurement and assessment have evolved. I present this perspective in Chapters 1 through 5, which contain descriptions and interpretations of measurement issues that have been important over the lifespan of psychological science.

My second goal is to expand discussion of the possible directions of measurement and assessment beyond those typically considered. Chapter 6 contains a summary of traditional approaches along with newer concepts and procedures. In Chapter 7 I attempt to integrate the major themes that emerge from the historical survey with the ultimate purpose of reviewing and proposing new directions. I have at times been more speculative than careful, in the hope that other psychologists and students may be encouraged to experiment with innovative approaches. These speculations may appear naive to some, but I think it is important that more theorists, researchers, and practitioners begin thinking about measurement and assessment.

Graduate students are one group crucial to the creation and sustenance of innovation in measurement and assessment. My experience with some graduate students is that instead of referencing reading material by author, they refer to THE BOOK, as in "THE BOOK says this." Matarazzo (1987) observed that psychological knowledge is largely transmitted by the textbooks employed in psychology courses. I think it is important to expand the scope of topics typically presented in psychological measurement and assessment texts, and I offer this book as a complement to those works. At the same time, I attempt to present this material as simply as possible. Too much of measurement is uncommunicable because of its complexity. At the risk of offending some psychometricians, I have emphasized the conceptual, not the statistical; much of the data presentation involves simple frequency distributions and visual displays. Cronbach (1991) stated that "one need not be a skilled mathematician to advance methodology; you call upon an expert once you know what to call for. The crucial contribution—which mathematicians cannot be expected to make—is an adequate formal description of an interesting set of social or psychological events" (p. 398). My goal has been to approach the problems of measurement and assessment from the perspective of psychological theory. I hope to reconnect measurement with substantive theory to create "better, richer, thicker descriptions from which to generate deeper conceptions and, most importantly, better questions" (Snow & Wiley, 1991, p. 6).

I have also been surprised by the relative dearth of sources describing the history of nonintellectual testing. Most measurement and assessment texts present a bit of history, and a few excellent book chapters and articles exist (e.g., Dahlstrom, 1985; Dawis, 1992). But I could find few sources that systematically examined the evolution of measurement and assessment to the extent that, for example, Boring (1957) did with experimental psychology. Perhaps the relative youth of psychological measurement—barely 100 years old—is a partial explanation. One consequence of this gap is that accounts of major concepts and procedures tend to be scattered throughout the literature. For example, I found different sets of references discussing the problem of social desirability in the clinical and industrial-organizational literatures. One of my goals has been to retrieve and reorganize seemingly unrelated material around long-standing measurement issues. At the same time, I expect that readers familiar with the measurement and assessment literatures will find portions of the presentation repetitive and will also find significant omissions. I hope such readers take the opportunity to educate me.

Many historical references quoted in this book contain sexist language, naming generic persons in terms of male pronouns. Rather than have a book of *sic*ked quotes, those references were left unaltered, with this disclaimer as an explanation. Also, I have referred to persons interested in measurement and assessment exclusively as psychologists. Professionals in areas such as sociology, economics, social work, and psychiatry have obviously been interested in and made important contributions to measurement and assessment.

I thank the large number of faculty and students who read portions of this manuscript and/or provided helpful material, including Drs. Stan Cramer, Jim Hansen, LeAdelle Phelps, Robert Rossberg, and Felicia Wilczenski. I am grateful to Robert Davis for his excellent graphics work. I thank Dean Hugh Petrie and Chairperson S. David Farr for approving a sabbatical leave that made possible the integration of this material into a book. Thanks to the underfunded SUNY Buffalo Lockwood Library, and especially, Susan Palmer, the latest and longest suffering graduate assistant to assist in the gathering of needed journals and books. Finally, I give special thanks to the book's editor, Nikki Fine, and her assistant, Diane Scott; to Mike Rutherford, the book's production editor; to Dr. Doug Schneidt and Dr. David Steinweg, who reviewed early chapter drafts; to Dr. Susan R. Davis, who provided a clinician's reaction to much of the material; and to the book's reviewers, Dr. J. Ronald Gentile and other anonymous sources.

To a significant extent, this book wrote itself. Reading publications such as Danziger's (1990) *Constructing the Subject*, Embretson's (1985) *Test Design: Developments in Psychology and Psychometrics*, Nelson and Hayes's (1986) *Con-*

ceptual Foundations of Behavioral Assessment, and Snow and Wiley's (1991) *Improving Inquiry in Social Science* has been like opening a chest containing many treasures. My final goal for this book is that it will communicate a sense of the interest and fascination that some psychologists find in measurement and assessment.

Scott T. Meier

1 HISTORY

THE SEEDS OF CONFLICT

Unknown to many outside the profession, a small war is waging among American psychologists that is the result of tensions existing since the beginning of scientific psychology. The war is between those who primarily identify themselves as scientists and those who identify themselves as practitioners. The numbers and influence of practicing or applied psychologists—whose specialty areas include clinical, counseling, school, and industrial or organizational psychology—have grown dramatically during psychology's brief history. Fretz and Simon (1992) noted that the previous division between scientists and practitioners "seems to have become more of a chasm" (p. 31). Scientific psychologists' alarm (e.g., Howell, 1993) at the practitioners' growing influence in the American Psychological Association (APA), the major United States psychological organization, recently led to the formation of an entirely new group, the American Psychological Society.

One of the most puzzling aspects of this split is the groups' inability to recognize that for both to survive, they need one another (cf. Danziger, 1990). Throughout psychology's history, financial support for scientific psychology (typically housed in academic departments in colleges and university) has often been provided on the premise that the work of such scientists would ultimately improve the lives of individuals. Similarly, credibility for the interventions implemented by practicing psychologists has often been based on the belief that those interventions were determined through scientific methods (e.g., VanZandt, 1990). Dawis (1992) noted, for example, that early clinicians, armed with psychological tests, "had a technology for client assessment that had the decided appearance of professionalism . . . [and] the scientific substance as well" (p. 11). Thus, despite their different goals, the science and practice of psychology complement one another. Most psychologists recognize the importance of meshing the two identities, as witnessed by the adoption by some specialties of a scientist–practitioner training model in which graduate psychology students are trained in both research and practice skills (Barlow, Hayes, & Nelson, 1984; Gelso, 1979). That integration, however, has never been very successful: relatively few psychologists conduct research beyond that required in graduate school; relatively few express interest in psychological science jobs at the beginning or end of the graduate school career; and very few clinical practitioners

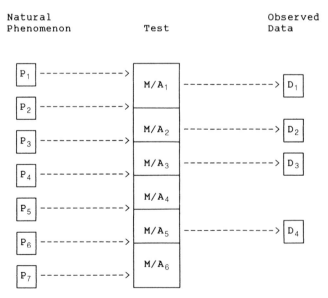

FIGURE 1   The function of measurement: Representing a phenomenon as data. M/A refers to measurements and assessments (e.g., M/A_1–M/A_6) that may be employed individually or as an aggregate to transform natural phenomenon (P_1–P_7) into data (D_1–D_4).

base their work on research information (Barlow, 1981; Herman, 1993; Joint Commission on Mental Health and Illness, 1961; National Institute of Mental Health, 1976).

The struggle between those who wish to be scientific and those who wish to be socially relevant has had profound effects on this book's subject, psychological measurement. Measurement is usually defined as the process of assigning numbers to objects according to agreed upon rules (e.g., Stevens, 1951). The assignment process is the crucial aspect of the definition. Krantz, Luce, Suppes, and Tversky (1971) defined measurement as assigning numbers to objects "in such a way the properties of the attributes are faithfully represented as numerical properties" (p. 1). In other words, data that result from the measurement process should reflect the differences inherent in the objects themselves. Psychological measurements are typically produced by tests, systematic procedures for observing behavior and describing it with a numerical scale or category system (Cronbach, 1970). As shown in Figure 1, psychological tests—measurements and assessments—provide a method of describing a natural phenomenon, of transforming phenomenon into data. As a result, the data resulting from any measurement procedure reflect only some part of the characteristics of the phenomena under examination.

The Desire to Be Scientific

In 1992, the APA marked the 100th anniversary of its annual convention. Some evidence suggests that the first APA convention was organized to help Joseph Jastrow provide examples of psychological measurement for an exhibit at the world's fair (Cronbach, 1992). In 1979 psychologists celebrated the 100th anniversary of the opening of Wundt's laboratory in Germany, an event often cited as the birth of scientific psychology. Organized scientific psychology is barely a century old. The fact that psychology is a young science must be emphasized in any study of the history of psychological measurement.

Although psychology came to be more formally recognized as a scientific discipline in the late 1800s, events were taking place earlier in that century that shaped the early practices and procedures of scientific psychology. The most important events were related to developments in physiology, biology, and astronomy.

The Model of Physiology.   In the 1800s, success in research and measurement of physiological processes provided examples of ideas and techniques that psychologists could apply in their work. Wundt produced what some considered the first psychology book, *Physiological Psychology* (Heidbreder, 1933), describing how psychological experiments could be patterned after physiological ones: the scientist employs a controllable stimulus and records the objective responses of subjects. Similarly, Helmholtz provided practical demonstrations in his research on the eye and ear, demonstrating that the experimental methods and measurement techniques of physiology and the natural sciences could be applied to psychological phenomena (Heidbreder, 1933).

Another early psychological researcher, Fechner, viewed studies of just noticeable differences—for example, distinguishing between objects of slightly different weights—as revealing a mathematical relationship between the physical objects themselves and a person's perception of those objects. A physicist and philosopher, Fechner's goal was to apply the methods of physical measurement to psychological phenomena (Falmagne, 1992). Fechner proposed that a person's ability to perceive a physical stimulus could be described by a logarithmic (curvilinear) function between the perceived sensation and measured stimulus value. With evidence of such a general relation (which he called Weber's Law, after E. H. Weber, who provided the data used by Fechner), Fechner felt encouraged that psychological phenomena could be studied with the scientific method. As Heidbreder (1933) noted,

> To Fechner's contemporaries, the remarkable feature of the psychophysical methods was the fact that they were quantitative. To measure mental processes was considered a startling innovation; to experiment with them in a manner that gave quantitative data marked the dawn of a new day. (p. 83)

As the methods and measurements of the physiological laboratory became available to psychologists, the phenomena studied with these tools—sensation and perception—appeared at that time to be likely candidates for the raw elements from which all important psychological entities were constructed. Galton, for example, thought that sensory discrimination might be a sign of an individual's capacity for intelligent judgment. James McKeen Cattell employed tasks such as grip strength, detecting the smallest differences in weight between two objects, and reaction time (RT) to sound in an attempt to develop predictors of intelligence.

Biology and Individual Differences.   Darwin's publication in 1859 of *Origin of Species* provided another model for psychology. Two ideas seemed particularly relevant. First, individuals had to be considered in light of their abilities to adapt themselves to their environment. Second, humans passed on to their descendants a genetic history. Interestingly, individual offspring displayed slight differences from their parents, differences that Darwin believed could be the source of materials for the processes of natural selection (Dawis, 1992).

Mental testers have a long history of viewing their work as assisting in the selection of individuals to fit the requirements of institutions. Cronbach (1957) put it this way:

Institutions, by demanding adaptation, serve as instruments of natural selection among men. . . . To Spencer, to Galton, and to their successors down to the present day, the successful are those who have the greatest adjustive capacity. The psychologist's job, in this tradition, is to facilitate or anticipate natural selection. He seeks only to reduce its cruelty and wastage by predicting who will survive in schools and other institutions as they are. He takes the system for granted and tries to identify who will fit into it. His devices have a conservative influence because they identify persons who will succeed in the existing institution. By reducing failures, they remove a challenge which might otherwise force the institution to change. (p. 679)

In contrast to the politically conservative testers, psychological experimenters and interveners tended to assist individuals in finding the best environmental fit and to challenge institutions to adapt to individuals.

Darwin's cousin Sir Francis Galton became interested in the role of heredity in intelligence and developed methods that inquired into personal and family history. Galton is often considered to be the first to introduce items that required psychological ratings. His measurement methods included tests of imagery in which individuals were asked to recall a previous experience in as much detail as possible. Galton also recognized differences in intelligence among individuals, an approach that required tests to quantify such differences and statistical procedures, such as standard scores and correlations, for analyzing the quantitative data such tests produce. Interest in individual differences had also been fed by a controversy during the early part of the century in astronomy (Rosenthal, 1976). The astronomer Nevil Maskelyne fired his assistant David Kinnebrook, whose timing of the transit of stars across a line in a telescope did not match those of the senior astronomer. It later became apparent that individual differences in RT explained the discrepancy, not the supposed incompetency of the junior astronomer. The idea that such individual differences were not restricted simply to RT was quickly accepted under the label of the personal equation.

Following the lead of scientists in other disciplines, Galton in the 1880s established a testing laboratory to assess individual differences (Danziger, 1990). Soon other laboratories appeared, with psychologists such as Joseph Jastrow, Axel Oehrn, Hugo Munsterberg, J. A. Gilbert, and James McKeen Cattell demonstrating new tests and collecting data (Boring, 1957). The APA in the 1890s formed a national committee to further cooperation between the laboratories. As Boring (1957) noted, testing was the natural development of the period. Psychologists began to recognize that different individuals could behave differently on the same tasks or in the same situations.

Thus psychologists adopted some of the forms of the natural sciences. They emulated the physiologist's laboratory and experimental methods; they employed physical and physiological tests with which they presumably could measure psychological attributes. They adopted some of the then-current philosophical assumptions about the role of heredity, particularly heredity's role in determining intelligence. They emphasized the quantification of individual differences in psychological measurement. With these imitations the field could act scientifically and appear scientific to psychologists and the lay public alike.

The Desire to Be Relevant

Psychologists also wished to be socially relevant. As a profession, psychology has always been acutely aware of its social responsibilities. Those responsibilities, however, have been interpreted differently throughout the history of psychology.

Schools and Wars.   Around 1900, in response to the French government's need for a procedure to classify students as appropriate or inappropriate for formal schooling (i.e., to identify the mentally retarded; Wolf, 1973), Alfred Binet developed a set of items that came to be called an intelligence test. Binet may be credited with setting in motion a set of events with the most profound repercussions for measurement methods.

Given the predominance of physiological measurements and experimental methods in psychology at that time, it would seem natural to apply physiological methods to the problems posed by school selection. But Binet soon began to doubt the usefulness of such sensorimotor tests as RT as measures of intelligence (Freeman, 1955). Binet came to believe that intelligence was constructed not of simple elementary processes, but of the unified whole of mental processes. An experimental psychologist, Binet took the risk of abandoning the psychophysical tasks of the experimental laboratory. The 1905 Binet-Simon test, although excluding tasks with direct schoolroom content (Dahlström, 1985), did include many practical, academic-like tasks, such as naming parts of the body and recalling pictures of familiar objects after they were displayed for 30 s (Freeman, 1955). Given that Binet's task was to determine students' likelihood of success in school, it is perhaps no surprise that these tests often resembled the criteria they were supposed to predict (Frederiksen, 1986). More recent analyses of intelligence test items and school tasks suggest that students employ similar processes to solve both sets of problems (Snow & Lohman, 1984).

Stella Sharp in 1898 indicated that for the measurement of intelligence, Binet's approach was superior to Cattell's physiological measures because Binet's tests better predicted school achievement (Boring, 1957). Wissler's (1901) review of Cattell's testing with college students, for example, showed that RT correlated $-.02$ with class standing and .16 with a test of logical memory. In comparison, intelligence tests typically demonstrate validity estimates in the .60 to .80 range (Maloney & Ward, 1976) and reliability estimates near .90 (K.R. Murphy & Davidshofer, 1988). Cronbach and Meehl (1955) maintained that Binet's tests were also valued because they were correlated with schoolteachers' judgments of intelligence, thus providing a more objective confirmation of those judgments. In any event, Binet's tests became the prototype for *all* psychological tests (Dawis, 1992). The need to classify students was not limited to the realm of educational selection. Parsons began the vocational counseling movement with his 1909 publication, *Choosing a Vocation* (Shertzer & Stone, 1980). Parsons believed that students required systematic help in choosing a vocation. Parsons' approach assumed a matching model in which students' traits (i.e., abilities and interests) were compared to the requirements of potential vocations (Super, 1957). Such traits could be measured via intelligence tests and questionnaires, such as Strong's Vocational Interest Blank (Strong, 1943).

The next major social events to influence psychological measurement were the two world wars. During World Wars I and II, the military required procedures for classifying the abilities of a large number of recruits to fit its occupations and to provide individual attention to soldiers in personnel selection, classification, and training (Dawis, 1992). Interviews are the oldest form of psychological measurement, but they are time-consuming and inefficient with groups. Psychologists such as Arthur Otis responded by adapting the tasks and procedures of Binet and others so they could be administered to large groups of adults (Freeman, 1955; K. R. Murphy & Davidshofer, 1988). The resulting Army Alpha and Beta intelligence tests were designed to screen out the duller recruits and identify brighter ones for more responsible work (Boring, 1957). Similarly, Woodworth's Personal Data Sheet, the precursor to modern personality and clinical tests, was developed as a device to screen WWI recruits for their susceptibility to shell shock or "war neurosis" (K.R. Murphy & Davidshofer, 1988). Military requirements did not wholly center on selection issues, however. World War II and the Korean War were the impetus for the development of task analysis, a procedure designed to specify the learning objectives for training soldiers in such tasks as assembling and disassembling an M-1 rifle (Bloom, Hastings, & Madaus, 1971).

In summary, the efforts of applied psychologists in the first half of the twentieth century were largely devoted to solving pressing administrative and selection problems (Danziger, 1990). Specifically, school and military administrators needed procedures for classifying large groups of individuals. The primary measurement needs of those administrators were (a) efficiency, obtaining as much information in as short a time as possible, and (b) control, obtaining sufficient predictability so as to assign individuals to appropriate school programs, jobs, and so forth. Because of these selection needs, tests were designed to be (a) as short as possible, (b) measures of psychological traits present in all individuals, (c) administered to large groups, and (d) evaluated primarily by their ability to predict important criteria. Interestingly, psychologists later applied the same criteria to psychological tests the purposes of which were not administrative in nature.

CONSEQUENCES OF THE SUCCESS
OF PSYCHOLOGICAL MEASUREMENT

Breaking away from their origins in physiological and experimental methods, early measurement psychologists developed tests that met the selection purposes of the first half of the twentieth century. The assumptions and methods employed to develop and evaluate these tests shaped the paradigm for psychological measurement during the first 50 years of this century. Psychologists have spent the past 40 years attempting to deal with the issues and problems of the original measurement paradigm, some of which are discussed below.

Prediction over Explanation

Although Binet's tests did allow some prediction of school performance, psychologists reached little consensus about how or why the tests worked. The test itself did not describe how individuals arrived at correct or incorrect responses. The emphasis for early testers, however, was on making predictions for selection decisions rather than understanding the meaning and causes of those scores. Cronbach (1992) framed this difference in terms of employing tests for decisions or for understanding. If decisions for selection purposes were to be the major use of a test, then the accompanying validation procedure was correlational, as when testers examined the correlation of a test with a concurrent measure or an external criterion. The search for causality and understanding of theory that accompanied experimental procedures was relegated to the background.

Binet and others employed the construct of intelligence to address this issue. That is, people who were more intelligent were more likely to answer a question correctly. The test, along with the school criteria, were assumed to be indicators of intelligence. Nevertheless, it soon became apparent that no consensus could be reached about what constituted intelligence. To justify their efforts, mental testers adopted a philosophy that one could value a procedure without understanding it (Cronbach, 1992). Freeman (1926, cited in Cronbach, 1992), for example, indicated that psychologists could measure intelligence even if they did not know what intelligence was. Intelligence became defined as what was measured by an intelligence test. If the measurement procedure predicted something of interest, psychologists assumed that they would come to understand how it worked later. Sixty years later, psychologists can still avoid examining the meaning of what tests measure. Discussing personality measurement, R. Hogan and Nicholson (1988) indicated that the issue of what an item means to the respondent is irrelevant or misapplied to measurement. In support of this position they cited Meehl's (1954) argument that "item endorsements are interesting

bits of verbal behavior whose nontest meanings remain to be determined"
(p. 625). Epstein (1979) observed that "Psychologists seem to take great
pleasure in developing new scales (e.g., the nearly 500 MMPI [Minnesota
Multiphasic Personality Inventory] scales), but little interest in determining
what scores on them mean" (p. 381).

Early psychologists had little interest in knowing what specific tests actually measured, taking test labels at face value (Cronbach, 1992). Gould
(1981) quoted Binet: "One might almost say, 'It matters very little what the
tests are so long as they are numerous'" (p. 329). Gould (1981) suggested
that psychologists committed an error of reification: they believed that because the term intelligence was employed to label what tests supposedly
measured, intelligence came to have an independent existence of its own.
Historically, psychologists seemed aware that other factors might be influencing scores on a test. Questions about and methods of investigating a
test's validity—defined as whether a test measures what it is supposed to
measure—did not become important until the 1950s.

The issue of test meaning, however, has critical implications. R. P. Martin
(1988) noted that quite different social implications occur if one presents
intelligence tests as partially flawed predictors of scholastic or occupational
achievement as opposed to tests of one's stable capacity to learn. R. P.
Martin (1988) suggested that if psychologists understand intelligence tests
in terms of a stable capacity to learn, they will be inclined to use those
scores in a policy of selection. On the other hand, if intelligence tests measure culture-specific cognitive skills, abilities, or aptitudes (cf. Gronlund,
1985, p. 296) that result from individuals' unique learning history (as proposed in the works of E. L. Thorndike; cited by Dahlström, 1985), psychologists will develop intervention programs to improve those skills.
Historically, psychologists have assumed that intellectual ability is indicated
by scores on intelligence tests, regardless of test-takers' cultural origins
(Helms, 1992). Helms (1992) found that little research has been conducted
to determine, for example, whether the ideas and concepts contained in
intelligence test items are presented in language equally understood by all
cultural groups. Helms maintained that good performance on such tests
requires knowledge of White, rather than Black, English language conno-
tations and denotations. Given that historically, few measurement theorists
have paid attention to the processes involved in test response, it is not
surprising that researchers have failed to investigate the test-taking processes and strategies of different cultural groups. But how many years of
controversy in intelligence testing might have been avoided if the descendants of Binet had discussed their work in less general and more circum-
scribed terms?

The problem may partially result from the desire to be scientific, that is,
to formulate general laws that hold across time and persons. As Danziger
(1990) noted, "the early investigators in educational psychology were never

content with a simple statement of practical expediency but always claimed that their statistical findings reflected on the nature of fundamental human functions or capacities, like memory or intelligence" (p. 150). Matarazzo (1992), for example, suggested that Binet "stumbled on classes of verbal and performance items that were infused for the most part with what Spearman (1904) already had begun to identify as a *general* intelligence factor" (p. 1009). Loevinger (1957) cited Guttman (1955) as indicating that Spearman created a test of general intelligence by removing items during the item-selection process that did not fit the general factor criterion. To qualify psychology as a science, psychologists desired laws that generalized as much as possible, laws about persons that went beyond specific individuals, time periods, or situations. Intelligence tests were assumed to measure a phenomenon assumed to be inherited, stable across time, and the presumed cause of one's success in life or lack thereof.

Intelligence thus became the first important psychological *trait*, that is, a phenomenon assumed to be relatively stable, enduring, and resistant to environmental influences. The crucial point about the concept of a trait is its *consistency*: if most psychological phenomena were traitlike, then one should find consistency wherever one looked. Traits meant that one should expect to find an individual's behavior consistent over such conditions as time and situations. If an item on a psychological test measured a trait the individual possessed, the individual should respond to that item identically whenever asked. The entire human population was assumed to be consistent in that psychologists assumed that traits were shared by all individuals. Throughout psychology's history, most measurement psychologists have agreed that the first principle of measurement is reliability, typically defined as the consistency of measurement. Interestingly, the second major principle, validity, is commonly assumed to hinge upon the first: an unreliable test cannot be valid (e.g., K. R. Murphy & Davidshofer, 1988). First and foremost, measurement psychologists have searched for consistency. Once that consistency was found, the search for universal laws could become relatively straightforward. One merely needed to develop a catalog of all possible traits and tests that could classify individuals by the amount of their respective traits: a Periodic Table of Psychological Elements, as it were.

Handling Error

Older sciences possess deterministic models in which one or more independent variables account for most of the variation in dependent variables (F. M. Lord & Novick, 1968). In a new science such as psychology, however, considerable uncertainty exists about the subject matter, prompting the use of probabilistic models and error terms. In other words, error exists in the descriptions developed by scientists in any new discipline. Factors other than one(s) proposed by the scientists to affect the phenomena—one definition of error—will affect the variable in question. As Loevinger (1957) stated, "When an item of behavior is viewed as an indication of a trait, all other traits and influences which determine it operate as errors" (p. 648). This is the foundation of the classical theory of psychological measurement: test scores came to be conceptualized as a combination of true scores and error.

A model is a set of ideas designed to reflect one's current working knowledge of the phenomena. It simplifies matters to describe the model in terms of a formula, as in the following:

$$Y = X - e, \tag{1}$$

where Y is the score that reflects the test-taker's true score on the phenomenon, X is the score the test-taker actually received on a test, and e is error. Again, measurement psychologists employ the term error in a special way: They mean error to be unknown factors that influence test scores. Psychologists have proposed two types of error: random and systematic. *Random errors* are those that occur by chance; they appear to have no pattern or order. *Systematic errors* do possess some pattern or order. If students attempt to fake good on a survey of attitudes toward their instructor, for example, they are committing a systematic error. The resulting scores will be systematically distorted away from scores indicative of their true beliefs.

As indicated earlier, early psychologists appeared to hold the following measurement model:

$$Y = X, \tag{2}$$

where the observed score was assumed to be the true score. But Binet's test only moderately correlated with school performance, and so some notion of error had to be introduced to account for the discrepancy between these two indicators of intelligence. How could psychologists account for this error?

At least three possibilities existed. First, one could apply mathematical principles that cope with error. Second, one could require the testing psychologist to observe and perhaps interview the test-taker to ascertain what factors besides the test stimuli affected the test score. Third, one could assume that most errors are systematic and establish a set of experiments to investigate the errors. As will be seen below, psychologists largely chose the first two options and only recently have been pursuing the third.

Statistics.　Given military, educational, and occupational selection requirements—that tests be developed, administered, and scored as quickly and efficiently as possible—statistical procedures and principles made the most pragmatic sense for dealing with error. Statistics is a branch of mathematics where one describes populations numerically on the basis of partial samples and partial descriptions of the factors affecting the population.

An important statistical procedure developed by Spearman and others in the early 1900s was the correlation coefficient. A correlation summarizes the extent of any linear relation between two variables. A correlation of .50 between a psychological test and a course grade, for example, indicates a moderate relation between the two. One could square the correlation to obtain an estimate of the variability in one score accounted for by the other. In this example, squaring .50 equals .25, indicating that 25% of the variance in the course grade can be accounted for by the psychological test. Seventy-five percent of the variance, however, is caused by error (i.e., unknown factors). Later, a related procedure, factor analysis, would become widely perceived as the procedure necessary to reveal the true nature of psychological phenomena hidden in test data. Statistical techniques like correlations and factor analysis could be employed during test construction to identify and eliminate test items and tasks that were too noisy, that is, contained too much error and too little signal (Coombs, Dawes, & Tversky, 1970).

An important statistical principle quickly utilized to handle error was aggregation. Psychologists such as Binet and Spearman recognized that error could be reduced through the use of large numbers of individuals and test items (Dawis, 1992). This was a result of the observation that in large samples, *random* measurement errors tend to balance each other, thus increasing our ability to detect some amount of the trait in question. Thus, if one individual's intelligence test score changed because of fatigue, that error-filled score would not have much effect on the correlation between test score and job performance if it was included in a sample of 100 persons. Similarly, if an individual misread one item, that incorrect response would not have much effect on the reliability of a total score reflecting the sum of 100 items. Test construction became dependent upon using large samples of individuals and initially large numbers of items.

The use of large samples to minimize measurement error, however, had several side effects (Danziger, 1990). It meant that research efforts with one or a few subjects were gradually abandoned. Such studies, particularly in the beginning of a research program, tended to provide qualitative insights into important causes, such as how the subject perceives and deals with experimental tasks and demands. Also, early experimental research, such as that conducted by Wundt, employed one of the members of the research team or another trained observer to function as subject. The assumption in these studies was that a naive observer could not provide reliable information. Naive observers, for example, might be more open to errors of interpretation of items or in the accurate recall of psychological data. Psychometric researchers, however, accepted naive observers. Danziger (1990) suggested that "the simple device of multiplying the number of subjects seems to have been resorted to as a compensation for their lack of skill and experience" (p. 78). Again, the assumption was that whatever errors the subject brought to the scale would be balanced or canceled in the aggregation of many subjects' responses.

Gradually, an individual's score came to be seen as meaningful only in relation to others' scores. That is, tests became norm-referenced, meaningful only in the context of the normal, bell-shaped distribution of many natural variables. As shown in Figure 2, such a graphic can illustrate the mean of the scores and contrast high and low scores with each other. Galton's scale of individual differences became the predominant basis for making sense of test data. This *Zeitgeist* continues in contemporary discussions of psychological measurement. For example, Epstein (1983, p. 381) stated that "it is meaningless to interpret the behavior of an individual without a frame of reference of others' behaviors," whereas Kleinmuntz (1967) maintained that "all meaning for a given score of a person derives from comparing his score with those of other persons" (p. 47). Large samples, then, were necessary both to cancel measurement errors *and* to scale individuals in relation to one another. No matter what the purpose of testing, psychologists came to pay attention to aggregated scores in aggregated individuals.

Assessment as a Complement to Measurement. Observing individuals during testing and conducting an interview (e.g., to determine history) were other methods of discovering factors that influenced test scores. This was usually not an option for large-scale selection operations, but it might be feasible in smaller clinical, educational, and occupational settings. Binet found it useful to think of the intelligence test as a clinical interview in which the examiner could get a sense of the methods and processes by which the examinee responded to items. Terman and Merrill (1937, cited in K. R. Murphy & Davidshofer, 1988) suggested that Binet's intelligence test was "a method of standardized interview which is highly interesting to the subject and calls forth his natural responses to an extraordinary variety of situations" (p. 4). Certainly, including a task such as removing the wrapper from a piece of candy was highly interesting to the children taking Binet's tests (Dahlstrom, 1993). In contrast, educational testing before Binet was essentially an unstructured interview conducted between pupil

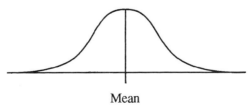

Mean

FIGURE 2   A normal distribution. The line down the center of the distribution represents the mean. Low and high scorers fall to the left and right of the mean, respectively.

and teacher (R. L. Thorndike & Hagen, 1961). Binet's method became an important demonstration of the benefits of combining testing and clinical judgment. This combination is typically what psychologists mean when they employ the term *assessment.*

Since Binet's time it has been standard practice for psychologists who give psychological tests to interpret those results, when possible, in the context of the additional information they obtain from test-takers. In a clinical context, this information includes a history of the presenting problems, family background and social supports, current medical problems, education, current employment, and financial resources. R. P. Martin (1988), however, suggested that test examiners must design their assessments to control unwanted factors in the information-gathering process. Ideally, assessors should use multiple settings, multiple sources, and multiple instruments to minimize error. Assessors must also pay attention to test-taker characteristics that may influence scores, including motivation to respond accurately, age, ability to read, socioeconomic status, cultural and family values, and motor ability. When the assessor cannot control for any of these factors, they must note alternate explanations in their test interpretations. In addition, contemporary psychologists face a new problem because of the increasing use of computers to administer tests and generate automated interpretations. Because such interpretations are based on evidence of varying reliability and often conflict, it is the responsibility of the assessor to decide which statements in computer-generated reports are valid (cf. Eyde & Kowal, 1984).

Given this history, it would be reasonable to suggest that clinical assessment would be more useful than testing alone. Surprisingly, adding clinicians' judgment to the mix often appears to hinder prediction, not help it. As will be discussed in detail in Chapter 3, research has documented the problems that arise when it is the psychologist who combines test scores and other assessment information to make predictions about an individual's behavior. Considerable evidence exists to suggest that test scores alone should be employed to make behavioral predictions.

De-emphasizing Measurement Theory.   The third method of handling error is to investigate the multiple factors that influence test scores. Instead of seeing test scores as reflecting some combination of true score and error score, one can see tests as reflecting multiple validities (Wiley, 1991). One goal of any science—perhaps the major goal—is to increase the complexity of the relevant theory by investigating errors, making them substantive factors in a theory (Kazdin, 1980). In other words, the statistician's error becomes the researcher's substance.

The early investment in prediction instead of explanation may also explain the relative dearth of measurement theories in psychology's first 50 years. From Binet onward, little agreement has been reached regarding explanations of the processes of psychological measurement. Substantial psychological systems have existed throughout psychology's history, of course, but they typically have not been applied to the problem of measuring psychological phenomena of interest. In addition, some early measurement psychologists clearly de-emphasized theory. Gould (1981) reported that Spearman, for instance, suggested that psychologists should forsake theory, instead taking psychology as the "barest empirical science. These he takes to be at bottom nothing but description and prediction. . . . The rest is mostly illumination by way of metaphor and similes" (Gould, 1981, p. 268). Similarly, Jessor and Hammond (1957) observed that "it is an artifact of tradition that theories have been utilized to derive experiments but not to derive tests" (p. 162).

By the mid-twentieth century, however, evidence of more widespread interest in the processes of psychological measurement began to appear. The first technical recommendations for measurement produced by the APA were published in the mid-1950s. Cronbach and Meehl (1955) and D. T. Campbell and Fiske (1959) published their classic works on construct validity. A major description of the concepts of Item Response Theory appeared in a 1968 publication by F. M. Lord and Novick, and Cronbach, Gleser, Nanda, and Rajaratnam described Generalizability Theory in a 1972 book.

Despite this progress, contemporary measurement authors continue to cite lack of theory as a major obstacle to developing better measurement and assessment instruments. Observations such as the following are plentiful in the measurement and assessment literature:

> There are hundreds of psychological tests but no analysis in terms of basic explanatory principles, with no methodology for producing that connection. Personality theories arise either within naturalistic study—as in psychotherapy—or in the construction of psychometric instruments. (Staats, 1988, p. 4)

> Not only is there a need for more reliable and valid personality tests, but improvements in the theoretical bases of these instruments and in the criteria against which they are validated are necessary. . . . Many of these techniques represent relatively crude attempts to measure characteristics of human behavior. . . . It is generally recognized, however, that none of the available methods of assessing personality is completely satisfactory. The solution to the problem clearly lies in better research and development. (L. R. Aiken, 1989, p. 418)

> Not only are new insights in short supply, but it is clear that not much thought of a theoretical nature has gone into the question [of psychological measurement]. . . . Self-report personality research has had a strong emphasis on empiricism to the partial or total exclusion of theory. (Epstein, 1979, pp. 364, 377)

Yet some sort of theory is implicit in every scaling approach and every test (Coombs, 1964). Proponents of the selection approach appear to assume, for example, that useful data are available only at the aggregated level, not with individual items; that traits were the major targets of psycho-

logical measurement, and that criteria to evaluate tests had to relate to
consistency; and that test scores were linearly related to the criteria they
were designed to predict. It would seem that opportunities exist, for example, to reconsider measurement phenomena at the level of the individual
task or item, in terms of states and situations, and in the context of possible
nonlinear relations (cf. Gleick, 1987) between tests and criteria.

Loss of Experimental Methods

Freeman (1955) noted that Binet's test development process could in
some sense be seen as experimental: Binet selected test tasks on some basis
and then tested their usefulness. But Binet demonstrated that one could
predict school performance without resorting to traditional experimental
techniques or methods. One consequence in the decades that followed was
an increase in mental testing unconnected to traditional experimental inquiry. Aided by Fisher's developments in sampling theory, which allowed
results to be generalized from samples to whole populations (Heppner,
Kivlighan, & Wampold, 1992), experimenters in the early 1900s shifted
their attention from measurement concerns to investigating the effects of
educational and therapeutic treatments (Cronbach, 1957). Thus began a
split between experimental and psychometric traditions in psychology that
continues through the present (Cronbach, 1957, 1975b).

Experimentalists tend to treat individual differences as error, whereas
psychometricians ignore situational factors (Cronbach, 1957; Danziger,
1990). As Danziger (1990) wrote, "In the one case the idealization was that
of a collective organism that exhibited only modifiability; in the other case
it was that of a collective organism that exhibited only stable traits" (p. 87).
Regarding treatments, experimentalists and correlationalists tend to be an-
tagonistic: the former searches for the best intervention to apply to all
individuals, whereas the latter searches for individuals who might best benefit from a single treatment (Cronbach, 1957). Throughout its history, experimental psychology has paid little attention to the construct validity of
its dependent variables; in contrast, construct validity has increasingly become the focus of measurement validation efforts. The result of these differences are incomplete descriptions of psychological phenomena that
hinder theory and measurement in experimental and measurement
psychology.

Heidbreder in 1933 could already distinguish between the traditional
experimentalists, who preferred the elaborate apparatus of the laboratory,
and the mental testers who were allied with the applied psychologists working in industry, education, and clinics. Thus, not only did experimental
and psychometric work become separated, but psychological measurement became closely associated with applied psychology. This link continues today and can be seen in contemporary measurement texts, which

typically begin with a few chapters describing basic principles, followed by chapters describing testing applications in such areas as counseling and clinical psychology, personnel psychology, and educational and school psychology.

Historians of psychological science tend to agree that the loss of experimental methods hindered measurement progress. Heidbreder (1933) maintained that without experimental methods, measurement psychologists lost the capacity to study process, that is, the factors that give rise to individuals' performance on psychological tests. Heidbreder (1933) defined a test as a device for

> revealing an individual's ability in a given performance, not for analyzing the process. It thus differs in intention from the typical experiment, which is directed toward finding out something not about the individual, but about the process that is being examined. (p. 108)

In addition, Danziger (1990) wrote that "because the phenomena to be studied were not treated as processes to be analyzed, no special observational skill or experience was required from the data source" (p. 92). Individual differences in the ability to observe psychological processes in oneself or others were no longer important. Errors were simply aggregated. If the purpose of the measurement was selection, one did not need to pay much attention to experiments, test processes, or individuals' observational skills.

The Gain of Traits and Loss of Situations

Psychologists interpreted Binet's results as evidence of an intelligence factor, which Spearman labeled *g*. Noting the intercorrelations of different components of intelligence tests, psychologists assumed that individuals applied *g* in all domains. *g* was assumed to be a hereditary factor, thereby largely stable and immune to situational influences. It was a psychological trait. Thus, intelligence testing, which came to be the model and standard for all psychological testing, emphasized the importance of enduring psychological attributes—traits—over environmental influences.

Although research has provided support for the importance of heredity in intelligence and temperament, many psychologists believe that situational and environmental factors must also be taken into account. In the measurement area, this controversy has been discussed more recently in terms of the consistency of behavior across situations. That is, if psychological phenomena are traits, individuals who are honest, for example, should be honest across all of the situations they encounter. Behavioral psychologists, on the other hand, maintain that environments and situations change behavior, influencing individuals to be honest in some situations and dishonest in others.

Loss of Precision

Although Binet thought that his tasks were more valid than the physio-logical measures, he also believed that he had lost the precision of the laboratory tasks (Freeman, 1955). Precision has been described as the de-gree of exactness with which a quantity is measured (J. T. Murphy, Hollon, Zitzewitz, & Smoot, 1986) or the ability of a measurement device to detect small differences (Babor, Brown & Del Boca, 1990). I employ precision in this book to refer to the ability of a measurement device to produce data that reflect the ordering, range, and distinctions of the phenomena in question (cf. Nay, 1979).

Binet *did* sacrifice some precision. Psychophysiological tasks such as RT could reliably detect small differences. Binet indicated that his tests would yield a classification or hierarchy of intelligences that would suffice for practice. The practicing psychologist, then as now, needed a procedure that could produce gross, but reliable differences between subjects who were high, medium, or low on various abilities. With Binet's tasks, psychologists possessed a reasonable, data-based procedure for selection purposes.

Many psychological tests can successfully place individuals into broad but distinct categories. For example, suppose we have a hypothetical test that classifies individuals into possessing low, medium, or high amounts of a psychological characteristic. We can be fairly confident, for example, that individuals who score at the top and bottom of that test (a) really differ by a substantial amount on the measured characteristic and (b) are likely to behave differently on some criterion that the test has been demonstrated to predict. We are considerably more uncertain, however, that the test could distinguish between the people who score in the middle range and the extreme groups. For example, Kendall, Hollon, Beck, Hammen, and In-gram (1987) reviewed research with the Beck Depression Inventory that found that over 50% of individuals classified as depressed or not depressed change categories, even when retesting occurs only within hours or days. Unfortunately, "one feature which all psychological tests share in common is their limited precision" (K. R. Murphy & Davidshofer, 1988, p. 2).

Figure 3 displays frequency distributions of hypothetical natural phe-nomenon and data produced by tests. Values of the phenomenon are des-ignated by the first distribution and show ordered, equal intervals. Test A's data reflect the range and ordering of the phenomenon but fail to produce sufficient distinctions. In Test B_1, test scores are too narrow and reflect only the central points of the phenomenon. Such data might appear when raters commit a central tendency error. Test B_1's data could be moved up the scale to illustrate a ceiling effect or down the scale for a floor effect. Test B_2's data reflects the results of a second administration of Test B: although the scores should remain stable, values shift from the first administration to the sec-ond. Such an effect might occur in a pre-post study where individuals learn

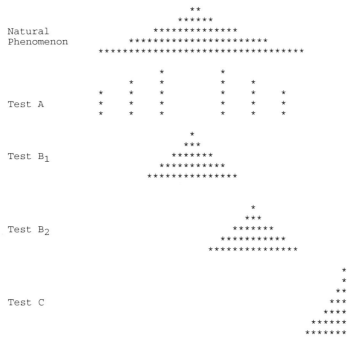

FIGURE 3   Tests change the distribution of phenomenon values. (Adapted from figures in Chapter 1 of B. D. Wright & Stone, 1979. Reprinted by permission.)

during an intervention what the investigator wishes to find in the study and adjust their posttest scores accordingly, independent of any real change. Test C produces values that fall outside the phenomenon's real values. Such data might occur when an ability test is too easy or difficult and produces scores that do not reflect examinees' real abilities.

Stevens (1951) introduced the concept of scale types or level. Nominal scales are those that contain qualitative categories (e.g., red, blue, or green) but do not have information about differences in amount. Ordinal scales describe objects that differ from each other by some amount, that is, they may be ranked. Test A displays ordinal data. As shown in the real-world phenomena in Figure 3, interval scales describe objects with differences that are marked by equal intervals. Ratio scales are like interval scales but have a zero point.

Stone, Stone, and Gueutal (1990) found that test-takers' cognitive abilities affected the reliability of the questionnaires they completed: examinees with lower abilities produced questionnaires with lower coefficient *alphas*. Stone et al. (1990) observed that if a subset of test-takers differs from the rest of the sample on a variable (such as cognitive ability) that affects the reliability of measures, correlations between measures will be different for the subset and the remaining subjects. They suggested that researchers in such a situation may erroneously conclude that a moderator variable other than the systematic measurement error is influencing the correlations. Researchers may thus embark on a fruitless search for such moderators, unaware that it is the interaction of subject characteristics and measures that is altering correlations. Potentially, any systematic error could affect measurement precision and the resulting sequence of events.

The important question about imprecision is, what causes it? I suggest that imprecision is caused by the presence of multiple invalidities. That is, every psychological test is influenced by more than one factor; a score on a psychological test reflects several causes. If item responses are affected by more than one factor, then those responses are likely to change, for example, when the test is administered twice. With contemporary psychological testing, some aspect of the test-taker or testing condition is likely to be different from one occasion to the next, thereby changing test responses over time.

CONSEQUENCES OF THE PROBLEMS OF PSYCHOLOGICAL MEASUREMENT

Despite the successes of psychological measurement and assessment, serious problems remained. Several of the most important consequences of these problems are described below.

Scientific Crises

Kuhn (1970) proposed that scientists in any discipline possess expectations about the results of their research. When these expectations are violated, the attention of the scientific community focuses on the source of the violations. If the violations cannot be explained in a satisfactory manner, a crisis is precipitated. I suggest that the failure to find expected consistencies in different measurement areas has caused recurring crises.

The term *crisis* also has a second meaning in this book. Psychologists who work in mental health settings frequently deal with clients in crisis. Crisis in this context is often seen as time-limited, that is, individuals cannot maintain the intensity of a crisis for more than a few weeks. Crises must be resolved in some manner before the individual becomes physically and emotionally exhausted. My use of the word *crisis* then, reflects these two meanings: (a) measurement efforts have often violated the expectations of the scientific community and precipitated crises, which are (b) later discarded or prematurely "solved" when the psychological community ceases its pursuit or becomes exhausted. The crisis is likely to reappear if and when the community recovers sufficient interest to renew the debate or when a new event indicates that the previous solution was insufficient. Meehl (1991) proposed a similar cycle for theories in the soft areas of psychology: (a) a new theory produces initial enthusiasm that (b) leads to considerable empirical investigation, but with ambiguous results, followed by (c) a proliferation of hypotheses designed to fix unexpected results, and eventually leading to (d) abandonment of the theory and research as investigators lose interest. I believe that measurement problems related to precision and validity are a major source of such cycles.

The historical pattern in psychological measurement has been for an event to occur that ignites controversy, only to fade away as psychologists fail to reach a consensus. For example, personality psychologists have spent the past 25 years attempting to rebut Mischel's (1968) claim regarding the instability of personality traits. Although some psychologists now claim victory regarding the existence and important of traits (Epstein, 1979; Goldberg, 1993), it is unlikely that contemporary behavioral assessors would concede the potency of trait influences over situational factors. For most psychologists this issue evolved into a problem of the interaction of traits and situations, but what began as a promising solution to this problem has also run into difficulties (Cronbach, 1975; R. B. McCall, 1991). Such controversies are common in psychology. Recently, for example, rifts have developed regarding the adequacy of psychological assessment and diagnosis as it is presented by expert witnesses in legal testimony (Faust & Ziskin, 1988; see also Bulkley, 1992; Matarazzo, 1990, 1991; Ziskin & Faust, 1991).

What are the consequences of repeated crises in areas related to psychological measurement? Two outcomes are likely: (a) psychologists might neglect measurement and assessment in important ways, and (b) psychologists will become very cautious in their use of measurement procedures, overrelying on traditional tests and methods.

The Neglect of Measurement

Training. Psychology educators know that most students, particularly those in the applied specialties, begin graduate school with more interest and competence in qualitative matters than quantitative. Surprisingly, this situation changes very little by the end of graduate school, according to a recent survey of graduate departments of psychology (L. S. Aiken et al., 1990; see also Davison, Damarin, & Drasgow, 1986). About 25% of the departments rated their graduate students as skilled with psychometric methods and concepts: students were most knowledgeable about methods of reliability and validity measurement, less so with exploratory factor analysis and item analysis, and nearly ignorant of item-response and generalizability theories. Only 13% of the departments offered test construction courses. Howell (1992) wondered "how many of today's new doctorates in psychology really understand the psychometric underpinnings of the instruments they use. . . . or what they are doing when they—or their 'statistical experts'—apply a statistical package to a set of data" (p. 21). Cliff (1992) maintained that "among all the variants of theory in our discipline, measurement must rank as the oldest in tradition, the deepest in formal development, but, for the majority of psychologists, the lowest in comprehensibility" (p. 88). Lambert (1991) believes that this situation constitutes a "crisis in measurement literacy" (p. 24).

Scale Development and Reporting. Given this context, it is not surprising that many studies have reported a tendency by researchers to be lax in their development of research scales and the reporting of scale characteristics. R. Hogan and Nicholson (1988) stated that

> the literature is replete with examples of researchers testing substantive hypotheses with homemade and unvalidated scales; when it is later discovered that the scales did not measure what they purported to measure, the entire line of research is called into question. (p. 622)

Meier and Davis (1990) examined trends in the reporting of psychometric properties of scales employed over the previous three decades in the *Journal of Counseling Psychology.* Although researchers increased the amount of reliability and validity data they reported over the sampled periods, the majority of scales described in the 1987 volume were still accompanied by no reliability and validity estimates. Meier and Davis (1990) also found that one-third of all scales were either investigator developed (for the particular study) or investigator modified. The modal number of items in all scales equaled 1. Interestingly, reliability estimates reported over the three decades remained near .80, thus providing some evidence that little progress has occurred in psychological measurement. Figure 4 displays histograms of reliability values for the years sampled. Median values were .82 for 1967 ($n = 7$), .85 for 1977 ($n = 19$), and .85 for 1987 ($n = 47$).

Similar results have been reported in other journals and specialty areas. Babor, Stephens, and Marlatt (1987) found similar infrequent reporting of scale reliability and validity estimates in the *Journal of Studies on Alcohol.* D. J. Tinsley and Irelan (1989) conducted a study of measurement reports in the *Journal of College Student Development.* During the 1981–1987 period, they found that 70% of the articles contained scales and that 87% of the scales were used only once during the 7 yr examined. Fifty-six percent of the scales were developed by the investigators for the reported study. Although investigators often provided information about scale format and number of items, only 39% reported reliability information and 27% validity information. Tinsley and Irelan concluded, "It is clear that the emerging empirical base upon which the [counseling] profession is being built is founded to a substantial degree on instruments that have enjoyed little or no rigorous 'scientific' scrutiny" (p. 446).

The Wisdom and Tyranny of Tradition

As previously noted, psychologists appear to ignore problems with a measurement procedure if the device fulfills some purpose. Despite our collective ignorance of what those tests actually measure, psychologists have long employed intelligence tests because of the tests' predictive capacities. Although they admit that it does not possess the predictive validity of intelligence tests, MMPI proponents point to the 10,000 published studies (Graham, 1990) as evidence that we know something about the meaning of its scales. In the context of repeated scientific crises that go unresolved, considerable safety exists in the use of a traditional test, particularly if no viable or distinct alternative exists.

Surveys of clinicians find that they continue to rely on traditional measures such as the MMPI and the clinical interview (Lubin, Larsen, & Matarazzo, 1984; May & Scott, 1989; K. R. Murphy & Davidshofer, 1988; Piotrowski & Keller, 1984, 1989; Piotrowski & Lubin, 1990). When they

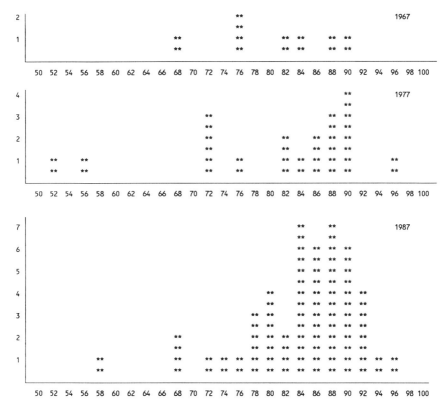

FIGURE 4 Histogram of reliability values reported in the *Journal of Counseling Psychology* by year. Reliability values are those cited by authors for research scales employed in their studies.

create new tests, researchers often imitate previous measures. For example, developers of new intelligence tests have even tended to borrow the same items from previous tests. Jackson (1992) reported that Wechsler used items from the Army Beta in the Wechsler-Bellevue intelligence test. Hathaway (1972) noted that psychologists continue to employ 1940s technology in the use of the MMPI; it took nearly 50 years before a revision of the MMPI was accomplished. Similarly, Gynther and Green (1982) suggested that traditional self-report methodology has advanced no further since the scales of the 1940s and 1950s. Buros (1970) suggested that "it is sobering to think that our most widely used instruments in personality assessment were published 20, 30, 40 or even more years ago" (p. xxv). R. P. Martin (1988) maintained that "personality assessors are using the equivalent of the first designs of the airplane flown by the Wright brothers" (p. 17).

Moderate success, repeated crises, and a lack of alternatives may motivate psychologists to stick with traditional instruments. But the side effect is that psychologists tend to minimize the problems of the original devices and fail to explore and experiment with new approaches that represent potential improvements. As A. Kaplan (1964) noted, "A conspicuously successful technique in some area of behavioral science is not only identified with 'scientific method,' but comes to be so mechanically applied that it undermines the very spirit of scientific inquiry" (p. 29). If problems do become so severe as to force an abandonment of a particular measurement procedure, psychologists have tended to recycle the procedure again at a later date. Interviews, for example, have been employed throughout psychology's history, but they fell into disfavor when research suggested that interview data could be influenced by numerous factors, such as interviewer race and gender (K. R. Murphy & Davidshofer, 1988) and that interviews were more reactive than questionnaires (Stone, 1978). Goldstein and Hersen (1990) recently observed, however, that "Following a period when the use of the interview was eschewed by many psychologists, it has made a return. It would appear that the field is in a historical spiral, with various methods leaving and returning at different levels" (p. 4).

MEASUREMENT AND THEORETICAL ADVANCES

Measurement problems are noteworthy because of measurement's crucial role in fostering scientific progress. As Tryon (1991) stated, "The history of science is largely coextensive with the history of measurement" (p. 1). Cone (1988) agreed: "It is certainly beyond argument that the building of all science rests on a foundation of accurate measurement" (p. 42). Even a cursory review of the history of science indicates that new measurement techniques drive scientific development (Cone & Foster, 1991; Forbes & Dijksterhuis, 1963). Meehl (1991) provided several examples: in chemistry, spectroscopy made possible knowledge about the composition of the stars; in biology, refinement of methods of measuring adenine and thymine along with advancements in X-ray technology made possible Watson and Crick's discovery of the structure of DNA. Philosophers of science note that scientific progress is not solely dependent upon measurement advances, but new measurement techniques have allowed refined tests between rival theories and hypotheses (cf. B. Ellis, 1967). Continuous innovation in measurement theory and techniques seems to be important for progress in any science (Judson, 1980; Kuhn, 1970). Tryon (1991) indicated that this progress is enabled by measurement's capacity to provide new data for ideas, extend human senses into new domains, and correct for limitations of the senses.

Dramatic examples of the link between measurement and scientific progress can be seen in astronomy. Galileo did not invent the telescope, but he employed it to observe Jupiter and its revolving moons, thus setting the stage for acceptance of a heliocentric view of the solar system. Galileo also encountered a validity problem familiar to measurement psychologists. Forbes and Dijksterhuis (1963) wrote, "No one yet understood the operation of the telescope and it is doubtful whether Galileo did so himself. In any case he made no attempt to prove that what he saw in his telescope really existed" (p. 210). Galileo could make basic observations and predictions with his telescope, but he could provide little evidence to verify the truthfulness of what he saw. Progress in astronomical observation has been particularly rapid within the past two decades. Instruments aboard the *Voyager* spacecrafts revolutionized astronomers' knowledge of the outer planets with such discoveries as volcanic eruptions on a moon of Jupiter, and the Hubble telescope is aiding similar discoveries of such esoteric objects as suspected black holes.

Figures 5, 6, and 7 show the striking observational advances made in the observation of Saturn. The first photo displays drawings of Saturn made in the seventeenth century by early observers, such as Galileo and Divini, who debated whether the object(s) surrounding Saturn were rings. The second photo, made by an 100-in. telescope at the Mount Wilson Observatory in 1943, clearly shows several divisions of the ring. The third photo, made by the *Voyager* spacecraft in 1981, displays considerably more detail. I would place psychological measurement's progress at the level of the 1943 photograph: we can observe basic surface structure, but very little detail.

Traditional views of the research process typically describe a cycle where theory produces inquiry and the resulting data refine and change theory. Platt (1977), for example, described the desired process as follows:

1. Formulate two or more competing hypotheses.
2. Devise a study that unambiguously contrasts those hypotheses.
3. Run a clean study (i.e., free of methodological explanations for the results).

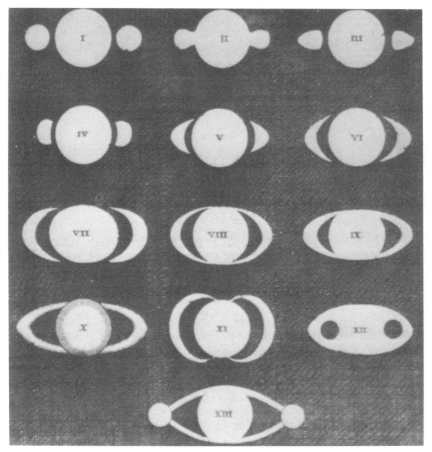

FIGURE 5 Seventeenth-century drawings of Saturn. (Reprinted by permission from Alexander, 1962.)

4. Use the results to reject unsupported hypotheses.
5. Recycle the procedure.

This sequence of steps is designed to produce a conclusion with few or no alternative explanations. Research data, however, heavily depend on the quality or lack thereof of the measurement procedures used to procure it. If measurement problems are substantial, it is impossible to successfully complete Platt's third component, run a clean study. Instead, problematic measurement presents a methodological alternative explanation.

Scientists deepen theory through the refinement, support, or abandonment of key concepts via empirical tests. The lack of methodological alternative explanations allows this process to proceed with confidence.

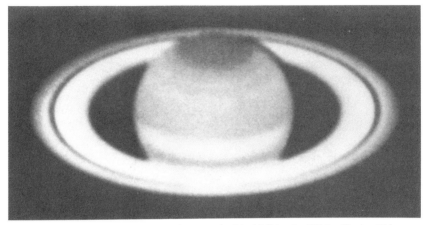

FIGURE 6   Saturn and ring system photographed in 1943 by the 100-in. *Hooker* Telescope, Mount Wilson Observatory. (Reprinted by permission from Alexander, 1962.)

Indeed, the presence or absence of any type of alternative explanation—not whether a study is experimental or correlational—ultimately provides the basis for evaluating the utility of a theory-research program:

> Manipulation per se is not the key to explanatory power. Given an observed relation between variables, what supplies power to a proposed explanation is the *absence of plausible alternative explanations*. . . . Experiments can be badly done—confounded—indicating that manipulation is no guarantee of strong inference. . . . The history of experiments in psychology has many examples of the following scenario: A long series of experiments is conducted, by several experimenters, with the rationale for each step being that the interpretation of the preceding experiment was somehow in error. The series does not end with a clear answer to the original question. (Dominowski, 1989, p. 1078)

Measurement problems complicate the process of challenging and disconfirming psychological theory. Meehl (1967), Kazdin (1980) and Dar (1987) observed that when researchers fail to confirm expected relations in their work, they frequently dismiss the findings on the basis of the scales' supposed low reliability or validity. Kazdin (1980) observed that "a common tactic among researchers is to lament the lack of sensitivity of a dependent measure as a possible explanation for the lack of findings" (p. 221). The investigator suspends judgment on experimental hypotheses by rejecting empirical results on the basis of suspected measurement problems. In cases where measurement problems are substantial, this may be a correct decision. In other cases, the decision may result in a missed opportunity to modify or reject a theory. As Evans (1986) noted, one can sustain an incorrect theory because of a lack of data sufficient to reject a hypothesis. The decision to accept or reject a hypothesis based on data from

FIGURE 7   *Voyager 2* photograph of Saturn ring system. (Reprinted, courtesy of the Jet Propulsion Laboratory, California Institute of Technology, Pasadena, CA.)

contemporary psychological tests is often difficult to make at this point in the history of psychological science.

   Given the number and complexity of demonstrated problems in psychological measurement, such alternative methodological explanations are plausible for many studies employing psychological measures. In experimental and treatment research in psychology, measurement scales typically form the dependent variables. In correlational research, the independent and dependent variables are often measurement scales. Substantial measurement problems, then, are likely to seriously impede the accumulation of knowledge in psychological research. Paul, Mariotto, and Redfield

(1986b) stated that "orderly, cumulative growth in knowledge is inhibited by the lack of a dependable empirical base" (p. 36). The accumulation of knowledge ultimately depends on the ability of measurement devices to provide meaningful information.

Knowledge Accumulation. Many psychologists believe that the field suffers from a lack of a substantial knowledge base. In 1886 Wundt (cited in Allport, 1937, p. 204) maintained that "there is no psychological law to which the exceptions are not more numerous than the agreements." Almost 50 years later Heidbreder (1933) suggested that "There is not enough fact in the whole science of psychology to make a single solid system" (p. 3). Contemporary observers offer similar laments. Danziger (1990) maintained that soft psychology has always had to contend with the problem that its knowledge base did not substantially diverge from common sense and that soft psychology has yet to develop expert knowledge in many areas. Meier (1991b) reviewed the research literature in vocational behavior and characterized that knowledge base as broad, but not deep; vocational researchers tended to continue research programs by adding demographic variables or generating novel constructs to investigate. Gardner (in C. Holden, 1988) suggested that "the areas of personality, consciousness, self, and will . . . are scarcely more developed now than in the days of James and Freud" (p. 1036).

Compared to all psychological measurement devices, intelligence tests typically possess the best psychometric properties (e.g., K. R. Murphy & Davidshofer, 1988). Yet the ability of those tests to make predictions has not substantially changed during the past 70 years. Discussing aptitude tests and validity, Cronbach wrote in 1957 that "we must be dissatisfied with our progress since 1920. As the Executive Committee of Division 5 itself declared this year, none of our latter-day refinements or innovations has improved practical predictions by a noticeable amount" (p. 675). Jackson (1992) noted that the validity of psychological tests has not substantially improved over the Army Alpha and Beta tests. Observing that the Scholastic Aptitude Test (SAT) predicts only about 10 to 15% of first-year college grade point average (GPA)variance, Wainer (1993) suggested that "predictive validity is too low and must be increased" (p. 2).

Kuhn (1970) predicted that once a scientific crisis is recognized, traditional rules will be loosened and more radical methods will be proposed to solve the problem. Such a situation certainly seems to exist in areas of psychology that suffer from a "relatively unimpressive degree of cumulative knowledge" (K. A. Feldman, 1971, p. 86). Meta-analysis, for example, has been proposed as a method of more systematically discovering knowledge in the psychological literature and thereby increasing our certainty and ability to generalize about substantive issues. Schmidt (1992) indicated that because of measurement and sampling error, psychologists conducting individual research studies are unlikely to make substantive discoveries. He suggested:

> Today, many discoveries and advances in cumulative knowledge are being made not by those who do primary research studies but by those who use meta-analysis to discover the latent meanings of existing research literatures. It is possible for a behavioral or social scientist today with the needed training and skills to make major original discoveries and contributions without conducting primary research studies—simply by mining the information in accumulated research literatures. This process is well under way today. (p. 1179)

At the other extreme, proponents of qualitative research (e.g., Hosh-mand, 1989; Polkinghorne, 1991) suggest that natural language methods be employed to supplement or as a substitute for traditional research methods. In the case of both meta-analysis and qualitative research, insufficient time has passed to judge their impact on the advancement of psychological science and practice. However, to the extent that specific meta-analyses examine research employing invalid measurement devices, their conclusions will be suspect; it may be possible statistically to correct for range restriction, but no correction for a lack of construct validity has been developed. Qualitative researchers appear to pay even less attention to issues of measurement reliability and validity than do traditional quantitative researchers (cf. Maxwell, 1992; Yorke, 1989). Reviewers of the history of science also suggest that qualitative measurement precedes quantitative work. Quantitative measurement tends to be resisted by qualitative proponents, as when sixteenth century physicians expressed reluctance to quantify anatomical functions (Boorstin, 1983). Caspar Hofman, an important physician of that time, took the quantitative scientists to task for pursuing "a fact which cannot be investigated, a thing which is incalculable, inexplicable, unknowable" (Boorstin, 1983, p. 368).

Theoretical Accuracy.   In addition to depth of knowledge, theory can be categorized as to its accuracy in describing natural phenomena. Accuracy refers to the degree to which a measurement approaches the actual value of the phenomena measured (e.g., Kendall & Buckland, 1957, cited in Nay, 1979). High accuracy is ascribed when a theoretical prediction is shown to be true. High probability is a fundamental feature of strong theories (Green, 1992); such theories make highly accurate predictions. Green (1992) also observed that the accuracy of strong theories is at least a partial result of theoretical precision. Precise theories, in turn, depend on data produced by precise measurement procedures.

At present, many psychological theories, particularly in the applied, soft areas of psychology, make very global predictions. Such predictions often take the form of positing differences between groups, as in a prediction that suggests that a treatment group, compared to a control group, will show improvement on a set of psychological scales. Although useful, such a prediction fails to describe such important details as the size of the differences between the groups, the length of time necessary for differences to appear, which individuals in the treatment group demonstrate the greatest or least improvement, and changes in measurement instruments that might occur as a result of treatment.

Disunity. One of the important theoretical activities in any science is the making of conceptual connections between seemingly disparate phenomena. When one begins to explore any phenomena in depth, a more complete picture begins to emerge, particularly in regard to how events and characteristics that appeared unrelated do, in fact, have important connections. Zigler and Glick (1988), for example, proposed that schizophrenia is not a homogeneous disorder, but consists of distinct subtypes. They suggested that paranoid schizophrenia may be more accurately described as a camouflaged depression. If this connection between a type of schizophrenia and depression is valid, it has important implications for the treatment of paranoid schizophrenics.

Despite a wealth of psychological data and constructs, there exists "a rather serious shortage of important connections" (Torgerson, 1958, p. 5). Staats (1981) described psychology as separatist, meaning that the science is "split into unorganized bits and pieces, along many dimensions. . . . Our field is constructed of small islands of knowledge organized in ways that make no connection with the many other existing islands of knowledge" (p. 239). Staats maintains that schisms, such as the role of personality versus environment in determining behavior, abound in psychology. Even a cursory review of various psychological literatures reveals phenomena that investigators consider separate but that contain highly overlapping theory and methods.

Although Staats (1981, 1983) believes that the separatism of psychology is largely a result of the failure to seek unity, the concepts developed in this chapter suggest that the field as a whole may not yet possess the capacity to make important connections. That is, measurement problems' interference in the theory–data cycle may prohibit unification. The inability to deepen theory inhibits the accumulation of knowledge and the inevitable connections made when such accumulation occurs. This perspective matches S. M. Schneider's (1992) belief that we may not yet have the right sort of data to make integrative efforts. What we need is more precise data to create theory with finer distinctions.

SUMMARY AND IMPLICATIONS

Decisions made in the beginning of a science influence subsequent trends and events (Danziger, 1990). The concept of a trait was the primary unit adopted by early measurement psychologists. Although process and change were recognized in psychological phenomena, stable, enduring traits best fit early psychologists' assumptions about human nature and their methods of measurement. Consistency was understandable; inconsistency was error.

Consistency has been investigated in a variety of contexts and at a number of levels in psychological measurement. Table 1 displays a partial list of consistency issues.

Chapters 2–5 contain accounts of several of the problems encountered in the search for consistency. I describe the inconsistencies and consistencies found (a) across and within individuals in Chapter 2; (b) between raters and rating procedures in Chapter 3; (c) across situations in Chapter 4; and (d) across constructs in Chapter 5. In Chapter 6, I describe important areas in contemporary psychological measurement, with an em-

TABLE 1   Searching for Psychological Consistency

Consistency	Key measurement concepts
Traits across individuals	Nomothetic versus idiographic measurement
Traits within individuals	Ipsative measurement; correlation of attitudes and behavior
Traits across situations	Cross-situational consistency
Mind and body	Correlation of physiological, personality, and intellectual variables
Self and others' observations	Correlation of ratings by an individual with ratings by persons, such as significant others, employment interviewers, and clinicians
Test scores across different motivational contexts	Reactivity; social desirability; correlation of behavior in observed and unobserved situations
Cognitive ability across time, gender, culture, race, native language	Comparison of mean differences in IQ test scores across these dimensions, culture-free tests
Test scores over time	Test–retest reliability
Responses to items intended to measure the same trait	Factor analysis, coefficient *alpha*
Test scores across measurement modes and methods	Desynchrony, method variance
Psychological constructs with similar and different constructs	Convergent and discriminant validity
Predictions across raters	Interrater reliability
Predictions made by raters and statistical methods	Clinical-statistical prediction

phasis on the problems they do and do not solve. In Chapter 7 I review and propose concepts that I believe hold potential for improving psychological measurement and assessment. Finally, I briefly discuss several conclusions and implications.

2 CONSISTENCY OF MEASUREMENT ACROSS AND WITHIN INDIVIDUALS

CONSISTENCY OF MEASUREMENT ACROSS INDIVIDUALS

One of the persistent controversies in psychology involves nomothetic versus idiographic approaches to measurement. Although psychologists typically discuss this issue in the context of personality psychology, the nomothetic–idiographic debate has relevance across psychological domains. Nomothetic measurements observe attributes of populations, whereas idiographic measures focus on individuals. The objects of nomothetic measurement are assumed to be present in every person. A nomothetic theoretician would maintain that every person could be described as possessing some amount, for example, of the traits of neuroticism, extraversion, openness to experience, agreeableness, and conscientiousness (Goldberg, 1993; McCrae & Costa, 1985; Wiggins, 1982). Idiographic theorists believe that individuals possess unique characteristics that may be shared with all, some, or no other people. An idiographic account is concerned with how the characteristics of a person combine into a unified, unique personality (Allport, 1937). From an idiographic perspective, a particular person might be described as very neurotic and somewhat extraverted, but the dimensions of agreeable, open and conscientious simply would not be meaningful to the study of this individual. From an idiographic perspective, error occurs when a score is assigned to an individual for a category that has no relevance for that individual.

Idiographic researchers study one or a few individuals, often over a long period. Nomothetic researchers study large groups, often on one occasion. Nomothetic researchers search for and believe that their research results apply to all persons, although such goals are also common to some idiographic researchers; for example, C. McArthur (1968) maintained that "we need to know many human natures before we can hope that Human Nature will be revealed to us" (p. 173). Both groups have tended to disparage the other. Allport (1937) quoted Meyer (1926): "A description of one individual without reference to others may be a piece of literature, a biography or novel. But science? No" (p. 271). Allport replied: "The person who is a unique and never-repeated phenomenon evades the traditional scientific approach at every step" (1937, p. 5). Although nomothetic approaches dominate many areas of contemporary psychological measurement, it is not surprising that idiographic measurement has its strongest foothold in such areas as clinical assessment, where psychologists tend to work with single persons.

Large Samples and Individual Differences Equals Nomothetic Measurement

How did nomothetic approaches come to dominate measurement? As noted in Chapter 1, psychometricians developed statistical models to describe the relations among the psychological characteristics they studied. To reach sufficient power to detect such relations, statistical methods require large samples of individuals. The larger the aggregate of individuals, the more likely that random errors of measurement would balance each other, thus increasing the chance of detecting the characteristic. If measurement errors balanced or canceled, it did not matter who any particular subject was, as long as you had many subjects. If you required many subjects, however, you also needed to assume that everyone in the sample possessed the characteristic. However, if all persons do not possess the characteristic, you must identify an individual who does and study that individual. As Danziger (1990) wrote, "If the subject is an individual consciousness, we get a very different kind of psychology than if the subject is a population of organisms" (p. 88).

Psychologists such as Allport (1937) took the nomothetic approaches to task because of their emphasis on groups of individuals instead of the individuals themselves. Idiographic psychologists were interested in developing laws that generalized across persons instead of groups of persons (Lamiell, 1990). For Allport, there were no psychological laws to be found outside the study of individuals. Lamiell (1990) provided an example of such a strategy in a series of studies that investigated how individuals rate other persons along psychological dimensions. Lamiell found that subjects typically rate other people not by comparing them to others (i.e., looking for differences between individuals), but by comparing the information provided about the person to an imagined polar opposite of that information. Thus, this comparison is not a retrieval of information from memory, but "mental creations of the person formulating the judgment" (Lamiell, 1991, p. 8).

In practice, the nomothetic approach seemed to work—to a point. With large samples, one could produce bell-shaped distributions of psychological characteristics, thus mirroring the distributions found in other sciences. But psychologists often found only weak correlations between psychological characteristics and the behaviors they were supposed to predict. Although correlations of .30 aided selection decisions in large groups, they still surprised psychologists. Why did x and y only correlate at .30? Were internal psychological variables and behavior really correlated in nature at such a low level? Or had psychology reached the limit of its statistical-measurement capabilities? Idiographic proponents have cited the selection of a nomothetic approach to measurement as the major cause of this and other problems reflecting a lack of scientific progress in psychology. Progress in the accumulation of knowledge, they maintained, cannot be achieved with nomothetic approaches. Similarly, more valid prediction of individual behavior might also be possible if measurement were idiographically based (cf. Magnusson & Endler, 1977; Walsh & Betz, 1985).

From this discussion it is evident that the purposes of nomothetic and idiographic measurement can be considered complementarity, not antithetical. As shown in Table 2, the advantages of one approach appear to be matched with the disadvantages of the other and vice versa. For example, an idiographic approach was not well suited to assist in the selection and administrative decisions that provided the impetus to develop early psychological tests; efficient nomothetic tests, however, did work well for such purposes. Idiographic assessment usually occurs in the context of a relationship between assessor and assessee. Such a relationship allows a greater understanding of the interaction between an individual's perception of traits and other factors, such as psychological states and external situations, which change over time.

CONSISTENCY OF MEASUREMENT WITHIN INDIVIDUALS

A Brief History of Traits

Social statistics were developed during the eighteenth century for the purpose of linking social and economic variables to social reform (Danziger, 1990). Crime rates, for example, appeared related to geographic locale, with the attendant environmental influences (e.g., poverty) readily recognized. To explain these statistical regularities, Quetelet conceived of the idea that individuals might possess "propensities" to commit acts such as homicide or suicide. Buckle argued that "group attributes were to be re-

TABLE 2   Complementarity of Nomothetic and Idiographic Approaches

Advantages	Disadvantages
Nomothetic	Idiographic
1. Aggregation of items and individuals quickly decreases effects of random error and maximizes trait measurement.	1. Difficult to detect random errors quickly or separate them from state and trait influences
2. Efficient and inexpensive, thus useful for selection decisions involving large groups	2. Time-consuming and expensive; requires extensive involvement of assessor(s) with a single assessee
Idiographic	Nomothetic
1. Long-term relationship provides in-depth understanding of the interaction of an individual's trait, states, and situation.	1. Little attention paid to nontrait factors or factors that change over time
2. Potential to maximize prediction of an individual's future behavior and provide information relevant to interventions	2. Low to moderate predictability; low to moderate relevance for interventions

garded as nothing but summations of individual attributes" (Danziger, 1990, p. 77). Propensities and attributes became traits, and the application of social statistics to individuals seemed a natural progression.

Psychological measurement and assessment have long been guided by the assumption that psychological phenomena are traits (Maloney & Ward, 1976; R. P. Martin, 1988). This assumption provided psychologists with a set to find consistency in such phenomena. Most definitions of attitudes, for example, have assumed some consistency or persistence. Krech and Crutchfield (1948, cited in Scott, 1968) defined an attitude as "an enduring organization of motivational, emotional, perceptual, and cognitive processes with respect to some aspect of the individual's world" (p. 152). Similarly, D. T. Campbell (1950) wrote that "a social attitude is . . . evidenced by consistency in response to social objects" (p. 31). Many contemporary psychologists continue to assume they are measuring traits, as evidenced by the fact that psychologists typically observe individuals and administer tests in their offices and assume that the resulting behavior generalizes outside of that particular situation (R. P. Martin, 1988).

K. R. Murphy and Davidshofer (1988) suggested that the concept of a trait has three meanings. First, psychological traits are causes. Thus, persons who are introverted avoid extensive social interaction, that is, their introversion motivates them to avoid others. Historically, this is the meaning of traits employed explicitly or implicitly by most psychologists. Second, traits function as convenient organizational schemes for perceiving and remembering similar information. Thus, we might tend to term certain behaviors (e.g., turning in a found wallet, paying all of the taxes you owe) as "honest" although their relatedness may only be illusory. Or the relation may be real: individuals form concepts about how to act across situations, which others perceive as traits (e.g., Stagner, 1984). Third, traits can be considered descriptive summaries of behavioral consistencies or act frequencies (Buss & Craik, 1983). Anastasi (1985) suggested that this conception of traits is being increasingly accepted. The personality traits identified by factor-analytic studies, for example, can be seen as "summarizing behavioral consistencies, rather than as underlying, fixed, causal entities" (Anastasi, 1985, p. 121).

The problem with trait-consistency approaches to measurement is that human behavior is also variable. Behavior changes, yet measurement approaches predominantly depend upon trait ideas. It should be no surprise, then, that measuring change is one of the most difficult tasks for psychological measurement. Regression toward the mean (RTM), for example, is a frequently cited problem in psychological research (e.g., Cook & Campbell, 1979). When a measure is administered two times, it is often observed that scores falling at the extremes of a scale at the first occasion often move toward the mean at the second measurement. This can be a fatal alternative explanation when trying to interpret the results of research that contrasts psychological treatment and control groups that are not equal before an intervention.

Suppose, for example, that you design a study to test the effectiveness of an intervention to decrease classroom behavior problems. For the dependent variable, you choose a checklist of classroom behavior problems. Before the intervention, teachers of students in the treatment class and the control class complete the checklist daily for 1 wk. Figure 8 displays the range of daily behavior problems for the treatment and control classes. As shown in Figure 8, the mean score of students in the treatment group is higher at pretest than the mean score of control students. If the treatment students' problems decline from pretest to posttest, whereas the control group scores remain unchanged, two alternative explanations appear: (a) the treatment worked, thus decreasing behavior problems, or (b) RTM occurred. If the true mean of the problem checklist in this example is 10, then we would expect the treatment group scores to decline upon retesting even without an intervention. RTM is a strong possibility when the treatment and control groups are not randomly assigned, as often occurs in quasi-experimental designs.

Interestingly, tests with more measurement error display more regression toward the mean (Kazdin, 1980). In other words, the more error in a measurement (i.e., the more factors influencing the test score that we do not understand), the more likely that its scores will change.

SYSTEMATIC MEASUREMENT ERRORS: SOURCES OF INCONSISTENCY

Error refers to factors that influence measurement in ways we do not recognize or understand. Random errors are those that occur unpredict-

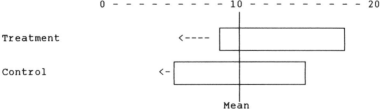

FIGURE 8   Regression toward the mean (RTM). If the mean score of classroom behavior problems is 10, then extreme scores at one administration should move toward that mean at a second administration, regardless of any intervention.

ably. Systematic errors occur in some regular manner and may accumulate, as does a trait, with aggregation. Historically, test theorists and developers have assumed errors in measurement to be random rather than systematic. That is, at the scale of the individual, errors might be systematic—one person may distort responses because of fatigue, another because of poor comprehension—but in large groups such a conglomeration of errors will behave as if they were random (K. R. Murphy & Davidshofer, 1988).

Psychologists have long sought to identify systematic errors in the measurement process. Table 3 displays errors, examined in the traditional psychological measurement and behavioral assessment literatures, that influence the consistency of individuals' test responses and observers' ratings. For example, individuals change their responses to test items when the items are rephrased from positive ("Do you feel the world is a good place to live in?") to negative ("Do you wish that you had never been born?") (Ong, 1965). Individuals behave differently when they are observed and unobserved (Webb, Campbell, Schwartz, Sechrest, & Grove, 1981). Changing the schedule of self-monitoring can influence the resulting data (R. O. Nelson, 1977b); retesting in as short a period as 1 day can reveal changes in test scores (Dahlström, 1969; L. A. Hough, Eaton, Dunnette, Kamp, & McCloy, 1990). Given the emphasis on traits, these inconsistencies are surprising.

Human Judgment Ratings

Human Judgment Ratings (HJRs) are defined here as qualitative or quantitative assessments made by individuals, about themselves or others, along a psychological dimension. HJRs consist of two types: self-reports and

TABLE 3   A Partial List of Measurement and Assessment Error Sources

R. L. Thorndike (1949) (in K. R. Murphy & Davidshofer, 1988)	Paul et al. (1986a)	R. O. Nelson (1972b)
Test-taking skills	Carelessness	Motivation
Ability to comprehend instructions and items	Fatigue	Valence
Response sets	Boredom	Instructions
Health	Information overload	Type of behavior
Fatigue	Emotional strain	Timing
Motivation	Attention shifts	Schedule of self-monitoring
Stress	Equipment failure	monitoring
Set for a particular test	Variations in lighting and temperature	Type of recording device
Examiner characteristics	External distractions	Number of behaviors concurrently monitored

other ratings. Self-reports have also been referred to in the literature as S data and observers' ratings as R data (Cattell, 1957, 1973). *Self-reports* are judgments made by individuals about some personal psychological attribute (e.g., rate your current job satisfaction). *Other ratings* occur when one person rates another on a psychological dimension, as when a manager rates an employee or a teacher rates a child on some attribute (e.g., rate how persistent a student has been over the past semester). Other ratings will be discussed in detail in Chapter 3.

As previously noted, the use of large samples in psychological research meant that one no longer needed to assume, as was the case in early experimental work, that the person who made the report was a psychological expert. As long as the person provided data of some validity, errors would cancel in the aggregation. With both self- and other ratings, Danziger (1990) observed that "during the early period of personality psychology, and to a considerable extent thereafter, it was simply assumed that personality ratings were an unproblematic product of attributes of the task, not attributes of the rater" (p. 160). Test items were assumed to be face valid across individuals and individuals were assumed to be able to respond in a valid manner to those items.

Given this history, it should be no surprise that self-reports and ratings by others constitute the method most frequently employed throughout the history of psychological measurement. With the exception of a few areas, such as behavioral assessment, most contemporary psychologists continue to rely on self-reports. Kagan (1988), for example, cited research indicating that most personality research during the past 10 years was based on self-report questionnaires. Noting that self-reports have been employed in alcohol research since the beginning of the twentieth century, Babor et al. (1987) observed that verbal reports remain "the procedure of choice for obtaining research data about patient characteristics and the effectiveness of alcoholism treatment" (p. 412). If self-reports are assumed to be credible and valid in some sense, their widespread use is inevitable given their ease of development, administration, and scoring. Indeed, investigators are continually tempted to create new instruments in their research area, as evidenced by a recent APA (1992) advertisement in the *Monitor* that estimated that 20,000 psychological, behavioral, and cognitive measures are created annually. Hartman (1984) noted that "if a behavior has been studied by two investigators, the chances are very good that at least two different self-report questionnaires are available for assessing the behavior" (p. 133).

Despite the widespread use of self-report, psychologists often seem to adopt one of the following dichotomous beliefs: (1) because individuals *can* self-report, self-reports must be valid, or (2) because self-reports can be distorted by test-takers, self-reports are useless. The first position represents that taken by most early measurement psychologists. In contrast, self-report critics espousing the second position have pointed to studies comparing self-reports to what the critics see as a more objective criteria, that is, overt behavior. Psychologists have consistently found discrepancies between self-reports of psychological phenomena and overt behavior indicative of or related to the phenomena (e.g., Doleys, Meredith, Poire, Campbell, & Cook, 1977; H. E. Schroeder & Rakos, 1978). Kagan (1988) summarized a variation on this perspective:

> A serious limitation of self-report information is that each person has only a limited awareness of his or her moods, motives, and bases for behavior, and it is not obvious that only conscious intentions and moods make up the main basis for variation in behavior. . . . Less conscious indexes, including facial expressions, voice quality, and physiological reactions, occasionally have a stronger relation to a set of theoretically predicted behaviors than do self reports. The reader will remember that when a large number of investigations were derived from psychoanalytic theory, the concept of unconscious ideas was prominent and self-report was treated as replete with error. (p. 617)

Although the discordance between behavior and self-report has led many psychologists to conclude that self-reports are untrustworthy sources of information, other explanations are available for these inconsistencies. Many psychologists have wondered if the prediction of behavior could be improved if systematic errors in the self-reports were identified and corrected in some manner. What are considered some of the most important of these errors are described below.

Response Strategies

Response strategies refer to the processes individuals employ to complete psychological items, problems, and tasks. Response strategies may be classified along an unbiased retrieval–generative dimension. At one end of this continuum are retrieval strategies used in the direct recall and reconstruction of extensive information about self or others from long- and short-term memory storage. At the other end are generative strategies, employed when individuals cannot or will not produce the relevant information from memory.

Test-takers probably employ strategies throughout the continuum when completing psychological tests, but many who use psychological tests often assume a predominance of unbiased retrieval strategies. That is, respondents are assumed to be retrieving valid information from memory as compared to creating distorted data. Considerable evidence exists, however, to suggest the frequent use of generative strategies. For example, when respondents answer questions that request information about events or beliefs that they do not possess, they create the information, as opposed to retrieve it from memory (A. F. Smith, Jobe, & Mingay, 1991). This may occur regardless of whether the items request specific data (as in the question, "How many visits to a physician have you made in the past

6 months?") or beliefs and attitudes ("How often should a person visit a physician per year to maintain good health?"). Whatever the cause, human judgment fallacies have been well documented (Dahlstrom, 1993; Nisbett & Ross, 1980).

FACTORS RELATED TO STRATEGY SELECTION

The degree to which respondents employ generative as compared to unbiased retrieval strategies appears to be related to a variety of cognitive, affective/motivational, and behavioral factors. These factors are discussed below.

Cognitive Influences

Cognitive factors refer to how individuals think about and process information related to tests. Cognitive psychology's relatively recent rise as an important paradigm has led many measurement psychologists to consider the role of cognitive factors in the testing process.

Level of Knowledge and Uncertainty. To the extent that respondents find ambiguous the elements of the testing situation—such as test items, instructions and format—they may be expected to employ more generative strategies. What do people do when asked a question for which they are uncertain about the answer? MacGregor, Lichtenstein and Slovic (1988) suggest that the simplest strategy to pursue, when estimating an uncertain quantity, is to intuitively produce a number based on whatever information comes to mind. Although inexpensive, simple, and often approximately correct, such intuitive judgments have been shown to lead to systematic biases (MacGregor et al., 1988). For example, MacGregor et al. note that such judgments tend to remain close to an initial value (Tversky & Kahneman, 1974) and may be influenced by recency, salience, and vividness effects.

Some evidence indicates that persons with less experience in a behavioral domain are more likely to exhibit greater attitude–behavior inconsistency in that domain (Fazio & Zanna, 1978; Regan & Fazio, 1977). Regan and Fazio (1977), for example, found that college students who personally experienced a dormitory housing crisis showed greater consistency between their attitudes and behavioral attempts to cope with the crisis than did students with similar attitudes but no direct experience.

Memory Processes. Many contemporary descriptions of the item-response process rely heavily on cognitive models (e.g., Babor et al., 1990;

Biemer, Groves, Lyberg, Mathiowetz, & Sudman, 1991). Theorists usually include the following stages in the item-response process:

1. Individuals, over time, notice their behavior or the behavior of others.
2. They store that information in memory, where it is subject to some degree of decay.
3. Individuals are presented with an item or task that they attempt to comprehend and then relate to information in memory.
4. Individuals retrieve the information and employ it in response to the item or task.

Distortion may arise from a number of complications during this process. For example, individuals usually do not know what information they will be required to retrieve for a subsequent psychological test, and consequently they cannot plan to systematically store relevant information. The longer the time period between information storage and recall on the test, the more likely the information will decay or be interfered with and retrieval altered in some manner. The most extensive production strategies must be employed when rating the past or the future because the information to make those ratings must be retrieved from memory or generated on some basis. The least generation should occur with ratings of the present, as when a person self-reports about current mood or a teacher rates a student's current classroom behavior. As the length of time increases between the rated event and the rating itself, so does the inaccuracy (cf. Paul, Mariotto, & Redfield, 1986a). Similarly, the number and complexity of the behaviors that observers must process about themselves or others appear to influence reliability. Nay (1979) reviewed research that found high negative correlations (in the -.50 to -.75 range) between the complexity of the categories recorded by an observer (defined as the number of categories employed divided by the total number of entries) and the reliability of those observations.

Schemas. Schemas are cognitive structures or networks that organize information. Usually functioning outside of awareness because they have been overlearned, these existing stores of knowledge and action sequences allow individuals to expect certain events, interpret new information, and solve problems (Gentile, 1990).

Test items and tasks reflect the language and schemas inherent in the culture of the test developer. To the extent that test respondents hold discrepant organizational schemas about test information, distortion from the reference frame of the test developer will occur. Such discrepancies are likely, for example, when the requirements of the test and the experiences of the respondent differ on such dimensions as language and culture. Some evidence suggests that a percentage of individuals store relevant information in a form incompatible with the measurement procedure. Tellegen

(1985) reported a study in which 23 subjects completed self-ratings of mood over a 90-day period. Subjects' responses were factor analyzed separately; for 21 of the subjects, a two-factor solution emerged. However, for 2 of the subjects, no interpretable result was found. To search for suspected differences in perceived item meaning, 15 subjects (including the 2 discrepant subjects) were recontacted and asked to sort the mood terms into subsets with similar meanings. Analysis of the discrepant subjects' sortings indicated that they were processing and understanding the terms in a manner different from the remaining individuals. Tellegen concluded that the two-factor model of emotion was valid "provided respondents are able to report emotional experiences in accordance with consensual semantic rules" (p. 704).

Summary. Cognitive factors such as knowledge level, memory processes, and schemas represent potential sources of systematic errors in psychological measurement. However, such internal factors, by themselves, cannot account for the presence of error. Rather, the interaction of these cognitive factors with test design and purpose increases the likelihood of generative responses. Thus, a test that requires the respondent to read at the eighth-grade level is likely to elicit retrieved responses from a group of eighth graders, but guesses or random responses from a group of second graders. I will discuss in more detail the results of such matches and mismatches at this chapter's conclusion.

Motivational and Affective Influences

These factors refer to the effects of individuals' affective characteristics and states on the testing process. Interestingly, even these influences tend to be discussed in the literature in terms of cognitive processes.

Testing Consequences. Given the widespread use of psychological tests for selection decisions, it would seem apparent that considerable emotion could result from an individual's perceptions of testing consequences. Tests can help decide whether a person obtains a particular job, is admitted to a desired school, or avoids an unwanted intervention. Cronbach (1984) noted that:

> Draftees have been known to report impressive arrays of emotional symptoms, hoping for discharge. In an ordinary clinical test, exaggerating symptoms may be a gambit to enlist sympathy and attention. An unsuccessful student may prefer to have the tester believe that his troubles are caused by an emotional disturbance rather than to be thought of as stupid or lazy. (p. 471)

In addition, when tests become the vehicle to create a label or diagnosis that becomes known to test-takers and other decision makers, their consequences can have effects that last long beyond any immediate decision. Such labeling can potentially influence individuals' self-concepts and behavior across a range of situations; for example, a student who is placed in a remedial class on the basis of a test may overgeneralize a lack of skill to other content areas (cf. Fairbanks, 1992). This type of effect is one reason psychologists have increased their attention to ethical issues in testing. For example, Messick (1980, 1989a, 1989b) discusses test validity in terms of the function of testing (interpretation and use) as well as the justification for testing (appraisal of evidence and consequence).

Attempts to cope with problems introduced by testing consequences have ranged from complete openness to concealing testing purposes (Cronbach, 1984). Cronbach (1984) suggested that making the testing purpose transparent is most common in situations where respondents are anonymous (as in some types of opinion polling) or when respondents may potentially benefit from valid self-disclosure (as in symptom reports in preparation for a clinical intervention). At the other extreme is a strategy of concealment where test developers attempt to hide the test purpose. For example, developers frequently create innocuous titles for tests (e.g., "Human Services Inventory" instead of the Maslach Burnout Inventory; Maslach & Jackson, 1981) or provide test-takers with a plausible but false rationale for the testing purpose (Cronbach, 1984).

Test Anxiety. Gregory (1992) provided a contemporary review of evidence and theory about test anxiety, the emotional experience of individuals who anticipate failure on a test. Although noting that past research has shown that test anxiety negatively affects test performance (e.g., Hembree, 1988), Gregory (1992) also questioned whether poor performance precedes and causes the anxiety. For example, Paulman and Kennelly (1984) found that test-anxious students had ineffective test-taking strategies, whereas Naveh-Benjamin, McKeachie, and Lin (1987) found that many test-anxious students also possessed poor study habits.

Gregory (1992) cited studies that indicate that test-anxious individuals appear to possess a threshold that once crossed, results in severe performance drops. For example, Sarason (1961, 1972) found no difference in performance on a memorization task between high- and low-anxiety individuals when the task was presented as neutral and nonthreatening. When the task was presented as an intelligence test, however, the high-anxious students' performance declined significantly. Similarly, Siegman (1956) found that high-anxious patients performed worse on timed as opposed to untimed Wechsler Adult Intelligence Scale (WAIS) subtests. The results may be explained by the cue-utilization hypothesis (Easterbrook, 1959), which indicates that emotional arousal alters individuals' ability to attend to environmental cues. As arousal increases, attention is narrowed to task-relevant stimuli; however, once arousal crosses a threshold, individuals lose their capacity to effectively process the cues related to the task. For individuals who perceive a topic or test situation as anxiety producing, completing the test quickly constitutes escape (negative reinforcement). Gentile (1990; see also Geen, 1987) argues that this is widespread in academic tasks, and it is likely to occur in clinical assessment as well. Similarly, Cronbach (1946) noticed that some students may speed through a test, giving the appearance of random responding.

Emotional States.   The emotional states that individuals bring to tests or that are induced by tests can affect test response. Brody and Forehand (1986) found that depressed mothers were more likely than mothers with low depression to interpret their children's noncompliant behavior as indicative of maladjustment. Neufeld (1977) observed that psychologists may avoid testing schizophrenics and some depressed persons because those groups are presumed to be unable to make valid judgments about their psychological attributes. Contrada and Krantz (1987) reported data indicating that illness and accompanying treatment can affect self-reports. Perceptual and cognitive distortions that may interfere with performance on measurement tasks are also apparent in such clinical phenomena as eating disorders (Halmi, Sunday, Puglisi & Marchi, 1989), stress, anxiety, and depression (Meier, 1991a).

Some authors have proposed an association between affective disorders and test response style. Freeman (1955), for example, suggested that (a) obsessive-compulsive persons provide test responses that are too detailed, but also full of uncertainty and doubt; (b) anxious persons have difficulty finding appropriate words or blurt out inappropriate replies; and (c) psychotic individuals demonstrate disorganized thinking and bizarre content in their responses.

Fatigue and Boredom.   As previously displayed in Table 3, authors who create lists of measurement errors typically include fatigue and boredom. These psychological-state effects are presumed to be an interaction between test-taker and test characteristics. Given that traditional personality and cognitive performance tests can require several hours of effort, it is not surprising that some respondents report fatigue and negative thoughts at the end of tests (cf. Galassi, Frierson, & Sharer, 1981). Fatigue effects have been observed, for example, in surveys of magazine readership, crime reports, and reports of symptoms (Sudman & Bradburn, 1982).

In general, humans attempt to minimize their cognitive-processing load (e.g., Fisher & Lipson, 1985). Sudman and Bradburn (1982) noted that questionnaire respondents who become aware that "yes" answers are followed by lengthy follow-up questions may quickly learn to answer "no." Similarly, questions may vary in the amount of detail they request respondents to recall (e.g., current salary vs. current interest on savings). As Biemer et al. (1991) noted, when questions become too difficult for respondents, they may prematurely terminate their cognitive processing.

Summary. Testing consequences, test anxiety, emotional states, and fatigue and boredom are potential sources of systematic errors. As with cognitive factors, individuals' affect and motivations interact with test design and purpose. Thus, an ability test administered to select new employees may evoke different motivational states and response styles than the same test administered in a research study investigating learning style.

Behavioral Influences

The testing environment can also influence test-takers' responses. Potential factors include the presence or absence of observers, test administrators' gender and race, the physical characteristics of the testing room (e.g., temperature and lighting), and the use of testing apparatus such as pencils or computer keyboards (which may pose difficulties, for example, for persons with physical disabilities). Probably the most studied problem involves the use of behavioral observers.

Reactivity. Although the term has been employed in the literature with slightly different meanings, *reactivity* is defined here as the possible distortion that may result from individuals' awareness that they are being observed by other persons for the purpose of measurement (Kazdin, 1980). The assumption is that as a result of learning (a) that testing or research is occurring, or (b) the intent of testing or research, individuals may respond differently than they would in unobserved situations. Hartman (1984) reviewed research that found that children's reactivity is influenced by such observer attributes as gender, age, and activity level, whereas adults are influenced by observers' tact and appearance.

Reactivity has also been described in terms of the transparency of testing or research; the purpose of test items, for example, can be described as more or less obvious to test-takers. The potential importance of reactivity can be illustrated by results reported in Smith and Glass's (1977) meta-analysis of psychotherapy outcome research. Smith and Glass calculated correlations between the amount of psychotherapy gain and such variables as client intelligence, therapist experience, and the reactivity of outcome measures. To gauge reactivity, Smith and Glass rated the transparency of each measure employed in the 375 psychotherapy studies they examined. Of all factors examined, reactivity correlated the highest at .30. This means that studies that employed the most transparent measures demonstrated the greatest therapeutic gain, leaving open an important alternative methodological explanation for study results.

Early work by Terman and Miles (1936, cited in Loevinger, 1957) indicated that traits could be measured more accurately when the intent of the measurement was hidden from the test-taker. Some research indicates that more subtle items may prevent socially desirable responding and make it more difficult for psychiatric patients to generate normal responses. The logical direction to move with such an approach is to make measurement unobtrusive, that is, to collect data from individuals without their knowledge. Unobtrusive measures have been proposed as a viable alternative and supplement to traditional assessment strategies (cf. Webb et al., 1981).

Unobtrusive Measurement. Examples of unobtrusive measurement include simple observation in naturalistic settings, observation in contrived situations, examination of archival records, or obtaining physical traces (Kazdin, 1980; Webb et al., 1981). Abler and Sedlacek's review (1986) provided several applied examples of unobtrusive measurement. In one study, researchers attempting to determine the effectiveness of an assertiveness training program posed as magazine salespersons and telephoned former participants to determine the program's effects (McFall & Marston, 1970). Another group of researchers found that prospective college students who made more errors filling out orientation applications were more likely to drop out (Sedlacek, Bailey & Stovall, 1984). Epstein (1979) reported a study in which students' self-reports of tension were significantly correlated with the number of erasures on exam answer sheets, number of absences, and number of class papers that were not turned in.

Several problems are inherent, however, with unobtrusive measurements (Kazdin, 1980; Meier & Wick, 1991; Webb et al., 1981). First, considerable effort may be necessary to obtain an unobtrusive measurement. It is much easier, for example, to administer a self-report scale to alcohol treatment participants than to create a simulated bar or observe subjects drink on weekend nights. Second, collecting unobtrusive measurements without arousing subjects' suspicions may be difficult. Third, construct validity is seldom addressed with unobtrusive measures. The behavior of individuals in naturalistic or contrived situations, for example, may not be direct reflections of a unidimensional construct. Finally, unobtrusive measures may pose ethical problems. Although researchers who employ unobtrusive measures may reveal this fact at debriefing, practitioners who wish to collect multiple unobtrusive measures (e.g., at the beginning, middle, and conclusion of multiple treatments) may be motivated to conceal the measures' true intent.

In experimental situations, researchers have documented that experimenters' expectancies and subjects' desire to receive experimenters' approval influence subjects' behaviors (Kazdin, 1980; Rosenthal, 1976). Several strategies have been employed to decrease experimenter expectancy and experimenter approval effects. One might attempt to keep the person who actually runs the study—the experimenter—as well as the subjects blind to the study's hypotheses. One might also include a control group whose expectations have been set similar or counter to the experimental group's; analyses would contrast the changes in such a control with those of the intervention. With such control groups, expectancies and desirability factors become objects of investigation rather than error.

Summary.   The environment and context of testing provide a third category for describing sources of systematic errors. The most central of these problems is reactivity, changes in behavior that occur in individuals who become aware of being observed or measured on some psychological dimension. Unobtrusive measures and concealing knowledge about testing purpose are among the strategies employed to circumvent these problems.

Examples of Generative Response Strategies

Generative response strategies such as socially desirable responding and random responding have been extensively studied by psychologists. As will be seen below, however, little consensus exists about the importance of such strategies, and with a few exceptions, about methods to minimize them.

Random Responding.   Systematic errors at the level of the individual may result in what appear to be random test responses. For example, respondents' lack of motivation to cooperate with testing may be manifested by responding to items randomly.

Test developers attempt to identify random responding by including items likely to be true or false for all persons (e.g., "I eat every day"). Clinicians may become experienced in recognizing random response profiles. Random response profiles, however, may also resemble those produced by persons with psychiatric diagnoses such as psychosis (K. R. Murphy & Davidshofer, 1988). Consequently, psychologists who administer tests will also conduct an interview to separate random responders from individuals with other problems.

Berry et al. (1992) investigated random responding in a series of studies with the MMPI-2. In a study of college students, they found that 60% gave one or more random responses to the 567 items. Seven percent reported random responding to many or most of the items; students who acknowledged some random responding averaged 36 such responses. Berry et al. found few correlations between self-estimates of random responding and subjects' demographic characteristics. In a second study, Berry et al. found that most subjects who admitted to random responding reported having done so at the end of the test, although another sizable group scattered responses throughout. A third study with subjects from the general population found that the number of self-admitted random responders dropped to 32%. Finally, a study of 32 applicants to a police training program found that 53% indicated that they had randomly responded to some items.

Dissimulation and Malingering.   Dissimulation refers to faking good or bad on test items (K. R. Murphy & Davidshofer, 1988), whereas malingering occurs when individuals simulate or exaggerate psychological conditions (G. P. Smith & Burger, 1993). Given that many test items and tasks are transparent in their intent to detect such phenomenon as psychopathology or dishonesty, test-takers may be motivated and able to generate answers that suit their purposes rather than reflect valid or retrieved information. For example, prejudiced individuals may very well tell a pollster that they would vote for an African-American presidential candidate when in fact they would not. Similarly, individuals who wish to receive disability payments may exaggerate their complaints and symptoms. Dahlström (1985) noted that as early as the 1930s investigators were able to demonstrate the ease of faking answers on psychological tests. Terman and Miles (1936), for example, found that the most discriminating items on a scale designed to show personality differences between men and women were also the most susceptible to change under explicit instructions to fake test answers in a masculine or feminine direction.

Test developers attempt to identify and reject items that may be easily faked during the test construction process. Developers have created scales to detect malingering (e.g., Beaber, Marston, Michelli, & Mills, 1985; Rogers, Bagby, & Dickens, 1992; Schretlen, 1986; G. P. Smith & Burger, 1993) as well as tests that include special items designed to detect dissimulation. Psychiatric patients, for example, appear less able to provide normal responses when item subtlety increases (R. P. Martin, 1988). R. P. Martin (1988) reviewed the best-known MMPI scales designed to identify distorted responding, including the (1) Lie scale, items in which the respondent may claim great virtue, (2) F scale, infrequently answered responses that may indicate a tendency to fake illness, and (3) K scale, subtle items intended to assess defensiveness and willingness to discuss oneself. A weighted derivation of the K scale is added to other MMPI clinical scales to correct for the generation of defensive responses. The problem with identifying items sensitive to dissimulation is that such items may also be sensitive to other factors. The F and Fb scales of the MMPI-2, made up of items reflecting clinically aberrant and statistically rare responses, are also affected by symptom exaggeration, psychosis, and random responding (Berry et al., 1992). The Variable Response Inconsistency (VRIN) scale (Tellegen, 1988) is composed of statistically and semantically rare item pairs and appears to be able to separate random responders from other groups (Wetter, Baer, Berry, Smith & Larsen, 1992).

Social Desirability. Social desirability (SD) is a type of response set, that is, a tendency to respond with answers that the respondent believes are most socially acceptable or makes the respondent look good (Edwards, 1953; Nunnally, 1967). Paulhus (1991) noted that psychometricians have been aware of SD effects since at least the 1930s (e.g., Bernreuter, 1933; Vernon, 1934). SD researchers maintain that it is a separate trait that varies among individuals (i.e., individuals have different needs for approval) and that it is SD that most personality tests actually measure. Edwards (1970), for example, summarized research demonstrating strong correlations between the probability of personality item endorsement (contained in tests such as the MMPI) and their SD value.

Although SD has been researched primarily with personality tests, the phenomenon has also been noted with other measurement methods, such as the clinical interview. Barlow (1977) described a patient who came to treatment with problems of anxiety and depression, which the patient indicated were associated with social situations. Over a 1-yr period the patient made progress in a treatment emphasizing the learning of social skills, but still complained of anxiety and depression. Finally, the patient blurted out that the real cause of the discomfort were strong feelings of homosexual attraction he experienced in some social situations. Asked why he did not report this previously, Barlow (1977) wrote that "he simply said that he had wanted to report these attractions all year but was unable to bring himself to do so" (p. 287). Although homosexuality may not be the taboo subject it was for many people in the 1970s, issues surrounding such sensitive topics as sexuality and substance abuse remain subject to SD errors. Hser, Anglin, and Chou (1992), for instance, found that self-reports of male addicts showed greater inconsistency between two interviews for more socially undesirable behaviors, such as narcotics use, than for socially desirable behaviors, such as employment.

Given the evidence that SD affects test responses, psychologists have attempted to eliminate its effects during scale construction and during test-taking (Paulhus, 1991). Although no consensus about best methods has been reached, strategies have included the following:

1. Instructing test-takers to respond honestly (e.g., Benjamin, 1988). Little research is available to document this instruction's effectiveness (R. P. Martin, 1988).

2. Developing instruments such as the Social Desirability Scale (Crowne & Marlowe, 1964) to identify and eliminate test items (during scale development) or test-takers (during concurrent administration of other tests), which correlate too highly with SD scores. Similarly, judges may rate new test items on a scale from extremely desirable to extremely undesirable in an effort to detect relatively neutral items. Research results suggest considerable agreement among groups of judges, including preschool children,

different psychiatric populations, and even judges from different cultures, on the desirability of specific items (Edwards, 1970; Jackson & Messick, 1969).

3. Providing items with two alternatives of equal SD value (Edwards, 1970). Some evidence suggests this strategy is ineffective (Waters, 1965).

4. Presenting subtle items that may be less transparent and therefore less easily faked (R. P. Martin, 1988). L. A. Hough et al.'s (1990) review of the literature provided little support for use of subtle items (e.g., Duff, 1965; R. R. Holden, 1989; Holden & Jackson, 1979; Jackson, 1971; R. J. McCall, 1958; L. D. Nelson & Cicchetti, 1991; Wiener, 1948). Graham (1990) reviewed studies of obvious and subtle items designed to indicate emotional disturbance that Wiener (1948) proposed for the MMPI. He concluded that obvious items are more highly correlated with nontest behaviors than subtle items and that MMPI Subtle–Obvious subscales do not accurately detect faked responses.

5. Warning respondents that methods to detect distortion exist. L. A. Hough et al. (1990) cited four studies that found support for the efficacy of these approaches (Haymaker & Erwin, 1980; Lautenschlager & Atwater, 1986; Schrader & Osburn, 1977; Trent, Atwater & Abrahams, 1986).

Despite an acknowledgment of the potential effects of SD, no consensus has been reached about the size of its effects. Dahlström (1969) suggested that SD may simply be another component of, instead of substitute for, factors such as neuroticism that are measured by scales such as the MMPI. SD, then, becomes not so much an error that must be eliminated or controlled but another component or type of psychological trait. Similarly, R. P. Martin (1988) suggested that socially desirable responses may not be invalid because most people typically do behave in a socially desirable manner. That is, individuals do attempt to manage the impressions they present to other people (Messick, 1991).

Problems such as SD bias may have persisted partially because of the dominating assumptions of selection testing. For example, McCrae and Costa (1983) wrote:

> As an item or scale characteristic, therefore, SD is a potentially serious problem in situations in which information is required about the absolute level of a response. For most psychological applications, however, absolute levels of scale scores are meaningless or difficult to interpret. Instead, normative information is used to compare the score of one individual to those of other persons from populations of interest. If the scores of all individuals are uniformly inflated or decreased by SD, it will make no difference in interpreting scores, since rank order and position in a distribution are unaffected. (p. 883)

But for many testing purposes, including selection, the absolute level of response *is* important.

In psychotherapy outcome research, it is quite plausible that SD effects would influence the mean of individuals' scores on such negative constructs as stress, anxiety, depression, and drug abuse. As shown in Figure 9, pretest scores on a socially undesirable construct such as anxiety might demonstrate a range restriction or floor effect (A). Many psychological interventions, however, teach clients to recognize and accept the experience of some amounts of anxiety as normal. If this education was the primary intervention effect—thereby reducing the socially undesirable perception of anxiety—posttest scores in the intervention condition might demonstrate a greater range as well as an increase in mean anxiety level from pretest to

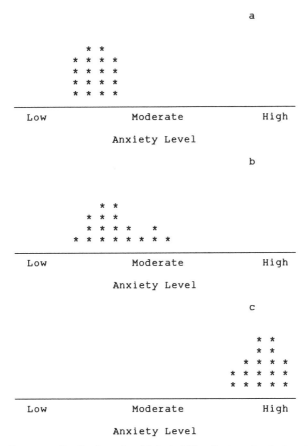

FIGURE 9   Frequency distribution of social desirability effects on level of anxiety at pretest (A), posttest (B), and retrospective pretest (C). In situation A, respondents consider anxiety to be socially undesirable and therefore minimize their reports, creating a range restriction or floor effect. An intervention that aims to eliminate the perception of anxiety as undesirable might produce posttest scores (B) that display a greater range and higher reported level of anxiety. Finally use of a retrospective pretest (C), in which respondents recall at posttest their level of pretest anxiety, might indicate that they were experiencing higher levels of anxiety than previously reported.

posttest (B). Use of a retrospective pretest (e.g., G. S. Howard, Millham, Slaten, & O'Donnell, 1981) might demonstrate the expected pretest–posttest decrease in anxiety (C), but the strength of placebo effects—the intervenee's expectation that change has occurred, regardless of the intervention's actual efficacy—makes acceptance of retrospective reports controversial.

To the extent that SD moves test scores toward the floor or ceiling of scale values and thereby restricts the range, interpretation of theoretical research and selection relations becomes problematic. As discussed in Chapter 1, theory development requires precise measurement that demonstrates the smallest distinctions (and therefore, greatest range) possible; to the extent that social desirability reduces such distinctions, measurements cannot reflect the full characteristics of the actual phenomena. The usefulness of selection testing depends on concurrent and predictive validity coefficients, correlations that will be attenuated when range restriction occurs. SD thus has the potential to affect many types of psychological measurement and assessment.

Response Styles.   Lanyon and Goodstein (1982) differentiated between response styles and response sets. They described a response set as a tendency to distort responses so as to generate a specific impression; thus, social desirability is a response set. Response style is a distortion in a particular direction regardless of item content; agreeing with all items regardless of what the item states is an example of a response style. Response style and set have often been employed interchangeably in the measurement literature, causing some confusion. In the discussion below, what researchers have termed both styles and sets refer to Lanyon and Goodstein's description of response styles.

The two most recognized response styles have been the tendency to agree with an item, called acquiescence, and the tendency to disagree with an item, called criticalness (K. R. Murphy & Davidshofer, 1988). Other proposed dimensions (see Messick, 1991) include uncritical agreement, where individuals agree because they lack the intellectual abilities necessary to critically respond to items, and impulsive acceptance, where individuals answer quickly and without much thought. A fifth type, acceptance, refers to individuals' willingness to accept personality characteristics on psychological tests as indicative of one's self-system (Messick, 1991). Acceptance relates to the nomothetic-idiographic split: if individuals do not accept particular dimensions as having relevance for them, how can they produce an answer to test items based on those dimensions?

Historically, interest in response styles has been cyclical. Messick (1991) credited reviews published by Cronbach in the 1940s (e.g., Cronbach, 1946) with calling attention to response sets in psychological testing. Sparked by Cronbach's reviews, hundreds of empirical studies investigating response styles were published, only to be followed by another set of publications that disputed the very existence of response styles (Messick, 1991). Interest in response styles has also been motivated by a desire to minimize such effects in popular psychological tests. Acquiescence became an issue in personality measurement when researchers noted that a major measure of authoritarianism, The California F Scale, was keyed so that all true responses were indicative of the trait (R. P. Martin, 1988; Messick, 1967). Thus, high scores could indicate a high level of authoritarianism or acquiescence. However, F Scale defenders suggested that acquiescent responding was itself one component of authoritarianism, a claim that never obtained much empirical support (Messick, 1967).

In the 1960s, acquiescence became a concern with the MMPI because 85% of its items are positively phrased (Messick, 1991). Several studies found that factor analysis of MMPI items revealed two factors that could be interpreted in terms of social desirability and acquiescence (e.g., Jackson & Messick, 1961, 1962, 1967). In other words, these researchers suggested that the MMPI did not measure its purported content as much as it reflected individuals' response sets and styles. Block (1965) responded to this criticism by revising MMPI items to reduce the effects of response styles and sets and then subjecting responses to the resulting items to factor analysis. Results indicated that the revised MMPI had a factor structure similar to the unrevised scale. This raised doubts about whether response styles actually confounded content measurement, suggesting instead that sets and styles were actually reflections of the very traits measured by the MMPI (see also Dahlstrom, 1969). The issue continues to be raised in present times, as in Messick's (1991) contention that problems caused by response styles have been documented in the measurement of mood states and androgyny.

Some response styles occur in the presence of certain item and test-taker characteristics. For example, acquiescence appears most pronounced when test-takers are presented with ambiguous items (Jackson & Messick, 1958). Berg (1955) suggested that acquiescence is a logical response of individuals in our culture who are presented with questions about matters they deem to be unimportant. Individuals with low verbal ability or high impulsivity are also more likely to employ response styles (Jackson, 1967).

To reduce acquiescence and criticalness, many test developers maintain a balance of items that can be scored true or false as indicative of the measured attribute. Suggestions have also been made to increase the content saturation of tests (Messick, 1991) and to write items that are clear and relevant to the test-taker (Jackson, 1967). Cronbach (1946) suggested that response sets could be reduced by any procedure that increased the structuredness of a test, such as better defining response alternatives or changing test instructions.

Interestingly, efforts to decrease response styles have been found to increase response sets and vice versa. R. P. Martin (1988) suggested that response sets partially result from the clarity of item content: the clearer the item, the more likely that a response set such as social desirability (SD) will occur. If the item is ambiguous, however, then the probability of a response style such as acquiescence increases. R. P. Martin (1988) noted that projective tests were partially constructed on the assumption that more ambiguous stimuli would lead to less faking and socially desirable responding. This assumption, however, has not received much empirical support (Lanyon & Goodstein, 1982). Similarly, test experts have debated the usefulness of more subtle but ambiguous items, the intent of which may be less transparent to test-takers, but which may also invite acquiescence or criticalness because individuals have little basis on which to respond. For example, K. R. Murphy and Davidshofer (1988) suggest that a question like "I hate my mother" is very clear and invites a response based on its content. Test-takers may also suspect, however, that such a question may be intended to measure neuroticism or psychopathology. A question like "I think Lincoln was greater than Washington" is less transparent, but a respondent who must generate a response may simply agree because of the positive item wording. Such a respondent might also agree with the statement that "I think Washington was greater than Lincoln." As noted previously, studies tend to favor the validity of obvious items over subtle ones. Consequently, the use of subtle items to diminish response sets may increase the likelihood of a response style and thereby diminish test validity.

ERROR SIMULATIONS

As noted above, most of the attention paid to systematic errors occurs during the item selection process. Test developers, for example, might examine correlations between test items and scores on an SD scale to eliminate items with a high SD relation. Few psychological scales contain items designed to detect systematic errors, and subscales designed to detect such errors often cannot differentiate between error types or their causes. Yet systematic errors are likely to be a function of persons and situations as well as items, so we should expect such errors even with items designed to minimize them. If errors such as random and socially desirable responding are present in test data, how could they be detected? Would such errors, for example, be apparent in the statistical procedures typically applied to describe and evaluate psychological scales?

One approach to this problem is to create a series of data sets containing ideal and error-laden values for comparison. Figure 10 displays responses to ten 5-point Likert items by 100 hypothetical individuals that form a unidimensional Guttman scale: all the persons in a higher level possess the characteristics of those at the next lower level, plus one more (Reckase, 1990). The data in Figure 10 have a mean of 30.00, a standard deviation of 14.00, and a coefficient *alpha* of 1.00.

```
1 1 1 1 1 1 1 1 1 1        3 3 3 3 3 3 3 3 3 3
1 1 1 1 1 1 1 1 1 1        3 3 3 3 3 3 3 3 3 3
1 1 1 1 1 1 1 1 1 1        3 3 3 3 3 3 3 3 3 3
1 1 1 1 1 1 1 1 1 1        3 3 3 3 3 3 3 3 3 3
1 1 1 1 1 1 1 1 1 1        3 3 3 3 3 3 3 3 3 3
1 1 1 1 1 1 1 1 1 1        3 3 3 3 3 3 3 3 3 3
1 1 1 1 1 1 1 1 1 1        3 3 3 3 3 3 3 3 3 3
1 1 1 1 1 1 1 1 1 1        3 3 3 3 3 3 3 3 3 3
1 1 1 1 1 1 1 1 1 1        3 3 3 3 3 3 3 3 3 3
1 1 1 1 1 1 1 1 1 1        3 3 3 3 3 3 3 3 3 3
1 1 1 1 1 1 1 1 1 1        4 4 4 4 4 4 4 4 4 4
1 1 1 1 1 1 1 1 1 1        4 4 4 4 4 4 4 4 4 4
1 1 1 1 1 1 1 1 1 1        4 4 4 4 4 4 4 4 4 4
1 1 1 1 1 1 1 1 1 1        4 4 4 4 4 4 4 4 4 4
1 1 1 1 1 1 1 1 1 1        4 4 4 4 4 4 4 4 4 4
1 1 1 1 1 1 1 1 1 1        4 4 4 4 4 4 4 4 4 4
1 1 1 1 1 1 1 1 1 1        4 4 4 4 4 4 4 4 4 4
1 1 1 1 1 1 1 1 1 1        4 4 4 4 4 4 4 4 4 4
1 1 1 1 1 1 1 1 1 1        4 4 4 4 4 4 4 4 4 4
1 1 1 1 1 1 1 1 1 1        4 4 4 4 4 4 4 4 4 4
2 2 2 2 2 2 2 2 2 2        4 4 4 4 4 4 4 4 4 4
2 2 2 2 2 2 2 2 2 2        4 4 4 4 4 4 4 4 4 4
2 2 2 2 2 2 2 2 2 2        4 4 4 4 4 4 4 4 4 4
2 2 2 2 2 2 2 2 2 2        4 4 4 4 4 4 4 4 4 4
2 2 2 2 2 2 2 2 2 2        4 4 4 4 4 4 4 4 4 4
2 2 2 2 2 2 2 2 2 2        4 4 4 4 4 4 4 4 4 4
2 2 2 2 2 2 2 2 2 2        4 4 4 4 4 4 4 4 4 4
2 2 2 2 2 2 2 2 2 2        4 4 4 4 4 4 4 4 4 4
2 2 2 2 2 2 2 2 2 2        4 4 4 4 4 4 4 4 4 4
2 2 2 2 2 2 2 2 2 2        4 4 4 4 4 4 4 4 4 4
2 2 2 2 2 2 2 2 2 2        5 5 5 5 5 5 5 5 5 5
2 2 2 2 2 2 2 2 2 2        5 5 5 5 5 5 5 5 5 5
2 2 2 2 2 2 2 2 2 2        5 5 5 5 5 5 5 5 5 5
2 2 2 2 2 2 2 2 2 2        5 5 5 5 5 5 5 5 5 5
2 2 2 2 2 2 2 2 2 2        5 5 5 5 5 5 5 5 5 5
2 2 2 2 2 2 2 2 2 2        5 5 5 5 5 5 5 5 5 5
2 2 2 2 2 2 2 2 2 2        5 5 5 5 5 5 5 5 5 5
2 2 2 2 2 2 2 2 2 2        5 5 5 5 5 5 5 5 5 5
2 2 2 2 2 2 2 2 2 2        5 5 5 5 5 5 5 5 5 5
2 2 2 2 2 2 2 2 2 2        5 5 5 5 5 5 5 5 5 5
3 3 3 3 3 3 3 3 3 3        5 5 5 5 5 5 5 5 5 5
3 3 3 3 3 3 3 3 3 3        5 5 5 5 5 5 5 5 5 5
3 3 3 3 3 3 3 3 3 3        5 5 5 5 5 5 5 5 5 5
3 3 3 3 3 3 3 3 3 3        5 5 5 5 5 5 5 5 5 5
3 3 3 3 3 3 3 3 3 3        5 5 5 5 5 5 5 5 5 5
3 3 3 3 3 3 3 3 3 3        5 5 5 5 5 5 5 5 5 5
3 3 3 3 3 3 3 3 3 3        5 5 5 5 5 5 5 5 5 5
3 3 3 3 3 3 3 3 3 3        5 5 5 5 5 5 5 5 5 5
3 3 3 3 3 3 3 3 3 3        5 5 5 5 5 5 5 5 5 5
3 3 3 3 3 3 3 3 3 3        5 5 5 5 5 5 5 5 5 5
```

FIGURE 10   A Guttman scale.

Suppose I simulate random responding by creating a computer program that takes these data and substitutes random numbers for 50% of the values. Table 4 displays means, standard deviations, and coefficient *alphas* for 10 such simulations. The means of these data are near the original's value; the standard deviations are considerably lower, but are relatively consistent within themselves. Surprisingly, the *alphas* are moderately high, near the median reported for actual scales sampled by Meier and Davis (1990). Given these results, I think it unlikely that most researchers and practitioners would be able to identify, in typical psychological test data, the type of systematic errors discussed above.

CONSISTENCY WITHIN HUMAN RESPONSE MODES: DESYNCHRONY OF BEHAVIOR, AFFECT, AND COGNITION

Binet and his contemporaries believed that physical and mental processes were closely linked. But Binet's cognitive tasks outpredicted Cattell's physical measures. Why should that be so? Should not individuals' performance on sensory and perceptual tasks be the first link in the chain of psychological processes? The lack of correlation between psychological and physiological measures surprised early psychologists and opened the way to fuller inquiry into the relations between different human systems.

Awareness of desynchrony—the lack of correlation between human systems that seemingly should be interrelated—has expanded over time. Social psychologists initially assumed that individuals' attitudes caused subsequent behavior, only to find that many attitude–behavior correlations are low (Liska, 1975). Researchers who wished to decrease alcohol and drug

TABLE 4   Statistics for Ten Simulations of 100 Test-Takers Providing 50% Random Responding

Simulation Number	Mean	SD	Alpha
1	30.27	8.40	.78
2	30.10	8.05	.78
3	30.48	7.61	.75
4	30.07	7.92	.77
5	29.67	7.69	.74
6	29.73	8.07	.76
7	29.76	7.45	.71
8	29.55	7.45	.70
9	30.10	8.04	.76
10	30.16	8.13	.77

use in adolescents by improving attitudes and knowledge about alcohol often find little behavioral change (Tobler, 1986). And psychotherapists who assumed that changes in clients' cognitions, affect, or behaviors would result in immediate changes across other systems have been wrong (Rachman & Hodgson, 1974). This is a measurement problem in the sense that psychological theories have often failed to describe what system should be measured when.

Psychological theorists have found it useful to divide human functioning and personality into distinct systems or modes. A large number of such modes have been suggested. A partial, overlapping list includes behavior (e.g., motor and interpersonal), affect, cognition, sensation, imagery, physiology, and communication (e.g., verbal and nonverbal) (Lang, 1968; Lazarus, 1981). Such divisions allow theorists to propose causal mechanisms to explain functioning. Other factors external to individuals, such as social, cultural, and physical environments, have also been discussed as causal factors, but they will not be included here.

Psychologists commonly discuss three modes as distinct and basic: behavior, affect, and cognition (B-A-C). B-A-C represents a simplified system that most psychologists understand. *Behavior* refers to the overt actions individuals perform; we may measure, for example, how frequently a manager speaks with an employee and the duration of those conversations. *Affect* is the emotion or mood a person experiences; an employee might experience such feelings as anxiety or satisfaction on the job. *Cognition* refers to the covert thought processes of an individual; a manager might think "Giving Jones a pay raise might increase her job satisfaction and keep her at this company."

Desynchrony refers to inconsistencies within an individual's B-A-C modes. For example, an adolescent might express, during a health educa-

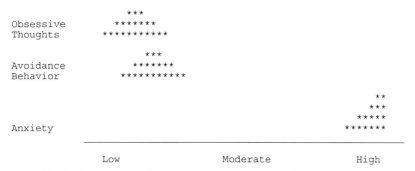

FIGURE 11 Evidence of desynchrony: Frequency distribution of measures of cognition, behavior, and affect for a hypothetical snake phobic following an intervention. A snake phobic who completes an intervention may show synchrony between two modes (e.g., few obsessive thoughts and avoidance behaviors) but desynchrony with a third (e.g., high anxiety).

tion class, a strong belief about the dangers of drinking and driving and then be arrested the following weekend on a drunken driving charge. A woman might know the importance of getting a mammogram but fail to schedule an examination. As shown in Figure 11, a patient completing systematic desensitization may no longer obsess about snakes, may be able to hold a snake, but may still report considerable anxiety about snakes when walking in the woods.

Desynchrony has measurement implications in terms of what to measure and when (Eifert & Wilson, 1991). If distinct modes exist, measurement of any one mode can provide only an incomplete model of human psychology. Suppose we are attempting to decrease drug abuse by at-risk adolescents and believe that behavior change should occur after an intervention that includes education and some type of affectively focused group discussion. In such a model, attempts to observe behavior change would be futile until the required cognitive and affective processes had occurred. If those modes are desynchronous, measurement of different modes must be guided by a theory of the desynchrony to make sense of the correlations that result. Such issues become only more complex if the processes of desynchrony vary idiographically.

History

Rachman and Hodgson (1974) first discussed the inconsistency of human modes using the term desynchrony. Working with phobic patients, they noticed that avoidance behavior and expressions of fear could correlate positively, negatively, or not at all. Rachman and Hodgson were also aware of Lang's (1968) work in which he referred to fear as a group of "loosely coupled components" (Rachman & Hodgson, 1974, p. 311). Rachman and Hodgson (1974) defined *discordance* as low correlations between measures at a single time point and *desynchrony* as low correlations between change scores across time. Rachman (1978) also suggested that desynchrony can be described as mode changes that occur at different speeds. Rachman and Hodgson (1974) suggested desynchrony will be minimized during intense emotional arousal and maximized when an external source influences one of the modes. They indicated that psychotherapy also appears to influence desynchrony; synchrony frequently is both a goal and outcome of therapy.

Desynchrony between physiological and cognitive measures constituted one of the first crises in the history of psychological measurement. As noted in Chapter 1, the success of physiology as a science strongly influenced early psychologists. Fechner and Cattell not only borrowed the methods of physiological laboratories, but viewed physiology as the foundation for the higher psychological processes. In 1896 Cattell asked, "To what extent are the several traits of body, of the senses, and of mind interdependent? How far can we predict one thing from our knowledge of another? What can we learn from the tests of elementary traits regarding the higher intellectual and emotional life?" (Sokal, 1987). Psychologists were interested in discovering general laws that would mark psychology as a legitimate science, and a genuine body–mind link would certainly qualify as an important instance of such a law.

It follows that psychologists would first employ physiological tasks such as grip strength in an attempt to predict such psychological phenomena as intelligence. But Binet's tasks, which were distinctly nonphysiological, better predicted school performance, leaving open the question of why physiological states did not better correspond with psychological ones. These issues remain important 100 years later. Psychologists still search for physiological markers and causes of psychological states, but this has proven to be a difficult task (cf. Cacioppo & Tassinary, 1990). For example, Goldstein and Hersen (1990) maintained that efforts to identify biological markers of most forms of psychopathology have been unsuccessful. Babor et al. (1990) similarly noted the lack of success in identifying biochemical markers of alcoholism. Matarazzo (1992) predicted that intelligence testing would become increasingly linked with physiological measures, particularly those assessing brain activity. He reviewed studies (Hendrickson, 1982; Reed & Jensen, 1991) that found moderate to high correlations between brain activity and intelligence scores. However, rather than demonstrating that biology causes intelligence, as hereditarians since Galton have believed, these studies illustrate the concurrence of brain activity and cognitive processes.

Surprisingly few gains in knowledge have occurred about consistency across human response modes. Psychologists have typically assumed that these modes work as we experience them, that is, as a unified whole, or that only one of the modes, typically behavior, is worthy of study. Regarding the latter, Loevinger (1957) maintained that "the common error of classical psychometrics and naively operational experimental-theoretical psychology has been to assume that only behavior is worth predicting" (p. 688).

Evidence for Mode Inconsistency

Evidence of desynchrony is plentiful. Behavioral, cognitive, and affective measures of fear and anxiety, for example, often demonstrate low to moderate intercorrelations (e.g., Abelson & Curtis, 1989; Craske & Barlow, 1988; King, Ollendick & Gullone, 1990; Leitenberg, Agras, Butz, & Wincze, 1971; Mineka, 1979). Measures of subjective sexual arousal do not always correspond to physiological measures of arousal (Hall, Binik, & diTomasso, 1985; Henson, Rubin, & Henson, 1979). Some psychotherapeutic and psychopharmocological treatments appear to produce desynchrony (Kincey & Benjamin, 1984), whereas others do not (McLeod, Hoehn-Saric, Zimmerli, de Souza, & Oliver, 1990). Desynchrony between cardiac responding and skeletal action has also been observed in animals (Gantt, 1953). In alcohol prevention programs, it is common to find a positive, but low correlation between measures of attitudes toward alcohol consumption and alcohol consumption itself (Tobler, 1986).

Mavissakalian and Michelson (1982; see also Barlow, Mavissakalian & Schofield, 1980; Michelson et al., 1990) studied patterns of change with 26 agoraphobics who were assigned to different 12-wk treatment programs. They measured clinical, behavioral, and physiological variables at pre-test, during treatment, and at a 1-month follow-up. Mavissakalian and Michelson found that the appearance of synchrony and desynchrony was at least partially caused by the examined interval between measurement periods. In general, behavioral and clinical measures changed most quickly, followed by physiological measures. Hodgson and Rachman (1974) reported similar findings for the order of mode change. The most common form of individual desynchrony during treatment was for self-reports of anxiety to decline while heart rate increased.

Hall et al. (1985) employed 20 heterosexual male college students in a study designed to assess physiological and subjective sexual arousal. While listening to audiotapes describing heterosexual intercourse, subjects moved a dial signifying low to high arousal; simultaneously, penile tumescence was measured by a strain gauge. Subjects demonstrated considerable variability on correlations calculated between physiological and subjective arousal measures. The highest correlations were present for individuals who were both most physiologically aroused and slower to report maximum levels of subjective arousal.

Causes

Why does desynchrony occur? Rachman and Hodgson (1974) reviewed three possibilities that remain viable. First, different modes could be linked to different types of reinforcement and reinforcement schedules (Gray, 1971). Thus, some agoraphobics maintain their avoidance behavior by attending to their home as a signal of safety; cognitive and affective states might not be reinforced by those same cues. This explanation has found support in studies that demonstrate that when highly motivated, phobic subjects can perform threatening behavior despite the accompaniment of fear (Hodgson & Rachman, 1974). Second, Schachter's (1966) research indicated that affect could be defined in terms of cognitive appraisal of physiological states. From this perspective, individuals could misinterpret their physiological status, thus resulting in desynchronous measures. Only at high arousal would individuals be unlikely to misinterpret their response modes, a hypothesis that has also received empirical support (Craske &

Craig, 1984; Kazdin, 1980; Marks, Marset, Boulougouris & Huson, 1971; Rachman, 1978; Watson, 1988) as well as disconfirmation (Kaloupek & Levis, 1983).

Watson (1988) reported that scales measuring positive and negative affect, often observed to be independent factors, exhibit higher (negative) intercorrelations during periods of greater emotion. Craske and Craig (1984) divided a group of pianists into high- and low-anxious groups and recorded self-report, behavioral, and physiological measures during a performance before an audience. The high-anxious group displayed increased anxiety across measures, whereas the low-anxious group was desynchronous. Such results seem to support a flight-or-fight stress response in which organisms oriented to a threat focus all their resources on coping with the threat (Selye, 1956). Finally, Lang (1971) suggested that verbal reports of affect may be more precise than data produced by measurement of autonomic systems. Intercorrelations between self-reports and physiological measures would be reduced because of range restriction in the latter. On the other hand, Kagan (1988) suggested it may be difficult to translate certain physiological phenomena into natural language items, and this may partially account for difficulties that respondents encounter when answering test items related to affect and physiology.

Psychologists often validate latent traits by correlating behaviors with self-reports of the construct representing that behavior. But Evans (1986) believes that "psychometric principles maintain the fallacy that behaviors are 'measures' of more fundamental underlying entities" (p. 149). Self-reports and behaviors may be organized by a third mechanism: reinforcement (Evans, 1986). Responses can form a cluster because they are under the control of a reinforcement contingency. Cognitions, psychophysiological responses, and overt behaviors "all interact in mutually dependent submodes of individual repertoires, not . . . alternative measures of a construct from different 'modes' of behavior" (Evans, 1986, p. 152). Evans suggested that reinforcement can create stable response repertoires across modes (i.e., synchrony) and that similar groupings may be shared by different individuals. In other words, stability that has been attributed to personality traits more accurately reflects, in Evans' view, the stability of environments inhabited by individuals.

Evans (1986) noted the common finding in the psychophysiological literature that individual differences exist in the ability to detect physiological processes. For instance, some individuals may be good judges of their heart rate, whereas others are not. Evans indicated that this variation may be partially explained by different strategies employed to monitor physiology. In a study of the correspondence between self-report and objective measurement of penile circumference during sexual arousal, some subjects appeared to observe their tumescence, whereas others made judgments on the basis of their appraisal of the erotic materials (Evans, 1986). Evans

(1986) also cited research indicating that some alcoholics and obese persons are poor judges of their relevant internal states.

Hodgson and Rachman (1974) offered three methodological hypotheses to explain desynchrony. First, B-A-C scales may differ in specificity, that is, the behavioral test may require a snake phobic to deal with a snake in the psychologist's office, whereas the cognitive self-report asks the phobic to predict behavior across a range of situations. Second, in treatment groups, a range restriction (not desynchrony) that exists at pretest will disappear at post-test when measures diverge because of differences between treatment responders and nonresponders.

Third, change scores are affected by the Law of Initial Values (LIV), which states that physiological responses to stimuli depend upon the prestimulus value of the physiological system (Wilder, 1957, 1967, cited in Andreassi, 1980). As shown in Figure 12, the higher the initial level, the smaller will be the response to stimuli that increase responding and the larger the response to stimuli that decrease responding. A person with a high pulse rate should show greater change to a relaxing stimulus than a person with a moderate pulse rate. Similarly, highly phobic patients should be more easily amenable to intervention as compared to moderately phobic patients. It is also possible that the LIV applies differentially to mode. Measures of affect and physiology may change according to LIV mechanisms, whereas cognition and behavior may be operating under different influences. In a similar vein, Kaloupeck and Levis (1983) proposed that desynchrony may partially be an artifact of the different scales employed to measure B-A-C. Changes of a certain magnitude on an affect scale may be not be matched by equivalent changes on a behavioral scale, with correlations correspondingly lowered.

Desynchrony may also occur because it presents individuals with significant opportunities for learning and adapting to their environment. Because environmental information may be differentially processed and acted

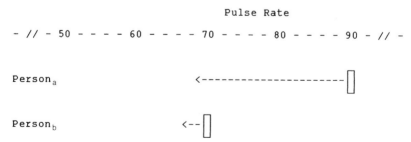

FIGURE 12   Law of Initial Values. Changes in scores on some physiological variables seem to depend on their initial values. For example, persons with high pulse rates are more likely to show greater decreases following a relaxation intervention than persons whose initial rate is lower.

upon, independence of modes expands the degrees of freedom afforded individuals. A child moderately frightened by a harmless pet cat can talk himself into touching the cat. An adult mildly obsessed with a thought can often stop the obsession by doing a behavior. A behavior may be delayed or modified while an individual considers its consequences.

Psychological Interventions

Desynchrony poses problems for theorists who devise psychological interventions and for practitioners who implement them. In the past, psychologists examining intervention effects have often assumed that treatments cause uniform effects across modes. Subsequent measurement has often focused only on one mode; misleading results occur, however, if intervention effects differ by mode. Even when multiple modes have been measured, they often did not correlate, thus raising questions about the construct validity of the scales and their constructs.

In psychotherapy outcome research, investigators attempt to change behavior, affect, and cognition as part of a therapeutic intervention (Bergin & Lambert, 1978). The effects of the intervention are assessed by measures of these three modes. The common desynchrony problem encountered in such research is that individuals often change on one, but not all of the measures, and sometimes in unexpected directions. Because the type of change produced by different forms of psychotherapy is difficult to predict, researchers typically include scales that assess all relevant domains (Bergin & Lambert, 1978). Although this enables researchers to describe the varying changes produced by therapy, it does not explain them.

In a study of desynchrony in 21 female agoraphobics, Craske, Sanderson, and Barlow (1987) found that high heart rate was strongly related to positive treatment outcome. Heart rate was associated in these patients with a willingness to approach a feared situation. Craske et al. interpreted these results as indicating the importance of patients' willingness to tolerate intense physical sensations in treatment success. It is also possible, however, that the patients employed awareness of their heart rate as concrete evidence of a phobia that they wanted to overcome. Rather than simply tolerating the physiological signs, these patients may have used those signs as motivation to change.

Assumptions of synchrony by psychological interveners have also been found to influence clinical judgment. Evans (1986) reported a study by Stark (1981) that examined staff ratings of the behavior of an autistic adolescent girl. Staff at the facility treating the girl reported that she frequently had off days in which they believed all aspects of her performance deteriorated and during which they believed it would be unsuitable to provide her with the usual educational programming. Stark found that staff judgments of off days were correlated only with the frequency of echolalic speech (i.e., involuntary repetition of speech said by others), but not with other measures of task performance. The professional staff, then, made the mistake of overgeneralizing from the speech problems to other modes: they assumed a consistency that did not exist. Chapter's 3 review will show that this is common problem with interviewers and raters.

SUMMARY AND IMPLICATIONS

Consistency assumptions have led psychologists to pursue such questions as, Are psychological dimensions common to all individuals? A better question might be: For what purposes are nomothetic tests best? One answer is to suggest that nomothetic tests seem to make the most sense for selection purposes where few resources are available for training or intervention. Idiographic assessment seems to fit better in intervention contexts with more resources to spend on individual data gathering.

In general, few resources are available in most testing situations, and the result has been a reliance on economical, nomothetic self-reports. The major question surrounding self-reports has been: What would cause individuals to respond inconsistently? A categorization of systematic response errors indicates that individuals employ item-response strategies influenced by such variables as cognitive, affective or motivational, and behavioral or environmental factors.

As shown in the decision tree in Figure 13, the possibility of such variables creating generative response strategies depends upon the degree of match between the test and the test-takers' cognitive, affective, and behavioral states and traits. If test-takers' reading levels preclude them from fully understanding items, for example, it is reasonable to assume that they may guess on such items. To the extent that test-takers' cognitive traits differ from test requirements and purposes—because of language or cultural differences, lack of education and cognitive skills, or insufficient knowledge— even objective tests may function like projective ones. That is, when the mismatch between test items and respondents' cognitive characteristics is sufficiently large, objective test items become ambiguous stimuli to these respondents, with the result being idiosyncratic associative responses. Such responses are desired in projective tests and error in objective tests.

Even when a cognitive match exists, however, test-takers' affective characteristics may not. Unmotivated individuals may respond randomly or employ a response style such as acquiescence; highly motivated test-takers may fake good or bad or employ a response set such as socially desirable responding. Finally, factors in the test environment, such as the presence of observers and test administrators as well as their characteristics, may influence responding. Even respondents who have appropriate motivation (e.g., few concerns about doing well or behaving properly) may restrict or alter their responses or behaviors until they become accustomed to the unusual aspects of the environment.

In general, the larger the number and degree of mismatches, the greater will be the use of generative response strategies. Correspondingly, more generative responses means lower validity for the test's designed purpose. If mismatches occur, it may be possible to intervene cognitively (e.g., explaining difficult words to a less educated test-taker), affectively (e.g., increasing motivation for valid responding by informing test-takers' that their responses will be checked for accuracy), or behaviorally (e.g., observing unobtrusively or allowing time for adaptation to the observer or administrator). Alternative methods, such as the interview, may be useful for determining mismatch causes or implementing an intervention. For example, listening skills are designed to increase a client's trust in the counselor, with one intent being that the client self-discloses more accurate information as the relationship develops (cf. Egan, 1990). Finally, it is also possible that type of generative response style (e.g., socially desirable responding) may be indicative of a specific type of mismatch (e.g., affective and motivational errors).

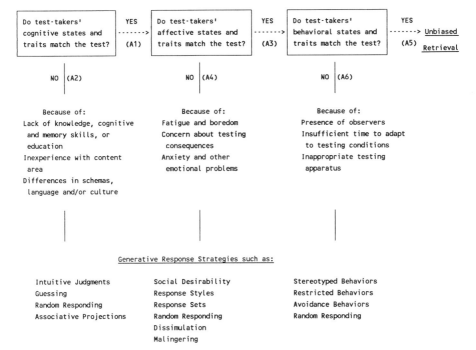

FIGURE 13 Decision tree of systematic errors for person variables. The use of generative response strategies depends on the degree of mismatch between the test and the test-takers' cognitive, affective, and behavioral states and traits.

TABLE 5   Desynchrony as a Result of Systematic Errors[a]

Answer	Test-Respondent Status			Outcome
	Cognitive	Affective	Behavioral	
A1	Match	—	—	Synchrony possible
A2	Mismatch	—	—	Desynchrony
A3	Match	Match	—	Synchrony possible
A4	Match	Mismatch	—	Desynchrony
A5	Match	Match	Match	Synchrony
A6	Match	Match	Mismatch	Desynchrony

[a]The answer column refers to the particular answer (1–6) to the questions posed in the flow chart in Figure 13.

The sequence of answers to the questions in Figure 13 also has implications for desynchrony. As shown in Table 5, matches and mismatches of tests and respondents can be examined in the cognitive, affective, and behavioral domains. Mismatches *within* any one mode mean that desynchrony is likely to be evident between that and any other mode. Synchrony can occur only when matches occur first within and then between modes. One solution to desynchrony has been to aggregate scores across modes, but this strategy may produce misleading data if synchrony and desynchrony are the result of systematic and not random errors. If theorists can specify when synchrony and desynchrony should occur in psychological and psychophysiological phenomena, more precise and valid measurement should result.

Desynchrony and systematic errors may be recurring problems partially because test developers and researchers have been guided by assumptions of consistency. Theorists working without consistency assumptions may be more likely to consider the roles and interrelations of cognitive, affective, and behavioral variables when they specify how constructs should be measured. From an idiographic perspective, systematic errors occur when the test developer assumes consistency across individuals, that is, when the test attempts to measure a cognitive, affective, or behavioral characteristic that either is not present or cannot be accessed by an individual. Nomothetically inspired items and tasks will thus lead to mismatches in many individuals and the use of generative response strategies.

3 CONSISTENCY ACROSS RATERS AND RATING PROCEDURES

If one does not entirely trust psychological self-reports, what then? A logical direction is to employ raters who do not share the biases of subjects and who have some experience or training in gathering information from individuals. In the history of measurement, the most commonly employed method of gathering psychological information has been the interview.

Interviews' greatest advantage and disadvantage is their face validity. That is, the data produced in an interview appear credible to the interviewer and the interviewee. Fremer (1992, p. 4) quoted R. L. Thorndike (1969):

> The teacher who is most critical of standardized testing is often endowed with unlimited faith in the accuracy of his own judgments. He knows! It is vitally important that we do not, in identifying the shortcomings of test data, manage at the same time to build up the teacher's view that his own judgment is infallible.

One can substitute clinician, employment interviewer, or whatever other rater role one wishes for teacher in the above quote. It is often difficult for interviewers to believe that the information they gather from interviewees may somehow be invalid.

As described in Chapter 2, other ratings are qualitative or quantitative assessments made by individuals about others along a psychological dimension. As was the case with self-reports, the search for consistency in data produced by interviews and other rating methodologies has proven problematic.

INCONSISTENCIES ACROSS RATERS

Employment Interviews

Interviews are often conducted in industrial-organizational (I/O) settings for the purpose of personnel selection. Studies show that over 95% of all employers use interviews and most see the interview as the most influential part of the hiring process (Guion, 1976; Miner & Miner, 1979; K. R. Murphy & Davidshofer, 1988). Similar ratings are also employed for measuring job performance and leadership evaluation.

K. R. Murphy and Davidshofer's (1988) review of the research literature examining the effectiveness of the employment interview suggested that no empirical basis exists for its popularity. Interviews have often been found to be unreliable, that is, interviewers exhibit little consistency in their judgments of applicants. Interviews also appear to lack high validity: many systematic sources of error, including the applicant's gender, age, ethnicity, and physical attractiveness, affect interview outcome. Little evidence exists to suggest that the interview adds to the effectiveness of selection tests. In other words, research results suggest employment decisions are best made on tests alone rather than tests *and* interviews.

Why do interviewing practices persist in the face of this evidence? K. R. Murphy and Davidshofer (1988) offered two reasons. Interviewers rarely receive feedback about the validity of their decisions and so may be likely to overestimate their judgment's effectiveness. Also, interviewers may feel more confident in their ability to conduct an interview than to employ more difficult techniques such as psychological tests.

Clinical Interviews

K. R. Murphy and Davidshofer (1988) noted that clinical and employment interviews are fairly similar. Both are usually less structured than tests and are often intended to obtain information unavailable from tests. During both types of interviews, interviewers pay attention to the interviewees' answers as well as their behavior. Like employers, clinicians rely heavily on interviews and typically place more weight on interview data than other sources. Yet empirical research does not support high validity for the clinical interview (K. R. Murphy & Davidshofer, 1988; Wiggins, 1973). Why not?

The hypothesis confirmation bias suggests that clinicians, like laypersons, may inappropriately crystallize on early impressions of other people (Darley & Fazio, 1980; Jones, Rock, Shaver, Goethals, & Ward, 1968). If clinicians' initial impressions of their clients are correct, interviewers will pursue useful lines of inquiry. But to the extent that hypotheses are misleading or incorrect, interviewers are likely to ignore important information contrary to their initial impression. As K. R. Murphy and Davidshofer (1988) observed, "there is a pervasive tendency to overestimate the accuracy of one's judgments, and clinicians do not seem to be immune from this tendency" (p. 374). Long-standing criticisms of clinical interviews and diagnostic techniques, however, have had little impact on the behavior of practicing clinicians (Peterson, 1968).

RATER ERRORS

Raters can make errors, that is, they may be influenced by systematic factors other than those intended for the rating process. K. R. Murphy and Davidshofer (1988) classified rater errors into three categories: halo errors, leniency errors, and range restriction errors. All three have been recognized at least since the 1920s (Saal, Downey & Lahey, 1980).

Halo Errors

One of the first rater errors to be studied (e.g., E. L. Thorndike, 1920), halo errors are those in which a rater's overall impressions about the ratee influence ratings about specific aspects of the person. In other words, a rater holds a stereotype about a ratee, and that global impression hinders a more precise or valid rating in specific domains. As shown in Figure 14, if a supervisor believes a particular employee is "good," then that supervisor may rate all instances of the employee's performance as good, regardless of the actual performance. The rating process is influenced by the supervisor's schema instead of data observed, stored, and retrieved from memory about specific behaviors. Nisbett and Wilson (1977) also distinguished between halo errors that cause global ratings even when specific information is held by the rater and errors made when only ambiguous data is available.

Saal et al. (1980) suggested that halo errors can be detected by (a) high correlations between performance dimensions that should not be highly related, thus indicating less discrimination among different aspects of behavior; (b) factor analysis of the ratings, in which the fewer factors that are

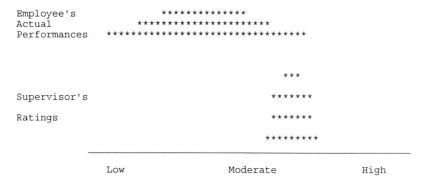

FIGURE 14   Halo effect. A supervisor's ratings may consistently exceed an employee's actual performance.

found, the greater the halo; (c) smaller variation across dimensions by a particular rater; and (d) a significant Rater X Ratee interaction in a Rater × Ratee × Dimensions analysis of variance (ANOVA). Although such evidence of halo effects is widespread, data that demonstrates raters' ability to discriminate are also available. For example, James and White (1983) found that some of the 377 Navy managers they studied were able to detect differences in employees' performances across situations.

Leniency and Criticalness Errors

In this class of errors, the rater is either under- or overestimating the performance of the ratee. Leniency errors might be detected by data whose mean deviates considerably from the midpoint on a scale or a data distribution that is positively or negatively skewed (K. R. Murphy & Davidshofer, 1988; Saal et al., 1980). Leniency errors may be a cause of ceiling or floor effects (Kazdin, 1980). In a ceiling effect, all ratings cluster near the top of the scale; with a floor effect, they cluster at the bottom. When an intervention is implemented, ceiling and floor effects can hinder the detection of the intervention's impact. For example, suppose a researcher designs a pretest posttest study examining the effects of a stress reduction program on air traffic controllers. As shown in Figure 15, an observer's judgments of controllers' stress significantly underestimates those levels at the pretest. How could a decrease resulting from the intervention be detected at posttest?

Range Restriction Errors

Raters' inability or unwillingness to distinguish the range of ratees' performance is reflected in range restriction errors. Raters who make this error

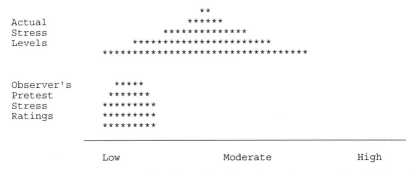

FIGURE 15   Leniency error causing a floor effect. If an observer's pretest ratings significantly underestimate individuals' actual stress levels, efforts to detect stress decreases after an intervention are likely to fail.

fail to discriminate ratees' level of performance; instead they consistently choose a rating near the scale midpoint. For example, a supervisor might rate all workers as average. A standard deviation near zero for a group of ratings would indicate the possibility of range restriction errors.

Halo and leniency criticalness errors also cause difficulties with range restriction. All three types of errors result in scores that do not reflect actual variation in ratees' performance. In these cases, specific raters show too much consistency and not enough valid variation relevant to the assessment's intended purpose. Scores that have restricted ranges attenuate correlations. For example, an employment test might actually correlate .70 with job performance, but range restriction in the test (and possibly, the criterion) would shrink the found correlation to .35. Statistical corrections for attenuation have been developed, but the transformed correlation can overestimate the actual relation (K. R. Murphy & Davidshofer, 1988).

IMPROVING INTERVIEWS AND RATERS

The traditional clinical interview has usually been unstructured, that is, the interviewer has few or no pre-established guidelines or procedures for gathering information. Contemporary assessors have targeted this lack of structure as a major source of interview problems (Mayfield, Brown, & Hamstra, 1980; Schwab & Heneman, 1969). For example, one of the major purposes of the clinical interview is to arrive at a diagnosis. Matarrazo (1983) reviewed studies indicating that interviewers, even two experienced clinicians with the same patient, could produce little agreement when using unstructured diagnostic procedures. Morrison (1988) suggested that such problems were primarily a result of two factors: (a) criterion variance, in which clinicians held different criteria for including and excluding patients into diagnostic groups, and (b) information variance, in which clinicians employed different questions with patients and thereby produced different information. Similarly, Swezey (1981) employed the term error of standards to describe inconsistencies among raters who all employ different standards when assessing individuals' behaviors.

Helzer (1983) defined a structured interview as one that describes

1. the clinical information to be obtained;
2. the order of questions;
3. the coding and definitions of symptom questions;
4. the guidelines for probing responses so as to obtain a codable answer.

In a number of areas clinicians have employed such procedures to develop explicit diagnostic criteria and a structured format for assessing them. Resulting interviews such as the Schedule for Affective Disorders and Schizophrenia (SADS; Endicott & Spitzer, 1978) and the Diagnostic Interview Schedule (DIS; Robins, Helzer, Croughan, & Ratcliff, 1981) have demonstrated significant increases in reliability over previous interviews (Endicott & Spitzer, 1978).

Wiesner and Cronshaw (1988) and P. M. Wright, Lichtenfels, and Pursell (1989) conducted meta-analyses that demonstrated that the addition of structure to employment interviews significantly increased validity estimates. P. M. Wright et al. (1989) found a validity estimate of .39 for structured interviews and suggested that this number "approaches that found for many cognitive ability tests" (p. 197) as reported by Hunter and Hunter (1984). Structured interviews work, P. M. Wright et al. (1989) maintained, because they (a) are closely based on a job analysis of the employment position, thus reducing error from information irrelevant to the specific job; (b) assess individuals' work intentions, which are often linked to work behavior; and (c) use the same set of questions and standards for scoring answers, thereby increasing reliability.

In the clinical area, however, little consensus has been reached about the validity of many structured interviews, partially because the criteria for diagnoses continue to be refined (Morrison, 1988). Nevertheless, structured interviews and relatively brief rating scales completed by the clinician, such as the Global Assessment of Functioning Scale (GAF; American Psychiatric Association, 1987; see also Endicott, Spitzer, Fleiss, & Cohen, 1976), appear to be multiplying in the same manner as self-report scales.

In such disparate areas as behavioral assessment (Hartman, 1984; Paul, 1986), performance appraisal (Gronlund, 1988), and process research (Hill, 1982), psychologists have increasingly focused on rater training as a method of decreasing rater error. As Paul et al. (1986a) observed, "The schema employed by untrained or minimally trained observers are generally loose, with fuzzy category boundaries based on prototypes" (pp. 1–50). Rater training is typically designed to reduce schema-produced biases, increase rater motivation, and improve observational skills (McIntyre, Smith & Hassett, 1984). Behavioral assessors record overt behavior, for example, in staff and clients (Paul, 1986). Observers are trained to record specific behaviors and then assigned to make those observations in specified settings. Describing the elements of one type of behavioral observational training, Hartman (1984) indicated that observers should do the following:

1. Complete a general orientation. In research studies, observers should be provided a rationale explaining that they should remain blind to study hypotheses, avoid generating hypotheses, and avoid private discussions of rating problems.

2. Memorize verbatim such information as the coding procedures and examples as contained in the observation training manual.

3. Be trained to criterion accuracy, first through written tests, and then with increasingly complex practice observations, each followed by feedback and discussion of rating problems.

4. Practice observations in the actual setting, with an emphasis on maintaining high observer motivation.

5. Receive periodic evaluation and retraining.

Elements (4) and (5) seem particularly important for maintaining the reliability of behavioral observers. Research has indicated that the reliability (i.e., inter-observer agreement) typically drops from a .70–.80 range under evaluation conditions to .30–.40 under nonevaluated conditions (Nay, 1979). In other words, when observers know their observations are being observed, they provide reliable observations; in other conditions, they do not.

What types of rater training work best? Dickinson and Baker's (1989) meta-analysis of 15 training studies found some support for rater discussion of material during training, rating practice, feedback, and discussion of feedback. Bowers (1973) found that some studies show greater consistency between self- and other ratings as raters' familiarity with the target person increases (Norman, 1969), whereas other research has demonstrated an increase in the judges' rating accuracy when they receive correct feedback about the target (Fancher, 1966, 1967). However, Fancher (1967) also found that judges with greater conceptual sophistication were less accurate in predicting behavior. Bowers (1973) interpreted this finding as indicating that when experienced judges encounter data discrepant from their schemas, they modify the information rather than their schemas. This would seem to be an instance of the hypothesis-confirmation bias.

One of the major problems in research with rater error is knowing exactly when ratings are in error. In a work setting, for example, what is there to compare a supervisor's ratings with? Laboratory studies in which actual performance is videotaped, however, allow comparison between ratings and actual performance (K. R. Murphy & Davidshofer, 1988). These studies indicate that valid ratings are related to a variety of factors, including supervisors' motivation to rate validly, variability of performance, memory aids, and the social context in which rating occurs (K. R. Murphy & Davidshofer, 1988). As displayed in Table 6, this list of factors is very similar to that provided by Boice (1983), Allport (1937), Taft (1955), Hartman (1984), and Hill (1982). Other authors (e.g., Groth-Marnat, 1990; P. E. Vernon, 1964), however, have suggested that differences on variables such as age and gender are subtle or nonexistent.

WHOSE RATING IS MOST VALID?

One of the basic questions still faced by psychological assessors is whether to employ the client's or the assessor's definition of the problem as the focus of assessment and intervention (G. S. Howard, 1981; R. P. Martin, 1988). In other words, whose rating is most valid? A similar issue centers on whether initial assessments should be geared to the presenting complaint only or made broader, perhaps including intelligence and personality testing. R. P. Martin (1988, p. 70) refers to these issues as requiring "artful decisions" based upon the "best guesses" of the assessor and client. Error is handled by the assessor.

Some evidence indicates that others see an individual more accurately than she or he sees her- or himself (e.g., Hollingworth, 1916, cited in Allport, 1937). Yet other researchers have shown the extent to which one person can hold a distorted view of another (Brody & Forehand, 1986; R. P. Martin, 1988; Vernon, 1964). Regardless of relative accuracy, social psychological researchers have documented differing perceptions about

TABLE 6   Characteristics of Skilled Observers[a]

K. R. Murphy and Davidshofer (1988)	Hartman (1984)	Allport (1937)	Taft (1955)
Motivation for accuracy	Women	Age—experience	Age—maturity
Variability of performance	Older persons	Similarity with observed	Intelligence
Memory aids	Social skills	Intelligence	Esthetic interests
Social context of rating	Perceptual-motor skills	Insight	Insight
	Morale	Personal complexity	Emotional judgment
	Intelligence	Detachment	Social
	Motivation	Esthetic attitude	perceptiveness
	Attention to detail	Social intelligence	

[a]The lists of Allport (1937) and Taft (1955) are cited in Boice (1983). Hartman's (1984) list is partially based upon Boice's (1983) review.

causality between persons who perform behaviors (called actors) and persons who observe those actors (Jones & Nisbett, 1971; Ross, 1977; Weiner, 1985). The basic finding, which Ross termed the *"fundamental* attribution error" (p. 183), is that actors attribute their actions to environmental factors such as task difficulty, whereas observers tend to view behavior as resulting from stable internal traits. Jones and Nisbett (1971) attributed different perceptions to the different salience of information available to actors and observers. Actors who perform what Jones and Nisbett (1971) termed "preprogrammed and prepackaged" (p. 85) response sequences tend to monitor the environmental stimuli that initiated the sequence. They concluded:

> In short, the actor need not and in some ways cannot observe his behavior very closely. Instead, his attention is directed outward, toward the environment with its constantly shifting demands and opportunities. (p. 85)

For the observer, however, the focus is the actor's behavior. Ross (1977) reviewed research that found that whatever or whoever was the focus of attention tended to be labeled as the causal agent. And given the human tendency toward cognitive balance and consistency, Jones and Nisbett (1987) argued that observers tend to impose trait conceptions upon other's behavior. Other research indicates that from the actor's perspective, good outcomes tend to be attributed to internal traits, whereas negative outcomes are attributed to external or transitory factors (Snyder, Stephan & Rosenfield, 1978).

Research comparing multiple raters often reveals at least some degree of inconsistency (Lambert & Hill, 1994). Botwin and Buss (1989; also see Cheek, 1982, and Quarm, 1981) instructed 59 couples to rate self and other behaviors along 22 personality dimensions such as responsible, secure, and extraverted. The self–other correlations of these sets of ratings ranged from .14 (secure) to .64 (emotional instability) with a mean of .43. Christensen, Margolin and Sullaway (1992) found considerable differences in mothers' and fathers' reporting on the Child Behavior Checklist about their children aged 3–13. Mothers reported more negative behaviors than did fathers, and parents disagreed about the occurrence of a behavior twice as often as they agreed. Christensen et al. (1992) found more consistency with behaviors described as more disturbed, overt, and specific. Similarly, Heppner et al.'s (1992) review of process research—which examines factors relating to client change from the perspective of the client, counselor, and outside observers—indicated inconsistencies across multiple perspectives. Tichenor and Hill (1989), for example, found near zero correlations among ratings by clients, counselors, and observers; other researchers have found that different types of observers assess different constructs, all of which relate to psychotherapy outcome (Heppner et al., 1992; Horvath & Greenberg, 1989; Marmar, Marziali, Horowitz, & Weiss, 1986). Studies of ratings by counselors in training, peer observers, and supervisors display similar inconsistency (Fuqua, Johnson, Newman, Anderson & Gade, 1984; Fuqua, Newman, Scott & Gade, 1986). Like Christensen et al. (1992), Heppner et al. (1992) suggested that agreement among observers should increase with more overt and concrete behaviors.

INCONSISTENCY ACROSS RATING PROCEDURES

Statistical versus Clinical Prediction

The question of valid perspectives has been superceded in the research literature by an issue slightly more complicated. The statistical versus clinical prediction debate refers to whether clinicians (intuitively using data from interviews and tests) or test scores alone (combined statistically) make better predictions or diagnoses. This debate, then, concerns not just the differences between self-reports and clinical judgment, but the differences between the processes clinicians use to make predictions and statistical methods used to make predictions. In a sense, the question may be reformulated as follows: Which is the better method for prediction, psychological measurement or clinical assessment? We could, of course, substitute an I/O psychologist or personnel manager in the place of the clinician.

Clinical-statistical prediction studies typically take the following form. For statistical prediction, one might obtain test scores (e.g., MMPI and WAIS scores) and diagnoses for a group of individuals. The researcher would then employ the scores in a multiple regression equation to predict diagnosis. Clinicians are also provided the same test information employed in the statistical equations, perhaps with case descriptions, and asked to provide diagnoses. The success rate of the two predictions are then compared.

History.   H. G. Hough (1962) presented a detailed history of the development of the statistical-clinical prediction debate. He noted that some of the earliest publications came in the form of exchanges between Viteles (1925) and Freyd (1925). Observing the tremendous growth in personnel selection testing after World War I, Viteles maintained that such tests should not be employed as stand-alone devices and that their scores should not be accepted at face value. In the tradition of Binet, Viteles maintained that tests required a psychologist for their proper interpretation. Freyd replied that such judgment should be left to employers who had more experience with their particular jobs. Clinical judgement, Freyd maintained, needed to be compared to statistical predictions to settle the matter.

Lundberg (1926) then published a classic paper in the area. Lundberg first noted the potential of statistical methods and the aversion to such methods by practitioners. Lundberg then proposed that the two methods were not in opposition, but that the clinical method was "merely the first step in the scientific method" (1926, p. 61). Lundberg (1929) later suggested that the clinical method represented only a crude and unsystematic form of the statistical method.

H. G. Hough (1962) described Allport as the first strong proponent of clinical prediction. Allport (1937) classified prediction into three types. The first was actuarial and consisted of finding statistical regularities (e.g., a mean number of deaths per city that is relatively stable by year). The second type of prediction was based on knowledge of general principles (e.g., normal individuals show increased skill on learning tasks after practice). Both of these types of prediction, it should be noted, were situation-free. The third type of prediction, Allport (1937) maintained, "forecasts what *one* individual man (and perhaps no one else) will do in a situation of a certain type" (p. 352). For this type of prediction Allport maintained that only clinical, *idiographic* methods would suffice. Nomothetic, trait-based measurement might predict psychological phenomena in large groups across situations, but change the scale of study—to one person, in different situations—and idiographic methods must be used. Allport (1942) also criticized statistical methods for (a) failing to distinguish between an event's frequency and its cause; (b) its assumption that an event has the same meaning for all individuals; and (c) its inability to deal with latent or unmanifested causes. He maintained that predictions must be made on the basis of perceived relations, the factors that give rise to change from the present situation, and recognition of contingent factors that cause exceptions to the predictive rules.

One of the first integrations of the two positions was offered by Horst (1941). Although acknowledging the usefulness of statistical prediction, Horst maintained an important role for clinical methods. That is, case studies provide a thorough understanding of individuals; they allow prediction in the absence of general knowledge about relationships necessary for statistical prediction; and they are invaluable to hypothesis formation.

Meehl's (1954, 1957, 1965) reviews are frequently cited as providing the most important impetus for consideration of this issue. In Meehl's (1954) initial review, 19 of 20 studies provided evidence that actuarial prediction equaled or exceeded clinical prediction. These conclusions have been confirmed and extended by subsequent research and reviews (e.g., J. S. Carroll, Wiener, Coates, Galegher, & Alibrio, 1982; Dawes, Faust, & Meehl, 1989; Holt, 1986; Sarbin, 1986a; Sawyer, 1966; Wedding, 1983; Wedding & Faust, 1989; Wormith & Goldstone, 1984). As H. G. Hough (1962) noted, Meehl also contributed to the debate by distinguishing between methods of *data collection* (by test or clinician interview) and methods of *data combination and prediction* (statistical and clinical). Although clinicians can be valuable data collectors, they rarely combine data in an optimal fashion.

Current Status.   The current resolution is to call for some combination of statistical and clinical procedures (cf. K. R. Murphy & Davidshofer, 1988). The best strategy involves collecting information through clinical interviews and tests and then combining data statistically to predict a criterion.

In the tradition of Binet, H. G. Hough (1962) and others have noted that clinical prediction might be used to supplement actuarial prediction. That is, a test is administered, scored, and predictions made; the clinician also interviews the test-taker to gain supplemental information and to be certain test results match the individual's history (which will not occur, for example, if the test-taker responds randomly). Although tests such as the MMPI provide validity indices designed to identify misleading responses, it is commonly considered the clinician's responsibility to interpret the truthfulness of the information provided (Ben-Porath & Waller, 1992). In actual practice, then, this combination of actuarial prediction and clinical confirmation is usually considered the best method of psychological testing and assessment.

Recognizing the pragmatic limitations faced by most clinicians, Wiggins (1973; see also Goldberg, 1970) suggested another approach to this issue. He proposed that (a) if data about a predictor-criterion relation exist, employ statistical prediction combining clinical and test data, or (b) if no data exist, combine the judgments of clinical raters, create a model based on the best raters, or use the model of the best rater instead of the rater her- or himself (Wiggins, 1973). Although the statistical approach may be the ideal, in the real world of clinical practice actuarial data relevant to the case at hand are often unavailable. Even if the relevant trait and environmental dimensions were known, it may also not be feasible to quantify this amount of information (Walsh & Betz, 1985).

Clinical Judgment.   Why do clinicians finish second? Clinicians in these studies often appeared unreliable, that is, when given the same information on two different occasions, they reach different conclusions. Considerable evidence points to an association between observer error and personal characteristics of the clinician (see Rosenthal, 1976, p. 7). Evidence exists to suggest that observers' reports of traits better reflect the observers' personalities than the observed (e.g., D. J. Schneider, 1973). Also, statistical methods are designed to maximize prediction. Clinical judgment could never exceed statistical prediction unless (a) the statistical model was inaccurate (e.g., the relationship being studied was nonlinear and the statistics employed to predict it were linear), or (b) the clinician had access to information not quantified by the tests. The latter could occur if clinicians interviewed clients in these studies, but typically clinicians only read case studies or test results to make their judgments.

Meehl's initial judgment of statistical superiority has not been over-turned, but the debate has often been reframed. In contrast to the nomo-thetic approach of most psychological tests, clinical assessment is often idiographic. A test like the MMPI or the Sixteen Personality Factor Ques-tionnaire (16PF) measures traits assumed to exist in all individuals. Mea-surement dimensions selected by a clinician with one client, however, may be shared with none, some, or all of the clinician's other clients. Skilled clinicians will also be open to modify or change their measurement dimen-sions after repeated meetings with clients. C. McArthur (1956, cited in H. G. Hough, 1962) suggested that clinicians attempt to create a unique model of each client they see. These conditions are not those typically found in the statistical-clinical prediction studies. Also, nomothetic measures typi-cally assess traits, not psychological states. To the extent that the predictors and criteria reflect traits, actuarial predictions based on nomothetic mea-sures should exceed clinical judgment. Clinicians, however, conceivably could be more sensitive to psychological phenomena that vary over time.

Clinicians' skills lie in the selection of variables to be measured and included in causal models to guide intervention (Meehl, 1954). Which tests to use and which variables to measure are decisions best made by clinicians. As noted in Chapter 1, tests provide descriptions, not causal explanations; clinicians and theorists provide the latter. Clinicians' weaknesses typically involve the lack of structure they employ when gathering and combining data. Tests (and presumably, structured interviews) should provide a better method of gathering data, and statistical analysis should provide a better method of combining data.

Clinicians would also enjoy an advantage over tests if they could detect information that tests could not. Shedler, Mayman, and Manis (1993) re-cently provided just such an example. They suggested that a group of indi-viduals exists whom they labelerd *defensive deniers,* that is, persons who deny and repress personal psychological distress. Shedler et al. proposed two hypotheses about this group: (a) they could be identified through inter-views with another person, and (b) their defensiveness would have a physi-ological cost, that is, it would be associated with autonomic reactivity.

In a series of studies, they first instructed research subjects to complete standard mental health scales (e.g., Beck Depression Inventory and the Eysenck Neuroticism scale). Subjects also completed a written version of the Early Memory Test (EMT); the EMT requested accounts of subjects' earliest childhood memories as well as their impressions of themselves, other people, and the mood in the memory. An experienced clinician then evaluated this material to determine each subject's mental health or dis-tress. Finally, the experimenters exposed subjects to laboratory stressors and recorded their changes in heart rate and blood pressure.

Shedler et al. (1993) found one group of persons who reported them-selves as distressed on the self-report scales and who were also rated as distressed by the clinician. However, another group who self-reported mental health was rated as distressed by the clinician. As hypothesized, this second group of defensive deniers did demonstrate greater reactivity on the physiological measures. Shedler et al. thus concluded that human judges could detect defensiveness that standard mental health scales could not. However, it is worth noting that of the 58 subjects who completed the EMT, 29 were judged distressed, 12 were judged healthy, and 17 were left unclassified "because their written responses to the Early Memory Test were too sparse for analysis" (Shedler et al., 1993, p. 1121). This unclassified group, nearly one-third of the total, may represent another subtype who were unwilling or unable to provide data that the clinician was able to process.

Selection and Psychotherapy. In the statistical versus clinical prediction debate, the *purpose* of testing is usually unstated, although it appears that the purpose usually is selection. That is, if one computes correlations between tests and clinicians' judgments of school or work performance and then the actual performance, the implied purpose of such testing in actual situations would be to assist in the admission or rejection of applicants into the performance situation.

Although administrators have had moderate success when using tests for selection, clinicians have experienced more difficulty. Tests are relevant for clinical selection in the sense that one could administer a test for the purpose of selecting an individual to a treatment or to one among many treatments. In regard to the latter, the question becomes, What individual characteristics (i.e., traits) will interact with which treatment environments to produce the best outcome? This is a long-standing intervention issue (e.g., Paul, 1969) that fits within the person-by-situation interaction debate discussed in Chapter 4. As is the case in other areas, research has yet to provide viable methods for matching clients and therapies (Hayes, Nelson, & Jarrett, 1987).

Selection, however, is only one reason clinicians may use tests. Clinicians (and many other types of psychologists) also desire tests that could assist them during the intervention process. That is, tests could assist clinicians to gauge progress during the course of therapy, and ultimately, assess therapeutic outcome. This use of testing, however, implies that one is administering tests repeatedly and for the purpose of detecting psychological phenomena that change.

The issues of using tests for selection and intervention may be combined under the rubric of the treatment utility of assessment (Hayes et al., 1987). The question here is, Do tests contribute to treatment outcome? Because outcome provides the ultimate justification for test use, tests should provide the intervener with information that improves the intervention (Korchin & Schuldberg, 1981; Meehl, 1959). Unfortunately, what little research that has been done suggests that traditional tests have a negligible impact on treatment outcome (Hayes et al., 1987).

Measurement and assessment may be considered treatment interventions in and of themselves. For example, clients' self-monitoring of such behavioral problems as smoking has been shown to decrease that behavior independent of other interventions (e.g., R. O. Nelson, 1977a, 1977b). Interestingly, Hayes et al. (1987) noted that assessment procedures could have treatment utility without possessing any amount of reliability or validity. This could occur, for example, when clinicians' observations of clients' test-taking behavior leads to an improvement in intervention or when the test-taking procedure increases clients' expectations that the intervention will indeed work. In both cases, the changes could occur even if the tests were psychometrically useless. It is a small step, then, to suggest that the widespread use of tests and assessments may be partially a result of their beneficial impact on clinicians' expectations for improvement. Tests may be clinicians' placebos.

The Negligible Effects of the Debate.   Given the results of the typical clinical-statistic review, one might expect clinicians to change their practice. Like employment interviewers, however, most clinicians have yet to suspend their judgment in favor of statistical predictions (e.g., Meehl, 1965, 1986). Proposed explanations for this phenomenon include the face validity of interviews, clinician overconfidence, and the need for the clinician to integrate test data and data not available from tests (K. R. Murphy & Davidshofer, 1988). Clinicians' overconfidence suggests that they do not differ from laypersons who have been shown to possess exaggerated confidence in what they know (e.g., Lichtenstein & Fischhoff, 1977; MacGregor et al., 1988). Professional reasons may also motivate psychologists to add their professional judgments to test data. Hilgard (1987) noted that in hospital settings where psychologists work with psychiatrists and social workers, psychological tests give clinicians something unique to say. He suggested that instead of being simple technicians who report test results in case conferences, tests such as the Rorschach require considerable clinical judgment and legitimize clinicians' desire to participate in group speculation about clinical hypotheses.

Although clinicians may acknowledge the superiority of statistical prediction, the difference between statistical and clinical prediction may be slight enough so as to preclude an acceptance of the former. Sechrest (1963) observed that a test may lack incremental validity, that is, its use does not improve the validity of a prediction. Peterson (1968) suggests that clinicians continue to employ familiar methods because no more effective methods have appeared to take their place.

For example, H. G. Hough (1962; see also Meehl, 1954) cited a study by Sarbin (1942), one of the first researchers to directly compare clinical and statistical prediction procedures. Sarbin examined the relative accuracy of methods of predicting 162 freshmen's first-quarter grade point averages (GPAs). Clinicians worked at a university counseling center and had access to interview data, personality, aptitude and career test scores, high school rank, and college aptitude test scores. The statistical prediction was made on the basis of the high school rank and college aptitude score. Sarbin calculated the following correlations, reported by student gender:

	Men	Women
Clinical prediction	.35	.69
Statistical prediction	.45	.70

The statistical procedure shows a slight advantage. A university administrator interested in selecting students for admission among a large group of applicants would be wise to employ the statistical procedure. A clinician dealing with a single client would probably see little practical difference between the two. Nevertheless, the statistical procedure would require less time than the clinical one, and for that reason alone the former would likely be employed. Few contemporary clinicians would be interested in using clinical prediction for answering a question about GPA or other cognitive abilities where tests have demonstrated predictive validity (C. McArthur, 1968). Clinicians would, however, be interested in clinical procedures for the many personality and related areas (such as interpersonal skills) where such validity is lower or absent.

H. G. Hough (1962) observed that "although statistical modes of prediction at the present time seem to have surpassed the clinical ones in accuracy, neither procedure has done very well" (p. 573; for a more contemporary example of low validity with statistical prediction, see Carbonell, Moorhead, & Megargee, 1984). Hough suggested this may partially be because for events with low occurrence (e.g., suicide or homicide), it is difficult to increase the success of predictions above the base rate. If suicide occurs, for example, in 3 of 100 persons of a certain age range and gender, then the base rate is 3%. Predicting that no one in this population will commit suicide will result in a successful prediction rate of 97%. However, psychotherapists (as well as family members, researchers, and attorneys, for example) are very interested in knowing which three persons will kill themselves. As indicated elsewhere, psychologists are far from that level of prediction. A good psychological test might identify 15 of the 100 who would be likely candidates to commit suicide, but it is unlikely that a test or clinician could differentiate the eventual 3 out of the pool of 15.

CLINICAL OBSERVATION OF TEST BEHAVIOR

As noted in Chapter 1, Binet found it useful to think of the intelligence test as a clinical interview during which the examiners could observe test-takers as they completed the test. These observations formed an important component of the process of psychological assessment, of which completion of the IQ test was only a part. Examinees' activity level, concentration, responses to stress and failure, persistence, and interpersonal behaviors with the examiner could be recorded (C. Kaplan & Owen, 1991). Thus, clinicians' failure to outperform tests alone might partially be a result of statistical-clinical studies' failure to allow clinicians to observe test-takers' behaviors. Is there any evidence to suggest that such observations are valid?

C. Kaplan and Owen (1991) found only three studies that examined the relations between test-takers' testing behavior, test performance, and behavior in nontest situations. Researchers in two studies (Glutting, Oakland & McDermott, 1989; Oakland & Glutting, 1990) found test behavior during completion of an intelligence test to be related to test score but not to classroom behavior. Glutting et al. (1989) suggested that test performance may be explained to some degree by the test-taker's persistence and motivation during testing. Gordon, DiNiro, Mettelman, and Tallmadge (1989) did find test behavior to be related to teacher assessments of behavior and classroom achievement, although they also found instances of disagreement among the three areas.

C. Kaplan and Owen (1991) developed a 43-item Behavioral Observation Scale (BOS) with which to record such testing behaviors as facial expressions, enthusiasm, and irrelevant verbal interruptions. The BOS was completed following the administration of an intelligence test, the Wechsler Preschool and Primary Scale of Intelligence—Revised (WPPSI-R), to 128 children. Although only a few of the correlations computed between the BOS and the criterion measures of WPPSI-R scores and classroom behavior indices reached statistical significance, several results were noteworthy. For example, the children's attention and cooperation during testing was related to teachers' ratings (6–9 months after testing) of their willingness to follow rules ($r = .35$, $p < .01$) and to their attention and persistence to schoolwork ($r = .33$, $p < .01$). These results provided evidence that clinicians' ratings could predict relevant future behaviors. C. Kaplan and Owen (1991) did not report correlations between the WPPSI-R and classroom behaviors.

Attention to the manner in which respondents process test stimuli is perhaps most explicit with the Rorschach, the major projective device. Rorschach examinees are presented with stimuli to which they respond and are later probed to gather more information about their experience of the stimuli. Exner (1978) suggested that the manner of articulation of the response to the projective stimulus can be as important as the content of the response itself. Exner (1978) maintained that "it does seem certain that different people will process the same stimulus cues differently; and the matter of articulation becomes one of the fundamental avenues through which some understanding of the processing may evolve" (p. 55). The clinician's observation of this processing and responding thus becomes central to the scoring of Rorschach responses.

SCIENTIST AS OBSERVER

What about the observational skills of scientists and researchers? As with clinicians, considerable evidence indicates that researchers (a) find what they expect or wish to find in experimental data, and that (b) those expectations may be communicated to subjects (Rosenthal, 1976). Rosenthal (1976) documented numerous cases throughout the sciences where data refuting accepted ideas were ignored or rejected. He noted that Newton did not see the absorption lines in the solar spectrum produced by a prism because he did not expect them to find them there. Similarly, Blondlot's 1903 discovery of N-Rays, which appeared to make reflected light more intense, was confirmed by other scientists, only to be later discounted as observer error. Observers' expectations have also led to faulty counts of blood cells by laboratory technicians and mistaken associations between cancer and cherry angioma, a skin condition.

A good rule of thumb is that the more interpretation and inference that must be made during an observational process, the more likely that error will occur. As Rosenthal (1976) observed, "Some observations require a greater component of interpretation than others" (p. 16). In most sciences, Rosenthal (1976) indicated, the eventual introduction of modern instruments reduces the effects of human observers. These procedures do not replace the human observer, but place the observation in a time or setting that reduces the likelihood of error. A tape recording of a conversation allows an experimenter to replay segments or record the entirety of the discussion—tasks impossible for most experimenters during the interview itself. Thus, the push is to increase the quality of research methodology so as to minimize the role of expectations and preferences in the interpretation of results.

One may also minimize expectancy problems by keeping subjects and experimenters blind to the purposes of the study. In the case of the latter, one may separate the role of the investigator who formulates study hypotheses from the experimenter who runs the study and interacts with subjects.

SUMMARY AND IMPLICATIONS

As with self-reports, raters' systematic errors made may be classified according to their cognitive, affective and motivational, and behavioral and environmental sources. Figure 16 displays a classification of such errors

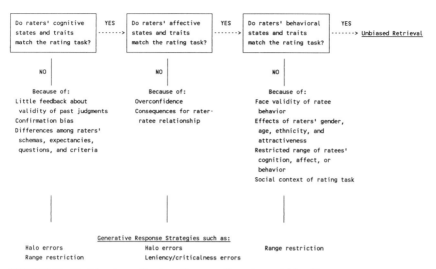

FIGURE 16   Decision tree of systematic errors for rater variables. Generate response strategies in raters result from the degree of mismatch between raters and the rating task.

listed in this chapter. In comparison to self-report errors (shown in Figure 13 in the previous chapter), relatively few motivational or affective errors have been discussed in the literature. This makes sense given that most raters should benefit from valid ratings. However, in some cases, as when the rater–ratee relationship might be adversely affected by the consequences of the rating, raters would be expected to display some of the generative response strategies (e.g., social desirability) found with self-reports.

It is worth noting that self-reports and other ratings share some similar problems. Raters make systematic errors based on their global impressions of the ratee (i.e., halo effect) just as persons completing self-reports make errors based on schemas. Similarly, researchers, clinicians, and lay persons all tend to notice confirming information more than disconfirmation. Interestingly, many of these generative response strategies frequently produce data that are too consistent. That is, raters and self-reporters fail to notice and report the full range of characteristics exhibited by the phenomenon (usually behavior) they are observing.

Yet interviews and self-reports continue to be the dominant measurement methods, probably because of their economy and face validity. Adding structure to interviews improves their psychometric properties just as standardization does so for psychological tests. Rater training is crucial in such areas as behavioral assessment in that it makes concrete the observational procedures. That is, the observer is provided with specific information and practice concerning what, who, where, how, and when to rate.

Providing individuals who complete self-reports with similar training is a possibility worthy of further investigation.

Although important differences exist between data produced by self- and other observers, few guidelines other than tradition and cost exist to direct the choice of observer. Aggregation of multiple observers can be useful, but may also be misleading if one of the observers produces more valid data than others. Actor–observer theory suggests that individuals may be better observers of environmental influences affecting their actions, and others may be better observers of intrapsychic traits. On the other hand, researchers have found that individuals may be unable to accurately identify situational factors that influence their behavior (Nisbett & Wilson, 1977). It would seem incumbent upon theorists and test developers to specify type of observer as one part of the construct explication process (i.e., specifying how the construct should be measured).

In general, psychologists frequently employ self-reports and interviews together to balance the strengths and weaknesses of both. When that is not possible, however, this chapter has provided information that may be employed to build tentative rules for the choice of self-report or interview. In general, I would suggest that a self-report test *only* be employed

1. if no significant mismatches occur between test and test-taker on cognitive, affective or motivational, and behavioral or environmental dimensions;
2. in any type of selection decision where predictor-criterion data exist.

If significant mismatches in (1) occur, then an interview would be preferred, given that (a) no significant mismatches occur between rater characteristics and rating task on the behavior, affect, and cognition (B-A-C) dimensions, and (b) the purpose is to measure intervention-related events.

As noted in Chapter 2, interviews may provide more flexibility than self-report tests when probing for idiographic material relevant to psychological interventions. The remaining question is, what should one do if substantial errors exist in both self-reports and interview data? I would suggest that ethical considerations must then guide whether a client is better served by the provision of no information or error-filled information.

Reviewers of studies comparing clinical and statistical prediction of future events agree on the latter's (typically slight) superiority, but the issue is complex. A key purpose of clinical measurement, hypothesis formation and testing, is often left unaddressed in these studies. That is, clinicians perform their work by forming hypotheses about factors causing client problems and using those hypotheses to guide interventions. Little evidence is available to support the proposition that psychological tests provide *better hypotheses* than clinical judgment, nor is there evidence that testing significantly contributes to the efficacy of psychological interventions. The tests employed in statistical-clinical comparison studies are instruments designed in the tradition of selection testing. As such, they can be very useful for answering questions that can be approached through the perspective of stable, individual differences. The issues of clinical assessment—such as measuring the interaction between type of intervention, intervener characteristics, and the psychological states likely to be the focus of the intervention—may require types of psychological tests yet to be developed.

4 CONSISTENCY WITHIN AND ACROSS SITUATIONS: TRAIT VERSUS ENVIRONMENT

HISTORY

Traditional psychological measurement and behavioral assessment represent one of many schisms found in psychology (Staats, 1983). Proponents of these two approaches tend to be interested in traits or behavior (D. Fiske, 1979). In one world spins traditional measurement, with its emphasis on traits, "real, relatively stable differences between individuals in behavior, interests, preferences, perceptions, and beliefs" (K. R. Murphy & Davidshofer, 1988, p. 17). In another is behavioral assessment, with its emphasis on psychological states as influenced by the environment. Rarely do the literatures of these worlds mix.

The tradition started by Watson focused on behavior. Behaviorists maintained that a psychological phenomenon was not real unless it could be directly observed. Given such assumptions, there was little need for measurement concepts: whatever could be operationally defined (in the laboratory) or observed (in the clinic), existed. On the other hand, the psychological phenomena of interest to the mental testers were almost always assumed to be unobservable: traits were *latent*. No single behavior could constitute intelligence, for example, but intelligence formed an abstract, useful construct that could explain clusters of behavior. Intelligence itself was not directly observable, and to this day the most advanced theories of mental testing discuss intelligence in terms of latent traits.

Some initial integration of the two positions has occurred (e.g., Silva, 1993), but the process remains incomplete. Behavioral assessors, for example, have more recently observed that fear is a construct. That is, fear itself cannot be directly observed, but the construct may be useful for certain purposes. In the clinic, many effective behavioral techniques have been developed to alleviate patients' fears. In the course of applying those techniques, however, assessors have observed a desynchrony between different indices of fear. At the conclusion of treatment, it is common for a snake phobic to be able to approach a snake and verbally report no fear, but still possess an accelerated heart rate. Unless we define *each* phenomenon by its measurement mode, we must resort to the use of a construct to make sense of this situation. As described in Chapter 2, Rachman and Hodgson (1974) cited Lang's (1968) definition of fear as a construct composed of "loosely coupled components" (Rachman & Hodgson, 1974, p. 311) that may covary or vary independently. Because of instances like these, behavioral assessors have become interested in applying traditional measurement concepts in their domain (e.g., Hartman, 1984).

As previously defined, traits are enduring, stable psychological characteristics of individuals. In the context of this chapter, traits are assumed to be

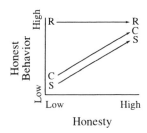

Honesty

FIGURE 17 Cross-situational consistency and inconsistency. R refers to a religious setting such as a church or temple; C refers to a classroom setting; and S refers to a store. As an example of cross-situational inconsistency, even persons with low trait honesty may behave honestly in a religious setting.

stable across *situations*. Thus, persons described as honest are expected to display honest behavior regardless of the situations they find themselves in. Figure 17 displays examples of cross-situational consistency and inconsistency. For example, individuals who score low on a test of honesty may behave dishonestly in classrooms and stores, whereas more honest individuals behave honestly in those settings. In religious situations, however, both high and low honesty individuals may behave honestly. Honest behavior in this case is situation-specific.

Use of the term *trait* implies that enough cross-situational stability occurs so that "useful statements about individual behavior can be made without having to specify the eliciting situations" (Epstein, 1979, p. 1122). Similarly, D. T. Campbell and Fiske (1959) stated that "any conceptual formulation of trait will usually include implicitly the proposition that this trait is a response tendency which can be observed under more than one experimental condition" (p. 100).

The assumption that psychological phenomena are traits has long guided psychological measurement, and the continued faith in trait measurement has been maintained at least partially by its success. For example, most measurement in vocational psychology is guided by trait-and-factor theory. Typically the tests employed by vocational psychologists measure interests, also assumed to be stable. Test-takers' interest scores are compared with the scores of successful workers in all occupations to determine the best fit. The Theory of Work Adjustment (Dawis & Lofquist, 1984; Lofquist & Dawis, 1969) proposes that to maximize worker satisfaction and production, individuals' abilities and needs must be matched with job requirements and reinforcers. Abilities, needs, job requirements and reinforcers are assumed to be relatively stable. Yet vocational counselors have also been influenced by a developmental concept, that of vocational self-concept crystallization (Barrett & Tinsley, 1977). Developmental theorists have suggested that vocational identities—beliefs about one's abilities and needs—tend to grow and shift until they crystallize, typically around age 18. That is, one's vocational identities become a trait, presumably stable for the remainder of one's life. A similar idea, the differentiation hypothesis (Anastasi, 1985), has been proposed to account for the emergence in individuals of group factors of intelligence.

As noted in Chapter 2, traits were first employed with the concept of intelligence, a phenomenon assumed to be transmitted through heredity and immune to environmental influences. Although measures of intelligence predicted school performance better than physiological measures, these mental tasks still fell considerably short of the mark of total prediction. If intelligence tasks fail, where is the next logical place to look for variables to assist in prediction? Personality and temperament were psychologists' answer to that question.

Developers of personality and temperament tests closely copied the assumptions and procedures of intelligence tests (Danziger, 1990). With both intelligence and personality tests, scaling involved aggregation, that is, a total score was obtained by adding the total number of correctly performed tasks or endorsed items. Most importantly, personality, like intelligence, was assumed to be consistent across persons and independent of environments.

THE CONTROVERSY OF MISCHEL AND PETERSON

But trait-based tests are not entirely consistent. Loevinger (1957) wrote that "circumstances contrive to keep behavior largely unpredictable, however constant its propensities" (pp. 688–689). The importance of environment was emphasized in 1968 with the publication of Mischel's *Personality and Assessment* and Peterson's *Clinical Study of Social Behavior.* These books ignited a controversy among measurement and personality theorists that continues to smolder.

Mischel (1968) contended that personality constructs were unstable, that is, the influence of traits was relatively small compared to the influence of situations or environments. He reviewed findings of measurement studies and proceeded to criticize personality psychologists for failing to account for environmental factors when measuring traits: "What people do in all situations and on all tests can be affected, often quite readily, by many stimulus conditions and can be modified substantially by numerous environmental manipulations" (p. 10). Mischel favored measuring behavior in specific situations as opposed to measuring signs of underlying mental processes that could presumably predict future behavior. Mischel believed that new theories of measurement needed to be developed that could account for human adaptability, perception, cognition, self-regulation, and self-modification.

Peterson (1968, p. 23) sounded a similar theme when he stated that research had "suggested very strongly that traditional conceptions of personality as internal behavior dispositions were inadequate and insufficient" because of the influence of situations. Peterson reviewed studies supporting this position in a number of areas, including research documenting the effects of examiners on the behavior of individuals taking projective devices. Whether Rorschach examiners were friendly or distant, Peterson noted, influenced the number and types of responses produced by examinees. Discussing personality assessment in the context of clinical applications, Peterson concluded that because "strong positive evidence for validity and utility is nowhere to be seen . . . it looks as if entirely new approaches to the clinical study of behavior will have to be developed" (p. 3).

Mischel's and Peterson's publications prompted many psychologists to reexamine trait-based measurement approaches. The violation of the expectation of personality consistency produced three major responses. Traditional theorists sought out more evidence for the consistency of traits. In contrast, some psychologists came to reject intrapsychic traits entirely. Most mainstream psychologists did not follow this extreme direction, however, preferring to search for explanations in the interaction between psychological traits and environments.

Reinforcing the Trait Argument

Some contemporary psychologists consider the attack to be repulsed and the battle won (e.g., Block, 1977; Epstein, 1990; Goldberg, 1993). For example, Anastasi (1985) stated that "the long-standing controversy between situational specificity and personality traits has been largely resolved" (p. 134). Anastasi's solution was to redefine traits as repositories of behavioral consistencies. Traits so defined are not causes, but simply convenient descriptions of psychological regularities that occur and may be influenced by environmental contexts.

Based on studies employing a variety of research methodologies and samples, personality researchers have become increasingly confident that long-term stability of personality traits exists. West and Graziano (1989) concluded that research studies have demonstrated substantial long-term stability of personality in children and adults. They also noted, however, that stability declines across longer measurement intervals, is lower in children, and depends on the particular traits measured. Moreover, predictions of personality from one time point to another typically account for only about 25% of the variance, leaving considerable room for environmental and person–environment influences. Examining the stability of vocational interests, Swanson and Hansen (1988; see also D. P. Campbell, 1971) found similar results: although individual variability and environmental influences existed, trait stability could be demonstrated over time. Similarly, Staw and Ross (1985) studied 5000 middle-aged men and found that job satisfaction remained stable even when employees changed jobs and occupation. In a laboratory study with 140 undergraduates, Funder and Colvin (1991) found behavioral consistency across laboratory and real-life settings, although consistency varied by type of behavior.

Epstein (1979, 1980) proposed that trait inconsistency results from insufficient aggregation of measurement observations. For example, one can aggregate 30 test items into a total score, and this total score is likely to predict a set of criteria better than any one of the individual items. Similarly, one can aggregate scores across different measurement occasions. Although acknowledging evidence that behavior changes as a result of situational variables, Epstein (1979) reviewed research that found that aggregating psychological measurements results in a substantial increase in validity coefficients. In terms of classical test theory, aggregation works because behavioral consistencies accumulate over multiple measurements whereas random errors do not (Rushton, Jackson, & Paunonen, 1981). Epstein (1979) also conducted a series of studies that found that through aggregation, intercorrelations of measures of behavior, self-reports, and ratings by others could exceed the typical .30 ceiling.

Most contemporary psychologists view the scores produced on intelligence tests as stable and as indicative of latent traits that operate across environments. For example, Schmidt and Hunter's (1977) work on validity generalization indicated that for general classes of occupational groups, tests of cognitive abilities may have validity across a wide variety of situations. Their research demonstrated that a significant portion of the variability among validity coefficients reported in the literature results from methodological problems such as small sample size, criterion unreliability, and scale range restrictions. When these sources of error are removed, cognitive tests have relatively stable validity within occupational groups. This work complements the position of Mischel (1968) who found that cross-situational consistency existed for behavioral correlates of cognitive abilities. However, validity generalization proponents' claim of negligible variation over sites has not been universally accepted (Tenopyr, 1992; also see Cronbach's [1991b] analysis of Hedges' [1987] data), and the question of situational interactions with cognitive abilities is probably not as closed as many psychologists consider it to be.

The Rejection of Traits: Behavioral Assessment

Behaviorists emphasized the dominance of environmental reinforcement in shaping individual's behavior, be it motor or verbal. In contrast with traditional psychological measurement, behavioral assessors are interested in measuring individuals' past learning histories and current environmental influences (R. O. Nelson & Hayes, 1986). Behavioral assessors observe behavior in natural or contrived settings and attend to stimuli, behavioral responses, and the consequences of those responses.

The processes, assumptions, and procedures of behavioral assessment differ from traditional measurement. Hartman (1984) emphasized that behavioral assessment is direct, repeated, and idiographic. Assessment is direct in that the psychologist measures observable behavior. Any observed behavior is considered to be a sample of potential behavior, as opposed to a sign of an underlying, unobservable trait (cf. Goodenough, 1950, cited in Cronbach & Meehl, 1955). Behavior is measured repeatedly for the purpose of demonstrating relative stability before intervention and change after intervention, thus demonstrating that the intervention is the cause of the behavioral change. Assessment may consist of continuous recording of behavior (when only a few behaviors occur) or some type of time sampling.

With the exception of areas driven by accountability concerns (e.g., psychiatric inpatients), nonbehavioral psychologists typically do little or no formal measurement during the intervention process.

Behavioral psychologists assess idiographic variables, that is, those unique to the individual in question, such as a behavior, affect, and cognition (B-A-C) mode sequence. Cone (1988) argued that nomothetic, trait-based measurements produce data remote from single cases. He suggested that idiographic instruments will be more sensitive to individual behavior change. In this context, idiographic measures are criterion-referenced (i.e., scores are compared to some absolute measure of behavior), whereas nomothetic are norm-referenced (i.e., scores are compared among individuals). Norm-referenced tests are constructed to maximize variability among individuals (Swezey, 1981). However, items that measure behaviors infrequently performed by the population are unlikely to be included in norm-referenced tests. Jackson (1970), for example, suggested that items checked by less than 20% of the test development sample be dropped because they will not contribute to total score variability. Yet those infrequent, idiographically relevant items may be the very ones of interest to change agents and to theorists.

Even the label behaviorists employ differs from traditional measurement. *Behavioral assessment,* rather than behavioral measurement, is the term employed to describe these measurement approaches because (a) psychologists (and to some extent, clients) typically perform the measurement in a clinical setting, in conjunction with behavioral interventions, and (b) psychologists gather different types of measurement data and integrate them in an assessment.

In contrast with traditional psychological measurement, where anyone can be a self- or other-observer if enough measurements are gathered to decrease measurement error, behavioral assessment involves training observers. Training consists of learning an observation manual (containing definitions of relevant behavior and scoring procedures), conducting analogue observations, on-site practice, retraining, and debriefing (Hartman, 1984; Nay, 1979; Paul, 1986). Hartman (1984) noted that research has indicated that better observers tend to be older, female, and to possess higher levels of social skills, intelligence, motivation, and attention to detail.

Behavioral assessors often express ambivalence about the utility of traditional psychometric analyses. For example, behavioral assessors have begun to attend to validity estimates of what are called higher order variables, such as anxiety and fear, that are likely to have more than one factor influencing their scores. For example, whether measures of eye contact, voice volume, and facial expression all relate to a client's complaint about shyness (Kazdin, 1985) can be framed as a question of construct validity. Yet Cone (1988) stated that:

Construct validity will be of no concern to behavioral assessors, in one sense since constructs are not the subject of interest, behavior is; in another sense, behavior can be seen as a construct itself, in which case the instrument will have construct validity to the extent that it "makes sense" in terms of the behavior as the client and the assessor understand it. (p. 59).

Cone (1988) also questioned the importance of discriminant validity, saying that it "is not relevant to an assessment enterprise that is built on the accuracy of its instruments. By definition, an accurate instrument taps the behavior of interest and not something else" (p. 61).

Cone (1988) and Pervin (1984) indicated that additional theoretical and psychometric criteria need to be established for behavioral assessment. For example, Cone (1988) proposed that a behavioral measure, to be considered accurate, must be able to (a) detect the occurrence of a behavior; (b) detect a behavior's repeated occurrence; (c) detect its occurrence in more than one setting; and (d) have parallel forms that allow detection of covariation to demonstrate that the behavior can be detected independent of any particular method. Cone also observed that no guidelines currently exist for selecting dimensions relevant to particular clients or for developing instruments to assess these dimensions; interestingly, both of these criteria are strengths of nomothetic approaches (cf. Buss & Craik, 1985). Cone proposed that such guidelines include (a) determining the environmental context of the problem; (b) determining how other people (or models) cope with the problem in that environment; and (c) constructing a template of those effective behaviors to match against the clients' current repertoire. Such a template could be used to guide therapy and as a gauge of therapy's effectiveness.

Person–Environment Interactions

Although the importance of person–environment interactions has been recognized for some time (Kantor, 1924; Lewin, 1935; Murray, 1938, cited in McFall & McDonel, 1986), interest has surged in the past two decades. Here behavior and environment are viewed as a feedback loop in which both factors influence the other (Magnusson & Endler, 1977). Instead of focusing on persons or situations, behavior must be measured in context, as a process that occurs in a steady stream. Bowers (1973) noted that from an interactionist perspective, individuals influence their environments as much as their environments influence them. To a significant extent, people create their own environments to inhabit (Bandura, 1986; Wachtel, 1973).

Bowers (1973) approached interaction from the perspective of Piaget's concepts of assimilation and accommodation. Individuals assimilate observations from the environment into preexisting cognitive schemas. At the same time, those schemas are modified to accommodate new information in the environment. Bowers (1973) stated that "the situation is a function of the observer in the sense that the observer's cognitive schemas filter and organize the environment in a fashion that makes it impossible ever to completely separate the environment from the person observing it" (p. 328).

Most interactionists assume that cognition mediates the perception of the environment. This is important because it means that behavior that appears inconsistent may actually be indicative of a single construct. For example, Magnusson and Endler (1977) observed that high anxiety may motivate a person to speak excessively in one situation and withdraw in another. The behaviors differ, but the causal construct (anxiety) is the same across situations. As shown in Figure 18, the relation between behavior and construct may be nonlinear. Thus, anxiety may motivate an individual to increase the amount of talking until it reaches a threshold where the individual begins to decrease speech and finally withdraws.

Magnusson and Endler (1977) discussed this type of consistency using the term *coherence.* They suggest that coherent behavior can be understood in terms of the interaction between an individual's perception of a situation and the individual's disposition to react in a consistent manner to such perceived situations. The factors that influence this interaction, such as intelligence, skills, learning history, interests, attitudes, needs and values, may be quite stable *within* individuals. As shown in Figure 19, individuals C and D, who score highly on a test of honesty, may show more honest behavior across two situations than individuals A and B who obtain low scores. However, C and D may also display differences between themselves in honest behavior across situations—perhaps because of slight differences in their perceptions of those situations—even though their mean behavior score is the same across situations. From the perspective of the individual, the behavior appears coherent. From the perspective of the observer who looks only at group differences, the behavior appears consistent. From the perspective of the observer who looks at individuals across situations, the behavior appears inconsistent.

Appropriate techniques for measuring and analyzing the processes suggested by interactionist theory remain in dispute (Golding, 1975; McFall & McDonel, 1986; Walsh & Betz, 1985). For example, McFall and McDonel

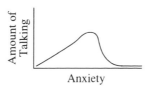

FIGURE 18   Nonlinear relation between anxiety and amount of talking. Anxiety may cause an increase in the amount an individual talks until a threshold is reached. Then the individual talks less and finally withdraws.

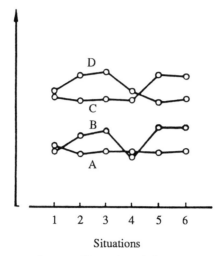

Situations

FIGURE 19.   Coherent, consistent, and inconsistent behavior patterns. Two individual (C and D) who score highly on a test of honesty may show more honest behavior across two situations than two individuals who obtain low scores (A and B). However, C and D may also display differences between themselves in honest behavior across situations even though their mean behavior score is the same across situations. (Reprinted by permission from Magnusson and Endler, 1977.)

(1986) stated that (a) analysis of variance (ANOVA) procedures that examine statistical interactions fail to investigate the theoretically central question of how person–situation variables interact over time; (b) investigators can easily manipulate experiments to show the relative importance of person, situation, or interaction factors; and (c) problems of scale remain, that is, no framework exists for how to determine the meaning of different units or chunks of the person–situation process. Bowers (1973) maintained that a rigid adherence to research methodologies has obscured the interactionist perspective. Experimental methods help investigators primarily understand the influence of situations, and correlational methods assist in the understanding of person differences.

Aptitude-by-Treatment Interactions

Treatments can be conceptualized as types of situations (Cronbach, 1975b; Cronbach & Snow, 1977). In a study where an experimental group is contrasted with a control group, both groups are experiencing different types of situations. Persons can also be conceptualized as having aptitudes, that is, individual characteristics that affect response to treatments (Cronbach, 1975a). As shown in Figures 20 and 21, in an aptitude-by-treatment interaction (ATI) study researchers attempt to identify important individ-

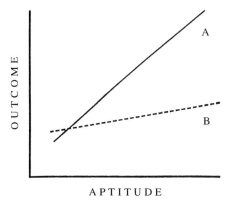

FIGURE 20   Aptitude-by-treatment interaction—1. In an ATI, the aptitude of subjects inter-acts with treatments to produce different outcomes. Here individuals high on an aptitude enjoy a much better outcome when completing treatment A than treatment B. (Reprinted from Cronbach, 1957.)

ual differences that would facilitate or hinder the usefulness of various treatments (Snow, 1991). From a common sense perspective, ATIs should be plentiful in the real world. From the perspective of selection, intervention, and theoretical research, finding ATIs would seem to be of the utmost importance.

ATIs were Cronbach's answer to the problem of unifying correlational and experimental psychology (Snow & Wiley, 1991). Cronbach (1957, 1975b) noted that the battle over the relative dominance of traits versus environment was maintained by ignoring the possibilities of interactions. For example, Cronbach (1975b) reported a study by Domino (1971), which investigated the effects of an interaction between learning environment and student learning style on course performance. Domino (1971) hypothesized that students who learn best by setting their own assignments and

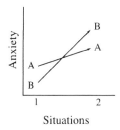

Situations

FIGURE 21   Aptitude-by-treatment interaction—2. Here A refers to a group of individuals with high anxiety and B to a group with low anxiety. Situation 2 causes an increase in anxiety for both groups, but the change is disproportionately larger for group B. Note that treatments and situations are interchangeable.

tasks (independent learners) might show the best outcomes in a class when paired with teachers who provided considerable independence. Similarly, students who learn best when provided with assignments by the teacher (achievement through conformity) might perform better when paired with instructors who pressed for conformity (e.g., teachers stressed their own requirements). Domino did find empirical support for this interaction.

But Cronbach (1975b) and others (cf. D. Fiske, 1979; McFall & Mc-Donel, 1986; Scriven, 1969) have largely abandoned the search for general laws via ATIs in favor of local, descriptive observations. Cronbach (1975) noted that results supporting ATIs are inconsistent, often disappearing when attempts to replicate occur. He saw time and history as the major culprits: many psychological phenomena change over time, frustrating attempts to fix them in terms of general laws. Cronbach (1975) indicated that trait conceptions do not hold to the extent necessary to demonstrate consistent ATIs. This may also be interpreted as support for the position that situations have stronger effects than traits or trait–situation interactions.

I conducted unpublished research that demonstrates the difficulty of finding ATIs. I investigated whether college students' comfort with computer use interacted with one of two interventions designed for alcohol education. The interventions were a computer-assisted instruction (CAI) program for alcohol education and a set of written materials on which the CAI program was based. The interaction hypothesis suggested that students most comfortable with computers and who completed the CAI program would demonstrate the greatest improvement. Students were pretested and posttested on measures of alcohol attitudes, knowledge about alcohol, and alcohol consumption. Given the resources necessary to run the interventions, data were collected over a period of several years, with preliminary analyses occasionally conducted. Analyses at various stages of data collection found the expected interactions, but when the n per cell reached about 15, only an alcohol attitude scale showed a significant interaction. Given these results and a change in my access to a major source of research subjects, the project was suspended.

Environmental Assessment

Instead of searching for stability in individuals, another group of theorists and researchers sought to find consistency in environments and situations. Attempts to categorize and measure environments form the essence of this measurement approach (Conyne & Clack, 1981; Walsh, 1973).

One of the major tasks of environmental assessment is an analysis of environment types, and many classifications systems have been proposed to accomplish this task (cf. Goodstein, 1978; Huebner, 1979; Steele, 1973). Conyne and Clack (1981) proposed that an environment consists of physical, social, institutional, and ecological-climate components that shape and are shaped by people. Moos (1973) classified human environments into ecology, behavior setting, organizational structure, inhabitants' behavior and characteristics, psychosocial climate, and functional reinforcements (i.e., environmental stimuli).

Many vocational psychologists hold a similar assumption about the relative stability of work environments. An occupational setting may attract certain types of individuals on the basis of the setting's *fit* with the needs and abilities of the worker. One of the best-known and well-researched occupational classifications has been proposed by Holland (1959, 1985). He suggested that work environments may be classified as involving one or more of the following dimensions:

1. Realistic environments, where work entails mechanical skill, physical strength, motor coordination, and concrete problems
2. Investigative environments, with an emphasis on research activities, scientific accomplishments, mathematics ability, and abstract problems
3. Artistic environments, involving artistic activities and competencies, and an emphasis on expressive, original, and independent behavior
4. Social environments, where work involves social interactions, liking others, cooperation, and help-giving
5. Enterprising environments, involving selling and leading activities, self-confidence, aggressiveness, and status
6. Conventional environments, involving recording and organizing records and data, conformity, and dependability

Holland (1985) believed, however, that individuals' characteristics may change the climate of the work setting. The most important variable in this regard is the extent to which an individuals' needs and abilities are congruent with the work environments in which individuals find themselves. Very incongruent individuals leave environments, whereas moderately incongruent individuals will change, moving toward the dominant persons in the environment.

As shown in Table 7, most person–work environment fit theories suggest that the degree to which individuals fit their work environment determines their level of productivity and job satisfaction. Thus, realistic individuals working in realistic occupations will be most productive and satisfied, Investigative individuals in investigative occupations, and so on. Holland's theory provides for similarity of occupational types (e.g., investigative and artistic occupations are more similar than investigative and conventional) so that different fits may be rank ordered in terms of their degree of expected productivity and satisfaction.

A crucial question in environmental assessment is whether to classify environments or perceptions of environments. The person many consider the founder of person–environment interaction, Kurt Lewin, continued a Gestalt perspective in which behavior was believed to occur in the context

TABLE 7   Rank Order of Expected Productivity and Satisfaction Indices by Person–Environment Fit[a]

	R	I	A	S	E	C			
R	1								
I	2	1						R	
A	3	2	1				C		I
S	4	3	2	1			E		A
E	3	4	3	2	1			S	
C	2	3	4	3	2	1			

[a]R refers to realistic occupations, I to investigative, A to artistic, S to social, E to enterprising, and C to conventional. The hexagon at right shows the degree of similarity among these different occupational types; adjacent occupations are more similar. Thus, R occupations are more similar to I and C than to S. The matrix at left displays the resulting rank order of expected productivity and job satisfaction indices based on the similarity of person–work environment fit.

of an individual's total perceptual field of an environment (Lewin, 1951). That is, people are surrounded by a self-generated psychological environment and a nonpsychological environment. As in other person–environment theories, cognition has been proposed as a significant mediator of how environmental events are perceived, understood and transformed by individuals (Bandura, 1986; Conyne & Clack, 1981). From this perspective, an understanding of how an individual thinks about a situation is necessary for a person–environment analysis. For example, R. B. McCall (1991) observed that after completing a Marine Corps' confidence course, recruits may view the course as a confidence builder or as intimidating. Some theorists had hoped that cognition might prove to be stable across situations, but research results have not been supportive. For example, attributional style—characteristic ways individuals explain and interpret life events (S. Fiske & Taylor, 1984)—appears to possess little consistency across situations (Bagby, Atkinson, Dickens, & Gavin, 1990; Cutrona, Russell, & Jones, 1984).

What kinds of measurements are undertaken in environmental assessment? Conyne and Clack (1981) provided several examples. Cognitive maps are spatial representations of individuals' psychological environments. Conyne and Clack described a researcher who instructed students to plot where in their neighborhoods they felt high and low stress. The resulting map helped to explain truancy by showing that a city school bus route stopped at many high-stress areas where students were afraid of being physically attacked. Geographic maps can be used to locate individuals with psychological characteristics and events (e.g., academic achievement, depression) to examine potential relationships between environment and person. However, many environmental assessment procedures consist only of self-report questionnaires that ask respondents to rate environments along different theoretical dimensions. In Moos' (1979a, 1979b) social climate scales, for example, individuals rate such environments as their college residence hall, classroom, family, and work along such dimensions as relationships, personal growth, and system maintenance and change. Similarly, vocational psychologists typically measure environments by assessing (via self-reports) the interests and abilities of persons successful in specific occupations.

Moderators of Cross-Situational Consistency

Moderator variables are those that change the nature of the relation between two other variables. For example, one may propose that investigative individuals would be most productive and satisfied in an academic or scientific environment as compared to other occupational situations. However, one might find that other variables, such as ethnicity or gender, affect that relation. Female and male academics might produce equal number of publications, but females might also experience less job satisfaction.

A variety of potential moderating variables have been proposed and investigated. Research has suggested differences in consistency by response mode and by levels of aggregated measures (Diener & Larsen, 1984; Epstein, 1983; Mischel & Peake, 1982; Rushton, Brainerd, & Pressley, 1983). For example, Violato and Travis (1988) found that male elementary school students demonstrated more cross-situational consistency on the variable of behavioral persistence. Similarly, Connell and Thompson (1986) found infants' emotional reactions were more consistent across time than their social behavior. Variables such as age (Stattin, 1984), gender (Forzi, 1984), socioeconomic status, and cognitive abilities (Violato & Travis, 1988) have also been found to moderate cross-situational consistency.

Bem and Allen (1974; also see Diener & Larsen, 1984; Lanning, 1988; Zuckerman et al., 1988) suggested that individuals themselves are moderators of cross-situational consistency. That is, some persons may act consistent across situations, and others may not; cross-situational consistency could be considered an individual difference variable. Thus, in person A, the trait of honesty is manifested across all situations; with person B, honesty occurs only at church; and person C exhibits little honesty in any situation. Investigators who conduct studies averaging these individuals would find no support for cross-situational positions, but a disaggregation of the data might demonstrate such consistency for pairings of similar individuals such as A and C. Bem and Allen (1974) found that students' ratings of their cross-situational consistencies often did match their behaviors in different situations. For example, students who said they were friendly across situations did show more consistency. However, more recent research has provided mixed support for this position. Chaplin and Goldberg (1984) failed to replicate Bem and Allen's results, whereas P. A. Burke, Kraut and

Dworkin (1984) found that subjects' ratings of personal traits, cross-situational consistency, and the traits' importance to their self-schemas were highly correlated. Greaner and Penner (1982) found a low reliability estimate for the 1-item consistency measure previously employed by Bem and Allen.

States and Traits

Psychologists have also suggested that psychological phenomena may be manifested through traits and states. States are transitory psychological phenomena that change because of psychological, developmental or situational causes. Spielberger (1991) credited Cattell and Scheier (1961) with introducing the state–trait distinction. Even theorists interested in measuring traits acknowledge the presence of state effects in psychological testing. F. M. Lord and Novick (1968), for example, observe that in mental testing "we can perhaps repeat a measurement once or twice, but if we attempt further repetitions, the examinee's response changes substantially because of fatigue or practice effects" (p. 13).

State constructs have occasionally been invoked to explain the inconsistencies found in psychological measures. For example, Matarazzo suggested that the MMPI measures states, not traits, and that it "reflects how you're feeling today, or how you want to present yourself that day" (Bales, 1990, p. 7). Similarly, Dahlstrom (1969) indicated that MMPI scales' reliability should not be assessed through test–retest methods because since "there is scarcely any scale on the MMPI for which this general assumption [of temporal stability] is tenable for any period of time longer than a day or two" (p. 27). Even intelligence may possess state properties: IQ test scores have been shown to be affected by amount of schooling (Ceci, 1991; see also Bandura, 1991, and Frederiksen, 1986). Retest of intelligence scores at 1-yr intervals show high stability but decrease substantially when the retest interval lengthens beyond that period (Humphreys, 1992).

Although trait conceptions have historically dominated measurement, psychologists have always recognized states and struggled to integrate them into measurement theory and practice. Loevinger (1957), for example, reviewed D. W. Fiske and Rice's (1955) theory for explaining intraindividual response variation. Fiske and Rice suggested that individuals will change their response to an item because

1. something changes within the individual (e.g., the individual matures),
2. the order of item presentation changes, or
3. the stimulus situation changes.

Fatigue, for example, is a physiological variable that might produce inconsistent responding on psychological tests. D. W. Fiske and Rice (1955) suggested that such variability is lawful, although Loevinger (1957) noted that such a belief is at variance with the classical test theory assumption that these errors are random. Loevinger also reviewed studies that demonstrated, over retests, improvements in personality functioning and intelligence. Such improvements, Loevinger suggested, are a function of practice effects and learning by the organism. In other words, psychological phenomena treated by traditional measurement approaches as traits may also demonstrate state effects.

Perhaps the most well-known state–trait measure is the State–Trait Anxiety Inventory (STAI; Spielberger, Gorsuch, & Lushene, 1970). The STAI consists of two 20-item Likert scales to measure state anxiety (i.e., situation-specific, temporary feelings of worry and tension) and trait anxiety (i.e., a more permanent and generalized feeling). Both scales contain items with similar and overlapping content: state scale items include "I am tense," "I feel upset," and "I feel content," whereas trait scale items include "I feel nervous and restless," "I feel secure," and "I am content." However, the state scale asks test-takers to rate the items according to how they feel "at this moment," whereas the trait scale requests the ratings to reflect how the test-takers "generally" feel. The instructions do seem to produce the desired difference: test–retest reliabilities for the state scale, for example, are considerably lower than for the trait. Spielberger (1991) also developed the State–Trait Anger Expression Inventory. Spielberger described state anger as a condition that varies over time as a result of such factors as perceived injustice and frustration. He distinguished state anger from trait anger, the latter being a disposition to perceive many situations as frustrating or annoying and to respond in those situations with state anger. Thus, the two constructs are related: persons high in trait anger will experience more frequent state anger.

Process Research

Psychotherapy researchers often distinguish between outcome research, designed to test the efficacy of various interventions, and process research, designed to detect variables that change during the intervention. Process research typically consists of single-subject, within-subject, or between-subject designs that assess such variables as counselor verbal behavior and aspects of the client–counselor relationship (Heppner et al., 1992).

Process research focuses on changes in the counselor, client, or counselor–client relationship within (e.g., treatment sessions) and across (e.g., different types of treatments) situations. The hope is that these changes will be related to intervention outcome, although it has been difficult to demonstrate a strong process–outcome link (Elliott et al., 1987; Heppner et al., 1992; Hill et al., 1988). The failure to show such a relation may partially result from researchers' emphasis on studying counselor variables to the exclusion of client variables (Heppner et al., 1992; Hill, 1982). Heppner et al. (1992) observed that process research typically assumes the client to be a passive agent instead of an active information processor. Measurement of process variables is performed by trained raters who assess segments or all of the counseling sessions. How much to measure has been one of the central questions of process research, and it appears that the purpose of the research can suggest answers (Friedlander et al., 1988; Heppner et al., 1992). For example, if the researcher is interested in process variables that apply across groups of counselors and clients, small segments of sessions (totaling as little as 10% of the session) have been found to be representative of the process in groups. If the researcher is interested in a single case, however, it appears necessary to sample entire sessions.

SUMMARY AND IMPLICATIONS

Situational influences on human behavior have been the most noticed sources of trait inconsistency. In response, psychologists have proposed the following:

1. Reinforcing arguments that traits exist, as in work on aggregation
2. Rejecting traits, as in behavioral assessment
3. The existence of person–environment interactions, where traits and environments influence each other in a continuous system
4. ATI, where aptitudes interact with environments, the latter conceptualized in terms of treatments
5. Environmental assessment, involving classification of environmental types
6. Moderators of cross-situational consistency, variables that facilitate consistency of traits across situations
7. Psychological states, constructs defined as variables that change over time
8. Process research, where researchers attempt to isolate and study variables that change during psychological interventions

Many psychological phenomena demonstrate trait and state characteristics. In other words, these phenomena are likely to demonstrate some stability (that is, to be a reflection of psychological traits) and change (that is, to be influenced by environmental and developmental factors). Goldberg's (1993) question, "Do traits exist?" may be rephrased as Cone's (1991), "What levels of aggregation of tests and criteria are needed to demonstrate trait properties?" To demonstrate trait consistency, it appears necessary to aggregate items, persons, and occasions of measurement. In addition, some people and dimensions appear more stable than others (Bem & Allen, 1974; R. P. Martin, 1988).

Idiographic approaches appear to have been more successful than nomothetic procedures for displaying cross-situational consistency. For example, C. G. Lord (1982) found that idiographic measures of conscientious behavior were consistent across situations, whereas nomothetic methods were not. Walsh and Betz (1985) maintained that behavior is "reasonably predictable, given knowledge of an individual's perception of the situation and of the individual's disposition to respond in that situation" (p. 13). The problem may center primarily on handling error: so many unknown factors operate in the interaction between person and situations that only repeated idiographic assessment may provide some sense of how any particular individual will behave across situations. Under these conditions, Magnusson and Endler suggested (1977, p. 11) that "individual behavior across different situations provides a consistent, idiographically predictable pattern." Clinical assessment, for example, provides a unique perspective on individual and situational factors. However, clinical assessors still cannot, for example, make predictions of person–environment interactions that would result in suicidal or homicidal behavior by a specific individual at a particular time.

Despite their initial promise, approaches such as ATIs and person–environment interaction theories have had relatively little impact on psychological measurement. The problem, Walsh and Betz (1985) believe, "is one of measuring and describing the multidirectional transactions. Currently this is a measurement task that has been very difficult to operationalize and make real" (p. 13). Measurement error is a plausible explanation for the failure to find person–environment interactions (Cronbach, 1991b). Imprecise measurement may obscure interactions, and measurements not guided by theory may lead to inappropriate or insensitive measurement (R. B. McCall, 1991). Partially because of cost and the fact that investigators have yet to settle upon a taxonomy for situations (McFall & McDonel, 1986), person–environment approaches have yet to command the attention given to traditional measurement.

McFall and McDonel (1986) saw the person–situation question as "inherently unresolvable" (p. 238) and suggested that the debate should be dropped. Instead, psychologists should continue elsewhere their search for the "meaningful units with which to describe, predict, and explain behavior" (p. 238). Tryon (1991) reached a similar conclusion. He maintained that situational specificity simply involves different mean levels of behavior in one situation compared to another. As shown in Figure 22, individuals may demonstrate, in general, more anxiety in two testing situations (situations 2 and 4) than in two lectures (situations 1 and 3). Arguments for traits, Tryon suggested, involve persons maintaining their rank on a construct within the distribution. If Persons A, B, C, and D rank first, second, third, and fourth on the amount of anxiety they display in a lecture, and then maintain that ranking in other settings, trait arguments will be upheld

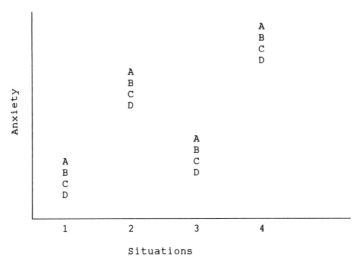

FIGURE 22   Situational specificity and traits. Situations 1 and 3 are lecture periods for two different classes (e.g., English and mathematics). Situations 2 and 4 are testing periods for the same classes. It is possible that groups of individuals will show differences between the lecture and testing situations (thus supporting situational specificity), but that individuals' levels of anxiety will remain in the same rank order across situations (thus supporting trait concepts).

even if overall levels of anxiety change. Tryon (1991) believed that it is possible to hold both the situational specificity and trait positions because "activity is both very different across situations yet predictable from situation to situation" (p. 14). He concluded:

> Situational differences are so large that they stand out immediately. Person consistency is more subtle and requires aggregation to reach substantial effect size. The Spearman-Brown prophecy formulate indicates that either effect size can be made arbitrarily large depending upon the level of aggregation chosen. The implication for research and clinical practice is that one should choose the level of aggregation that provides the necessary effect size to achieve the stated purpose of the empirical inquiry at hand. (p. 14)

5 CONSISTENCY ACROSS CONSTRUCTS: LACK OF DISCRIMINANT VALIDITY

HISTORY

According to the classical definition of validity, a valid test is one that measures what it is supposed to measure; Cronbach (1992) reported that such a definition was officially noted in a 1921 publication by a group that became the American Educational Research Association (AERA). From this perspective, a test of honesty that actually measures honesty is valid; an honesty test that measures social desirability and honesty is less valid; an honesty test that measures only social desirability is invalid. Validity has been contrasted with reliability: Reliability is the consistency of scores on the same test, whereas validity is the consistency of scores between related tests (D. T. Campbell & Fiske, 1959). Similarly, Mischel (1968) defined reliability as agreement between tests under maximally similar conditions, whereas validity is agreement under maximally dissimilar conditions. It is

113

important to recognize, however, that tests themselves do not possess reliability or validity. Rather, reliability and validity estimates are based on data provided by a sample of individuals who complete the test under certain conditions. Consequently, reliability and validity estimates are not static, but assume a range of values that partially depend on variables other than the test itself.

Current definitions of construct validity, from one perspective, tend to be less rigorous than previous ones (Moss, 1992). The focus has moved from what a test measures to whether evidence exists to support whether a test can be put to a certain use; the validity focus has shifted away from the test itself and toward the inferences drawn from test scores (American Psychological Association [APA], 1985). Current use of the term *construct validity* refers to efforts to justify a particular interpretation of a test score (Cronbach, 1969; Moss, 1992) as compared to knowing what a test actually measures. With the new definition, investigators examining the construct validity of a test of executive leadership might present evidence to suggest that the test *could* be interpreted as a test of leadership. These researchers might conduct research that finds (a) a .30 correlation between leadership test scores and current management level, and (b) a single strong factor, in a factor analysis, that contains items pertaining to leadership behavior. Since tests may have multiple purposes, evaluations of validity in this example would center on whether the test score interpretations are valid for selecting management leaders.

Types of Validity

Validity during the first 50 years of organized psychology was typically conceived of as the ability of a test to predict a criterion (Cronbach, 1957). Thus, criterion validity refers to validating a test by correlating its scores with those of a relevant criterion. For example, if you wish to predict who will succeed as a manager in a company, you need a test that correlates highly with managerial success. Similarly, if you develop a test to measure psychopathology, you might validate the test by comparing its scores with those of psychiatrists' ratings.

At least two factors influenced psychologists to refine their thinking about test validity. Before 1950, little consensus existed about a theory of validity (Cronbach & Meehl, 1955). Psychologists proposed numerous types of validity, including intrinsic (Gulliksen, 1950), logical and empirical (Cronbach, 1949), factorial (Guilford, 1946), and face (Mosier, 1947). Thus, it was difficult to know how to develop or recognize valid tests. Psychologists needed some structure to organize and make sense of the diverse ways of thinking about validity.

Criterion validity also posed problems. From a scientific viewpoint, a test that could predict managerial success was seen as having little generalizability to other nonmanagerial situations. Thus, data from this test would offer limited utility for formulating general scientific laws (Loevinger, 1957). In the clinical area, psychologists did not wish for their tests to be ultimately validated against criteria such as psychiatrists' ratings (Cronbach, 1992). Finally, criteria are also measurements that share many of the difficulties of predictors. These issues provided an impetus to develop other methods of test validation.

In response to the disorganization of validity concepts and the overemphasis on criterion validity, the APA published in 1954 its *Standards for Psychological Tests*. Those standards recognized four types of validity: predictive, concurrent, content, and construct. Concurrent validity was identical to predictive validity, except that with concurrent validity, predictor and criterion were measured at the same time. Later versions of the *Standards* (e.g., APA, 1985) combined predictive and concurrent validity into criterion validity.

Content and construct validity were concerned with whether a test measured what it was supposed to measure. Content validity focused on the content of the test items and their relation to the intended domain of the test. To be valid in this sense, a test developer had to demonstrate that the content of a test's items was representative of the universe of relevant content. In achievement testing, for example, content validity results when test items match the instructional topics. Construct validity focused more on the abstract construct the test actually measured, regardless of test item content or other factors. For example, an honesty test might be composed of self-report items that apparently have little to do with honest behavior (e.g., "I always get up at 6:30 A.M.") but when aggregated are significantly correlated with honest behavior in some situations. As K. R. Murphy and Davidshofer (1988) put it, "Content validity is established if a test looks like a valid measure; construct validity is established if a test acts like a valid measure" (p. 107).

Initially, content and construct validity were viewed as unrelated to the two other sorts of validity proposed in the APA document. Predictive and concurrent validity were evaluated by the validity of decisions based on tests. For example, if the criterion was first-year college grade point average (GPA) and Test A correlated with GPA at .60, it would possess greater predictive validity than a test that correlated at .30. Nevertheless, attempts to estimate the construct validity of Test A might well fail: that is, we might not understand what the test measured, even if it could predict GPA. As described in Chapter 1, much effort during the first 50 years of psychological measurement was devoted to finding tests that predicted socially relevant criteria.

Despite this initial split, the contemporary view places construct validity as the fundamental type of validity on which the other types depend (Anastasi, 1992; Kagan, 1988). Predictive validity depends on construct validity because it is the psychological phenomena that test and criterion measure which determines the relation between the two. I use the term *phenomena* deliberately to indicate that any particular psychological test reflects multiple influences. As indicated previously, test scores do not simply reflect item content, but also cognitive, affective and motivational, and behavioral processes, characteristics of the modes assessed (e.g., behavioral, affective, and cognitive), states, traits, situations, and raters and ratings processes.

In other words, tests have multiple validities (Meehl, 1991; Wiley, 1991). If the factors that affect test scores are irrelevant to the test's purpose, those factors may be termed invalidities (Wiley, 1991). If one does not understand the multiple factors affecting test scores—that is, if construct validity estimates are unavailable—then estimates of predictive validity are likely to be inconsistent because of respondent characteristics, environmental characteristics, scale characteristics, their interactions, and so forth. The test developer must have knowledge of a test's validities and invalidities, in regard to a particular testing purpose, to understand how the predictor–criterion relation generalizes across situations. In addition, test developers concerned with predictive validity typically start the test development process with a large pool of items and determine which items (or aggregations of items) correlate with the criterion. Some of those correlations are likely to reflect actual predictor–criterion relations and some are likely to occur by chance. Indeed, if the initial estimate of predictive validity capitalizes on chance (which is likely to occur when the test developer uses the same individuals to evaluate test items and then correlates the resulting items with an external criterion), subsequent estimates are likely to be lower. This is the typical outcome of cross-validation studies.

More than predictive validity depends on construct validity. Cronbach and Meehl (1955) maintained that construct validity was the approach investigators needed to take when they could not operationally define their variables of interest. Similarly, if no adequate criteria or universe of content were available to validate a test against, Cronbach and Meehl suggested that construct validity was the necessary approach. They indicated that construct validity is also necessary when theory development is the purpose of testing: "Typically, however, the psychologist is unwilling to use the directly operational approach because he is interested in building theory about a generalized construct" (p. 284).

Constructs, Theories, and Valid Measurement

To understand construct validity, one must first understand the meaning of the word *construct*. Cronbach and Meehl (1955) defined a construct as an attribute of individuals evidenced by test performance. K. R. Murphy and Davidshofer (1988, p. 98) defined constructs as "abstract summaries of some regularity in nature" indicated by observable events. Both of these definitions connect unobservable, latent constructs to observable events or behaviors.

Why do measurement psychologists employ constructs? Constructs allow generalizations beyond any specific situation at any particular point in time. They enable theorists to create scientific laws and to appropriately name phenomena. Cook and Campbell (1979) indicated that demonstrating the validity of constructs is crucial to all types of psychological research, experimental and correlational. They wrote that "it should be clearly noted that construct validity concerns are not limited to cause and effect constructs. All aspects of the research require naming samples in generalizable terms, including samples of people and settings as well as samples of measures or manipulations" (Cook & Campbell, 1979, p. 59).

As indicated in Figure 23, some constructs may not be directly related to behaviors but to other constructs that have such connections. The process of describing the relations between abstract constructs and observable events is known as construct explication. K. R. Murphy and Davidshofer (1988) offered one description of this process:

1. identify behaviors related to the constructs
2. identify related constructs
3. identify behaviors of these other constructs and see if they overlap with behaviors of original construct

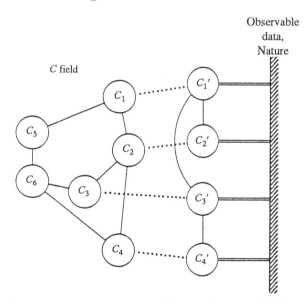

FIGURE 23 Relations between constructs and data. As Torgerson (1958) explained, constructs on the right lie close to real-world phenomena. Those on the left have no operational definition, but are connected to observable data via another set of constructs. (Reprinted by permission.)

Suppose, for example, a research team develops a measure of depression. They might begin by reading the research literature and discovering that other researchers have proposed a number of behaviors thought to be associated with depression, such as disturbed sleep, loss of self-reported interest in usual activities, significant changes in weight, fatigue, and diminished cognitive abilities (American Psychiatric Association, 1987). Related constructs include fear and anxiety, associated with such behaviors as excessive worry, irritability, trouble with concentration, and physical discomforts such as palpitations, sweating, and shaking (American Psychiatric Association, 1987). Given the relative separateness of the behaviors on the two lists, the researchers should be able to develop a depression scale that does not correlate with measures of fear or anxiety. If they employ depression and anxiety measures with a group of individuals and find low intercorrelations, they would have produced a useful start on construct explication and a nomological net. The latter is a description of relations among constructs and behaviors that constitutes a theory (Cronbach & Meehl, 1955). If they find unexpectedly high correlations, however, a problem exists with the measurement devices or with the theory that suggested such construct-behavior links.

Nomological networks are desirable for constructs that we do not believe should be linked to one specific behavior. For a construct such as aggressiveness, theorists might not wish to define it solely as the occurrence, for example, of one person physically striking another. As K. R. Murphy and Davidshofer (1988) wrote,

> We cannot say precisely what aggressiveness *is*, but we can describe how an aggressive child might act and we can make reliable and meaningful statements about children's level of aggressiveness by observing their behavior. The more detail included in descriptions of the nomological network, the more precision there will be in describing constructs. (p. 101)

Few or no "incontrovertible indices" (Cone, 1988, p. 58) exist that enable us to operationally define psychological phenomena. Peterson (1968) stated that few "clear-cut types of behavior disorders . . . seem to occur in nature" (p. 5). We may also say that ordinarily, behavior is multiply determined and that measurements have multiple validities.

So far this discussion presents constructs as abstract phenomena and behaviors as concrete, observable events. This dichotomy mirrors the assumption in much of the traditional measurement and behavioral assessment literatures that constructs are latent and behaviors are overt. R. P. Martin (1988) observed, however, that even behavior "has unclear boundaries and arbitrary characteristics, as do the other units of analysis" (p. 13). In an important sense, behavior can be considered a construct. That is, behavior becomes a construct if we assign a name to two instances of a behavior. If we observe a person smoking a cigarette on one occasion, we can call that behavior "smoking." However, if that same person smokes again, smoking becomes a construct because the two instances cannot be exactly the same. For example, which of the following constitutes smoking: (a) taking one puff of a cigarette and putting it out? (b) putting a cigarette in one's mouth without lighting it? (c) chewing smokeless tobacco? or (d) smoking tobacco in a cigar? Nicotine consumption might be a better labeling of the four behaviors above than smoking. Some definition or description of the behaviors must be offered to classify instances as smoking or nicotine consumption, and the production of those definitions and descriptions are the essence of explicating constructs.

The question of whether a phenomenon is a behavior or a construct may have more to do with the construct explication process than the intent of the assessor. As part of a training exercise in clinical assessment, I instructed 54 students to complete two tasks while they watched a film of psychotherapist Carl Rogers with a client named Gloria (Shostrum, 1966). In the first task, as shown in Figure 24, they simply checked the number of questions they saw Rogers ask—a seemingly straightforward behavioral observation. In the second task, students rated *emotion experienced* by Gloria along the scale shown in Figure 24. My expectation was that students would demonstrate much more consensus (as indicated by less dispersion of scores) with the question counting task than with the global rating. As shown in Figures 25 and 26, however, the opposite occurred. Although other explanations could be proposed for these results (e.g., fewer categories in the rating task), I suggest that the global rating was less ambiguous for the students because of (a) the relatively clear explication of the rating task and (b) the difficulties students encountered when attempting to decide whether Rogers actually asked a question, paraphrased a response, or so forth in any particular exchange.

```
1.  # of questions Rogers asked:

1  2  3  4  5  6  7  8  9  10  11  12  13  14  15  16  17  18  19  20  21  22  23

24  25  26  27  28  29  30  31  32  33  34  35  36  37  38  39  40  41  42  43


2.  Rate Gloria on the construct of emotion experienced:

        1            2            3            4            5

Clear resistance to feeling probes      Responds to probes
Many intellectualizations                 with feelings
Feelings denied                         Few intellectualizations
Frequent incongruence of                Feelings acknowledged
     feeling/content                    Frequent congruence
No emotions expressed nonverbally       Emotions expressed
                                          nonverbally
```

FIGURE 24. Instructions for assessing questions and emotion experieced.

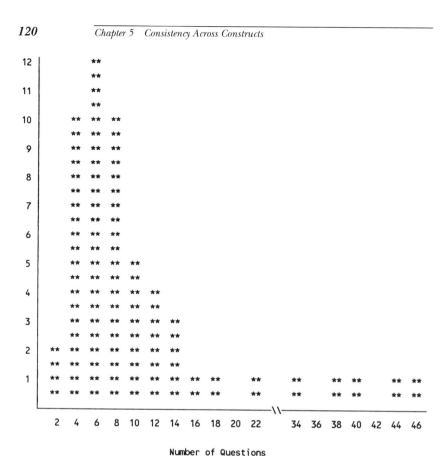

Number of Questions

FIGURE 25   Histogram of student count of questions asked.

Behavioral assessment texts describe instruction manuals for observers that contain procedures for creating and employing such descriptions. Nay (1979), for example, suggested that manuals should provide the following:

1. Rationale for observations
2. Description of applicable settings
3. Coding definitions
4. Rules for sampling behavior
5. Rules for observer behavior
6. Methods for assessing observer reliability
7. Methods for assessing observation validity

In essence, the manual defines what is *included* and *excluded* as a recordable behavior. The procedure is very similar to that typically described in construct explication.

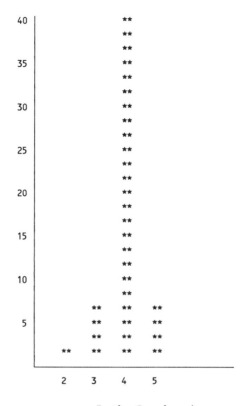

FIGURE 26   Histogram of student ratings of emotion experienced.

Knowledge accumulation is a matter of elaborating or deepening a nomological network as well as increasing confidence in the certainty of its components (Cronbach & Meehl, 1955). Initially, the network will be limited in the number and connections of its components. As research data become available, constructs should be modified and dropped. New constructs and new connections among existing constructs should be added.

The strength and weakness of this approach is that theories and measurements are inexorably linked. Its strength lies in the fact that measurement content and procedures can be produced from theory. The weakness results from instances when unexpected or disconfirming results occur: in such cases, the data may result from measurement or theory problems, and no clear guidelines exist for separating the two. One must possess a theory valid enough to predict how test data should appear. Without such theory, demonstrating the validity of measurement becomes difficult.

Theoretical and measurement precision are also linked. Again, precision is the ability to detect small differences. If a test score is multiply determined and the construct of interest is but one of the determining factors, then it is likely to be difficult to detect small instances of that construct in test scores. Imprecise measurement occurs when we fail to adequately isolate a particular construct for which we are employing a measurement device.

MULTITRAIT–MULTIMETHOD MATRICES

If construct validity is the key type of validity, how should it be evaluated? K. R. Murphy and Davidshofer (1988) observed that when assessing validity, test developers typically have no standards to compare tests against; it is for that reason that measurement psychologists seldom use the term *accuracy* when discussing tests. Instead, psychologists gather evidence from a variety of sources to demonstrate validity. Cronbach and Meehl (1955) suggested that construct validity could be investigated through studies of group differences, correlation matrices and factor analysis, the internal structure of tests (e.g., item intercorrelations), change over occasions, and studies of individuals' test-taking performance. Cronbach (1989) later amended that list to include the examination of items, internal correlations, score stability, protocol analysis of tests, varying test procedures experimentally, attempts to improve scores, correlation with practical criteria and other tests, and studies of group differences. Similarly, K. R. Murphy and Davidshofer (1988) wrote that laboratory and field experiments, questionnaires, and unobtrusive observations might provide construct validity data. Murphy and Davidshofer concluded that "it would be fair to say that any type of data or statistic might be useful in determining construct validity" (p. 103). Anastasi (1986) reached a similar conclusion: "Almost any information gathered in the process of developing or using a test is relevant to its validity" (p. 3). All of these methods could provide data to compare against theoretical expectations and predictions.

Thus, criteria for evaluating the construct validity of any test would seem to be plentiful. The problem, however, is how to weight various pieces of evidence for validity, particularly if the pieces are contradictory or possess substantial error.

Campbell and Fiske

Two of the key ideas to emerge from the study of construct validity were convergent and discriminant validity. A valid test should converge or correlate with another test that measures the same or a similar construct.

Scores on the test of interest should diverge from scores on a test that measures a different construct.

D. T. Campbell and Fiske (1959) culminated the validity efforts of psychologists in the 1950s by providing a theoretical framework and pragmatic methods for evaluating the construct validity of a test. First, they emphasized the importance of convergent and discriminant validity for evaluating any test's construct validity. Campbell and Fiske proposed that to be valid, a test of a particular construct should be more highly related to another test of the same construct than to tests of other constructs or tests. For example, if leadership and aggressiveness are conceptualized as two distinct traits, then two measures of leadership should correlate more highly with each other (convergent validity) than with any measure of aggressiveness (discriminant validity).

Second, D. T. Campbell and Fiske (1959) observed a consistent finding in experimental and applied research: how data are gathered strongly influences the data itself. Method variance is present in all psychological measures. If one changes how a construct is measured—say, from self-report to behavioral observation—the score will change. Something about the test item or task itself—in addition to item content—contributes to the observed score. As Cronbach (1957) put it, "Every score mixes general construct-relevance variance with variance specific to the particular measuring operation" (p. 676).

Campbell and Fiske suggested that any test of a construct should be treated as a trait–method unit. Method and trait could be considered different influences or multiple validities. Thus, two measures of leadership should intercorrelate highly even if they are measured by different methods (e.g., self-report and ratings of observed behavior). Intercorrelations of identical traits should be higher than any of the correlations between different traits measured via identical methods.

Criteria for Construct Validity

Using these principles, Campbell and Fiske proposed that construct validity be evaluated through the construction of a correlation matrix that displays correlations between tests of at least two different constructs and at least two different methods. They employed the term *multitrait–multimethod* matrices (MTMMs) to describe such correlation tables. To clarify the convergent validity of a construct, a similar construct to the one in question should be included as well as a dissimilar construct. They also indicated that the methods employed to measure constructs be as different as possible so that no reason exists for believing that they share method variance. If such diversity is not possible, D. T. Campbell and Fiske (1959) suggested that "efforts should be made to obtain as much diversity as possible in terms of data-sources and classification processes" (p. 103).

D. T. Campbell and Fiske (1959) proposed five specific criteria to demonstrate convergent and discriminant validity. Regarding convergent validity, reliability values of tests of the examined construct should first be high. Second, correlations between measures of the same trait should be substantial and significantly different from zero. These validity coefficients should indicate how the same trait is predictable by differing measurement methods.

For discriminant validity, the first criterion indicates that the convergent validity value for a construct should be higher than the correlations between that construct and any other construct having neither trait nor method in common. Second, a construct should correlate more highly with independent measurements of the same trait than with measures of different traits that employ the same methodology. Third, the pattern of intercorrelations among constructs should be similar across the MTMM matrix.

Ubiquitous Method Variance

D. T. Campbell and Fiske's (1959) criteria appear to be relatively simple qualifications for psychological tests to meet. However, if method variance is substantial, correlations between different constructs measured similarly are likely to be high. Likewise, if predictor and criterion measures are both assessed via self-report, it is likely that the resulting correlation will overestimate the true relation (i.e., the relation between constructs only) because both measures share method variance. Substantial method variance means low construct validity. As D. T. Campbell and Fiske (1959) stated, "To the extent that irrelevant method variance contributes to the scores obtained, these scores are invalid" (p. 84). The critical question then becomes, To what extent does method variance contaminate psychological tests?

The answer seems to be, to a great extent. D. T. Campbell and Fiske (1959) reviewed several studies in which the highest correlations found in the MTMM matrices were those of different constructs measured by the same method. They concluded that their conditions for construct validity "are rarely met. Method or apparatus factors make very large contributions to psychological measurements" (p. 104). Among Campbell and Fiske's examples of the influence of method on measurement were E. L. Thorndike's (1920) halo effects, the finding of apparatus effects on research with laboratory animals, and Cronbach's (1946, 1950) response sets. Nearly 30 years later, K. R. Murphy and Davidshofer (1988) noted that method bias is still frequently found.

D. T. Campbell and Fiske (1959) predicted that this problem would be resolved when measurement theorists described method variance more specifically in terms of constructs such as response sets. They wrote that "it will then be recognized that measurement procedures usually involve several theoretical constructs in joint application" (p. 102). For example, employees might complete a self-report measure of honesty and a self-report of work persistence—both of which contain transparent items—in a socially desirable fashion. However, supervisors who record those employees' honest behaviors and persistent behaviors might be very lenient in their ratings of such variables. The resulting correlation matrix would likely display high correlations between self-reports of honesty and persistence and between observations of honest and persistent behaviors. If those correlations equal or exceed the correlations between measures of honesty and persistence, the construct validity of the scale and constructs would be called into question. Discerning the influence of social desirability and lenient ratings, however, would require an analysis beyond that typically employed in construct validation studies.

Eliminating or controlling method variance to obtain a purer measure of the psychological construct in question remains an important goal in psychological measurement. If test scores largely reflect measurement procedures, it becomes impossible to create constructs that generalize across methods. In such a context, scientific theory-building is severely limited.

INCONSISTENCY ACROSS CONSTRUCTS

Since D. T. Campbell and Fiske's (1959) publication, demonstrations of the type of construct validity they proposed have been infrequent and typically disconfirming of the validity of test and construct. As shown in Table 8, failure to demonstrate strong discriminant validity is evident across diverse constructs. Substantial questions about construct validity remain even with intelligence tests and cognitive traits (e.g., Lohman, 1989). The lack of evidence for discriminant validity, coupled with the fact that scale developers infrequently perform rigorous evaluation of scales' divergent qualities, casts doubt about the foundations of many psychological research programs.

A Multitrait–Multimethod Example

Clinicians and theorists have long wondered—and disagreed—about the distinctness and overlap between the constructs of anxiety, depression, and stress (e.g., Moras, Di Nardo, & Barlow, 1992; Tellegen, 1985). These psychological phenomenon are widespread in the population (American Psychiatric Association, 1987) and are believed related to a host of other psychological traits and states (e.g., Zigler & Glick, 1988). Clinical lore and some empirical evidence indicates that persons experiencing high levels of stress are more likely to become physically ill (e.g., S. Cohen & Edwards, 1989; R. A. Martin, 1989), but depressed persons also seem more prone to illness (Anisman & Zacharko, 1992; Harris, 1991). Researchers in the area of stress and depression, however, tend to treat each area as relatively distinct.

Meier (1984) employed Campbell and Fiske's MTMM approach in a study of the construct validity of occupational stress. In addition to stress, measures of depression and personal orderliness (i.e., personal neatness, chosen as a discriminant construct) were selected. Because these constructs are primarily measured through self-reports, methods selected for this study were differences in self-report response mode. That is, measures of stress, depression, and orderliness were chosen by the formats of Likert scale, true–false response, and one-item simple self-ratings. Subjects were 320 university faculty members who spent at least 50% of their time in teaching.

The resulting MTMM correlation matrix is displayed in Table 9. Given that D. T. Campbell and Fiske's (1959) approach is designed to test the validity of stable constructs, it follows that their first criterion for construct validity is that all scales be reliable. In Table 9, reliability values are shown

TABLE 8   A Partial Listing of Constructs Lacking Support for Discriminant Validity

Construct	Sample citation(s)
Anxiety and depression	Gotlib (1984); Tanaka-Matsumi and Kameoka (1986); Watson and Kendall (1989)
Psychopathology and neuroticism	Dohrenwend, Shrout, Egri, and Mendelsohn (1980); Reich (1987); Shedler, Mayman, and Manis (1993); Tellegen (1985)
Optimism	T. W. Smith, Pope, Rhodewalt, and Poulton (1989)
Stress	Meier (1991a); Watson and Pennebaker (1989)
Social support	Payne and Jones (1987)
Coping	F. Cohen (1987, 1991)
Masculinity and femininity sex roles	Lubinski, Tellegen, and Butcher (1981); Wong, McCreary, and Duffy (1990)
Vocational constructs	Macnab and Fitzsimmons (1987); H. E. A. Tinsley, Bowman, and York (1989)
Job satisfaction	Landy (1989); Tenopyr (1993)
Organizational strategies	Venkatraman and Grant (1986)
Psychological hardiness	Funk and Houston (1987)
Self-esteem	Winne, Marx, and Taylor (1977); Wylie (1974, 1979, 1989)
Irrational thinking	B. F. Nelson (1991); Zurawski and Smith (1987)
Assessment center constructs	Sackett and Dreher (1982)
Self-efficacy expectations and other cognitive constructs	Clark, 1988; Eastman and Marzillier (1984)
Personality scales	Ben-Porath and Waller (1992)
Motivational constructs	Klinger (1987)

TABLE 9 Total Multitrait–Multimethod Matrix[a]

Method	Likert			True–False			Self-Ratings		
	1	2	3	1	2	3	1	2	3
Likert									
1. Stress	**88**[b]								
2. Depression	57	88							
3. Order	−18	−13	87						
True–False									
1. Stress	*61*[c]	65	−09	**76**					
2. Depression	57	67	−13	69	**80**				
3. Order	−17	−17	74	−14	−23	**86**			
Self-Ratings									
1. Stress	*65*	53	−14	*63*	59	−12	**73**		
2. Depression	55	62	−12	54	63	−13	60	**57**	
3. Order	−14	−23	70	−12	−20	73	−10	−13	**60**

[a]Decimal points are omitted.
[b]Reliability values are set boldface along the diagonal.
[c]Italicized numbers are convergent validity estimates.

in boldface along the diagonal. With the possible exception of the self-rating values for depression and order, these estimates, whose mean equals .77, are typical of psychological measures.

Also shown in Table 9 are the italicized convergent validity estimates. D. T. Campbell and Fiske (1959) suggest that different measures of the same trait should correlate highly. The three stress intercorrelations of .61, .65, and .63 meet this criterion.

Table 10 is a deconstructed version of Table 9 showing the appropriate correlations for D. T. Campbell and Fiske's (1959) first discriminant validity criterion. Each convergent validity coefficient (italicized) should be higher than the correlations between that variable and any other variable having neither trait nor method in common. Eleven of 12 comparisons meet this criterion. Only the .65 correlation between Stress/True–False and the Depression/True–False scales exceeds the Stress/True–False and Stress/Likert correlation of .61.

Table 11 displays the relevant correlations for the second discriminant criterion. Each convergent validity coefficient (italicized) should be higher than the correlations between that variable and different traits that employ the same method. Ten of 12 comparisons meet the criterion. The .69 correlation between Stress/True–False and Depression/True–False scales exceeds the .61 correlation between the Stress/True-False and Stress/Likert scales and the .65 correlation between Stress/True-False and Stress/Self-rating.

TABLE 10   First Discriminant Validity Criterion[a]

Method	Likert			True–False			Self-Ratings		
	1	2	3	1	2	3	1	2	3
Likert									
1. Stress									
2. Depression									
3. Order									
True–False									
1. Stress	*61*[b]	65	−09						
2. Depression	57								
3. Order	−17								
Self-Ratings									
1. Stress	65	53	−14	*63*	59	−12			
2. Depression	55			54					
3. Order	−14			−12					

[a]Decimal points are omitted.
[b]Italicized numbers are convergent validity coefficients.

Finally, in Table 12, the rank order of correlations within the triangles should be the same. In the nine triangles, six rankings are identical: the stress–depression correlation is the highest, followed by the depression–order correlation and the stress–order correlation.

In sum, the measures of stress appear reliable, intercorrelate highly, but also overlap with measures of depression. The data indicate that measures

TABLE 11   Second Discriminant Validity Criterion[a]

Method	Likert			True–False			Self-Ratings		
	1	2	3	1	2	3	1	2	3
Likert									
1. Stress									
2. Depression	57								
3. Order	−18								
True–False									
1. Stress	*61*[a]								
2. Depression				69					
3. Order				−14					
Self-Ratings									
1. Stress	65			*63*					
2. Depression							60		
3. Order							−10		

[a]Decimal points are omitted.
[b]Italicized numbers are convergent validity coefficients.

TABLE 12   Third Discriminant Validity Criterion[a]

	Likert			True–False			Self-Ratings		
	1	2	3	1	2	3	1	2	3
Likert									
1. Stress									
2. Depression	57								
3. Order	−18	−13							
True–False									
1. Stress		65	−09						
2. Depression	57		−13	69					
3. Order	−17	−17		−14	−23				
Self-Ratings									
1. Stress		53	−14		59	−12			
2. Depression	55		−12	54		−13	60		
3. Order	−14	−23		−12	−20		−10	−13	

[a]Decimal points are omitted.

of stress meet approximately the same number of validity and reliability criteria as do the measures of order and depression. Meier (1984) concluded that to the extent that depression and order have gained acceptance as constructs, occupational stress merits similar regard.

But does the construct of occupational stress have adequate construct validity? In a second study, Meier (1991a) administered measures of occupational stress, depression, and physical illness to 129 college students. Stress and depression measures were again highly correlated with each other (r's near .60) and with a measure of physical symptoms (r's near .30). In a hierarchical multiple regression analysis with symptoms as the dependent measure, gender and stress accounted for a significant amount of the variance (Adjusted *R Square* = .17). Depression accounted for no additional variance. These findings echoed the conclusions of D. H. Schroeder and Costa (1984; see also Watson and Pennebaker, 1989) who suggested that previously found relations between stress and illness are largely a result of neurotic responding by subjects to self-report measures. In other words, neurotic subjects—persons prone to negative mood states—were more likely to agree with items assessing stress, depression, and illness regardless of the actual occurrence of the thoughts, behaviors, or feelings measured by the different scales.

PROBLEMS WITH CONSTRUCT VALIDATION

As indicated in the stress–depression example, considerable ambiguity can exist in the application of Campbell and Fiske's criteria. No specific level exists for determining when differences between correlations are sufficient to proclaim a test-construct as possessing adequate convergent or discriminant validity (e.g., Jackson, 1975). One could perform a z test to determine if correlations significantly differed, but most MTMM researchers choose not to, presumably because of the triviality of the results. In addition, researchers select the constructs and methods employed to demonstrate similarity to and differences from the construct in question. Selection of similar methods (as in Meier, 1984) or similar constructs make tests of discriminant validity more difficult. The reverse can be true: researchers can choose dissimilar methods and constructs to make Campbell and Fiske's criteria easier to attain. Given the history of observational bias in all sciences and the variety of methods for assessing construct validity, it is not surprising to find that developers of tests and constructs frequently interpret results as supportive of construct validity. On the other hand, critics of the same tests and constructs often interpret similar or identical validity data in the opposite direction. In any event, much is left to the judgment of researchers. Evaluations of construct validity are hindered by a lack of consensus about acceptable procedures for evaluating discriminant validity (Burisch, 1984).

Campbell and Fiske's methods have also been criticized for the use of observed instead of latent variables (Kenny & Kashy, 1992). Latent variables produced by statistical techniques such as factor analysis presumably should be closer to true values than the untransformed observed scores. The predominant solution adopted by researchers to this problem has been the use of confirmatory factor analysis (CFA; Joreskog, 1974; Kenny & Kashy, 1992; Schmitt & Stults, 1986). In CFA, researchers specify in advance which measures of a trait should load on a single trait factor and which measures assessed by a particular method should load on a single method factor. Yet unresolved issues remain about the use of particular analytic procedures (Kenny & Kashy, 1992; Millsap, 1990), leaving questions about CFA's usefulness for determining construct validity.

SUMMARY AND IMPLICATIONS

Although discussions of test validity have clearly evolved through the past 50 years of measurement history (cf. APA, 1954, 1966, 1974, 1985), many of the problems present in the beginning of this century remain. A major cause is that traditional test developers have tended to eschew concern about what tests measured in favor of a pragmatic emphasis, typically on predictive validity (Burisch, 1984). As described in Chapter 6, however, a renewed emphasis on construct validity is in evidence among several contemporary approaches to psychological measurement. The most important question remains: What is it that a particular test measures? Contemporary theorists suggest that multiple factors cause scores on psychological tests and that these factors may be considered valid or invalid depending on the test's purpose.

Perhaps the most rigorous criteria proposed for evaluating validity were those of Campbell and Fiske (1959). D. T. Campbell and Fiske judged a test's validity by contrasting test scores with those of similar and different tests. One can make the extreme argument that few self-report, nonintellectual tests have fully passed their discriminant validity criteria. This makes sense if (a) the psychological tests in question are self- and other-reports, and (b) method variance can be largely explained by the generative response factors described in Chapters 2 and 3. If this reasoning is accepted, three recent trends concerning validity practices can be explained. First, relatively few contemporary investigators even attempt D. T. Campbell and Fiske's (1959) type of MTMM validity evaluation. Second, a number of investigators have rejected the Campbell and Fiske criteria when their tests have failed to meet these standards (e.g., Dahlstrom, 1969). Finally, more recent validity standards have been eased to require only that evidence be presented to justify the use of test interpretation for a particular purpose.

When creating and evaluating tests, psychologists should draw from theory about the construct in question *and* from measurement theory. Construct explication is the process of connecting theory to observable events. A test's construct validity results from proper construct explication; thus, construct validity problems possess information about how to modify the construct explication. Construct explication should be an iterative process in which theory is employed to create a measurement procedure, which in turn is employed to produce data, that is then used to refine the theory and the procedure. Method variance has been proposed as a major culprit in construct validity problems, but often left unaddressed is the question of why method variance exists in the first place. One solution involves an analysis of the measurement characteristics of the triple response system of behavior, affect, and cognition (B-A-C). If individuals do process information differently in these three systems—that is, B-A-C differences do explain method variance—theorists and test developers must specify the pattern of mode relations for the construct and the resulting best methods of measurement in those modes. Similarly, method variance may be explained by the effects of different situations and their demand characteristics. For example, transparent self-reports of different constructs may all be influenced by a social desirability bias, whereas all ratings may be affected by raters' desire to be strict in their evaluations.

Figure 27 summarizes the theoretical components of test validity discussed in previous chapters: traits, cognitive, affective, and behavioral mismatches, situations, and error. It may be that in any particular application, one or two of these factors may have a disproportionately large influence on test scores. To the extent that a factor is ignored in a test, however, it

```
TEST VALIDITY  =    (1)   TRAITS

                    (2)   COGNITIVE, AFFECTIVE, AND
                          BEHAVIORAL MATCHES

                    (3)   SITUATIONS

                    (4)   ERROR
```

FIGURE 27   Theoretical components of validity for psychological tests. Scores on a test depend on the influence of these four factors.

becomes a source of invalidity. Note that test refers to any type of psychological test, task, or rating, and can include the criteria used to validate tests. Measurement precision is positively correlated with validity. If test data possess considerable invalidities, detecting small differences among the remaining valid variance is likely to be difficult. Tests with many invalidities, by definition, lack construct validity. Little evidence for discriminant validity will result if (a) invalidities on a test, such as those associated with self-report (e.g., recall inaccuracies or socially desirable responding), are substantial compared to the relevant validity, and (b) invalidities are shared by supposedly different tests and criteria.

6 PROMISING APPROACHES[1]

[1]Portions of this chapter are reprinted from Meier (1993) by permission of the American Psychological Association. © 1993 by the American Psychological Association.

This chapter contains descriptions of important existing and innovative approaches in psychological measurement and assessment. I discuss theory and methods in terms of five major categories: traditional approaches (e.g., MMPI and neuropsychological assessment), statistically oriented approaches (e.g., item response theory), cognitive approaches, behavioral assessment, and computer-based methods.

TRADITIONAL APPROACHES

Traditional measurement devices such as the WAIS-R, Rorschach, and MMPI-2 continue to be widely used by psychologists to assist in selection decisions in education, mental health, medicine, business and industry, and the legal system. As many authors have noted (Buros, 1970; Gynther & Green, 1982; Hathaway, 1972; Jackson, 1992; R. P. Martin, 1988; K. R. Murphy & Davidshofer, 1988), few innovations introduced since the 1940s have been powerful enough to alter the use of traditional tests and procedures employed by psychological practitioners and researchers.

Traditional tests share certain methods, concepts, and statistical assumptions. In classical test theory, an observed test score is composed of true score and error. The true score usually represents a trait, a relatively enduring personal characteristic that influences behavior across settings. The goal of classical test theory is to maximize the true score component and minimize error. During test construction and evaluation, classical measurement approaches attempt to identify and minimize error through statistical methods. Typically, self-report items completed by many individuals are aggregated to produce an estimate intended to discriminate traits and individuals from other traits and individuals.

MEASUREMENT OF PERSONALITY AND TEMPERAMENT

Act-Frequency Analysis

A central problem in personality psychology has been the identification of important personality traits (e.g., Cattell, 1946a, 1957; Eysenck, 1947; D. Fiske, 1949; McCrae & Costa, 1985). Buss and Craik (1983; see also Angleitner & Demtroder, 1988) described a procedure they termed an act-frequency analysis. In contrast to factor analysis, which attempts to reduce and isolate traits by focusing on items that covary, an act-frequency analysis involves a series of studies to identify prototypic acts characteristic of trait categories. Subjects first nominate acts (e.g., starting a fight) that are examples of a trait or disposition (e.g., aggressiveness). A group of judges evaluates these acts to produce a smaller set most representative of the specific disposition. Subjects then complete the item pool to determine if the items possess sufficient frequency (i.e., a base rate greater than zero) and variation (i.e., individual differences in frequency) in the sample to be meaningful.

R. Hogan and Nicholson (1988) suggested that a test of a disposition could be correlated with ratings of these prototypic acts to gauge the test's construct validity. Some evidence, however, suggests that act-frequency data may be particularly susceptible to socially desirable responding (Block, 1989; Botwin, 1991). Act-frequency analysis appears to be a type of construct explication based on natural language rules.

The Big Five

Given the desire for a taxonomy of important traits, personality psychologists have reached a consensus about what are termed the Big Five factors (Cattell, 1946b; Digman, 1990; Goldberg, 1990; McCrae & Costa, 1989; Norman, 1963; Tupes & Christal, 1961; Wiggins & Pincus, 1989). These orthogonal or independent factors—neuroticism, extraversion, openness to experience, agreeableness, and conscientiousness—have been proposed as nomothetic structures to guide the measurement of personality and interpersonal behavior. Factor analyses of trait descriptors, produced by different methods (e.g., self-report and ratings by others) and with different samples (including cross-cultural), have resulted in the identification of five factors (Botwin & Buss, 1989; John, Angleitner & Ostendorf, 1988; McCrae & Costa, 1985, 1987b). Two major components of the circumplex model of interpersonal behavior, dominance and nurturance, have also been connected to the Big 5 factors of extraversion and agreeableness (Trapnell & Wiggins, 1990).

Empirical results, however, provide some ambiguity about the Big Five model. Botwin and Buss (1989), for example, instructed 59 couples to report self and other data about previously performed behaviors corresponding to the five-factor model. Factor analyses of self and partner data yielded similar results. Botwin and Buss concluded that the resulting factors, labeled responsible-stable, insecure, antagonistic-boorish, sociable, and culture, departed substantially from the five-factor model. When ratings data were adjusted for the frequency level of the behaviors, however, the resulting factors closely matched the five-factor model.

Predicting Occupational Criteria

As noted in Chapter 1, interest in the measurement of personality and temperament began when limits were found to intelligence tests' ability to predict school and vocational success. Although some research has suggested that affective variables may influence cognitive development (Anastasi, 1985), personality and temperament researchers have continued to develop such measures in the hope that they might complement intelligence in such predictive tasks. Given the discrepancies between constructs measured by personality tests and constructs represented in many occupational criteria, it is unsurprising that such efforts have often been unsuccessful (Guion & Gottier, 1965; Schmitt, Gooding, Noe, & Kirsch, 1984).

L. A. Hough et al. (1990; see also J. Hogan & Hogan, 1989; Lohman, 1991) developed an inventory to measure six constructs previously found to be useful predictors of job-related criteria. The six constructs—surgency, adjustment, agreeableness, dependability, intellectance, and affiliation—are closely aligned with the Big 5 personality factors described above. Hough et al. administered this instrument to over 9000 military personnel to obtain correlations between scale scores and criteria, which included knowledge tests, supervisory ratings, letters of recommendation, and disciplinary actions. Temperament scales correlated in the .15–.25 range with such criteria as effort, leadership, personal discipline, and physical fitness. Correlations with technical knowledge criteria were near zero.

L. A. Hough et al. (1990) also examined self-report distortion, a problem thought to interfere with real-world personnel selection. Hough et al. constructed scales to measure social desirability, poor impression, self-knowledge, and random responding. These validity scales did significantly correlate with job criteria, although at lower levels than the temperament scales. Hough et al. also found that random responding reduced predictor–criteria correlations, with random responders averaging approximately .07 lower than careful responders. The social desirability and poor impression scales also demonstrated some moderation of predictor-criteria correlations.

Clinical Measures

Graham (1990) listed a number of problems that led to the recent revision of the MMPI, including (a) a small, relatively homogeneous initial norm group of 724 persons, and (b) items that contained archaic, inappropriate, or sexist language. The revised test, the MMPI-2, contains a more representative normative sample of 2600 subjects and a relatively small number of altered items.

Butcher (1990) described the MMPI-2 as a useful screening device to provide information about an individual's strengths and weaknesses. Only weak evidence is available, however, supporting use of the MMPI in decisions about assignment to psychological treatments (e.g., Alker, 1978). Treatment-related data that could be provided by the MMPI-2, Butcher (1990) indicated, include symptoms of which an individual was unaware as well as motivations, fears, and defensive styles. As an example, Butcher (1990) cited a psychotherapy client who failed to disclose significant problems with substance abuse that were revealed by an MMPI-2. Butcher (1990) also suggested that the MMPI-2 could be employed during therapy for the purposes of accountability and monitoring of progress. He referred to a 29 year-old man who presented with problems of occupational stress. His initial MMPI-2 scores showed elevations on scale 2 (depression) and scale 7 (psychasthenia). After eight sessions of supportive and problem-solving therapy, scale 7 showed a significant decline.

Butcher (1990) maintained that "clinicians and researchers using the MMPI in treatment evaluation have long been aware of the stability of MMPI profiles over time" (p. 10). Graham (1990) reviewed data pertaining to stability and to other psychometric properties of the MMPI-2. Test–retest data of 1 wk for 13 MMPI-2 scales, as cited in the MMPI-2 manual (Hathaway et al., 1989), ranged from .58 to .92 with a median value of .81. In contrast, the stability of a more frequently used MMPI score, the two-point code (i.e., the highest two scales), was fairly low: only about one-fourth to one-third of subjects in research studies show the same two-point code. Most MMPI-2 scales also appear to be multidimensional, given that a sample of coefficient *alphas* for 13 MMPI-2 scales ranged from .34 to .87 with a median of .625. Two major factors that emerge from factor analyses of the MMPI-2 are maladjustment–psychoticism and neurotic characteristics.

Another traditional instrument, the Rorschach, has enjoyed a resurgence as a result of efforts by Exner (1978, 1986) and colleagues to establish more standardized procedures for administering and scoring the instrument. Published in 1921, the Rorschach was also developed to assist in differentiating between normal and clinical groups (Groth-Marnat, 1990). During the test, examinees provide a description of what they see in the inkblots and then clarify their responses (i.e., explain why the inkblot looks like a certain object). The major assumption is that how test-takers organize and respond to ambiguous stimuli in the testing situation reflects similar processes in nontest environments.

The clinician must attend to both the object description and the clarification, which Exner (1978) termed the articulation of the response, to understand the individual response process. Exner (1978) emphasized the multiple factors that influence examinee responses:

> The skilled Rorschacher . . . appreciates the fact that the response process in itself consists of the perceptual mediation factor, the decision to deliver or not to deliver what has been perceived, plus the manner of delivery. Articulation, as such, is as vital to the overall interpretation of a record as is the response itself. (p. 54)

Exner (1978) also stressed that the clinician must attend to the verbal behavior of the examinee rather than to the clinician's beliefs about that behavior. He suggested that "the strength and accuracy of the interpretation proceeds from what the subject says about the blot rather than what is inferred about his percept" (1978, p. 55).

Parker, Hanson, and Hunsley (1988) compared the published psychometric properties of the MMPI and Rorschach. Using a meta-analytic approach, they collected data about test reliability (including internal consistency and rater agreement estimates), stability (test–retest), and convergent validity (correlations with relevant criteria). Interestingly, Parker et al. found an insufficient number of discriminant validity reports to be able to report a comparison of the two instruments in this category. Parker et al. (1988) combined test subscales to produce the following psychometric estimates: (a) for reliability, an overall r of .84 for the MMPI and .86 for the Rorschach; (b) for stability, an overall r of .74 for the MMPI and .85 for the Rorschach; and (c) for convergent validity, an overall r of .46 for the MMPI and .41 for the Rorschach. Parker et al. concluded that despite the MMPI's reputation as the superior instrument, both the MMPI and Rorschach appear to possess comparable psychometric values.

Cognitive Abilities and g

Although many psychologists "act as though 'intelligence is what intelligence tests measure' . . . few of us believe it" (Sternberg, 1984, p. 307). The construct validity of cognitive traits and abilities remains a topic of interest in the seminal measurement area of intelligence testing (Lohman, 1989). Although measures of cognitive abilities can predict educational and occupational performance (e.g., Austin & Hanisch, 1990; Hunter & Hunter, 1984), what these tests actually measure remains in some doubt. On the basis of strong positive correlations among intelligence measures, Spearman introduced g as a general factor of intelligence (Nichols, 1980). Thurstone (1938) and Guilford (1967) believed that more specific group factors accounted for the operations of cognitive abilities, a conceptualization that some researchers believe is supported by the findings of contemporary cognitive psychology. Ascertaining the structure of intellect remains an important but elusive goal for those who desire to improve the measurement of cognitive abilities and skills.

Gould (1981) claimed that intelligence testing is a misnomer because no one has yet to demonstrate that what intelligence scales measure is a unilinear, single phenomenon. Despite this fact, Gould suggested that Terman's original work became the standard against which test developers compared new scales, which they then labeled intelligence tests. Thus, "much of the elaborate statistical work performed by testers during the past fifty years provides no independent confirmation for the proposition that tests measure intelligence, but merely establishes correlation with a preconceived and unquestioned standard'' (Gould, 1981, p. 177).

What cognitive ability tests measure has also been central to more recent controversies about the roles of race and ethnicity in ability scores. Humphreys (1992) summarized research on differences between Blacks and Whites that indicated that (a) Whites as a group score about 1 standard deviation higher; (b) Blacks as a group have demonstrated improvement on national educational measures in such areas as reading, mathematics, and science; and (c) ability tests equally predict Black and White success in education, industry, and military service. Dana (1993) noted, however, that group differences tend to be reduced when the tested sample is matched on sociodemographic variables and that factor analyses of intelligence tests tend not to produce the same number of factors or factor structures across cultures. Dana (1993) indicated that changes in the use of traditional cognitive ability tests are more likely to result from political than psychometric considerations:

> The continued use of intelligence tests that provide for a rank-ordering of persons against an Anglo-American criterion must be recognized as part of a societal demand for acculturation and acceptance of Anglo-American standards. This demand can only be modified or changed by political decisions that result from realignments of power following shifts in the population composition during the next century. In the interim, however, the use of these tests should be on the basis of the current multicultural research literature, an appreciation/understanding of multicultural clients, and consistent use of appropriate social interaction styles, including first languages. (p. 191)

On the basis of work by J. B. Carroll (1992), Humphreys (1992), and Jensen (1992), Estes (1992) summarized the current consensus about ability tests:

1. Such tests do make excellent predictions in many domains, including school and occupational performance.

2. Such tests are correlated with socioeconomic status and familial factors.

3. SES and background factors are associated with different opportunities to learn material measured by such tests, thus handicapping some individuals' scores on the tests.

4. Work in cognitive psychology has improved theory about such tests but has yet to improve substantially the tests themselves.

Cognitive psychologists have applied their theory and experimental methods to ability testing (e.g., J. B. Carroll, 1992; Sternberg, 1988), although this merging is still in its initial stages (Hunt, 1987). As described later in this chapter, cognitive psychological theory and methods also appear to have influenced other types of measurement.

Neuropsychological Testing

Goldstein (1990) cited Reitan as describing neuropsychological tests as those that are "sensitive to the condition of the brain" (p. 197). Neuropsychological testing refers to a wide range of measures employed to discover brain damage. Neuropsychology became particularly important during World War II when thousands of brain-injured soldiers required assessment and rehabilitation (Gregory, 1992). When it became apparent that brain injury was revealed by performance on psychological tests, neuropsychologists became successful heirs of the tradition started by early psychologists who sought relations between physiology and psychology.

Because neuropsychology has roots in a variety of disciplines, many different techniques are employed as neuropsychological tests (Franzen, 1989). These tests evaluate individuals' capacity for sensory input, attention and concentration, memory, learning, language, spatial ability, reasoning and logical analysis, and motor skills (Bennett, 1988; Gregory, 1992). Although brain injuries can affect all of these areas, a one-to-one relation between an injury and a dysfunction is seldom apparent (Lynch, 1985). Two important consequences are that (a) diagnosis often involves score profiles, with their accompanying psychometric difficulties (K. R. Murphy & Davidshofer, 1988), and (b) a thorough patient history and interview are still required to make sense of the neurological information provided by different tasks and sources (Lynch, 1985).

The most common change after brain injury is a general intellectual impairment, that is, the patient seems less bright or less capable of abstract thinking (Goldstein, 1990). Consequently, cognitive tasks and tests such as the WAIS-R and Wechsler Memory Scale are frequently employed for screening as well as perceptual and motor skills tests such as the Bender-Gestalt. The Luria-Nebraska Neuropsychological Battery (Golden, Hammeke, & Purisch, 1980) and the Halsted-Reitan Neuropsychological Test Battery (Reitan & Wolfson, 1985) present a more extensive set of tasks assessing a larger domain of neuropsychological categories.

Given the strong links between neuropsychological and cognitive ability testing, it is not surprising that questions have also arisen about the construct validity of neuropsychological tests. Although reliability estimates are as high as those exhibited by cognitive ability tests (Franzen, 1989) and neuropsychological tests do discriminate between brain-injured and other individuals, what the neuropsychological tests actually measure remains in doubt (Gregory, 1992; Kolb & Whishaw, 1990). This situation may be alleviated more quickly in neuropsychological testing than in other measurement areas because of the sophisticated validation criteria, such as brain imaging techniques, that are becoming increasingly available (Goldstein, 1990). It is also likely that theoretical progress in cognition and neuropsychology will continue to benefit measurement and assessment in both areas (Goldstein, 1990).

Aggregation

Aggregation refers to the summing or averaging of multiple measurements. Spearman (1910, cited in Rushton et al., 1983) appears to be the first psychologist to note the advantages of obtaining multiple measures, although Rushton et al. (1983) observed that averaging of multiple observations was the solution adopted by astronomers to handle Maskelyne's problem of individual differences in observing star transits.

The chief contemporary architect of this work has been Epstein (1979, 1980, 1983, 1990). His research has focused on the effects of aggregating measurements of such variables as unpleasant emotions, social behavior, and impulsivity. Although Epstein acknowledges evidence that behavior varies as a result of situational variables, his studies indicate that averaging measurements of behavior, self-reports, and ratings by others over time dramatically decreases measurement error and increases validity coefficients well above the average .30 ceiling. Measurements can also be aggregated over sources and methods (R. P. Martin, 1988). In terms of classical test theory, aggregation works because behavioral consistencies accumulate over multiple measurements and random errors do not (Rushton et al., 1981).

Although Epstein has presented his research as demonstrating renewed support for the existence of psychological traits, others have not fully accepted his arguments (Day, Marshall, Hamilton, & Christy, 1983; McFall & McDonel, 1986; Mischel & Peake, 1982). McFall and McDonel (1986), for example, criticized Epstein for (a) failing to control for method variance, that is, Epstein's measures were primarily self-reports; (b) failure to demonstrate discriminant validity for personality measures; and (c) failing to notice, in one study, that the best predictor ($r = .80$) of actual amount of time spent studying was not aggregated personality items, but a single item asking students to rate (from 1 to 5) how much time they typically spend studying.

Rushton et al. (1983) suggested that insignificant correlations in psychological research may partially result from a failure to aggregate measurements. They reviewed research in such areas as judges' ratings, cross-situational consistency, personality stability, and cognition–behavior relations which indicated that aggregation improved validity estimates. Rushton et al. noted that researchers typically find low correlations between measures of attitudes and behavior. However, Fishbein and Ajzen (1974) observed that such correlations may be increased by aggregating different measures of behaviors: attitude scales and single behaviors correlated around .15, whereas aggregated measures correlated in the .70–.90 range. Aggregation, however, may be misleading when components of the aggregated data differ substantially in reliability and validity. R. P. Martin (1988; see also Epstein, 1981) provided an example where a mother may accurately rate a child as moderately emotionally expressive, whereas the father, because of his emotional difficulties, rates the child as extremely expressive. The aggregation of mother's and father's score may be less correlated with other variables (such as teachers' ratings) than the mother's score alone. In addition, the discrepancy score between mother's and father's ratings may contain useful clinical information about the family system. R. P. Martin (1988) suggested that when discrepancies occur—whether across source, time, setting, or methods—the assessor must produce an explanation.

Summary

Many of the traditional approaches described above grew out of a history of testing aimed at identifying stable traits for selection purposes. Except when political and legal forces intervene, these traditional approaches, given their demonstrated effectiveness and fairness, are likely to be increasingly employed in the future for such decisions. For example, if pressure to reduce health care costs continues to shrink mental health benefits, it would not be surprising to see traditional tests such as the MMPI used to screen individuals to determine the degree of psychological disturbance (cf. Goldberg, 1965, 1968) and thus decide the amount or type of treatment they subsequently receive. As will be discussed in more detail in the next chapter, however, I expect traditional tests to be employed less frequently in the future for guiding psychological interventions.

STATISTICALLY ORIENTED APPROACHES

Glass (1986) suggested that psychometric investigations began to move away from the mainstream of psychology around 1940. To put it simply, statistically oriented approaches attempt to make sense of existing measurement data through statistical analyses and transformations, whereas more theoretical approaches are concerned with understanding how the data came to be created in the first place (i.e., a search for causes). Statistically oriented approaches such as item-response theory (IRT) do tend to assume that the psychological entities being measured are traitlike. IRT, confirmatory factor analysis, structural equation modeling (Joreskog, 1974), and, to some extent, generalizability theory (GT), can be included in this category.

Item-Response Theory (IRT)

Of all the measurement approaches described in this chapter, IRT has generated the most interest among test developers. Given this enthusiasm, it is not surprising that a number of descriptions of various IRT theories and procedures exist (e.g., Hambleton, Swaminathan & Rogers, 1991; F. M. Lord, 1980; F. M. Lord & Novick, 1968; Rasch, 1980; Weiss, 1983; B. D. Wright & Stone, 1979). Hambleton and Swaminathan (1985) traced initial IRT work through the 1930s and 1940s, but noted that publications by F. M. Lord (1952, 1953a, 1953b) are generally credited with providing the modern impetus for IRT development.

IRT proposes that item responses allow inferences about hidden or latent traits. IRT assumes that a relation exists between an observable item response and the unobservable trait that underlies performance, and that this relation, in cognitive ability items, can be described by a mathematical function, a monotonically increasing curve (see Figure 28). Analyses based on this ideal curve have demonstrated considerable utility in test development and item analysis (Cronbach, 1991a).

For example, two different item characteristic curves (ICCs) can be expected for discriminating and nondiscriminating verbal ability items. With a discriminating item, persons with good verbal skills should be more likely to correctly answer the question. A nondiscriminating item, however, would show no difference between persons of high and low verbal ability. Similarly, persons at the same ability level should provide different answers to items of different difficulty levels; for example, two persons of moderate ability should both answer an easy item correctly and a difficult item incorrectly. Identification of poorly discriminating items allows their deletion at no loss of measurement precision. In addition, IRT analyses also permit the development of a calibrated item bank. From this bank may be drawn sub-

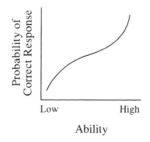

FIGURE 28 An item characteristic curve. An item characteristic curve shows the relation between the probability of choosing the correct answer to an item and the level of the latent attribute being measured by the item (K. R. Murphy & Davidshofer, 1988). In general, as the person's attribute increases, so does the probability of a correct response.

sets of items that yield comparable latent trait scores, a useful benefit in many measurement applications.

The IRT test developer collects item data and compares it to the statistical model proposed for those items. If the fit is good, then (a) the resulting ability estimates are not dependent upon a particular test (because they are based upon the underlying trait, not the test), and (b) the resulting item estimates are not dependent upon a particular sample (because the slope and intercept of the demonstrated ICC remain the same despite the value of a score contributed by any particular individual). Item and ability parameters produced through IRT analyses are invariant because they include information about items in the ability-estimation process and about examinees in the item-estimation process.

Item subsets with comparable scores are necessary for another IRT application, computer adaptive testing (CAT). IRT indicates that a test most accurately measures ability when test difficulty level and examinee ability level are closely matched; easier items do not provide useful information about high-ability examinees and difficult items do not provide useful information about low-ability examinees. With CAT, an individual first completes a subset of items. Based on those responses, the testing program selects more difficult or easier items to better fit the examinee's abilities. The program administers items with known difficulty and discrimination levels until the standard error of the examinee's ability score reaches a specified level or stops decreasing by a predetermined amount. CAT produces an estimate of individuals' ability with fewer items, providing a more efficient measurement method, particularly for examinees of very low or high ability. Thus, CATs produce shorter tests of equal measurement precision as well as greater test security, a testing pace set for the examinee that may minimize frustration, and reduced time for test supervision (Hambleton et al., 1991). Adaptive testing is not intrinsically dependent upon automation—Binet introduced the procedure (Dawis, 1992)—but with CAT, computers facilitate the administration and storage of test data.

Although many IRT examples can be found in educational measurement, a few applications of the theory with attitude and personality measurement are scattered throughout the psychological and educational measurement literatures (e.g., Gibbons, Clark, Cavanaugh, & Davis, 1985; Hoijtink, 1990; Koch, Dodd, & Fitzpatrick, 1990; Kunce, 1980, cited in Reckase, 1990; Reise & Waller, 1990; Thissen & Steinberg, 1988; Waller & Reise, 1989). Waller and Reise (1989), for example, employed CAT and IRT procedures to identify extreme responders on a personality scale with an average 25% of the available items and a 100% accuracy rate.

Generalizability Theory (GT)

Shavelson, Webb, and Rowley (1989; Brennan, 1983; L. Crocker & Algina, 1986; Cronbach, et al., 1972; Shavelson & Webb, 1991) describe GT as a framework for examining the dependability of psychological measurement. GT approaches differ from classical test theory in several respects. The concept of reliability is replaced by generalizability, the ability to generalize a score from one testing context to others. GT recognizes that error is not always random; systematic error can be identified by examining variability of measurement data over conditions, called facets in GT. GT suggests that multiple sources, including persons, content, occasions, and observers, can affect measurement devices; GT provides a theoretical and statistical framework for identifying and estimating the magnitude of those sources. Given this information, researchers can then compare the relative effects of different measurement conditions. By knowing the most important sources of measurement variability, measurement devices and procedures can be designed to minimize undesired sources.

Shavelson et al. (1989) described an application of GT in a study of disaster survivors' psychological impairment (Gleser, Green, & Winget, 1978). Two interviewers assessed 20 survivors; two raters then used the resulting interview to determine survivors' impairment. Gleser et al. (1978) estimated variance components for the effects of survivors, raters, interviewers, and their interactions. Two components produced the largest variance: survivors (indicating individual differences among subjects) and the survivor by interviewer interaction (indicating measurement error, i.e., the interviewers produced inconsistent information from their interviews with different survivors). These results suggest that to improve the generalizability of measurement, the researchers should standardize the interviewers' procedures. Other potential sources of variation that might have been investigated include the different occasions of interviewing and the interview questions.

Unlike IRT, GT proposes no particular model of item response. Instead, GT suggests that with any particular test, a universe of conditions exist that may affect test scores. Investigations of the relative effects of such conditions are called *G studies*. The results of G studies can then be used to design studies to identify sources of variability and error in situations where test scores will be employed to make real decisions about individuals. These latter studies, termed *D studies*, can help modify some aspect of the testing conditions to provide the most precise data possible (e.g., standardize interviewer training, as noted in the previous example).

Does Measurement Equal Statistics?

B. Ellis (1966) described measurement as "the link between mathematics and science" (p. 1). Many good reasons exist for the close relations between measurement and statistics. With few measurement theories available, statistical methods played an important role in helping early psychologists efficiently describe the distributions and relations they found in their measurement data. Galton's work around 1870, for example, provided the basis for the standard score and the correlation (Dawis, 1992). Statistical concepts such as aggregation and regression toward the mean (RTM) helped cope with and explain the large amount of error produced by the new science's measurement procedures. Quantifying general theoretical propositions often forces theorists to be more specific and concrete, thereby positioning the theory for better tests of confirmation and refutation. F. M. Lord and Novick (1968) observed that "it is a truism of mathematics that strong assumptions lead to strong results" (p. 25); once psychological theories have been placed in mathematical form, manipulation of the elementary constructs can produce new deductions (F. M. Lord & Novick, 1968). Quantification in measurement offers a vehicle for translating different experiences into a universal language of numbers. And given that modern sciences are quantitative, adoption of statistical and mathematical descriptions and procedures enabled a new field like psychology to appear more scientific (Heidbreder, 1933).

But the merging of statistics and measurement also produced difficulties. In much of psychological measurement, the link between measurement and statistics became a chain. Statistics and measurement have become functionally equivalent in the minds of many graduate students and psychologists. Psychometric approaches focus more on statistical procedures than on psychological theory (cf. Glass, 1986); the teachers of measurement courses, more likely than not, are statisticians. Davison et al. (1986) wondered "how many students fully understand what psychometrics entails other than statistics" (p. 586). Over time the line between statistical description and psychological explanation has been erased: psychologists have often failed to distinguish between psychological and statistical reality and to note that statistical models implied certain psychological models of reality (Danziger, 1990). Many proponents of statistical and empirical approaches have been resistant to incorporate theories about causality into measurement (Wiggins, 1973). Contemporary personality researchers, for example, continue to employ statistically based descriptions that they acknowledge still require causal explanations (Lamiell, 1990; McCrae & Costa, 1987b; Wiggins, 1979).

As noted in Chapter 2, psychometricians describe RTM as a statistical phenomena in which scores that fall at the extremes of a scale on one occasion tend to move toward the mean at a second testing. Psychologists often have no idea about the cause of RTM other than it is proposed to be a result of measurement error (Kazdin, 1980). Measurement error, however, refers to unknown factors that randomly or systematically influence scores on a measurement procedure. We cannot explain RTM very deeply.

Figure 29 displays a graphic representation of RTM and the Law of Initial Values (LIV). The LIV indicates that the greater the initial value of a psychophysiological measure, the smaller the response will be to a stimulus

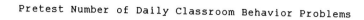

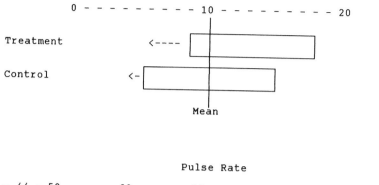

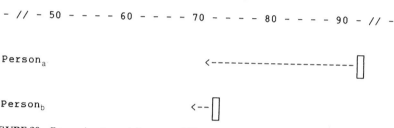

FIGURE 29 Regression toward the mean (RTM) and the law of initial values (LIV). In RTM, persons who score at the extreme of a phenomenon move toward the mean at retest. In the LIV, change in scores depend on their starting values. Are RTM and LIV separate or similar principles?

(Wilder, 1967). When the initial value is extreme, no response or even a paradoxical response can occur (Surwillo, 1986). For example, an individual with a resting heart rate of 100, when shown a threatening photograph, is less likely to increase heart rate significantly compared to an individual whose initial rate is 70. Many psychophysiologists believe negative feedback provided by homeostasis—the process of maintaining an organism's equilibrium—is responsible for the LIV (R. M. Stern, Ray, & Davis, 1980). These feedback mechanisms set limits on the degree to which the organism can move away from its homeostatic set point. The question remains: Is the LIV a theoretical explanation for some RTM effects?

If the answer is yes, then the LIV has important implications for measurement of constructs—such as stress, anxiety, and depression—that may be influenced by such mechanisms. On the basis of a homeostatic model, we might assume that individuals who score high on a measure of these constructs may be motivated to decrease their affect without further intervention or stimuli. Such spontaneous remission—improvement without treatment—is a frequent finding of psychotherapy outcome studies (Bergin & Lambert, 1978).

Long ago Boring (1919) criticized psychologists' "blind reliance on statistical samples, statistical conventions, and statistical assumptions for drawing substantial psychological conclusions" (p. 338), declaring that "inaccuracy of definition will never yield precision of result" (Boring, 1920, p. 33; see also Allport, 1937). Tukey (1950, cited in Loevinger, 1957) suggested that psychologists tend to rely on statisticians, instead of theory, to find significant relations between psychological variables. Cronbach (1991a) aptly described the tension between statistical and measurement concerns:

> One need not be a skilled mathematician to advance methodology; you call upon an expert once you know what to call for. The crucial contribution—which mathematicians cannot be expected to make—is an adequate formal description of an interesting set of social or psychological events. If you start with a mathematician's model not made for you, something in it probably distorts your real concern . . . and when you construct your own model, as the classical reliability or prediction theorist did, you are likely to leave out something that deserves attention. There is no sure procedure for deliberately locating the blind spots in a mathematical formulation; one must simply be on the alert for oversimplifications and trace their consequences. (p. 398)

Complex statistical procedures also decrease the communicability of results and the resulting spread of innovation (Burisch, 1984; J. Burke, 1978). W. J. Popham (1993), for example, contended that IRT tends to be perceived as magic. In such a context, W. J. Popham (1993) indicated, educators may defer all questions and issues about measurement to IRT specialists, thus resulting in a decline in educators' understanding of assessment. W. J. Popham (1993) exhorted "the IRT community to provide some type of intuitively comprehensible explanations to educators about what's going on when computers do their IRT dances" (p. 14).

Although the ability to translate qualitative statements into mathematic terms is often a sign of theoretical precision, complex statistical analyses of psychological data have often led to an *appearance* of precision. Using statistical significance testing, it is possible in any study to find significant results given a sufficiently large number of subjects and variables; this process is known as fishing (Cook & Campbell, 1979). At first glance the investigator appears to be detecting small nuggets of knowledge from a morass of data; such nuggets, however, often change or disappear upon replication. The finding of statistical significance in support of proposed hypotheses is the goal of most psychological investigations, and once found, often signals the end of analysis. Psychologists appear to share the judgment of lay persons that information that confirms propositions is more relevant than disconfirming information (J. Crocker, 1981).

Do the Measurement Properties of Objects Affect the Type of Statistical Procedure Employed?

Another controversy involves the relation between type of measurement scale and statistical procedures. Stevens (1951) indicated, for example, that parametric techniques such as correlations and *F* tests require at least interval level data. Others (e.g., Gaito, 1980) have argued that no relation exists between type of scale and the statistical technique used. Statisticians who support this perspective frequently cite F. M. Lord's (1953c) quote that "the numbers do not know where they come from" (p. 751).

Only the investigator who has explicated the link between the phenomena being measured and the numbers produced by the measurement procedures knows where the numbers come from. Strictly speaking, the results of statistical analyses apply only to the numbers produced by the measurement procedure, not to the phenomena itself (K. R. Murphy & Davidshofer, 1988). If the procedure does not reflect the phenomena adequately, subsequent analyses are not generalizable to the real world. In a similar vein, contemporary statistical approaches to measurement, such as confirmatory factor analysis (CFA) and structural equation modeling, uniformly work with latent variables. That is, observed variables are assumed to contain substantial amounts of error, and transformations of some sort are necessary to produce latent variables that presumably reflect real-world variables more accurately. However, the connections between observed variables and the latent ones are often weak (Cliff, 1992). Attempts to transform the results of analyses based on transformed data back to the real world will be successful only to the extent that we understand the factors in the measurement procedure that lead to the initial data alteration. Gould (1981) made a similar criticism of the use of factor analysis in research on intelligence. He indicated that intelligence had been reified to the status of a physical entity but that "such a claim can never arise from the mathematics alone, only from additional knowledge of the physical nature of the measures themselves" (p. 250; also see K. R. Murphy & Davidshofer, 1988, p. 32-33).

If measurement procedures cause real-world data to collapse from interval to ordinal level, results of statistical tests of the transformed data may be invalid when applied back to the real world. For example, suppose we are examining ratings on a seven-point scale made by managers of prospective employees completing tasks at a work assessment center. As shown in Figure 30, a substantial set of these raters may make a central tendency or range restriction error. Although the employees' performances might range from very poor to very good, most raters employ only the midpoints of the scale. This systematic error by raters results in the collapse of real-world interval level data to ordinal data. Real differences between individuals are lost during the measurement process. Even the latent variables produced by statistical procedures may fail to fully reflect the actual phenomena.

Statistics computed on the observed measurement data are likely to produce misleading results. In the example above, the standard deviation will have shrunk from its theoretical true value, as will correlations with other variables. Townsend and Ashby (1984) provided a similar example to demonstrate that statistical tests applied to ordinal level data produce meaningless results.

Advanced statistical procedures that transform manifest measurement data into latent variables may or may not accurately model reality (cf. Cliff, 1992). A correction for attenuation might produce useful data, but in a real world situation, multiple errors may intrude, depending, for example, upon the interaction of the sample and the measurement procedure. Given the knowledge of the desirable properties of interval level data, transformations of raw data raise the question of whether structure is being recognized in items or imposed upon them (Loevinger, 1957). Statistical tests may certainly be applied to observed data regardless of measurement scale type. But it would also appear that (a) those results would apply only to the observed data, not the real-world phenomena, or (b) results based on latent variables and transformed data apply to the real world only to the extent that these transformations accurately account for errors that occur during the measurement process.

Summary

Procedures developed in the popular IRT approach aid large-scale selection testing because they improve testing efficiency (i.e., they require fewer

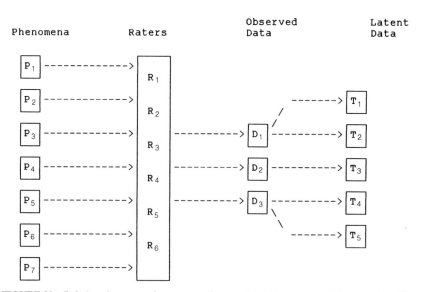

FIGURE 30   Relations between phenomena, data produced by raters, and latent values. Raters may only record a portion of the range of the phenomenon they observe. The observed ratings may be considered indicators of unobserved or latent values that may be produced through statistical transformations of the observed data.

items without loss of test reliability). IRT procedures do not, however, tend to improve validity. To do so, I suspect that much more must be known about the processes of measurement, and it is here that GT, with its ability to identify systematic error, offers useful analytic tools.

COGNITIVE APPROACHES

Scaling refers to "the assignment of meaning to a set of numbers derived from an assessment instrument" (Reckase, 1990, p. 41). The important issue here is who assigns the meaning to the numbers. Traditionally, the chief decision maker is the test developer who transforms the raw data provided by test-takers using statistical methods. For example, the developer may (a) sum all item responses to produce a total score, (b) examine correlations between individual items and summed scores to determine which items should be deleted from a scale because of low correlations, or (c) factor analyze the data to determine which items converge to form separate constructs. In each case, the developer assumes that the transformed data have more meaning than any particular response generated by the test-taker.

In addition to the test developer, the test-taker or observer assigns meaning to numbers. Test items and tasks are cognitively and affectively processed for meaning and subsequent response in a different manner by different individuals (cf. Cronbach, 1946). As Loevinger (1957) stated, "The naive assumption that the trait measured by a personality test item is always related in a simple, direct way to the apparent content of the item has long since been disproven" (p. 651). This approach represents a movement away from viewing questions and answers in a stimulus–response mode toward viewing them in terms of meaning and context (Mishler, 1986). The importance of understanding the processes employed by individuals when responding to tests has long been understood; for example, Cronbach (1946) cited work by Seashore (1939) and others which indicated that test results are not simply a product of individuals' ability (or personality), but also of the methods subjects employ when completing test items. This knowledge, however, has had relatively little impact on psychological testing (cf. Burisch, 1984).

Many contemporary psychologists have returned their attention to response processes (Guion, 1977). Experimental methodologies and theoretical constructs from cognitive psychology have begun to provide paradigms for investigating such processes in cognitive ability and other tests (Embretson, 1985). Embretson, Schneider, and Roth (1986) suggested that aptitude researchers have moved their focus from traits to the cognitive components underlying test performance.

Task Decomposition

Perhaps the most promising aspect of cognitive models for measurement is that these approaches seem capable of offering methods for examining the underpinnings of construct validity, particularly for the cognitive skills employed in intelligence tests (Embretson, 1985; also see Sternberg, 1977, 1988). Embretson (1985) suggested that understanding item or task responses requires a theory of the process factors that underlie performance along with research designed to explore those factors. From the standpoint of cognitive psychology, experiments must be designed to decompose those variables and determine their relative weights. The test developer becomes a researcher who creates tests on the basis of studies that examine the stimulus content of test items and the cognitive processes (such as strategies and level of knowledge) individuals use in response to those items. Researchers have employed this approach to examine the cognitive processes that underlie performance on tests of verbal ability, inductive reasoning, and spatial ability (Embretson, 1985).

Butterfield, Nielson, Tangen and Richardson (1985) provide an example of decomposition with letter series tasks, a measure of inductive reasoning common to intelligence tests. Letter series can be used to specify such relations as identity (AAAAA), next (ABCDE), and back (ZYXWV). Butterfield et al. conducted a series of theory-based decomposition studies in which they found that performance on letter series tasks could be explained by the examinees' level of knowledge and ability to perform multiple operations. The resulting ability test score, then, summarizes the particular weighting of these two cognitive variables for a particular set of letter series tasks. This score will correlate with other tests or criteria to the extent that they similarly weight the underlying cognitive processes. Using this type of research program, test developers should be able to select or construct items that measure specified components and combinations of components, thereby increasing the possibility of designing new tests with greater validity.

Task decomposition approaches may be limited, however, by the complexity of the response processes required by the test item or produced by the test-taker (cf. Lohman, 1989). If individuals employ substantially different processes to perform components of a task, attempts to isolate common processes will fail.

Protocol Analysis

Ericsson and Simon's (1984) research with protocol analysis exemplifies contemporary work on item and task response. In this structured, qualitative procedure, subjects are instructed to "think aloud" as they complete a task, and their verbal reports are recorded verbatim. In contrast to most measurement procedures, persons providing the reports receive a brief training period consisting of practice exercises (Ericsson & Simon, 1984). Protocol analysis is premised on the belief that information attended to and held in *short-term memory* can be accurately reported (S. L. Martin & Klimoski, 1990). Ericsson (1987; Ericsson & Simon, 1984) maintained that sufficient research has documented that the verbal reports produced through protocol analysis are reliable and valid. Essentially, this research has indicated that individuals' reports about how they solve problems or tasks predicts how well they are able to solve those problems. Research in protocol analysis, for example, has revealed differences between high- and low-aptitude subjects' ability to represent problems. Unskilled subjects experience difficulty in representing problems in a way that enabled them to access past knowledge.

Without verbal reports of how people solve problems or answer test items, Ericsson (1987) suggested that we have no way of knowing whether the items evoke the same response process: "Understanding what individual tests measure is a prerequisite for understanding the observed correlation between scores on two different tests. Protocol analysis would allow us to evaluate the importance of two different sources of correlation" (p. 222). In contrast, traditional intellectual and personality tests sum the products of those processes.

Jobe and his colleagues have applied protocol analysis methods to test and survey problems. They found that variables such as recall strategies, instructions, mood, time elapsed since target event, and response formats affected the accuracy of recall of medical visits, smoking levels, and dietary habits (e.g., Jobe & Mingay, 1991; Jobe et al., 1990; Lessler, Tourangeau, & Salter, 1989; Means, Swan, Jobe, Esposito, & Loftus, 1989; Salovey et al., 1989; A. F. Smith et al., 1991; Willis, Royston & Bercini, 1991).

Jobe et al. (1990) investigated the effects of different types of recall strategies on the accuracy of reported health care visits. Some theorists had suggested that forward (chronological) recall would be more accurate because earlier events could guide the recall of subsequent events; other theorists proposed that recent events would be more easily remembered and thus could prompt better recall of earlier events (backward or reverse chronological recall). Subjects were randomly assigned to recall visits using one of three strategies: forward recall, backward recall, or free (unstructured) recall. Using medical records from physicians, Jobe et al. then matched recalled with actual visits and found that the overall sample of 337 subjects underreported visits by 20%. Recall order was compared with 75 respondents who reported two or more visits during the 6-month reference period. Free-recall subjects were found to be more accurate (67% match) than forward- (47%) or backward- (42%) recall subjects. However, gender interacted with recall condition: women in the free-recall condition correctly recalled 60% of their visits, whereas men in the backward condition recalled 61%. Self-reported health status also interacted with recall condition: subjects in good health tended to recall best (85%) in the free-recall condition, whereas those in poor health recalled equally in the backward (50%) and free-recall (50%) conditions. Jobe et al. found no main effects or interactions with race, education, or income.

S. L. Martin and Klimoski (1990) employed protocol analysis to test propositions of attribution theory and cognitive appraisal models with 36 managers who made self- and employee-performance evaluations. They asked 36 managers to think aloud while providing four "'thorough, complete' open-ended performance evaluations" (p. 139) of themselves and three subordinates. Managers then provided summary ratings of the subordinates on a 1–5 scale (1 equaled poor, 5 equaled excellent). These evaluations were tape-recorded and then parsed into single ideas or thoughts so they could be coded by trained raters into categories such as positive evaluation, negative evaluation, external attribution, and trait attribution. Martin and Klimoski found that the number of positive evaluations found in the verbal reports correlated .49, .69, and .59 with summary ratings of the three employees.

Actor–observer theory indicates that observers are more likely to attribute others' actions to internal traits than situational factors (Ross, 1977). In contrast, actors are more likely to attribute their actions to situational than trait factors. S. L. Martin and Klimoski (1990) did find that managers made significantly more internal attributions on employee evaluations (10% of the phrases) than self-evaluations (5%). Managers also made more external attributions (12%) in their self-evaluations than for employee attributions (2%). Martin and Klimoski found that managers remembered negative behavioral episodes for good and bad employees, but that managers dismissed the negative episodes for employees receiving positive evaluations. During self-evaluations, managers tended to use external attributions to enhance their appraisal of their ability to perform despite environmental constraints.

Contrary to attribution theory and appraisal models, managers produced an evaluation immediately, that is, within 1 of 2 s following a request to do so. S. L. Martin and Klimoski (1990) maintained that theory suggests that considerable information processing should occur before the rating is reported. They proposed, however, that the managers retrieved the evaluations from memory rather than generated them as an end product of an employee evaluation task. Martin and Klimoski suggested that managers may have retrieved their most recent evaluation from memory and then attempted to confirm or disconfirm by retrieving relevant performance information about the particular employee.

Ericcson's (1987) work indicates that individuals produce a diversity of mediating thoughts when confronted with a simple task like memorizing individual nonsense syllables. Given the increased complexity of answering personality test items, one would expect an even greater diversity of cognitive processes (but see Ursic & Helgeson, 1989, for an exception). This diversity—the individual differences exhibited when humans construct meaning from seemingly simple stimuli—may dictate limits to the possible understanding of item-response processes. Similarly, practice on a test and learning of shortcuts and strategies by a test-taker may complicate research aimed at understanding item response. And like much qualitative research, it is labor intensive to produce and review the transcripts required by protocol analysis.

Item Characteristics

The issue of how respondents construe the meaning of the items extends beyond simple distortion. As Kagan (1988) noted, every question forces the respondent to decide on the meaning of the terms, and "the investigator cannot assume similar meanings" (p. 617). But that is an assumption shared by many test developers. Walsh and Betz (1985; see also Wiggins, 1973) stated that "it is assumed (at least to some extent) that each item on a test and all the words in that item have some similar meaning for different people" (p. 17). Test developers assume similar meaning chiefly for convenience: until recently, few methods have been available for studying differences in item meaning.

Item Ambiguity. As noted previously, respondents may generate information if they do not understand the psychological constructs being measured. Some evidence suggests that many items on psychological tests engender subtle differences among respondents in comprehension and recall of information (cf. Baker & Brandon, 1990; Watson, 1988). Such individual differences in item processing are likely to be compounded by the ambiguity found in self-report scales. Gynther and Green (1982) suggested that many self-report items are "stated in such a general fashion that test takers can only respond on the basis of their implicit personality theories rather than how they actually behave and feel in specific situations" (p. 358).

Helfrich (1986) found that item understanding may be influenced by the presence of negatives in the item, passive tense, ambiguity, and respondent age. Angleitner, John, and Lohr (1986) reviewed research that found (a) a negative correlation between item length and test–retest consistency and (b) a negative correlation between ratings of item comprehensibility and the number of letters and sentence clauses in items. They also found that (c) according to subject ratings of scales such as the MMPI and Sixteen Personality Factory Questionnaire (16PF), 25% of the items were ambiguous and 50% difficult to understand, and (d) in one study, almost 20% of subjects changed their item response over a 2-wk test–retest interval. Angleitner et al. concluded that "one cannot help but be impressed by the degree of response inconsistency elicited by most personality questionnaire items" (p. 97).

Response Formats. Ratings by self and observers are frequently employed to evaluate such psychological dimensions as job performance or attitudes (Landy & Farr, 1980, 1983). With ratings by others, individuals are evaluated on a particular format. As shown in Figure 31, raters may be asked to mark or circle a number along a Likert scale containing descriptive terms. Self-reports typically require test-takers to respond to true–false formats or Likert scales that contain three or more alternatives. The second Likert scale in Figure 31 contains a midpoint to allow a neutral or uncertain answer.

Formats can be described along a variety of dimensions. One such dimension is the number of response alternatives. A test such as the MMPI offers two possibilities to the test-taker (true or false) and an additional category to the test scorer (items left blank). Because Likert scales theoretically should increase the variability of responding, most contemporary tests employ such scales, using between five and nine possible responses (cf. Dawis, 1987; K. R. Murphy & Davidshofer, 1988). Increasing the number of response alternatives, however, may increase the cognitive processing demand required of the respondent. Two likely results of such increased demand are (a) a lengthening of item completion times and total test times when large numbers of items are involved (cf. Lohman, 1989), and (b) an increased likelihood of unmotivated or unskilled respondents generating, as opposed to retrieving, responses.

Concreteness or ambiguity is a second dimension along which rating scales can be described. Thus, rating scales may be anchored simply by two global descriptors (e.g., poor or excellent) or they may include a number of explicit behavioral descriptions (e.g., to receive a rating of 1 on a dimension of promptness, an employee must always meet the required deadline). Considerable ambiguity seems to exist in the content and format of most

		Performance Level			
Poor		Average			Superior
1	2	3	4	5	6

		Attitude		
Agree		Uncertain		Disagree
1	2	3	4	5

FIGURE 31   The ubiquitous Likert scale. Likert scales offer measurement of phenomena with multiple values.

rating scales (K. R. Murphy & Davidshofer, 1988). In response, researchers have attempted to create rating scales with descriptor terms that are as explicit as possible. Reviews of studies using these Behaviorally Anchored Ratings Scales (BARS), however, have not demonstrated their superiority over other types of scales in terms of validity (K. R. Murphy & Davidshofer, 1988).

BARS are likely to be subject to the same sorts of production strategies described for self-reports in Chapter 2. In addition, some studies have asked raters to assess expected behaviors rather than observed behaviors (Latham & Wexley, 1977). Latham and Wexley (1977) proposed a substitute for rating scales in the form of a Behavioral Observation Scale (BOS). Rather than rate behavior along a scale, observers simply count the frequency of important job behaviors. Particularly if it is done immediately after a behavioral observation, a BOS should be more valid than BARS (cf. Paul et al., 1986a). However, under certain conditions a BOS may be functionally equivalent to BARS. If supervisors must recall worker behavior over long periods, they may generate such data on the basis of their impressions of workers (K. R. Murphy, Martin & Garcia, 1982). Similarly, raters who possess strong beliefs about workers may be motivated to notice positive behaviors in individuals they perceive as "good" and to ignore negative behaviors in "bad" workers (K. R. Murphy & Balzer, 1981, cited in K. R. Murphy & Davidshofer, 1988).

The Interaction of Cognitive Ability and Item Characteristics. Stone et al. (1990) noted that test researchers rarely study the ability of test-takers to understand test instructions, item content, or response alternatives. They proposed that if respondents lack the cognitive ability to read and interpret questionnaires, their motivation and ability to complete the questionnaire will be impaired. Stone et al. (1990) suggested that such effects could be detected by comparing the psychometric properties of questionnaires completed by groups with different levels of cognitive ability.

Stone et al. (1990) used the Wonderlic Personnel Test to classify 347 Army Reserve members into low-, medium-, and high-cognitive ability groups. Subjects also completed an additional 203 items in a test battery of 27 measures that included the Job Diagnostic Survey, which contains scales to measure such constructs as task identity, autonomy, extrinsic feedback, satisfaction with job duties, and organizational commitment. Stone et al. found significant differences in coefficient *alpha* for 14 of the 27 constructs. In 12 of those cases, *alpha* rankings were as predicted, from lowest to highest reliability estimates matching low- to high-cognitive ability. Stone et al. also found a significant correlation ($r = -.23$) between cognitive ability and the number of missing questionnaire responses. Finally, they observed that the scales most adversely affected by low-cognitive ability were composed of only three or four items.

Stone et al. (1990) recommended that test developers devise items capable of being understood by all levels of respondents. This may be particularly important in areas such as industrial-organizational psychology where questionnaires may be completed by subgroups with moderate- to low-cognitive ability. Stone et al. noted that estimates place one-third of the United States work force as functionally illiterate and that job titles may provide rough estimates of cognitive ability.

Berk and Fekken (1990) reported a similar finding about the relation between cognitive ability and scale properties. They investigated a person reliability index computed with the scales of the Jackson Vocational Interest Survey. This index, which results from producing two scores per scale (each based on half of the items) and then correlating scores across pairs of scales, was significantly correlated across two administrations of the scale ($r = .60$). This result indicates that the person index can function as a reliable measure of whether a profile will remain stable over a brief time period. Interestingly, a measure of verbal ability was significantly correlated ($r = .28$) with a measure of scale stability, suggesting that verbally more skilled subjects possessed more stable scores.

Constructivist Assessment

Test-takers may perceive measurement devices as ambiguous because it is usually the test developer who creates and selects test instructions, item content, and response alternatives. Respondents who differ from the test developer on such variables as culture, gender, age, and cognitive ability may represent the testing task in unintended ways. Proponents of constructivist assessment believe that humans construct their psychological realities and that it is the linguistic constructions of individual persons—instead of the test developer—that should be measured (G. J. Neimeyer & Neimeyer, 1993).

These assessment approaches are descendants of the work of George Kelly (1955), who developed a theory of personal constructs. Kelly proposed that constructs are bipolar (i.e., expressions of opposites) *distinctions* that enable the perceiver to construct discrete meanings out of the vast amount of perceivable stimuli (G. J. Neimeyer & Neimeyer, 1993). Constructivist proponents believe that meaning is constructed through language organized into narratives, metaphors, and stories (Sarbin, 1986b). Reactivity is not viewed as a problem in constructivist approaches as much as an inevitability (G. J. Neimeyer & Neimeyer, 1993). That is, assessments are perceived as interventions that cause the individual to reconsider the constructs being assessed. In contrast to cognitive behavioral assessments, which tend to focus on isolated negative self-statements, constructivists examine interconnected constructs through repertory grid techniques (Beail, 1985; Kelly, 1955; R. A. Neimeyer, 1993).

R. A. Neimeyer (1993) called the repertory grid "the Rorschach or MMPI of constructivist assessment" (p. 72). The grid is typically administered in an interview: Individuals are asked to select elements from a personal domain (e.g., potential careers such as construction worker, park ranger, and electrical engineer) and then rate those elements on personally selected constructs (e.g., low or high starting salary, indoor or outdoor work, low or high opportunity for advancement). The resulting content and numeric ratings provide qualitative and quantitative information. Qualitative data such as elicited constructs can be coded on such factors as interpersonal content or level of abstractness. Quantitative data are typically analyzed to determine (a) differentiation, the number of different dimensions of judgment employed; (b) integration, the organization or correlation among dimensions; and (c) conflict, the amount of negative correlation among the dimensions (G. J. Neimeyer, 1988, 1989a, 1989b). In vocational psychology, differentiation, integration, and conflict constructs have been related to vocational choice, vocational identity development, and quality of career decision-making skills (G. J. Neimeyer, Brown, Metzler, Hagans, & Tanguy, 1989).

G. J. Neimeyer et al. (1989; see also Borgen & Seling, 1978) maintained that research has demonstrated that individuals process experimentally provided constructs (as in standard vocational interest items) and personally elicited constructs in fundamentally different ways. As idiographic proponents would argue, constructs created by individuals carry greater personal meaning and thereby facilitate greater understanding and more accurate recall of vocational information. Referring specifically to vocational research literature, G. J. Neimeyer et al. (1989) suggested that if differences between information generated through experimenter provided and personally elicited constructs are sufficiently large, many research findings may be undependable (see also Schulenberg, Vondracek, & Nesselroade, 1988).

Summary

Cognitive approaches' great promise would seem to lie in their potential for illuminating important cognitive components that partially form the basis for construct validity. That is, these approaches offer tools for investigating such problems as how test-takers construe the meaning of items and how individuals' cognitive abilities interact with test item characteristics. Historically, motivational and affective influences have also been recognized as important influences in testing processes, and it is here that cognitive psychology may have less to offer in the way of theory and methods.

BEHAVIORAL APPROACHES

As described in Chapter 4, behavioral assessment focuses on environmental stimuli, behavioral responses, and the consequences of those responses. Such assessment focuses on obtaining repeated samples of observable behavior, often in conjunction with an intervention.

Assessment in Mental Health Institutions

Decision makers in settings such as mental hospitals, community mental health centers, and residential facilities need information to make rational decisions (Paul et al., 1986a). Given the range of measurement and assessment procedures available—interviews, intelligence tests, behavioral observation, personality tests, vocational tests, progress notes—the question becomes, What is the best method or combination of methods? When these decisions are made by behaviorally oriented assessors, it should come as no surprise that direct observation of behavior, not trait-based approaches, is heavily emphasized.

Paul (1986, 1987a, 1987b) described a comprehensive assessment system designed to produce clinical and administrative data in a residential treatment setting. Paul et al. (1986a) suggested that information should be assessed in three domains:

1. Clients, including problem behaviors, stable personal-social characteristics (e.g., age, gender, education), and physical-social life environments (i.e., the context in which problems occur)
2. Staff, including therapeutic techniques, stable personal-social characteristics, and physical-social life environment (i.e., the context in which treatments occur)
3. Time, the moment when an assessment is obtained and the period of time to which it applies.

Given these dimensions, who might best provide this information? Paul et al. (1986b) listed six potential sources:

1. Clients and staff who can provide information about themselves
2. Significant others
3. Residential clients who could provide information about other clients and staff
4. Clinical staff who could provide information about all three domains
5. Records and archives
6. Trained staff whose only responsibilities are to function as observers. Such staff can be interactive (i.e., they interact with target individuals) or noninteractive.

When should information be obtained and recorded? Paul et al. (1986b) classified observational schedules into programmed (i.e., scheduled or unscheduled) and discrete or continuous. Recording can be accomplished immediately after behavior or delayed, on single or multiple occasions, and with stable or transitory phenomena. Actions or interactions can be monitored as well as individuals or aggregations of individuals. They recommended that observations be recorded as soon as possible because accuracy and precision tend to decrease as the time period between event and recording increases. Although measurement error increases with sampling, continuous recording of data in all three domains is usually impractical.

Paul et al. (1986b) also suggested that the units of observation be established before the observation period so that observers are able to focus on important elements. Such units should be discrete samples of behavior, as opposed to global signs, because greater amounts of interpretation by observers are more likely to reflect characteristics of the observer. Error arising from such factors as carelessness or fatigue by the rater will be minimized when measurement data can be aggregated from multiple occasions. Observation of clients and staff may be reactive, but independent raters should be less so than clients or staff because their ratings will have less personal significance and evaluative potential. Paul et al. (1986b) concluded that the accuracy and relevance of observations can be maximized using multiple, discrete, and scheduled observations made by trained observers as soon as possible following a behavioral event.

Paul et al. (1986b) described their chief assessment tools as Direct Observational Coding (DOC) procedures. DOCs require explicit sampling of individuals and occasions by trained observers. Mariotto and Licht (1986) suggested that such training include the following:

1. An orientation stressing the purposes and confidentiality of measurement
2. Technical manuals that describe coding content and procedures
3. Practice coding behavior
4. Objective feedback to coders
5. In vivo coding practice
6. Certification, through a work sample, of the observer's readiness
7. Procedures to maintain observer skills

Paul et al. (1986b) noted two important sources of error that should be monitored with observers: (a) decay, random changes in the observer's reliability or consistency of observation, and (b) drift, systematic changes in the definition or interpretation of coding categories. Paul et al. (1986b) maintained that such errors could be minimized by obtaining converging data from different assessment procedures, conditions, and operations.

Licht, Paul, and Power (1986) reported that such DOC systems have been implemented with more than 600 clinical staff in 36 different treatment programs in 17 different institutions. The resulting flood of data has produced results of interest to researchers as well as to clinicians and administrators in the studied agencies. Data from DOC systems have produced evidence of substantial differences in the behavior of different clinical staff and treatment programs. For example, staff–client interactions in 30 studied agencies ranged from 43 to 459 interactions per hour; over a full week, staff members were responsible for as few as four clients or as many as 33. DOC data also demonstrated changes in staff behavior resulting from training and development procedures and the maintenance of such behavior. Licht et al. (1986) reported that how staff interact with clients— that is, specific intervention programs—was highly correlated with client functioning and improvement (r's range from .5 to .9 on different variables). In addition, the quality of staff-client interaction was more important than the quantity of that interaction. Licht et al. (1986) noted that DOC information may not only aid in the monitoring of treatment implementation but may be employed as feedback to adapt treatment for improved effectiveness.

Behavioral Physics

Observing that "we tolerate substantial measurement error in psychological tests and rating scales" (p. 11), Tryon (1991) attempted to reduce such error by selecting highly reliable and accurate measurement devices. Tryon (1991) coined the term *behavioral physics* to describe how important aspects of psychological behavior can be studied through measures of activity, time, and space. Monitoring devices can record the frequency, intensity, and duration of exercise and other activities, thus providing information for clinical and research purposes. Such instruments have the ability to provide longitudinal, continuous measures of individuals in their natural environment. Examples of activity measurement devices include the following:

1. Actometers, mechanical wrist watches that record kinetic energy produced by body movements
2. Heart rate recorders, portable devices that can measure heart rate over days
3. Body temperature sensors that transmit temperature data to nearby receivers

Tryon reviewed research examining the relations between activity and such problems as mood disorders, hyperactivity, eating disorders, sleep, substance abuse, and disease. For example, he found that exercise alleviated reactive depression in over a dozen studies, with samples that included postmyocardial infarction patients (M. J. Stern & Cleary, 1982), college students (Greist, Klein, Eischens, & Faris, 1979), and psychotherapy clients diagnosed as depressed (Klein et al., 1985). In the Klein et al. (1985) study,

60 depressed individuals were randomly assigned to exercise and cognitive-interpersonal and meditation-relaxation therapies. Although completion rates differed (56%, 67%, and 48%, respectively), all three groups demonstrated significant reduction in depression at treatment conclusion. Although these studies did not do so, Tryon (1991) suggested that activity monitors could document the presence and intensity of therapeutic exercise. Tryon also proposed that further research be conducted to examine the relation of depression and activity over long periods.

Simulations, Structured Assessments, and Work Assessment Centers

With cognitive ability tests, respondents *perform* tasks that often resemble the criteria the test is designed to predict. Personality and temperament tests, in contrast, require respondents to *report* on relevant tasks. In addition, personality tests have been characterized as artificial and restricted in range (Hilgard, 1987). Given the substantial differences in reliability and validity between cognitive ability and personality tests (e.g., K. R. Murphy & Davidshofer, 1988; Parker et al., 1988), it would appear logical to develop personality tests that require respondents to perform relevant behaviors in naturalistic settings.

The idea of simulating aspects of real life as a measurement procedure is as old as psychological science. Allport (1921) cited Galton as advocating the representation of "certain problems of actual life, and of observing the individual's adjustment to these situations" (p. 451). Theory and research do support the idea that tests that function as simulations of criteria may maximize predictive validity (Cronbach & Gleser, 1965; Paul et al., 1986b; Wiggins, 1973). Asher and Sciarrino's (1974, cited in K. R. Murphy & Davidshofer, 1988) review of research on work sample tests found that the greater the similarity between test content and job, the higher the predictive validity. Wernimont and Campbell (1968) maintained that "an implicit or explicit insistence on the predictor being 'different' seems self-defeating" (p. 373); they described procedures for detailing critical job duties and assessing applicants' history relative to those behaviors. Gronlund (1988) advised developers of achievement tests to "*use the item types that provide the most direct measures of student performance specified by the intended learning outcome*" (p. 27). Danziger (1990) observed that in general, psychological tests best predict performance on other psychological tests:

> When one applies intelligence- or aptitude-test results to the prediction of future performance in the appropriate settings, academic or otherwise, one is essentially using a simulation technique. The more effectively the investigative context simulates the context of application, the better the prediction will be. (p. 188)

Contemporary reviewers of cognitive ability tests such as Lohman (1989) have noted trends toward increased study of simulations (Frederiksen,

1986), performance assessments (Gronlund, 1988; Shavelson, Baxter, & Pine, 1991), and the criteria such tests are attempting to predict (Cronbach, 1984; Glaser, Lesgold, & Lajoie, 1987). Cronbach (1992) emphasized that a major focus of measurement work in the 1990s will be improving the psychometric properties of test criteria.

Hilgard (1987) reported that the potential of structured assessments, seen in Murray's work and that of other psychologists, led to efforts during World War II to create extended observations in naturalistic situations. K. R. Murphy and Davidshofer (1988) described the program developed by the Office of Strategic Services (OSS; the CIA's precursor) to select and train intelligence agents. Recruits performed in lifelike situations over a three-day period so that observers could record their responses to stress. Recruits completed such tasks as (a) building a simple structure with the help of two uncooperative assistants who were assessment confederates; (b) functioning as a recruiter who interviewed an applicant/confederate; and (c) improvising during a role play of various interpersonal situations.

K. R. Murphy and Davidshofer (1988) described similar methods employed by the Peace Corps. Suitability screenings consisted of questionnaires and tests assessing the applicant's previous training, experience, and language aptitudes as well as academic transcripts and letters of reference. These screenings were followed by field selection procedures consisting of two to three months of training. During this period applicants completed interviews and psychological tests such as the MMPI and were observed and rated by staff. At the end of training a selection board reviewed all information and decided who to accept and reject for the corps.

K. R. Murphy and Davidshofer (1988) noted that it is difficult to evaluate the relative effectiveness of the OSS and Peace Corps assessment programs, partially because of a lack of suitable criteria. They reported that the OSS concluded that little evidence existed to support the predictive validity of their assessments (Office of Strategic Services Staff, 1948). However, later analyses of OSS data (Wiggins, 1973) indicated that the assessments produced a modest increase in the number of correct selection decisions made. With the Peace Corps, only 9% of those selected returned prematurely from their assignments, with 1% of the total returning because of psychiatric reasons. This result compared favorably to the 10–15% of volunteers' age cohort expected to experience some type of emotional impairment that would have interfered with assignment completion. Noting the results of the statistical versus clinical debate, K. R. Murphy and Davidshofer (1988) concluded that little evidence supports the use of diagnostic committees to integrate data and make selections over statistical methods.

The OSS and Peace Corps programs provided a foundation for contemporary work assessment centers. Gaugler, Rosenthal, Thornton, and Bentson (1987) estimated that since AT&T began the first center in 1956 (Bray & Grant, 1966), more than 2000 organizations have utilized such facilities.

Such centers typically assess individuals in small groups, utilizing multiple methods, including situational tests (such as the in-basket work sample and the leaderless group discussion), interviews, and personality tests, on multiple dimensions, such as leadership and resistance to stress.

Reviews of the reliability and validity of work assessment centers are generally positive (Gaugler et al., 1987; R. Klimoski & Brickner, 1987; K. R. Murphy & Davidshofer, 1988). Gaugler et al.'s (1987) meta-analysis of 50 assessment center studies revealed a corrected mean of .37 for 107 validity coefficients. Gaugler et al. (1987) found that validities were higher when (a) multiple evaluations were used, (b) assessees were female, (c) assessors were psychologists rather than managers, (d) the study was methodologically sound, and (e) peer evaluation was used. K. R. Murphy and Davidshofer (1988) noted that predictors and criteria in assessment center studies frequently are observer ratings; Gaugler et al. (1987; also see R. J. Klimoski & Strickland, 1981, cited in Hunter & Hunter, 1984) found that assessment centers better predict ratings of work potential than performance or ratings of performance. Sackett and Dreher (1982; R. Klimoski & Brickner, 1987), however, questioned the construct validity of assessment center measures, noting that factor analyses of exercises and dimensions more closely relate to distinct exercises than to dimensions or constructs.

Another significant limitation of assessment centers and other performance measures is their failure to exceed the predictive validity of cognitive ability tests for occupational criteria. Hunter and Hunter's (1984) meta-analysis, for example, found comparable validity estimates (.43 to .54) of predictors such as work sample tests, ability tests, peer ratings, behavioral consistency experience ratings, job knowledge tests, and assessment center ratings. The greater cost of assessment centers and simulations, compared to ability tests, sets limits on their utility in educational and occupational domains. Assessment center costs, however, are not fixed, as it is unclear just how much of the criteria must be simulated to obtain valid predictions (cf. Motowidlo, Dunnette, & Carter, 1990). Frederiksen (1962) proposed a set of five such distinctions that gauge the fidelity of psychological tests in comparison with actual behaviors:

1. The first category, *opinion*, requires the test-taker to state an opinion about an individual's performance. Given the multiple factors that can influence such opinion, this level represents the lowest fidelity when actually compared to performance.

2. *Attitude* scales presumably correlate with performance. These correlations, however, are often low to moderate.

3. *Knowledge* measurement is similar to Bandura's (1977) outcome expectation variable. Both reflect an individual's knowledge of the information and skills necessary to perform a behavior. The correlation between such knowledge and actual performance is often low.

4. *Related behaviors* are concomitants that are presumed to covary with performance and that are often employed because of practical considerations.

5. *Simulations* are constructed situations where respondents indicate what they would do if they were actually in the performance situation.

6. Finally, *lifelike behavior* refers to respondents' performance under conditions similar or identical to the situation in question.

Summary

These approaches offer well-developed methods for observing psychological phenomena. To the extent that behavioral assessment retains its radical roots, however, it is likely to resist exploring the usefulness of well-developed traditional concepts such as constructs, reliability, and validity. Such concepts seem indispensable for theory development and measurement evaluation (cf. Silva, 1993).

COMPUTER-BASED APPROACHES

Scientific progress is inseparably linked to the state of measurement theory and procedures. Measurement, in turn, is limited by the technologies available to gather data. Throughout most of psychology's history, the predominant measurement technologies have been printed materials and pencils. Danziger (1990) maintained that other sciences came to rely on reliable witnesses as the key to credible knowledge; nonetheless, technology can also increase observer reliability (cf. Rosenthal, 1976). The moons of Jupiter, for example, are invisible to all except individuals with exceptional eyesight in excellent atmospheric conditions. A telescope, however, allows any sighted person to easily view those moons at leisure.

The introduction of microcomputers has resulted in widespread interest in measurement uses of this technology. With the exception of IRT applications, most contemporary developers of computer-based testing procedures have focused on adapting traditional tests so that one or all test components—administration, response recording, scoring and data analysis, and interpretation—is done by computer (Butcher, 1987a; Hedlund, Vieweg & Cho, 1984). Many of these applications were published in the 1980s when it appeared that testing software would be an economic boon for developers and publishers. Automated procedures were created, for example, for the MMPI (Anderson, 1987; Butcher, 1987b; Honaker, 1988), 16PF (Harrell & Lombardo, 1984; Karson & O'Dell, 1987), Rorschach (Exner, 1987), Strong Interest Inventory (Hansen, 1987; Vansickle, Kimmel & Kapes, 1989), Self-Directed Search (Reardon & Loughead, 1988), neuropsychological tests (Adams & Heaton, 1987; Golden, 1987; Heaton, Grant, Anthony, & Lehman, 1981), interviews (Erdman, Klein & Greist, 1985; Fowler, Finkelstein, Penk, Bell & Itzig, 1987; Giannetti, 1987), intelligence and aptitude tests (Elwood, 1972a, 1972b, 1972c, 1972d; Harrell, Honaker, Hetu, & Oberwager, 1987), behavior rating systems (Thomas, 1990), psychophysiological research (Blumenthal & Cooper, 1990; D. L. McArthur, Schandler, & Cohen, 1988), attention deficits and hyperactivity (McClure & Gordon, 1984; Post, Burko & Gordon, 1990), and diagnostic procedures (Stein, 1987).

Given that the basic objective of much of this work has been the transfer of paper-and-pencil tests to computer, a logical research question to ask concerns the equivalence of procedures, particularly with computer administration of test material (Skinner & Pakula, 1986). That is, does the automation of test procedures affect the instrument's reliability and validity? Given the economic potential of testing software (Meier & Geiger, 1986), these questions have tended to be investigated *after* software has been developed and marketed. Some studies have found no differences between traditional and computer-administered versions of tests (e.g., Calvert & Waterfall, 1982; Elwood, 1972d; Guarnaccia, Daniels, & Sefick, 1975; Hitti, Riffer, & Stuckless, 1971). However, some who take computer-administered tests show elevated negative affect scores (C. E. George, Lankford, & Wilson, 1990), indicate more anxiety with computer-based procedures (Hedl, O'Neil, & Hansen, 1973), alter their rate of omitting items (Mazzeo & Harvey, 1988), and increase their "faking good" responses (Davis & Cowles, 1989). Given the equivocal findings, the equivalence issue currently must be addressed by test administrators on a test-by-test, sample-by-sample basis.

Although straightforward automation of traditional tests often improves the reliability and efficiency of testing procedures and scoring, computerization has yet to advance basic measurement theory and technology. The existing and growing base of microcomputers, however, offers a platform from which to support a second phase of new measurement procedures that more fully utilize computer capabilities. Experimental procedures and measurements that have previously been laboratory-based can now be economically transported to microcomputers for use in applied settings. As Embretson (1992) noted, tightly controlled experimental tasks may be implemented as test items. Computer-based measurement can blur the distinction between experiments and tests, thus facilitating the unification of correlational and experimental psychology suggested by Cronbach (1957). Part of the success of neuropsychological testing results from the fact that many of the tasks contained in these tests have been derived from laboratory procedures (Goldstein, 1990). Automation may make such derivations possible in other domains, several of which are described below.

Response Latency

A variable usually associated with cognitive investigations in laboratory settings (Welford, 1980a), reaction time (RT) or response latency can easily be measured in computer-based tests and tasks (Ryman, Naitoh & Englund, 1984). Brebner and Welford (1980) observed that early psychologists hoped to use RT as a physical measure of mental processes. Contemporary psychologists have employed latency as indicators of cognitive ability (Jensen, 1982; Lohman, 1989), stress and fatigue (Nettelbeck, 1973; Welford, 1980b), and psychopathology (Nettelbeck, 1980).

Utilizing latency as a key component, R. R. Holden, Kroner, Fekken and Popham (1992) described a model to predict faking on personality test item response. In this model, test-takers respond to items by comparing test item content with self-information contained in a schema (R. R. Holden, Fekken & Cotton, 1991). Because schemas expedite the search for information, R. R. Holden et al. (1992) proposed that responses should be faster for schema-congruent test answers than incongruent responses. Previous research has found that individuals who possess high total scores on an anxiety scale respond more quickly when agreeing with anxiety-relevant items (R. R. Holden et al., 1991; S. M. Popham & Holden, 1990). Given the historical emphasis on distortion in self-report, R. R. Holden et al. (1992) extended this model to include dissimulation on personality test items. They reasoned that persons faking good would respond more quickly to socially desirable items (i.e., congruent schema) than undesirable items (incongruent). Conversely, persons faking bad should respond more quickly to undesirable items than desirable ones. Using microcomputer-presented items, R. R. Holden et al. (1992; also see R. R. Holden & Kroner, 1992) found support for both hypotheses in a series of studies utilizing the MMPI and Basic Personality Inventory with college students and maximum security prisoners. Other researchers (M. George & Skinner, 1990; Tetrick, 1989) have also described studies using subjects' response latency to individual questionnaire items to detect inaccurate responding.

Human Speech

As applications to record and transcribe human speech become available and economical in this decade, they have the potential to revolutionize interviewing and measurement procedures. A program that could recognize disruptions of normal speech patterns and relate that information to anxiety (cf. Mahl, 1987) would certainly be of interest to research and applied psychologists. Most theories of counseling and psychotherapy view language as crucial to understanding and intervening with clients (Meier & Davis, 1993). Researchers and practitioners have considerable interest in computer programs that could transcribe psychotherapy sessions and produce or assist in the production of qualitative and quantitative measures of that communication.

Research on speech applications appears to be in its initial stages. Friedman and Sanders (1992) described a microcomputer system, coupled with a telephone, designed to monitor pauses in speech. They analyzed long speech pauses (defined as ≥ 1 s) in relation to mood disorders. Friedman and Sanders (1992) maintained that pause measurement can be useful in studying and identifying such problems as depression, mania, dementia, and coronary-prone behavior. Canfield, Walker, and Brown (1991) described a microcomputer-based coding system to analyze sequential interactions that occur in psychotherapy. Using the Gloria films of Ellis, Perls, and Rogers (Shostrum, 1966), Canfield et al. (1991) explored whether this coding system could demonstrate differences among therapists with distinct therapeutic styles. Canfield et al. (1991) analyzed transcripts of the Gloria psychotherapy sessions for positive and negative emotion, cognition, and contracts (i.e., promises and commitments). As expected, they found that the three therapists' use of these categories differed in frequency. They also found that Gloria differed in her frequency of these categories across the three therapists and that therapists employed different sequences of categories when responding to client statements. For example, one therapist would respond to a client's positive emotion statement with a positive emotion, whereas another therapist would respond with a positive cognition. Canfield et al. (1991) noted that previous studies of these films have found differences in use of predicates (Meara, Shannon, & Pepinsky, 1979), reflection and direction (Hill, 1978), and language structure (Zimmer & Cowles, 1972).

Simulations

Computers make increasingly realistic simulations of the type discussed above an economically viable possibility now and in the near future. Multimedia programs that utilize audio and visual material in addition to text may be used to create assessment simulations for use in business, industrial, educational, and clinical settings. These simulations can also function as unobtrusive measures to supplement reactive self-report scales (Johnson, Hickson, Fetter, & Reichenbach, 1987). Computer-assisted instruction programs (CAI) can employ simulations to perform the dual functions of teaching and assessment (Fulton, Larson, & Worthy, 1983; Meier & Wick, 1991). Meier and Wick (1991) described a simulation designed to demonstrate blood alcohol levels for subject-selected drinking experiences. Unobtrusively recorded reports of subjects' alcohol consumption in the simulation was (a) significantly correlated with self-reports of recent drinking behavior, drinking intentions, and attitudes toward alcohol, and (b) uncorrelated with a measure of social desirability. Similarly, Worthen, Borg, and White (1993) discussed the use of computers in continuous measurement in educational settings. If a particular curriculum was computer-based, testing could be embedded in the instructional material and thus be relatively unobtrusive. Worthen et al. noted that such an approach fits very well with mastery learning where progression to the next level of instruction depends upon demonstration of successful performance on the current material.

Being relatively resource poor, psychology usually must wait for new technology to become available in the mass marketplace before such devices can be applied to measurement and assessment problems. Such is the case with virtual reality, a set of computer-based devices that allow simulations of visual, auditory, and tactile phenomena. According to Potts (1992), the devices typically include (a) a helmet for projecting three-dimensional views and stereo sound; (b) a joystick for controlling the user's movement in the virtual world; (c) a glove that allows the user to manipulate objects in the virtual world; (d) a Polhemus sensor, suspended above the user, that tracks the positions of the helmet, joystick, and glove, and relays that information to the computer; and (e) a computer to create sensory input for the user and track the user's actions. If the validity of simulations depends upon the closeness of their match to real situations (Motowidlo et al., 1990), then virtual reality holds great potential for psychological measurement. Like much of the technology described in this section, however, the cost of a virtual reality system is high (down from $200,000 a few years ago to $20,000 currently, according to Potts, 1992) and availability is low.

Summary

Computer-based approaches will be increasingly employed in the future for no other reason than they offer increased efficiency in test development, administration, scoring, and interpretation. Automation in psychological testing has occurred, however, with relatively little attention to such theoretical considerations as human factors issues (cf. Meier, 1988b; Meier & Lambert, 1991; Rosen, Sears, & Weil, 1987) or fully employing computer capabilities in the testing process.

SUMMARY AND IMPLICATIONS

This chapter has described current work in traditional measurement, statistically oriented approaches, cognitive approaches, behavioral assessment, and computer-based approaches. Much of the work in traditional measurement appears to center on confirming the Big Five factors of personality and extending this model to other areas such as clinical assessment (e.g., McCrae & Costa, 1987a; Wiggins & Pincus, 1989). Behavioral assessment continues to thrive even with a greater focus on its relations to traditional psychometric concepts (e.g., Silva, 1993). As described in this chapter and in Chapters 2 and 3, cognitive theory and procedures hold considerable promise for the investigation and explanation of such measurement processes as item response; cognitive models, however, tend to neglect the motivational and affective influences of measurement processes. Computer-based approaches would seem important if for no other reason than technological innovations tend to reduce the amount of interpretation in measurement and assessment. Content analysis and qualitative research, for example, are facilitated by tape recording of conversations, which allows the listener to replay phrases and sentences for coding instead of performing the task as the activity occurs.

Theoretical and statistical approaches need greater reintegration, but that may not happen until the former has grown in strength sufficient to function as a full partner in such a merger. Brennan (1983) noted that IRT is a scaling theory, that is, useful for determining which items fit a theoretical model. With ability tests, good items should fit the shape of the appropriate ICC. GT, in contrast, is a sampling theory, useful for investigating the multiple factors that influence item and test scores. Brennan summarized these differences by observing that IRT attends to "individual items as fixed entities without specific consideration of other conditions of measurement," (p. 122), whereas GT's emphasis "is placed on viewing an item as a sampled condition of one facet in a (usually) larger universe of conditions of measurement" (p. 122). It makes sense that IRT's major applications have been with cognitive ability tests that measure a single dominant factor (Hambleton et al., 1991). Noncognitive tests with multiple validities, resulting from method and construct-related influences, would seem more amenable to study utilizing GT procedures. Nevertheless, both approaches seek increased precision in psychological tests. Although IRT and GT may eventually be merged in a more complete measurement theory, GT deserves more attention than it has received. Loevinger's (1957) comment remains apropos: "There is extraordinarily little empirical evidence for raising validity by improving scalability, considering the amount of interest in scale analysis" (p. 663).

This chapter contains an important omission that deserves at least a brief emphasis. Work on fundamental measurement theory (Krantz et al., 1971; Luce, Krantz, Suppes, & Tversky, 1990; Suppes, Krantz, Luce, & Tversky, 1989) attempts to understand the foundations of types of measurement across the sciences through an analysis of measurement axioms (i.e., self-evident principles). Such principles include the rules for (a) assigning numbers to two manifestations of a phenomenon that differ in some respect and (b) performing mathematical operations on those numbers, such as addition and division. Knowledge of the properties of these numbers may help evaluate the usefulness of the scales and actual objects they are intended to represent. For example, Cliff (1992) noted that Luce and Tukey (1964) demonstrated that interval scales could be defined when ordinal consistency appeared among three or more variables. Such a conclusion, Cliff (1992) observed, "seemed to open the way to define the truly psychological nature of many variables" (p. 186). However, psychologists' knowledge of work in this area has been hampered by its mathematical complexities, lack of demonstrated empirical usefulness, and difficulties in coping with error (Cliff, 1992).

7 INTEGRATION

The major concern of validity, as of science more generally, is not to explain any single isolated event, behavior, or item response, because these almost certainly reflect a confounding of multiple determinants. Rather, the intent is to account for consistency in behaviors or item responses, which frequently reflects distinguishable determinants. In contrast with treating the item responses or behaviors in question separately as a conglomeration of specifics, these behavioral and response consistencies are typically summarized in the form of total scores or subscores. We thus move from the level of discrete behaviors or isolated observations to the level of measurement. (Messick, 1989a, p. 14)

Tests are used to make decisions. (K. R. Murphy & Davidshofer, 1988, p. xi)

Counseling psychology research has almost exclusively been, and still is, individual differences research. (Dawes, 1992, p. 13)

THE IMPLICATIONS OF MEASUREMENT HISTORY

The above quotations describe several of the most important current assumptions resulting from the evolution of psychological measurement and assessment. Messick indicated, for example, that measurement consists

173

of the aggregation of items. Little attention is given to the possibility that consistency may be possible at a scale other than that of the aggregated total. The error that occurs at the scale of the single item is considered random and unavailable to investigation. Loevinger (1957) noted the belief about the futility of single-item analysis when she wrote that "the many sources and many meanings of every response induce scepticism about the value of searching for rigorously structured, pure, unidimensional patterns" (p. 644).

Danziger (1990) suggested that during the historical development of psychology, certain methods became the only acceptable alternatives available to investigators. The decision to select these methods, Danziger noted, was not necessarily rational and was certainly influenced by political forces within the profession. From the historical review provided in previous chapters, psychological measurement and assessment can be seen to have been primarily influenced by administrative selection purposes. Psychologists have underappreciated the role that selection pressures and procedures have played in measurement and assessment. One can frame the purpose of tests in terms of cost-effective decision making, but such a perspective can also obscure and complicate the use of tests for other purposes.

Tests constructed for selection purposes now dominate theoretical and intervention research in all of soft psychology. I would interpret Dawis' statement to mean that psychological researchers, whatever their purpose, employ tests designed to measure stable traits that distinguish between individuals. I will argue in greater depth that psychologists' purposes should influence the design strategy of their measurement devices. For example, rather than employing tests containing items measuring stable traits, researchers interested in evaluating the efficacy of psychological interventions might more appropriately construct tests on the basis of items' ability to distinguish between groups of individuals exhibiting treatment success and failure.

As illustrated in Figure 32, the procedures of selection testing have exerted a dominant influence on the four major components of testing: test

---

	Test Component			
Purpose	Construction	Administration	Scoring	Interpretation

SELECTION	
	Should procedures developed
Theory-Building	with selection tests be
	employed with tests intended
Intervention	for other purposes?

FIGURE 32   Major testing purposes and components.

construction, administration, scoring, and interpretation. Although exceptions can be found, in the typical psychological test:

1. test items have been selected and evaluated with only a loose connection to psychological theory;
2. tests have been designed to be administered economically, which often translates into quickly and in large groups;
3. test items are aggregated to produce summary scores, thus minimizing the "errors" of individuals;
4. test scores are interpreted in terms of some placement decision (e.g., should this person be classified as mentally retarded? admitted to this school?), with little attention to how scores could provide information about intervention.

Test validity must be evaluated in the context of its purpose (Cronbach & Gleser, 1965). In addition to selection, tests may be employed for the purposes of intervention and theory building. One can certainly employ tests for selection into an intervention: for example, a test might be useful in determining degree of psychopathology and thus deciding whether an individual requires an intervention (e.g., Hayes et al., 1987). One could also employ a test to determine which type of intervention would be most effective. However, tests might also be used to develop a model or theory of the target of intervention, be they individuals, groups, or organizations. Finally, selection and intervention testing would certainly be applicable to theory building, but researchers also seek data for the purpose of accumulating explanatory knowledge independent of any immediate application.

Below I discuss four components of testing—construction, administration, scoring, and interpretation—within the context of three major test purposes: selection, intervention, and theory building.

CONSTRUCTING TESTS

The first step in test construction is to decide on the form and the content of the test. In traditional measurement, this involves creation of a pool of items and selection of items from that pool. In behavioral assessment, the "test" is constructed by selecting behaviors to be targeted by the intervention. Other types of testing, such as performance appraisal, focus on selecting appropriate tasks for testing.

Measurement for Selection

Selection tests are typically used for the purpose of classification and subsequent prediction. R. P. Martin (1988) indicated that such measurement focuses on broad, relatively stable traits. Under this heading, R. P.

Martin (1988) included testing for the purposes of screening (i.e., isolating a subgroup for further assessment or intervention), differentiating between normal and abnormal behavior, differential diagnosis (i.e., classification into one type of psychopathology), and delineating normal individual differences. Again, psychologists historically have been interested in creating measures that show differences among individuals in order to classify them into academic, occupational, or therapeutic groups. For example, Hathaway and McKinley originally developed the MMPI to function as a substitute for the individual interview in assigning psychiatric diagnoses (Graham, 1990). They selected MMPI items on the basis of their ability to discriminate between normals and hospital patients who possessed some type of psychiatric illness as indicated by clinical judgment (Graham, 1990). However, researchers found that the MMPI could not adequately fulfill its diagnostic role in that individuals who scored highly on a scale matching their initial diagnoses (e.g., depression) also tended to score highly on other clinical scales (Graham, 1990). Graham (1990) suggested that instead of seeking diagnoses, MMPI users came to rely on profiles of MMPI scores that were associated with specific behaviors and traits. But because of the limited reliability of subscales and the difficulties clinicians encounter in reliably applying complex decision rules, the validity of profiles used in classification and prediction tasks remains controversial (K. R. Murphy & Davidshofer, 1988).

Given that cost remains the major element in psychological measurement and assessment (R. P. Martin, 1988), selection tests for the military, business, and education have usually been empirically developed. That is, large numbers of items are written and administered to a representative sample. Items are then evaluated against a criterion such as job performance or grades. The time-consuming task of developing items and tasks that follow from a theoretical construct or a task analysis is avoided. Selection procedures represent the least expensive method of test construction. The source of items is relatively unimportant, as long as the initial pool is relatively large and a criterion to correlate with those items is available.

If a theory is employed in selection test development, it is likely to be trait-based. The construct in question is assumed to be stable and consistent over time; test developers seek items that show differences among individuals. The testing format is likely to be the most economical available (i.e., self-report), unless differences between methods show a significant improvement for a more costly procedure (as is the case with cognitive ability testing versus self-report of ability; see Hunter & Hunter, 1984).

Criterion-Referenced and Norm-Referenced Tests.   In criterion-referenced tests, scores are compared to some absolute measure of behavior, a criterion; norm-referenced scores are compared among individuals (Glaser,

1963). Gronlund (1988) indicated that developers of norm-referenced tests seek items with the greatest possible variability. With achievement tests, these items are pursued through a selection process that retains items of average difficulty; easy and hard items are likely to be discarded. Aggregation of such items increases the possibility of making valid distinctions among individuals. With criterion-referenced tests, however, items are retained because of their relation to a criterion, regardless of the frequencies of correct or incorrect responses. Since maximizing the similarity between test and criterion tends to increase predictive validity (e.g., Cronbach & Gleser, 1965; Danziger, 1990; Paul, 1986; Wiggins, 1973), selection tests might be improved by following guidelines provided for criterion-referenced tests (and, interestingly, behavioral assessment), where item selection is based upon performance objectives or criteria the test is designed to measure (Swezey, 1981).

Swezey (1981) observed that criterion-referenced tests have received widespread attention only since the 1960s. A plausible guess is that cost played a major role in delaying the development of this approach. Criterion-referenced tests cost more than norm-referenced tests because the former (a) require considerable effort in the analysis and definition of the performance criteria to be measured and (b) may necessitate special facilities and equipment beyond self-report materials. If one is interested in predicting performance on a criterion—the major purpose of selection testing—then criterion-referenced approaches would seem a logical choice. However, norm-referenced testing has been the predominant approach in selection testing. Besides their lower cost, norm-referenced tests also seem more applicable when the test administrator desires to select some portion of a group (e.g., the top 10% of applicants) as compared to all applicants who could successfully perform a function. Thus, norm-referenced tests are useful in selection situations where individuals are chosen partially on the basis of scarce resources. Suppose you conduct a research study and find that 95% of all graduate students who score 600 or above on the Graduate Record Examination (GRE) Verbal scale are able to pass all required graduate school courses. From the perspective of criterion-referenced testing, everyone scoring 600 or above should be admitted. In many graduate departments, however, that would mean admitting more students than available courses, instructors, or financial supports. Such a situation certainly occurs in other educational, occupational, and clinical settings with fixed quotas. Norm-referenced testing, then, provides a solution: identify the top-scoring number who match the available resources.

To the extent that additional resources become available to test developers, selection testers are likely to increase their use of criterion-referenced procedures. Descriptions of the development of criterion-referenced tests (Gronlund, 1988; Swezey, 1981) typically include the following steps:

1. Task analyses of the criteria must be performed to create operationally defined objectives. Objectives include performances (what the test-taker knows or does), conditions (the testing situation), and standards (the level of satisfactory performance). W. J. Popham (1978) discussed this specification in terms of stimulus attributes (the material presented to the test-taker) and response attributes (the test-taker's selected or constructed responses). Descriptions of specifications for criterion-referenced items resemble, in spirit if not in detail, those contained in behavioral assessment manuals, structured interviews, and process research manuals. All are time-consuming.

2. Items must be planned in terms of cost (time and personnel constraints) and fidelity (realism of the items as compared to the performance criteria). W. J. Popham (1993) recommended multiple methods and definitions for criterion-referenced items to avoid test-specific instruction (i.e., teaching only material relevant to the subsequent test).

3. An item pool must be created, with twice as many items created as eventually needed.

4. Final items must be selected. The item pool should be administered in a pilot study to a group of mastery and nonmastery individuals to determine the extent to which the items can discriminate between the two groups. Content experts may review the items, and the items should be evaluated against psychometric standards of reliability and validity. Gronlund (1988; Kryspin & Feldhusen, 1974) suggested the following formula for evaluating an item's sensitivity to instructional effects:

$$S = \frac{R_a - B_b}{T}$$
(1)

where R_a is the number of test-takers correctly responding to an item after instruction, B_b is the number correctly responding before instruction, and T the total number of test-takers at a single administration. Values near 1 indicate items more sensitive to instruction. Gronlund (1988, p. 148) also described a method for computing the reliability of a criterion-referenced test.

During item development, Swezey (1981) emphasized the importance of precisely specifying test objectives. Criteria can be described in terms of variables such as quality, quantity, product or process, time to complete, number of errors, precision, and rate (Gronlund, 1988; Swezey, 1981). A criterion may be a product such as "student correctly completes 10 mathematics problems"; a process criterion would be "student completes division problems in the proper sequence." If the test objective is a product, then product measurement is appropriate. Process measurement is useful when diagnostic information is required, when the product always follows from the process, and when product data is difficult to obtain. An adequate specification describes which of these components are included and excluded as part of the task. Criterion-referenced tests should be reliable and valid to the extent that performances, testing conditions, and standards are precisely specified in relation to the criteria. For example, Swezey (1981) preferred "within 5 minutes" to "under normal time conditions" as a precise testing standard. In some respects, the criterion-referenced approach represents a move away from a search for general laws and toward a specification of the meaning of test scores in terms of important measurement facets. Discussing test validity, Wiley (1991) presented a similar theme when he wrote that the labeling of a test ought to be "sufficiently precise to allow the separation of components of invalidity from valid variations in performance" (p. 86). Swezey's and Wiley's statements indicate the field's increasing emphasis on construct explication.

Measurement for Explanatory Theory Building

Where Do Test Items Come from?   How do test developers create and select items and tasks for their measurement devices? Golden, Sawicki, and Franzen (1990) listed three sources: theory, nomination by experts, and other tests. Golden et al. (1990) indicated that whatever their source, items initially are selected on the basis of their face validity. That is, the items appear to measure what they are intended to measure. When test developers employ a rational or theory-based approach, item selection stops when theoretically relevant items are written. Most test developers, however, typically administer those items and score the responses according to empirical strategies. The initial item pool, which Golden et al. (1990) recommended should be two to four times the final number of desired items, is fitted empirically against a psychometric model. Test developers typically search for consistent item responses that consistently predict some criterion. Consistency is often evaluated by selecting only items (a) that are highly correlated with the total score (i.e., internal consistency), and (b) that contribute to total scores highly correlated with a second administration of the same test with the same subjects (i.e., test–retest reliability).

In another approach, items may first be subjected to factor analyses or other "complex analyses aimed at revealing the truth" (Burisch, 1984, p. 215). That is, the data are transformed statistically in an attempt to reveal a true, latent value, which theoretically should then demonstrate better psychometric properties (e.g., higher reliability and greater predictive validity). Next, scores that predict a criterion are retained. A more rigorous evaluation is passed when those same scores maintain some degree of predictability across samples and occasions. This cross-validation, however, is surprisingly rare (Schwab & Oliver, 1974, cited in K. R. Murphy & Davidshofer, 1988).

Given its importance in the construct explication process, a surprising looseness and lack of organization exists during the process of item selection for most psychological tests. Loevinger (1957) stated there exists an

idiosyncratic, *nonreproducible* process, the process by which the given investigator or group of investigators constructs or selects items to represent that content. Although this process, the constitution of the pool of items, is a universal step in test construction, it has not been adequately recognized by test theory. But this step in test construction is crucial for the question of whether evidence for the validity of the test will also be evidence for the validity of a construct. (p. 658) [italics added]

Similarly, Lessler, et al. (1989) maintained that questionnaire design "remains essentially an art" (p. 1). Some measurement psychologists have offered item-selection guidelines that attempt to integrate the theoretical and statistical strategies described above (e.g., Jackson, 1970). Little consensus, however, exists about a best method. In fact, Burish's review of the literature (1984; Goldberg, 1972; see K. R. Murphy & Davidshofer, 1988, and Paunonen & Jackson, 1985, for opposing views) found that few differences existed in the psychometric properties of scales produced by different test construction methods.

Although selection procedures have dominated measurement, I propose that test construction procedures should follow from the intended purpose of the test. Test developers should not default to traditional approaches, that is, searching for consistent items that contribute to aggregated scores and differentiate among individuals in linearly predicting a criterion. Traditional approaches perform well for selection tests, but different strategies are likely to be necessary for tests of explanatory theory building and for tests that assess the effects of interventions.

Response Process Validity. Response process validity (RPV) refers to knowledge about the processes employed by individuals when completing psychological tests and tasks. RPV would seem a critical component of construct validity. To the extent that we understand item- and task-response processes, we should understand what a test measures. RPV applies equally to tests and criteria and ultimately should have implications about the possibility of increasing correlations between any two operations. Embretson (1985) maintained that "understanding the nature of the relationship, as opposed to just its magnitude, puts test developers in a better position to increase validity" (p. 286).

What would constitute a RPV research program? A frequent criticism of single-subject research is that the idiosyncrasies of any particular individual will interfere with the ability to generalize to all persons. However, if your purpose is to investigate error, then the single subject (as well as the single item) is exactly the place to start. Qualitative approaches, such as naturalistic observation, interviews, and protocol analysis, should provide information about the processes employed during the production of task and item response. Messick (1989a) noted that a test's construct validity can be ascertained through probes of "the ways in which individuals cope with the items or tasks, in an effort to illuminate the processes underlying item response and task performance" (p. 6). Similarly, Cronbach (1989) suggested that one could learn about construct validity by administering a test to individuals who think aloud as they answer the items.

In N of 1 studies (Barlow & Hersen, 1984; Gentile, 1982), a baseline period (A) is followed by an intervention (B). Next, the intervention is removed during a second baseline period (A); finally, the intervention is instituted for a second time (B). In this ABAB design, the targeted behavior should be stable during the first baseline; behavior should change during the intervention and then revert to previous levels once the intervention is removed; when the intervention is again implemented, behavior should again change. The sequencing of repeated baseline and intervention periods helps to establish the intervention's causal effects on the desired behavioral change.

This type of N of 1 research may allow investigation of a test's characteristics as well as its effects as an intervention. Suppose that you were interested in understanding the processes by which self-monitoring affects behavior (R. O. Nelson, 1977a, 1977b), which in this example will be amount of anxiety as expressed by a highly anxious client. As shown in Figure 33, during a baseline period of 1 wk, an observer could daily and unobtrusively rate the individual's level of anxiety; the observer rating would continue during the remaining components as the dependent variable. The intervention might then consist of hourly self-monitoring of

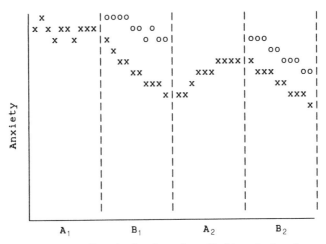

FIGURE 33 Investigating self-monitoring through an N of 1 study. A_2 refers to a baseline period, followed by the intervention (B_1), self-monitoring of anxiety. In A_2, self-monitoring ceases during the second baseline, followed by reimplementation of self-monitoring (B_2). In this example, x indicates an observer's ratings of a client's anxiety; o indicates the client's self-ratings.

anxiety by the client for a 1-wk period; the observer ratings would continue during this period also. The self-monitoring would cease for the second baseline period and then be reimplemented for the final intervention. If the self-monitoring functioned as an effective intervention, we would expect to observe the following sequence of observer anxiety ratings: (a) during the first baseline, stable, high observer ratings of anxiety; (b) during the intervention, a gradual decrease in observed anxiety; (c) during the second baseline, a gradual increase in observed anxiety; and (d) during the second intervention, a decrease in observed anxiety.

To increase our knowledge about the self-monitoring procedure, it would be useful to (a) ask the client to talk about how he or she is gauging anxiety while she makes the self-reports and (b) explore reasons (during and after the research) for the synchrony or desynchrony between the self- and observer ratings (particularly if the self- and observer ratings were conducted in a blind fashion to each other). Inquiry about how the client assesses anxiety might occur during the self-monitoring period or at the end of an intervention period (if one wished to avoid contaminating the effects of self-monitoring alone). Comparison of reports about self- and observer ratings might reveal similarities and differences in the basis for which those ratings were constructed. For example, it might be found that the observer rated anxiety on the basis of the client's facial expressions, whereas the client rated on the basis of physical sensations, such as sweating or upset stomach. In Figure 33, the observer's ratings of anxiety are always lower than the client's. Such differences might occur, for example, if the client tended not to be very facially expressive and the observer had no way of detecting the physiological conditions of the client.

Research with large numbers of subjects assumes that some of the variance contributed by one individual is uncorrelated with variance contributed by another individual (R. P. Martin, 1988). But investigation into such problems as self-report and rater errors suggests that individuals may share considerable error sources. Expansion of the investigation from a single subject to include additional persons (and items) is likely to lead to greater understanding of the etiology of systematic errors. Measurement psychologists who believe that useful research necessitates large numbers of subjects should note that Spearman employed ability data he collected from children at a small village school to develop the concepts and procedures of test error, correction for attenuation, *g*, and correlational methods.

Following small subject studies, experimental designs are likely to be useful. Research with relatively small groups provides an opportunity to experiment with interventions designed to reduce systematic errors. Cronbach (1957) and D. T. Campbell and Fiske (1959) both hoped that their work in construct validity would encourage such measurement experimentation. Cronbach (1957), for example, cited work by Fleishman and Hempel (1954) that found that practice in motor skills changed the factor structure of those skills. Cronbach (1957) maintained that Fleishman and Hempel's efforts "force upon us a theory which treats abilities as a product of learning, and a theory of learning in which previously acquired abilities play a major role" (p. 676). For the most part, however, experimental approaches have yet to be integrated into psychological measurement (cf. Tryon, 1991).

Why Are Items Dropped? The focus in traditional test construction is on finding items that meet the consistency-predictive validity model. Items that do not fit this model are dropped from the test. Little or no study is devoted to understanding *why* items do not meet test criteria. Test developers commonly assume that dropped items are poorly written, misunderstood by respondents, or fail to tap into the desired construct. In fact, developers seldom know why items fail to be retained.

Loevinger (1957) made a strong case for examining response processes in individual items. Although the empirical selection approaches that dominated at the time advocated against it, Loevinger (1957) maintained that "if theory is fully to profit from test construction as a part of psychology, every item included in a scoring key must be accounted for; a less strong case can be made for explaining the exclusion of items" (p. 657). Given the fact that more items are dropped than retained during item selection (Golden et al., 1990), the typical test development process may provide information about measurement theory as well as the substantive construct(s) under investigation. If the items are not theoretically based, as with empirical selection approaches, rejection of items has little potential import. But for the purpose of deepening measurement theory, it would be very useful to know *why* items are retained and deleted. If the items and tasks selected for the initial pool are theoretically based, they should have an equal probability of being selected for the test; an item that fails to meet inclusion criterion has the potential to inform theory.

Assume that a set of items measures a particular trait. If a subset of those items fail to show temporal stability, it would be useful to compare dropped and retained items on such methodological factors as item length and subjects' comprehensibility of items. It would also be useful to examine item content for state material and to compare the internal consistency of the temporally stable and unstable items. The unstable items may in fact be internally consistent, as is the case with the State form of the State–Trait Anxiety Inventory (STAI, Spielberger et al., 1970).

In the context of developing trait-based tests, Loevinger (1957) proposed two principles to guide this type of item selection. These principles are based on the idea that structuring the initial item pool allows testing hypotheses about the trait to be measured. First, a set of items should be drawn from a pool broader than the intended trait. Second, the items should sample all alternative theories of the trait. This is rarely performed in contemporary item selection because any contrasting of competing hypotheses occurs at the level of aggregate scores, not items. Both principles are similar to D. T. Campbell and Fiske's (1959) proposal for discriminant validity, although their idea pertained to scales and not individual items per se. In Loevinger's (1957) procedure, once the theoretical item pool has been created, items are selected for the trait scale on the basis of tests of structural validity. She suggested that if theory proposed certain relations between two types of nontest behavior, this relation should also be evident between test items measuring the behavior. Loevinger (1957) noted that aggregating items into total scores would obscure such interitem relations. It remains questionable, however, whether psychological test items have the capacity to function as stand-alone observations; individual items administered repeatedly and then aggregated might possess more utility. Loevinger (1957) believed that interitem correlations would not be subject to the problems associated with individual item response.

If a test developer can identify and control the important factors that influence item response, the developer should be able to reproduce the results of any item-selection process. For example, if the test developer creates, based on theory, an initial pool of 100 items, subsequent item analysis frequently results in the selection of 30 or so items. If the processes by which subjects respond to those 100 items are well understood, then the developer should be able to replicate the item-selection process. This procedure is not followed in contemporary item development: efforts to cross-validate (i.e., check predictive validity estimates in a new sample) remain at the level of the total score, not individual items. The failure to demonstrate a link between theory, item creation, and item selection, however, weakens the construct explication process and conclusions about construct validity.

Measurement for Intervention

Why conduct measurements and assessments as part of interventions? Given that one can have no knowledge of the success or failure of the intervention without some type of measurement, the answer seems obvious. But many practitioners who provide counseling and psychotherapy, for example, eschew formal tests, substituting their or the client's qualitative judgment for knowing when the process is complete. This is reasonable in the context that it is typically the client's (or a significant other's) judgment that initiated the intervention; such judgment is also inexpensive. Cost is important for all testing purposes, but particularly so in interventions.

The problem with this logic, of course, is that under the circumstances described in Chapters 2 and 3, clinicians and clients may be unable to produce valid judgments about treatment efficacy. Control groups consisting of persons who do not receive a treatment are typically included in research designed to test the efficacy of psychological interventions. Of relevance to this discussion are placebo control groups where individuals are led to believe they are receiving an effective treatment when, in fact, they are not. The placebo control group is designed to assess the effects of increasing individuals' expectancies for improvement on actual behavioral change. Placebos have been found to be as effective as other psychological interventions in such areas as smoking cessation, test anxiety, and speech anxiety (Heppner et al., 1992).

Model Building and Assessment. Three categories of intervention-related assessment can be described. In the first, practitioners employ a trial-and-error (eclectic) approach to intervention where they experiment with treatments until one works. Assessment is relatively unimportant in this process; to have a successful outcome, one simply needs the client to report feeling (or thinking or behaving) better. The second option, typified by Lazarus' (1973, 1981) multimodal approach, can be characterized as the reverse of the first in that everything is assessed. In his BASIC ID procedure, the intervener continually assesses behavior, affect, sensation, imagery, cognition, interpersonal relationships, and drugs or biological influences.

A third alternative, assessment of variables in a causal model of the client (Maloney & Ward, 1976), suggests that interveners conduct assessments with as little precision (and accompanying cost) as necessary. In an advanced science, an intervention decision could be made on the basis of decision rules involving test scores. In the clinical realm, for example, a certain profile on a psychological test such as the MMPI-2 might automatically result in the assignment of that individual to a fixed treatment (Cronbach & Gleser, 1965). At present, however, test results generally cannot be employed to make such decisions in psychological interventions (Cronbach & Gleser, 1965; Paul, et al., 1986a). Instead, an adaptive treatment is used where test results and other sources of information provide data for the formation of hypotheses about the causes of the problem, which in turn guide the selection of an intervention. To the extent that the intervention is unsuccessful, hypotheses are revised and a modified intervention implemented. The process is recycled until the intervention is concluded in success or failure. This type of model building for intervention is very similar to that of explanatory theory building, but on a smaller scale. Tests employed in this manner may be termed diagnostic and formative (Bloom et al., 1971).

An integration of different approaches to this model-building assessment suggests the following steps:

1. Select multiple constructs based on a causal model. Multiple operations and methods should also be included when possible.

2. Preplan observations. Although this step is assumed in theoretical research and in selection, it is often not included as part of intuitive clinical assessment.
3. Attempt to disconfirm and modify indicators of constructs and hypotheses of the model. Initial indicators of a construct may not be the only or best operations. Similarly, initial hypotheses are likely to be revised with additional data.
4. Apply such measurement rules as immediate recording of data and standardization of stimuli.

In the clinical realm, Maloney and Ward (1976; also see L. Goldman, 1971) discussed these procedures in terms of conceptual validity, that is, evaluating the usefulness of constructs relating to a client's functioning. Psychologists use assessments to test hypotheses and constructs about individuals instead of about tests or theories (Groth-Marnat, 1990). Ongoing assessment enables the intervener to test, disconfirm, and modify hypotheses about the causes of client distress. For example, a clinician might work with a pre-med college student who presents with severe test anxiety. The clinician administers an intelligence test and the MMPI to the student and finds evidence of average verbal ability and high depression. The working hypothesis, then, might be that the combination of depression and average ability is impairing the student's ability to adequately prepare for and perform on difficult tests. Given this hypothesis, it would make sense to attempt to alleviate the depression and determine if anxiety subsequently decreased and test performance improved. If anxiety remained high, however, the clinician should begin to explore and test alternative hypotheses about the causes of the student's anxiety. In the absence of general scientific laws, such as dependable aptitude-by-treatment interactions (ATIs), valid assessment of factors in a causal model is necessary to adjust treatment (Cronbach & Gleser, 1965; Licht, et al., 1986).

With more difficult problems in individuals, groups, and organizations, interveners must develop more complex causal models that require precise—and more expensive—measurement. The need for more precise measurement and assessment is likely to depend on two factors:

1. The knowledge base of the science. If a science is new, then relatively little knowledge will be available to guide interventions. Thus, interveners will frequently need to develop causal models and measure variables in the model.
2. The knowledge base of the individual intervener or intervention team. The more knowledge held by the intervener, the more automatic will be the application of knowledge to the intervention. Novices particularly require the skills of model building and intervention-related assessment.

Behavioral Assessment. Behavioral assessors believe that idiographic measures are more sensitive to behavior change in individuals (e.g., Cone, 1988; Hartman, 1984). Because no individual is likely to display all or just the right combination (i.e., a prototype) of the indicators of a construct, idiographic measures should better indicate change than nomothetic devices. In other words, unless a nomothetic measure has sampled the universe of a construct's indicators, it is unlikely to function with a specific individual as well as an idiographic measure. Bellack and Hersen (1988) suggested that idiographic approaches can aid in determining treatment targets and environmental contingencies. For example, three clients might define anxiety as the amount of hair-pulling, sweating, and self-reported tension, respectively. A therapist might observe or teach a client to self-monitor level of anxiety across different work tasks, social situations, or therapeutic interventions. Behavior would be assessed before treatment (to provide a baseline), during treatment (to guide treatment), and at the conclusion of treatment (to document outcome). To avoid error, assessors would be careful not to change the measurement procedure from one occasion to another (R. P. Martin, 1988).

But how are "items" selected in behavioral assessment? Interestingly, research indicates that selection of target behaviors varies by assessor (Evans & Wilson, 1983; Hartman, 1984). Hartman (1984) proposed that behavioral assessors disagree in their selection of target problems because of different beliefs about what is socially important, the relative desirability of alternative responses, different ideas about deviant behavior, and varying experience with the consequences of problem behaviors. Given these assumptions, Hartman (1984) suggested the following criteria for evaluating potential behavioral targets:

1. The behavior is important to the client or significant others.
2. The behavior is dangerous to the client or others.
3. The behavior is "socially repugnant" (p. 109).
4. The behavior interferes with the client's functioning.
5. The behavior clearly departs from normal functioning.

Precision. Cook and Campbell (1979) observed that measurement of precision can also be discussed in relation to the independent variables of intervention studies. Levels of the intervention can be specified imprecisely, such as when an investigator tests only two levels of an intervention, instead of potential levels 1 through 5. This underspecification may lead to statistically insignificant results and perhaps an improper generalization about the lack of efficacy of the named intervention (Cook & Campbell, 1979). For example, 6 wk of job enhancement may demonstrate negligible effects when compared with a placebo control. Significant effects might occur, however, when the intervention proceeds for 52 wk.

Item and Task Selection.   W. J. Popham (1993) maintained that because of their capacity to better evaluate interventions, educators prefer criterion-referenced over norm-referenced tests. The advantage of criterion-referenced tests partially results from differences in test construction. Norm-referenced tests are constructed to maximize variability among individuals (Swezey, 1981); such dispersion increases the efficiency of selection decisions. However, items that measure infrequent behaviors are not likely to be included in norm-referenced tests. Jackson (1970), for example, suggested that items endorsed by less than 20% of the test development sample be dropped because they will not contribute to total score variability. However, those dropped items may be the very ones of interest to change agents. Criterion-referenced tests, in contrast, are composed of items based on criteria for which the intervention is targeted, regardless of the frequency of endorsement.

Distinctions similar to norm- and criterion-referenced testing are apparent in formative and summative testing (Bloom et al., 1971). Summative tests provide an overall evaluation of an individual's performance in an intervention (e.g., a course grade); summative tests provide data convenient for administrative decision making. Formative tests, in contrast, provide feedback about an individual's performance on components of the intervention so that the intervention or the individual's place in it can be appropriately adjusted. Test data can be employed for formative and summative interpretations, but differences do exist in their respective test construction strategies. In particular, formative tests require some type of task analysis that separates performance into specific subtasks. Items or tasks tapping those components are then included in the formative test. Bloom et al. (1971) maintained that summative evaluations, often constrained by limited testing time, can sample only portions of the relevant content. In contrast, formative tests must sample all of the relevant content to be useful to the intervener.

Change-Based Measurement.   In research and practice that is not trait-based (e.g., intervention and longitudinal), it is unreasonable to employ measurements and assessment tasks that selected out state-type items during the test construction process. Collins (1991) noted that in the context of longitudinal research, it is possible to distinguish between static (trait) variables and dynamic (state) variables. Practitioners and researchers attempting to measure change examine intraindividual differences over time. However, Collins (1991) observed:

> Little in traditional measurement theory is of any help to those who desire an instrument that is sensitive to intraindividual differences. In fact, applying traditional methods to the development of a measure of a dynamic latent variable amounts to applying a set of largely irrelevant criteria. (p. 138–139).

As noted, traditional approaches to scale development retain items that display variability between persons and drop those that do not. For example, Collins and Cliff (1990) observed that no grade-school children may be able to perform certain division tasks at the beginning of the school year, but all will do so at the end of the year. Those items would show no variation at either testing point and might be dropped during development of a traditional test of mathematics skill. Collins (1991) suggested that traditional definitions of reliability and precision, which emphasize variance between individuals, may be misleading indicators of the usefulness of measures assessing change (and the lack thereof) over time.

Because many possible types of change patterns are possible, the theoretical task involves specifying the expected pattern as closely as possible. Schoolchildren, for example, may be expected to demonstrate certain patterns of change in their acquisition of mathematical skills. Children may first learn addition, then subtraction, multiplication, and division, in that order. Such a sequence can be characterized as cumulative (i.e., abilities are retained even as new abilities are gained), unitary (i.e., all individuals learn in the same sequence), and irreversible (i.e., development is always in one direction) (Collins, 1991). This theory, in turn, stipulates the form of measurement necessary to test the theory. As displayed in Table 13, Collins (1991) described a Longitudinal Guttman Simplex (LGS) model in which persons, items, and times can be ordered relative to one another. That is, not only can persons and items be combined, but the matrix can be expanded to include times of measurement. Such a model can be employed to test for developmental sequences. Again, the important consid-

TABLE 13 Hypothetical Example of a Longitudinal Guttman Simplex Model[a]

| Individual | Mathematics Test Results | | | |
	Addition	Subtraction	Multiplication	Division
Child A				
Grade 1	Pass	Fail	Fail	Fail
Grade 2	Pass	Pass	Pass	Fail
Grade 3	Pass	Pass	Pass	Fail
Child B				
Grade 1	Fail	Fail	Fail	Fail
Grade 2	Pass	Pass	Fail	Fail
Grade 3	Pass	Pass	Pass	Pass

[a]Reprinted from Collins (1991), copyright (1991) by the American Psychological Association. Reprinted by permission.

eration is that items are selected on the basis of their ability to reflect change, not their ability to show differences between individuals.

Criteria for Selection of Intervention Items. Given the above concepts, it seems possible to summarize and propose a set of criteria for the selection of items and tasks suitable for a test of an intervention. First, such items must show change resulting from the presence of an intervention; for example, items should demonstrate expected changes from pretest to posttest. Second, changes in scores from preintervention to postintervention demand that such alterations not be attributable to measurement error (Tryon, 1991); thus, pretest and posttest measures must show stability independent of treatment effects. Third, such items should not change when respondents are exposed to placebos or other types of control conditions; that is, item change should not occur solely as a result of expectations about treatment efficacy. Appropriate item change might occur, however, as a result of an intervention that alters individuals' expectations about (a) their personal competence for performing targeted behaviors, or (b) the skills and knowledge actually required to produce desired outcomes (cf. Bandura, 1977).

To gauge the reliability of instruments employed repeatedly, Tryon (1991) proposed the use of the coefficient of variation (CV):

$$CV = \frac{SD}{M} \times 100, \tag{2}$$

where SD is the standard deviation and M is the mean. Tryon (1991) suggested that stability will be demonstrated when repeated measurements show small standard deviations. CV represents the degree of error and is functionally equivalent to $1 - r^2$ (reliability squared). Thus, a CV of .05 indicates the measure has 5% error. A psychological test with an r of .80— approximately the median reliability value found for the data reported by Meier and Davis (1990) in Chapter 1—indicates that the scale has 36% error.

ADMINISTERING TESTS

Test administration refers to the procedures involved in the preparation and completion of a psychological test. Given that test conditions affect test performance (K. R. Murphy & Davidshofer, 1988), the central concern of test administration has been standardization, the establishment of identical or similar test procedures for each respondent. Dawis (1992) credited Binet with introduction of standardization, the major purpose being that test results be unaffected "neither by the bad humor nor the bad digestion of the examiner" (Binet, as cited in DuBois, 1970, p. 33).

Selection

Traits have been the primary focus of measurement psychologists interested in selection. For administrative decisions, psychologists have often assumed that no change in the phenomena is possible (e.g., because the trait is biologically based) or necessary (e.g., because the resources to intervene are lacking). Given the typical constraints on time and cost in administrative situations, selection tests typically must meet several standards. First, they are designed to be administered to large groups at a single administration. Thus, such tests measure stable, nomothetic constructs that should not change over time and that are possessed by all respondents. Instructions for such tests necessarily are brief, as are the response formats. True–false or multiple-choice tests are much more likely to be employed, for example, than performance tasks. As noted previously, some tests were initially developed as substitutes for time-consuming interviews.

Theory Building

Traditional, standardized psychological tests are externally structured and internally unstructured. Efforts to standardize tests emphasize the arrangement of the environment external to the test-taker. General instructions are frequently provided, including a brief description of the test's purpose, a sample item, and an explanation of response format alternatives. Many group-administered tests, however, have no mechanism to determine if test-takers read the instructions, understand the items, or employ the same strategies for answering items throughout the test. Traditional standardization does not guarantee uniformity of testing experience, as Gould's (1981) account of confused individuals completing the original Army Beta indicated. Clearly, more structure could be added to psychological tests and assessments, particularly regarding the test-taker's *internal* state. It seems possible that increasing the structure of self-reports could improve these instruments in much the same way additional structure has improved the reliability and validity of interviews.

Item-Response Strategies. When retrieving knowledge, MacGregor, et al. (1988) proposed that individuals use one of two methods: intuitive or analytic. Most people employ an intuitive strategy, which MacGregor et al. describe as holistic, inexpensive, portable, approximately correct—and empirically related to systematic biases. In contrast, analytic strategies produce more precisely correct judgments, but with a few large errors (Peters, Hammond & Summers, 1984). As an example of an analytic strategy, MacGregor et al. describe algorithms, a series of steps that produce a solution to a task. Algorithms provide an unambiguous approach to problem-solving and should lead to similar solutions to problems even when applied by different individuals. MacGregor et al.'s experimental comparison of analytic and intuitive strategies, employing college students who completed estimation problems, found the analytic groups to be more accurate, more consistent, and more confident of their estimates. The question remains, Could structured knowledge retrieval aides improve self-reports?

Research exploring the strategies employed by test-takers to answer items is relatively recent. Recall the work of Jobe et al. (1990) described in Chapter 6. They examined the effects of prescribing the order of re-call—forward (chronological), backward, and free recall—of health visits on the accuracy of that recall. Free recall subjects correctly remembered 67% of their visits, compared to 47% for forward recall and 42% for backward recall. It is important to note that the structure imposed on respondents in this study impaired their performance. Adding structure to tests may be counterproductive if it interferes with respondents' natural processes; on the other hand, identifying and enhancing such styles may potentially improve test performance. In a similar vein, Osberg and Shrauger (1986) reported the results of research that investigated the types of strategies subjects employed in self-predictions. They found that individuals' predictions were often based on knowledge of the past frequencies of personal behavior, current and expected conditions, knowledge of personal qualities, intent to perform the behavior, and the frequency of the behavior in the general population. Osberg and Shrauger also found that predictions based on subjects' knowledge of their past frequencies of behavior and subjects' personal qualities were the most accurate.

The Effects of Nontest Events and Interventions.   Evidence of the effects of nontest events on test behavior can be found in the literature on instrumentation (Cook & Campbell, 1979), response-shift bias (G. S. Howard, 1982), and alpha-beta-gamma change (Golembiewski, Billingsley, & Yeager, 1976). Instrumentation refers to changes in scores from pretest to posttest that occur because of changes in the measuring instrument, not as a result of an intervention (Cook & Campbell, 1979). Response-shift bias occurs when an intervention changes respondents' awareness or understanding of the measured construct (G. S. Howard et al., 1979). In response-shift research, respondents first complete an intervention. Respondents then answer a posttest as well as a retrospective pretest where they rate items in reference to how they perceived those items before the intervention (G. S. Howard, 1982). As predicted by the response-shift effect, different results are apparent between scores of persons who complete the usual pretest and posttest and persons who complete a posttest and a retrospective pretest (G. S.

Howard, 1982). In addition, some evidence suggests that retrospective pretests are free of response styles (G. S. Howard, et al., 1981; Sprangers & Hoogstraten, 1987).

Golembiewski et al. (1976) proposed that the pre-post changes demonstrated on measuring instruments can result from (a) alpha change, in which altered scores validly correspond to changes produced by an intervention; (b) beta change, in which respondents alter the intervals of the scale; and (c) gamma change, a shift in the entire meaning or conceptualization of the instrument, perhaps as a result of seeing scale content in a new light. Golembiewski (1989) noted that very little attention has been paid to these ideas when interpreting the results of intervention research in organizational development. While alpha-beta-gamma changes have been recognized as potentially important sources of error, researchers have been limited by a lack of methods appropriate for investigating and demonstrating such changes (Millsap & Hartog, 1988).

Similarly, research indicates that psychotherapy reduces desynchrony in individuals. Such an effect occurs in psychotherapy studies that examine correlations among pre- and posttreatment measurements of client affect, cognition, and behavior. Typically, such correlations are low at pretest but rise after therapy. Correlations should also be greater among members of a treatment group than in a control group. For example, Moore and Haverkamp (1989) reported a study designed to increase the emotional expressiveness of a group of men. Twenty-eight subjects were randomly assigned to treatment or control group in a posttest-only design. Subjects completed (a) self-report scales that assessed their perceptions of how often they experience emotion and how often they express emotion and (b) two behavioral tests that required subjects to produce written and oral responses to affect-laden situations presented through videotape and written materials. Moore and Haverkamp found that their treatment affected expressiveness as indicated by one of the two behavioral measures, but not on the two self-report measures. They then wondered whether the intervention "altered the experimental group members' perception of their level of verbal expressiveness" (p. 515). Substantially higher correlations were present in the experimental group between self-report and behavioral measures on three of four comparisons, lending indirect support to the proposition that the intervention increased awareness of verbal expression to the point where it matched actual expression. It may be possible that by teaching test-takers a basic emotional vocabulary, validity of report may be increased.

Active Measurement. Traditional testing procedures treat test-takers as passive respondents whose primary task is to validly respond to standardized stimuli. Test-takers can also be viewed, however, as active participants in a dynamic process where test stimuli and tasks can be altered.

Teaching test-takers to respond more appropriately to psychological tests is an old but relatively unexplored idea. In the laboratories of the early experimental psychologists, subjects were not naive observers, but members of the research team or other observers able to observe psychological phenomena in a methodical manner (Danziger, 1990). There were good reasons for this practice. Danziger (1990) reviewed research in psychophysics documenting the difficulty individuals experience when quantifying perception. Danziger (1990) cited Boring (1942, p. 482) who wrote that "the meaning of the judgment *two* is indeterminate unless the criterion has been established." In 1946, Cronbach suggested training for subjects to overcome response sets. Acquiescent students, for example, could increase their test-wiseness by learning how many false-marked-true errors they make. Cronbach (1946) similarly believed that "it is relatively easy to teach mature students what is desired in essay examination responses" (p. 489). In contemporary psychophysiological measurement, respondents first complete an adaptation or training period to allow stabilization of physiological variables (Sallis & Lichstein, 1979). Behavior therapists who teach their clients to self-monitor may instruct clients to keep a small notebook with them at all times, record incidents immediately after they occur, and record only a single response at a time (Hayes & Nelson, 1986). In all of these cases, test-takers receive training or employ procedures that increase their ability to perform the required measurement tasks. Assessors have also offered other proposals and conditions for improving test performance (e.g., Babor, et al., 1990; Fazio & Zanna, 1978; R. Klimoski & Brickner, 1987; Laing, 1988; Osberg, 1989; Regan & Fazio, 1977).

To the extent that a research program successfully identifies systematic invalidities in item responding, it may also be possible to manipulate the testing situation to minimize unwanted factors. For example, aggregation of item responses across an empirically determined number of occasions or period of time may eliminate state effects and increase trait variance of a construct (Cone, 1991). With the problem of social desirability, some research has provided evidence of the efficacy of a technique called the bogus pipeline effect (Jones & Sigall, 1971). Here respondents are led to believe that the test administrator possesses an objective method of ascertaining their true attitudes or beliefs; the result is often a decrease in socially desirable response tendencies (Botvin, Botvin, Renick, Filazzola, & Allegante, 1984; Brackwede, 1980; Mummendey & Bolton, 1981; Sprangers & Hoogstraten, 1987; 1988). Mummendey and Bolton (1981) compared subjects exposed and not exposed to bogus pipeline instructions and found that the former significantly reduced the frequency and intensity of their endorsement of socially desirable items. Sprangers and Hoogstraten (1987) found that a bogus pipeline procedure eliminated response shift bias in a pre-post intervention design, but failed to replicate these results in a second study (Sprangers & Hoogstraten, 1988).

Studying Temporal Inconsistency: Psychological States. As described in Chapter 4, one solution to the observation that behavior varies is to contrast psychological traits with psychological states. States vary, traits do not. Success in the measurement of transient psychological states has yet to reach the level associated with trait-based tests, as K. R. Murphy and Davidshofer (1988) noted:

> It is easier to make reliable inferences about stable characteristics of individuals than about characteristics which vary unpredictably. For example, it would be easier to develop a reliable measure of a person's basic values than of a person's mood state. (p. 84)

The difficulty in measuring mood and emotions, however, may have less to do with any inherent unpredictability than with the trait-based procedures that have typically been employed. The State–Trait Anxiety Inventory (STAI; Spielberger et al., 1970), for example, contains two 20-item scales to measure state and trait anxiety that differ mainly by instructions: the state measure asks respondents to answer according to how they feel "at this moment," whereas the trait measure requests responses that reflect how test-takers "generally" feel. The STAI, however, begs the question in an important respect. By imbedding the measurement in a questionnaire administered at one point in time, we still have little information about how or why the psychological characteristic varies. Heidbreder saw this in 1933:

> Even in those systems of psychology which reduce their material to elements, the elements, whether bits of consciousness or bits of behavior, are defined as processes. It is true that, having been defined as processes, they are often, in actual practice, treated as fixed units, for the habit of thinking in terms of fixed units is tenacious. But when attention is turned upon psychological material directly, the character of change presents itself as an inescapable fact. (p. 24)

Repeated measurements, then, may be the most effective method of studying psychological states.

Particularly in the measurement of emotions, motivation, and related psychological states, it may also make sense to measure individuals when they are in those states. Although research results have been equivocal, studies in the areas of mood-state-dependency and mood-congruent learning suggest improved recall when mood at testing matches mood at the time of learning (Bower, 1981; Bower, Monteiro, & Gilligan, 1978; H. C. Ellis & Ashbrook, 1989; Mecklenbrauker & Hager, 1984). For example, one of my psychotherapy clients was best able to recall and describe past incidents of obsessive behavior during periods within the session when he was feeling anxious. Similarly, Steinweg's (1993) review found research demonstrating that depressed inpatients (a) better recalled negatively valenced over positively valenced memories (D. M. Clark & Teasdale, 1982) and (b) recalled negative information more quickly (Lloyd & Lishman, 1975). Research with the Velten mood induction (Velten, 1968) indicated that mood states such as depression or elation can be induced in individuals. Isen, Shalker, Clark, and Karp (1978), for example, utilized success and failure on a computer game to induce elation and depression, respectively; they found that subjects in the success condition recalled more positive than negative words. Finally, Rorschach content and the behavior of the test administrator are designed to maximize the ambiguity experienced by test-takers so that they reveal how they organize stimuli (Groth-Marnat, 1990).

Intervention

One of the more interesting aspects of test administration to investigate is the extent to which tests function both as measurements and interventions. That is, measurements and assessments can alter the amount of the construct they are intended to measure. As Webb et al. (1981) observed, "interviews and questionnaires . . . create as well as measure attitudes" and other constructs (p. 1). Bailey and Bhagat (1987) reviewed research indicating that the act of completing questionnaires and interviews can create or alter the level of held beliefs and attitudes. For example, Bridge et al. (1977) randomly assigned individuals into distinct groups who were questioned regarding their opinions about cancer and crime, respectively. Respondents repeated the survey several weeks later. Although the initial survey did not find differences on attitudes toward cancer and crime between the two groups, Bridge et al. (1977) found that individuals initially questioned about cancer, compared to individuals questioned about crime, increased their assessment of the importance of good health on retest. Bailey and Bhagat (1987) also cited a study by Kraut and McConahay (1973) which found that prospective voters, randomly sampled for a preelection interview, showed a significantly higher turnout (48%) than the noninterviewed population (21%).

In behavior therapy, clients are frequently assigned to self-monitor (i.e., record) problematic behaviors in preparation for an intervention. Interestingly, the simple act of recording such behaviors often leads to a decrease in their frequency (R. O. Nelson, 1977a, 1977b). Research indicates that completing simulations can also provide measurement data *and* change test-takers' level of the construct (Fulton et al., 1983; Johnson et al., 1987; Meier, 1988a; Meier & Wick, 1991). Meier (1988b) described research with *If You Drink,* a computer-assisted instruction (CAI) alcohol education program. This CAI program consists of modules designed to teach high school and college students facts about alcohol, the effects of alcohol consumption on blood alcohol levels, the effects of combining alcohol with other drugs, and responsible decision making about alcohol. Two of these modules incorporate computer simulations that allow students to input data about alcohol consumption (e.g., number of drinks consumed at a hypothetical party) and receive feedback about subsequent consequences (e.g., blood alcohol level). Meier (1988a) found that this CAI program, compared to a placebo control group, significantly improved college students' attitudes toward alcohol. Meier and Wick (1991) employed the same program with seventh and ninth grade students to investigate the program's viability as an unobtrusive measure of alcohol consumption. As reported in Chapter 6, Meier and Wick found that unobtrusively recorded reports of subjects' alcohol consumption in a simulation was significantly correlated with self-reports of recent drinking behavior, drinking intentions, and attitudes toward alcohol.

SCORING TESTS

The purpose of measurement and assessment is to produce quantitative data that reflect the order and distinctions inherent in the measured phenomena. Most tests have explicit rules that allow objective scoring, that is, identical results are found whenever the rules are followed. Although formats such as multiple-choice allow such rules, essays tests and projective tests such as the Rorschach involve considerable judgment about scoring (K. R. Murphy & Davidshofer, 1988).

Selection

As noted, summing or averaging item responses is the most common method of scoring tests. If the test purpose is to measure traits, aggregating as many items and occasions of measurement as is feasible should increase the probability of detecting traits. From a practical standpoint, the primary problem with aggregation would seem to be cost. In Epstein's (1979) research, a large number of measurements were required to reach high validity coefficients; in one study, for example, 14 days of measurements completed daily were required to reach .80. R. P. Martin (1988) also noted that to increase the correlation between predictor and criterion, aggregate measurements of criterion and predictor are necessary to reduce unreliability in both measures.

Selection testers do aggregate items and individuals, but they tend not to aggregate measurements over time. Given any test's ability to measure traits, aggregation of measures over time and occasions would seem a useful step in minimizing error. In general, it would seem advisable for test administrators to administer tests and criteria more than once and to employ the average of those administrations as trait indicators.

Because the purpose of selection testing is to compare an individual with others for the purpose of making a decision, raw scores are transformed, often into percentile ranks and stanines (Gronlund, 1988). The most common transformation, z scores, are standard scores, that is, scores that reflect the position of an individual in relation to all individuals who took the test; Z scores allow such comparisons across different sets of test scores (even those which have different means and distributions). The following formula computes z:

$$z = \frac{X_1 - M}{SD} \tag{3}$$

where X_1 is an individual's score on a test, M is the mean of all individuals' scores, and SD is the standard deviation, a statistic indicating the degree of variability or dispersion among data. A z of 1, for example, indicates that an individual scored 1 standard deviation above the mean. A more familiar type of standard score is the IQ:

$$IQ = \frac{MA}{CA} \times 100, \tag{4}$$

where MA is mental age as determined by type of tasks successfully completed by the test-taker and CA is the individual's chronological age. Here mental age is scaled against chronological age, a procedure with an underlying assumption that CA reflects consistent cognitive developmental sequences for individuals, for example, across gender and culture.

The problem with z scores is that the units change depending on the individuals who complete the test (Tryon, 1991). Thus, changing the test sample is very likely to change the mean and standard deviation and thus the z-score units. Tryon (1991) observed that with z scores, persons are measured against other persons instead of other criteria or theoretically meaningful constructs. Thus, "z-score units are borne of desperation due to the absence of theoretically meaningful units of measure" (Tryon, 1991, p. 6).

Theory-Building

Approaches such as disaggregation, experimentation, and Generalizability Theory (GT) would seem the most appropriate procedures for deepening our understanding of how tests could be scored. Aggregation can be employed to study consistency across situations (Cone, 1991), but it can also mask the influence of situations (Schwenkmezger, 1984). Thus, investigators interested in situational effects could aggregate items, persons, and occasions, but disaggregate situations (i.e., examine variability over situations). At this point in psychology's history, measurement theory is likely to be deepened by studies that disaggregate combinations of items, persons, occasions, and situations.

To the extent that psychologists adapt laboratory-type tasks to function as computerized measurement, it may be possible to supplement or substitute for traditional scoring procedures through replication and experimentation. With replication, the same task is repeatedly presented to determine consistency of results. As shown in Figure 34, a simulation could be presented multiple times, with aggregated scores computed for stable trait constructs and stability of scores compared across administration to provide reliability estimates. Multiple administrations also provide an opportunity to study variables and constructs expected to show change, such as practice and fatigue effects.

In contrast to classical test theory, GT recognizes that individuals have more than one true score on a construct (Cronbach, 1984). That is, various factors influence individuals' test scores or provide a source of variance. Identifying these factors depends on specifying the conditions of testing we wish to generalize to. Cronbach (1984) provided an example of ratings of friendliness for a preschool child. An observer watches the child for 5 min each in the sandbox, on playground equipment, and drinking juice. Potential sources of measurement variation in this example include the observer, the situation, and the occasion (i.e., different instances within the situations, over time). Studies of these different sources could provide an indication of how much each source influences test scores. In general, GT

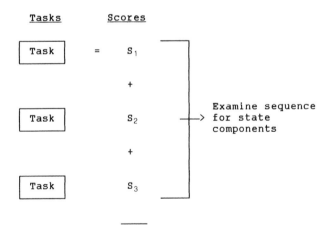

FIGURE 34 Increasing scoring options through repeated administrations. A simulation task could be administered repeatedly to examine trait and state effects. If the same task were used, scores could be employed to provide reliability estimates and to search for practice and fatigue effects. If different tasks tapping the same construct were employed (e.g., anxiety-provoking tasks in social, academic, and occupational situations), aggregation of scores might provide a trait estimate of anxiety, whereas score differences would reflect situational effects.

procedures might be useful to investigate variation contributed by (a) dynamic or state constructs, (b) different measurement methods and modes, (c) different types of test-taker characteristics, (d) different types of test structure and test-taker training, and (e) situational differences.

Intervention

Swezey (1981) reported two types of scoring systems for criterion-referenced tests. Noninterference scoring occurs when a test-taker completes an item or task without input from the test administrator. With assist scoring, the administrator corrects the test-taker when an error occurs, and the test-taker then completes the remainder of the task. Swezey suggested that assist scoring is appropriate in diagnostic situations where the test administrator wishes to discover which components of the task require further intervention for a particular test-taker.

As an example of the more precise data that can be provided by formative tests, Bloom et al. (1971) described procedures developed by E. R. Smith and Tyler (1942). Item-response categories can be designed to permit an analysis of errors. For example, students can respond to a test item by marking true, probably true, insufficient data, probably false, and false. These response categories allow identification of the following errors:

1. General accuracy, that is, how well students' responses match the correctly keyed responses
2. Caution, the extent to which students underestimate the data available to answer the item
3. Going beyond the data, the extent to which students provide answers with greater certainty beyond that inherent in the item
4. Crude errors, the number of true or probably true responses to items keyed false or probably false, and vice versa

Teachers who conduct an analysis of such student errors should be able to specify more precisely the type of instruction that should occur.

INTERPRETING TESTS

How test data are interpreted partially depends on the purpose of the test. Gronlund (1988) observed that "strictly speaking, the terms *norm referenced* and *criterion referenced* refer only to the method of interpreting test results" (p. 11). Suppose an individual received a score of 95% on a classroom test. A norm-referenced interpretation would restate that score as "higher than 94% of the rest of the class"; a criterion-referenced statement would be "correctly completed 95 of 100 questions." Criterion-referenced interpretations simply describe task performance or state performance in relation to a standard other than other persons.

Selection

Norm-referenced tests allow comparison of an individual's test score with all others who have taken the test. When interpreting tests, this is the usual approach to making sense of scores. For example, students who score 600 and above on the Verbal and Quantitative components of the GRE might be retained among a pool of students who receive further consideration for graduate school admission.

The purpose of testing also affects who receives and acts upon the test interpretation. H. G. Hough (1962) considered the hypothetical case of a personality test, employed to match couples for marriage, which could reduce the divorce rate by 10%. Despite this benefit, Hough suggested few individuals would place the choice of spouse in the hands of such a test. If social administrators decided to decrease the divorce rate, however, I venture they would use such a test. Paul et al. (1986a) indicated that assessment in mental health settings can provide information for the clinician, facility director, government facility monitor, researcher, client, and family members. All of these individuals may be interested in different components and levels of test data. Clients, for example, may be concerned about whether the assessment data indicates they can be discharged from treatment, whereas facility directors may focus on the relative efficacy of different treatment units in reaching client discharge by target dates or periods. Tests' utility may partially be evaluated on the basis of the number of relevant interpretations provided to decision makers (Cronbach & Gleser, 1965).

Theory-Building

Construct Explication. From the perspective of theory building, one of the most important interpretations of test data concerns the extent to which the test adequately measures a construct. The key questions are, What constructs does the test measure? How well does the test measure the construct(s) of interest?

Selection measurement is concerned with predicting outcomes (such as performance on a criterion), whereas measurement for explanatory theory building is focused on process, the system of operations that produces the outcome. Understanding process means that you can create a model of that phenomenon and connect the variables in that model to the real world. Torgerson (1958) believed that "the development of a theoretical science . . . would seem to be virtually impossible unless its variables can be measured adequately" (p. 2). The initial step in developing adequate

measurement is explication of constructs in terms of measurable operations, and it is this task that is most crucial and difficult in new sciences
such as psychology (Torgerson, 1958). Until constructs are precisely explicated, scientists in any new discipline will devote "an immense amount
of time . . . to construction of complex and elaborate theoretical super-
structures based on unexplicated, inexact constructs" (Torgerson, 1958,
p. 8). The scientific literatures will be broad and unconnected.

Cronbach and Meehl (1955) maintained that "unless the network makes
contact with observations, and exhibits explicit, public steps of inference,
construct validation cannot be claimed" (p. 291). Similarly, Cone (1991)
stated that "when scores on an instrument are totally controlled by objective features of the phenomenon being measured, we say the instrument
is accurate" (p. viii). As shown in Figure 35, test validity—and the corresponding usefulness of that test data for such purposes as theory development, intervention, and selection—significantly depends upon the linkages
between the phenomenon being studied, the data produced by the test
process, and any transformations of that data. In many research areas, psychologists do not possess a very detailed understanding of the processes of
responding to psychological test items and tasks. In other words, we do not
know with much certainty whether those tests are good explications of the
constructs they are intended to measure. And without knowledge of a test's

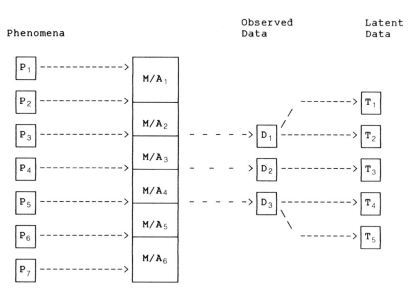

FIGURE 35   Validity depends on the processes of transforming phenomena into observed
and latent values. The validity of observed and latent data depends on measurement, assessment, and statistical procedures employed to produce observed data and to transform observed data into latent values.

construct validity, it becomes difficult to evaluate and modify the construct in question (Mischel, 1968).

Psychological researchers often assume that their constructs can be measured through any procedure, with the default method being self-report. Dawis (1987) is among those, however, who have suggested that the method of measurement should be an integral part of construct definition and explication. If the meaning of a construct is affected by the form of its evidence (Kagan, 1988), then theorists must realize that in practice, there is no such thing as a construct or a method, but only construct-methods.

Precision. The construct explication process frequently focuses on whether or not operations accurately reflect the *named* construct. The methods described by D. T. Campbell and Fiske (1959) and Cook and Campbell (1979) attempt to evaluate the naming of a construct through two criteria: (a) convergence, whether different measures of the same construct correlate, even when measurement methods are different, and (b) divergence, whether measures of different constructs fail to correlate even when measurement methods are similar. Here we are searching for the method bias commonly found to affect psychological measurement. Studies of convergence and divergence produce a nomological net of relations that assist the researcher in naming the construct. Finding the predicted relations does not finish the task, however, as another construct may also explain those relations (Cook & Campbell, 1979). In this case, an additional study would be necessary to construct competing explications of the two constructs and then compare them (Platt, 1977). Regardless of the procedure, the first task of construct validity is to name the construct by referencing it to other related and distant constructs (Torgerson, 1958).

A second and underappreciated reason constructs may fail to be represented adequately by measurements is imprecision. The goal of measurement theory and practice should be to generate devices that produce data that mirror the distinctions that occur in nature. In contrast, many test developers validate tests by simply contrasting groups who possess more or less of the construct in question. For example, developers of a measure of depression may contrast mean scores of depressed patients with normal controls. Although such differences certainly support validity of the test as a selection device, they constitute weak evidence for other purposes. Theoretically, we would expect to find more than simple mean differences between depressed and nondepressed individuals. High scores on a depression inventory would also provide little information for deciding between types of treatment.

Cook and Campbell (1979) maintained that an inadequate preoperational explication of constructs is a major threat to the construct validity of studies and measures. Cook and Campbell (1979) proposed that "a precise explication of constructs is vital for high construct validity since it permits tailoring the manipulations and measures to whichever definitions emerge from the explication" (p. 65). In a new science, however, constructs tend to be operationalized inadequately; thus, the initial goal of most research programs should be to create more precise measurement devices. This is the essence of the process of theory leading to data and the data enabling the theorist to refine theoretical constructs.

Cook and Campbell (1979) presented such an example in the work of R. Feldman (1968). Feldman employed five measures—giving street directions, mailing a lost letter, returning money, giving correct change, and charging the correct taxi fare—to determine whether foreigners or compatriots would be more likely to receive cooperation. Feldman found that two of the measures, giving directions and mailing the letter, related to the experimental manipulation differently than the other three measures of cooperation. Feldman interpreted these results to mean that cooperation should be differentiated into low-cost favors and foregoing financial advantage. Work such as Feldman's, however, tends to be the exception. The construct-data-construct revision process can be short-circuited when researchers (and journal reviewers) view data that disconfirms the study's operations as a failure rather than an opportunity for revision and replication. Although Cook and Campbell (1979) noted that often "the data force one to be more specific in one's labelling than originally planned" (p. 69), they also believed that since Feldman's "respecification of the constructs came after the data were received we can place less confidence in them than might otherwise have been warranted" (p. 69). Because such results may or may not be due to chance, the next step would be a replication of the more precise construction of cooperation. This is the process of making error into substance (McGuire, 1969).

During the item-development process, test developers often appear to assume that they have access to the entire domain or at least a representative sample of the construct's operations and relations with other variables. Golden et al. (1984) stated that:

> A thorough understanding of what the test is expected to measure will guide both initial validation research and later clinical interpretation of individual results. Such theoretical understanding of what a given test is expected to produce also guides the development of an initial item pool. (p. 22).

The explication of a construct, however, begins with only a partial knowledge of the construct. This is the major reason for employing error in the measurement models that dominate psychological testing. To deepen knowledge, test developers must explicate constructs, test them empirically, revise the constructs, and recycle the process. Until the process reaches a sufficient degree of precision—as evidenced, for example, by replication of the item pool—researchers employing the measurement device who encounter negative results will not know whether those results should be attributed to incorrect theory or invalid measurement (Torgerson, 1958).

R. Feldman's (1968) method is one of disaggregating constructs to increase validity: that is, two types of cooperation fit the data better than one. Cook and Campbell (1979) called this construct underrepresentation. But there also exists the problem of surplus construct irrelevancies (Cook & Campbell, 1979), which refer to operations containing factors unconnected to the construct in question. Underrepresentation and irrelevancies are other ways of stating that the two primary concerns of construct validity are appropriate naming and sufficient precision. We must be able to say what a construct is and is not, and we must be able to match the natural levels of the construct with data produced by measurement devices.

As an example of a construct being underrepresented in measurement, Cook and Campbell (1979) noted that attitudes are typically defined as consistent responses to an object across cognitive, affective, and behavioral domains or across time. They observed that most measurements of attitudes are one-shot measures that do not meet these requirements. As an example of construct irrelevancies, Cook and Campbell (1979) discussed hypothesis guessing by subjects in studies. If subjects guess how the experimenter wants or expects them to behave, subsequent scores may not solely represent the construct of interest. In addition, measurements can both underrepresent constructs and contain irrelevancies. Cook and Campbell (1979) suggested that this occurs with single measures of constructs: aggregating more than one measure of a construct should decrease error due to invalid factors and increase the possibility that more aspects of the construct are tapped. Similar problems are created when only one method (e.g., self-report) is employed to measure a construct; the single method may contain factors irrelevant to the construct.

Multiple methods, like multiple operations, should decrease error in the construct explication process. But the process is not always straightforward. Although multiple operations and methods may strengthen validity, it is also true that changing one's method and operation of measurement may alter what is measured. Examples include (a) Arisohn, Bruch and Heimberg's (1988) findings that the magnitude of self-efficacy ratings for assertive behavior was influenced by method of situation presentation and response generation; (b) Cacioppo and Tassinary's (1990) explanation of how psychophysiological effects can change radically according to different measurement procedures; and (c) Watson's (1988) report that relatively small changes in affective descriptors and response format led to significant changes in correlations between scales measuring positive and negative affect. For some purposes, one may aggregate across methods and operations, but that leaves open the questions of (a) why the methods and operations differ and (b) whether one of the methods or operations is a better measure of the construct.

Expecting broad classes of psychological and physiological phenomena to correlate may represent a contemporary extension of the mistake committed by early psychologists. They expected to find relations between many different types of physical tasks, physiological activities, and intelligence, but discovered that such correlations were largely absent. Over 100 years after early psychologists began the task, Cacioppo and Tassinary (1990) found that attempts to link physiological states to psychological operations remain problematic because of confusion about the relations among the categories of events measured. As shown in Figure 36, they proposed that such relations be conceptualized as:

1. outcomes, where many physiological events vary as a function of a single psychological operation within a specified context or group of individuals;
2. markers, where a single physiological event varies with a single psychological operation within a specified context or group of individuals;
3. concomitants, where many physiological events vary with a single psychological operation across a broad range of situations and individuals;

Depiction of Logical Relations Between Elements in
the Psychological (Ψ) and Physiological (Φ) Domains

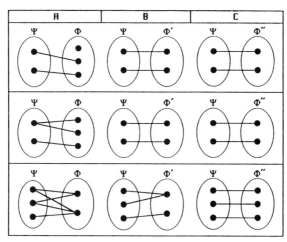

FIGURE 36   Depiction of logical relations between elements in the psychological (ϕ) and physiological (ψ) domains. (A) Links between the psychological elements and individual physiological responses. (B) Links between the psychological elements and the physiological response pattern. (C) Links between the psychological elements and the profile of physiological responses across time. (Reprinted from Cacioppo and Tassinary, 1990. Copyright (1990) by the American Psychological Association. Reprinted by permission.)

4. invariants, where a single physiological event varies with a single psychological operation across a broad range of situations and individuals.

Desynchrony and Construct Explication. Desynchrony has important implications for the validity of measurement. If individuals were totally synchronous, then measures of behavior, affect, and cognition (B-A-C) would be substitutable. One could validate a measure of behavior, for example, by correlating that measure with a corresponding measure of cognition or affect. A more extensive validation procedure, involving a multitrait–multimethod correlation matrix (D. T. Campbell & Fiske, 1959), would consist of evaluating two or more psychological phenomena along the modes of B-A-C. For example, one might attempt to validate a measure of job satisfaction by (a) explicating B-A-C indicators of job satisfaction and then (b) correlating those measures with B-A-C indicators of similar (e.g., occupational stress) and different (e.g., personal orderliness or neatness) constructs. But if the Law of Initial Values influences affective measures of job satisfaction and occupational stress, correlations with cognitive and behavioral measures may be attenuated.

Human response modes may also be idiographic. That is, the interrelations among modes may differ by individual. Bandler and Grinder (1975), for example, proposed that individuals differ in their mode preferences for perceiving environmental information and expressing psychological states. Some individuals may think about a stimulus and ignore their feelings before executing behavior. Idiographic desynchrony has important implications for anyone conducting psychological interventions. If desynchrony is caused by idiographic ordering of response modes, then it becomes crucial to understand these linkages in the individuals for which you wish to facilitate change. The B-A-C causal sequences would influence the intervention design and the assignment of individuals to those interventions. Although no standard procedure exists for measuring the B-A-C sequence, Evans (1986) noted that clinical assessment involves a great deal of effort at understanding how individuals response modes are organized. In Lazarus' (1981) BASIC ID system, the assessor attempts to observe sequences among modes to develop intervention strategies (Lazarus, 1981; Nay, 1979).

Most contemporary theorists appear to assume that self-reports of B-A-Cs are sufficient operationalizations of the psychological constructs they propose. If self-report requires primarily cognitive activities, however, then most theorists are assuming that cognitive reports of all modes are adequate. The evidence for desynchrony, however, suggests that (a) theorists must specify what mode(s) should be measured to detect those phenomena, and (b) that theorists should consider the possibility that cognitive reports may be less valid when applied to other modes. Desynchronous individuals may not have cognitive access to valid information about their affect and behavior.

One of the major tasks of the measurement theorist may be to develop precise models that allow prediction and explanation of synchrony and desynchrony. In this context, it is important to emphasize that synchrony does occur (Evans, 1986). For example, decreases in pupil diameter are highly correlated with cognitive task demands (Beatty & Wagoner, 1978). Cardiac deceleration is correlated with an intention to perform a voluntary act (Lacey, 1967). Obrist (1981) conducted extensive research to map out synchronous processes among physiological modes. Pennebaker, Hughes and Uhlmann (in DeAngelis, 1992) found that 50% of their subjects demonstrated a significant covariation between their written expressed affect and skin conductance recorded simultaneously.

Desynchrony Implications for Explanations and Predictions.   If theory and research indicate that under certain conditions human modes function independently (i.e., they are parallel and nonredundant), the practical implication is that two very different measurement approaches should be employed for *explanatory* and *predictive* purposes. If the research objective is to explain relations among human modes, it would be important to include measures of all modes to detect desynchrony effects. Examples of such research include studies to determine the causal sequence of B-A-C operations in individuals or the effects of psychotherapy. Researchers conducting these studies are likely to be those concerned with general psychological laws.

On the other hand, researchers interested chiefly in prediction might choose a priori which mode they aim to assess and measure that mode only. Not only might past behavior best predict future behavior, but past cognition might best predict future cognition, and so forth. To the extent that modes operate independently, discriminant validity would be not an issue because no correlation should exist among the modes of B-A-C. One would still be well advised to employ multiple measures (Cook & Campbell, 1979), but multiple measures in the same mode. To maximize prediction, the task would involve specifying the mode one is interested in measuring and measuring the mode in a setting that approximates as closely as possible the criterion setting. Predicting which potential clients might make the best group therapy participants, for instance, could involve establishing a simulated group in which group behavior could be observed. In fact, Yalom (1985) described research that found that direct sampling of relevant group behaviors is a better predictor of individuals' group behavior than personality inventories. The success of work assessment centers may also be explained by the fact that such centers typically employ tasks closely matching those found in the workplace (A. Howard, 1983; R. Klimoski & Brickner, 1987).

Construct Explication and Phenomenon–Data Distance. A major argument of idiographic proponents is that the scores of large groups of individuals are too distant from the psychological phenomena being measured to inform any theory of those phenomena (Cone, 1988; Loevinger, 1957). As illustrated in Figure 37, traditional self-reports combine the item responses of individuals, thereby aggregating such systematic errors as social desirability and acquiescence. The resulting scores contain difficult to separate validities and invalidities (Meehl, 1991; Wiley, 1991).

In contrast to such phenomenon-distant research, seminal work in such areas as learning, sensation and perception, and cognitive development has been performed using repeated observation of single subjects. The history of psychological science contains many examples (e.g., Fechner, Wundt, Piaget, Ebbinghaus, Pavlov, and Skinner) in which investigators' work with one or a few subjects produced data sufficient for the start of important research programs or for practical applications. Such research, while time-consuming, can be phenomenon-close: that is, the investigator observes the phenomenon as it occurs. The phenomenon may be multiply determined

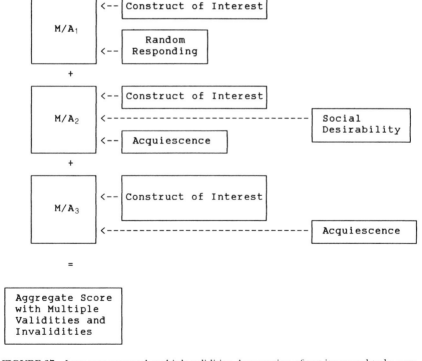

FIGURE 37 Item response and multiple validities. Aggregation of test items and tasks accumulates trait constructs and generative response styles.

and the observer may commit errors. Nevertheless, systematic, repeated observation of a single subject, in naturalistic and experimental settings, often represents the simplest available system in which to study a phenomenon. The data provided by methods such as single-subject designs, qualitative research, and protocol analysis is likely to be of sufficient quality to permit more precise construct explications. In contrast, an investigator who *begins* a research program by creating and administering a test to large groups may ultimately possess little sense of how the phenomenon operates, particularly when interpreting test scores influenced by multiple, difficult to identify factors.

Intervention

Criterion-referenced tests allow intraindividual comparisons of progress toward performance of specific criteria or objectives. Like Gronlund (1988), Swezey (1981) observed that norm- and criterion-referenced tests can appear identical in terms of instructions, items, and format. The purpose of testing directs the types of data employed in test interpretation.

Criterion-referenced tests have considerable utility in evaluating interventions (Swezey, 1981). The typical procedure is to develop a criterion-referenced test and administer it pre- and postintervention. Pretest scores might help select individuals in or out of the intervention. Post-test scores indicate who has reached the necessary performance level as well as who requires additional intervention. As noted previously, selection tests can also be useful at the beginning and end of interventions. To the extent that resources are limited, placement tests may be employed to decide who should receive a treatment, job, or school admission. Similarly, summative tests may be useful in certifying the completion of an intervention or training; in certain circumstances, summative, norm-referenced tests may be appropriate.

Ideally, tests employed for intervention should be able to provide diagnostic and formative information. That is, test data should be able to provide diagnoses of problems (in personal-emotional tests) and errors committed (in cognitive ability tests) to suggest appropriate interventions. During the intervention, formative tests provide feedback to the intervener and client that reveal progress and guide adjustment of the intervention. An individual's success or failure on formative test items provides feedback about progress and the focus of intervention efforts. In education, Cross and Angelo (1988) described this process as a loop "from teaching technique to feedback on student learning to revision of the technique" (p. 2). Whereas summative tests focus on an aggregate score (of items and components), administrators of formative tests tend to examine item-response patterns (Bloom et al., 1971). Summative tests can suggest initial hypotheses relevant to interventions: for example, a standardized achievement test can describe a student's strengths and weaknesses (compared to other students) across subject areas, information that may be relevant to inclusion or exclusion from an intervention. More sensitive measures will be needed to develop and test those hypotheses, however, and it is here that formative tests can be useful (Bloom et al., 1971; Cross & Angelo, 1988).

Formative tests provide data relevant to individuals and groups. Bloom et al. (1971) discussed how a series of formative tests completed by students correlated with those students' eventual summative scores. Different classes demonstrated different patterns. In one class, only 20% of students demonstrated mastery across seven summative tests, and Bloom et al. (1971) indicated that about the same percentage achieved mastery on the summative test. In another class, an increasing percentage of students demonstrated mastery on the formative tests, with 67% achieving mastery of the final formative test. Bloom et al. (1971) reported that about the same percentage achieved mastery on the summative test.

Bloom et al. (1971) suggested that formative tests can provide teachers and students feedback about progress in learning. Such feedback may be particularly reinforcing to students as they master small units of learning. A similar effect occurs when behavior therapy clients who begin self-monitoring demonstrate improvements in the monitored behavior (R. O. Nelson, 1977a, 1977b). Formative evaluation also allows for correct pacing of learning, indicating when more difficult material should be introduced and when additional time is necessary to master material.

SUMMARY AND IMPLICATIONS

Because tests may have multiple purposes, evaluations of validity focus on whether test score interpretations are valid for a particular use. Selection tests have influenced many test developers to embrace nomothetic, norm-referenced, trait-based, single administration, and aggregated measurement procedures. These characteristics, however, may not be optimal even for selection purposes; criterion-referenced tests, for example, may hold more potential for increasing selection tests' predictive validity. Given the influence of selection procedures, most contemporary psychological tests would seem to be more valid for decision making than for explanatory theory building or assisting psychological interventions.

Clearly, the link between substantive theory, measurement procedures, and empirical data in psychology must be strengthened. Measurement approaches have relied heavily on analyzing data *after* it has produced by human subjects, employing statistical techniques to break the code presumably encrypted in the data. Measurement psychologists, more so than any other specialty, have believed that "inaccurate data could be made to yield accurate conclusions if the proper statistics were applied (Boring, 1950)"

(Barlow & Hersen, 1984, p. 6). I propose that we better understand how those data are produced in the first place. Substantive models of measurement processes must continue to be developed, and substantive psychological theories must be examined for potential measurement implications. Researchers and theorists should spend more resources on explicating and investigating how their constructs should—and should not—be observed and measured. The purpose of measurement should be the major consideration of theorists considering construct explication.

Tryon (1991) discussed the problems that result when scientists have yet to settle upon and employ standard measurement units. He believes that "to say that intelligence is what an intelligence test measures both begs the question and is a correct evaluation of the current conceptualization of intelligence" (p. 4). In contrast, Tryon noted that a component of intelligence such as information processing could be defined as information correctly processed within a set time period (e.g., correct bits per second). Whatever unit is constructed will possess different implications for theory. One can study correct bits per second or the time period it takes to produce one correct bit; the two units are likely to possess different implications for theory. Similarly, Evans (1986) observed that the time intervals aggregated for data analysis can have considerable impact on the interpretation of research results. Citing work by Baerends (1972), Evans (1986) noted that birds' nest building and preening behaviors are (a) negatively correlated at short time intervals, because the behaviors are topographically incompatible; (b) uncorrelated at intermediate intervals, because preening, the higher frequency behavior, serves multiple functions; and (c) positively correlated over longer intervals because preening and nest building are both related to reproduction. Evans (1986) observed similar effects of aggregation in the study of the behavior of severely handicapped children (Evans & Voeltz, 1982; Evans, Voeltz, Freedland, & Brennan, 1981).

Without fundamental measurement units, reliable and valid measurements may also be inaccurate (Tryon, 1991). Tryon provided the following hypothetical experiment in which five investigators independently investigate temperature by filling a glass tube with mercury. They assess reliability by repeatedly placing the tube in ice water and recording the height of the mercury in the tube, with appropriate resting periods between the procedure. This process would likely demonstrate high test–retest reliability for each of the five investigator's measurements. Similarly, the investigators place their tubes in beakers with ice water, water at room temperature, and boiling water. All find that the height of mercury is highest with the boiling water, moderate at room temperature, and lowest with ice-water: a 1.00 correlation. Yet when the five investigators meet together and place their respective tubes in the same beaker of water, all register different temperatures. Because no standard unit of measurement was employed, each investigator's tube will show different heights of mercury depending upon the tubes' different volume and the different amount of mercury employed by each.

I have described in previous chapters numerous constructs that might form the basis for the creation of units of measurement for psychological phenomena. Such constructs include:

1. Persons
2. Response modes (e.g., cognition, affect, and behavior)
3. Gender
4. Group status (e.g., culture and ethnicity)
5. Measurement methods (e.g., physiological, self-report, behavioral)
6. Observer status (e.g., self or other)
7. Reactive or nonreactive methods
8. Traits
9. States
10. Situations (e.g., environmental types, such as those proposed in vocational choice theories such as Holland, 1985)
11. Time (e.g., occasions, frequency, duration)
12. Level of aggregation (items and aggregated scores)

Further theoretical and empirical work is needed to explore the utility of combining these units. Such efforts in applied psychology have already yielded substantial progress. Most measurement psychologists would agree that D. T. Campbell and Fiske's (1959) conception of tests as trait–method units has been very useful for thinking about and evaluating tests. Selection tests have benefited through maximizing the aggregation of persons and items. Validity generalization suggests that if persons, items, and tests are combined within appropriately defined occupations, such aggregation is sufficient to permit moderate to high levels of predictive validity (Schmidt, 1992; Schmidt & Hunter, 1977). Collins (1991) demonstrated the utility of constructing person-item-occasion measurements for the study of longitudinal change.

To the extent possible, the goal of science is to develop a dependable theory-measurement basis upon which to make selection and intervention decisions. Psychology is a new science, and this kind of knowledge base is available for relatively few problem–treatment combinations. In most contemporary intervention contexts, the intervener's task is to develop a model of the client, measure the variables in that model, and implement treatments in a trial-and-error fashion. It should be no surprise that the majority of psychotherapists and counselors identify themselves as eclectic (Meier & Davis, 1993). As the knowledge base deepens, one would expect fixed treatments to replace adaptive ones, and eclectic practitioners to be replaced by specialists. This process, however, heavily depends on the quality of the science's measurement theory and methods.

8 CONCLUSIONS AND SPECULATIONS[1]

Accepting any successful paradigm carries with it benefits and costs.[1] The promoters of a successful paradigm will obviously emphasize its benefits, but eventually other groups will attempt to demonstrate and publicize the accompanying costs. To the extent that a paradigm cannot explain the phenomena of interest, calls for revisions and modifications, and revolutions are likely to be increasingly heeded.

A paradox exists between the sharp criticisms of psychological measurement by academic scientists and others and the widespread use and acceptance of current tests by practitioners and researchers. The paradox may be understood by noting that psychological measurement devices appear adequate for some purposes, but not for others. For example, selection testing is one of psychology's most important societal functions. In education, business, and the military, psychological measurement, particularly cognitive ability tests, represent the best and fairest approach to selection decisions. That success led psychologists to apply selection assumptions and procedures to tests in other areas, such as explanatory theory building and intervention, where the results have been less successful. Thus, ample reason exists both to respect contemporary tests and to work toward their improvement.

I disagree with those who believe or imply that important psychological constructs are largely immeasurable (cf. L. Goldman, 1990; Mayer, 1966). The evidence does not support Faust and Ziskin's (1988) assertion that human behavior "resists objective, direct, or reliable observation and measurement" (p. 33). No other set of procedures exceeds the utility of psychological measurement and assessment in their proper applications. To improve measurement's effectiveness, what is required is a renewed emphasis on theoretical and technological development, application of existing substantive theories to measurement procedures, experimentation with new procedures, and programmatic research. In turn, these goals should be supported by increased grant funding, additional attention to measurement and assessment in graduate coursework, and greater attention to these issues in scholarly publications. I am astounded at how little grant support is available for measurement and assessment research, particularly from nonmilitary sources. For example, a 1970 plan to revise the MMPI—

[1]Portions of this chapter are reprinted from Meier (1993) by permisison of the American Psychological Association. © 1993 by the American Psychological Association.

probably the most important noncognitive psychological test in the world—was delayed until recently partially because of a lack of funds (Graham, 1990). The issue of sufficient resources to study measurement and to do applied assessment is a "what-comes-first?" problem. Without the additional resources necessary to improve measurement and assessment, little progress in these areas can be expected. Yet better measurement and assessment will be expected by those who will judge our requests for additional resources in science and practice. Economics is likely to be a critical factor in applied measurement innovations: for example, as long as costs are the primary factor in deciding the extent to which assessments should be conducted in practice settings, the most inexpensive methods, self-reports and interviews, will continue to reign. It is ironic that the managed care companies now dominating psychological practice, who publicly profess to value solid evaluations of health care, show so little interest in paying for psychological assessment, research on assessment innovation, or training practitioners in effective assessment.

Dawis (1987) maintained that "researchers should not be reluctant to experiment with different scale construction approaches—and should report their results, so that the rest of us can find out what method is best" (p. 488). D. T. Campbell and Fiske (1959) expressed similar hopes:

> Psychologists today should be concerned not with evaluating tests as if the tests were fixed and definitive, but rather with developing better tests. We believe that a careful examination of a multitrait–multimethod matrix will indicate to the experimenter what his next steps should be: it will indicate which methods should be discarded or replaced, which concepts need sharper delineation, and which concepts are poorly measured because of excessive or confounding method variance. (p. 103)

Sidman (1960) observed that much important work in experimental psychology is devoted to ". . . improvements in measuring instruments, advanced methods of recording data, sophisticated data analysis, the design of specialized apparatus to do a particular job or generalized apparatus to perform many functions, and the extension of old techniques to new areas" (p. 16). Sidman (1960) also reported that Skinner suggested that apparatus (and measurement) failures could be a source of new discoveries.

When measurement and assessment advance, my guess is that testing will move away from its strict reliance on self-report. For example, several researchers have begun to investigate the potential benefits of combining self-reports with the response latencies of those reports (e.g., R. R. Holden et al., 1992; Scheidt & Meier, 1993). Test construction will focus not just on maximizing individual differences, but on other criteria as well. For example, test developers might construct a measurement device containing items and tasks that differentiate between adolescent, minority women who respond and fail to respond to a particular psychological intervention. If they are theory-based, items and tasks retained and dropped during test development will contain information relevant for theory revision. I believe that scale construction will become more specialized and closely linked with substantive and measurement theories. Different types of instruments will be designed for different tasks.

Kuhn (1970) implied that one essentially gambles when choosing between paradigms. My bets are on the theories and procedures, such as cognitive approaches and GT, that pay the most attention to construct validity and construct explication. I suspect that the validity procedures proposed by D. T. Campbell and Fiske (1959) and Cronbach and Meehl (1955) won over other proposals because their methods dealt with measurement at the level of the total score. In contrast, proposals by Loevinger (1957) and Jessor and Hammond (1957) to evaluate construct validity at the item level received less attention because no theory or methodology was available to handle the variability of responses at the item level. Cognitive and cognitive-behavioral theories are now available that have the capacity of guiding investigations at the item level.

Although students still require instruction in such basics as reliability, validity, norms, and item analysis, recent developments argue for a revision and possible expansion of the measurement curriculum. I would argue for greater attention to approaches that emphasize construct validity and construct explication. To diminish the artificial science–practice split in the graduate curriculum, faculty should also increase the measurement emphasis in applied and practice courses. Instructors could construct assignments in which students apply basic and advanced measurement procedures to important problems in their subspecialties. Such practical applications might increase students' interest in measurement and assessment and intrigue some students sufficiently to investigate the utility of new measurement procedures in their areas. Few students realize that the investigator-developed scales frequently employed in basic research (Meier & Davis, 1990) lack sufficient evaluation in terms of reliability and validity, thus presenting alternative methodological explanations that weaken confidence in research results. In general, measurement instructors should teach students how to (a) evaluate the psychometric properties of measurement devices employed in published studies and (b) routinely evaluate and report the psychometric properties of students' measurement devices.

Throughout the history of the science and the profession, psychologists have been presented with a pressing need for useful measurement and assessment. At present many psychological measures produce data comparable to a map that contains the names and relative locations of towns and villages, but little information about scale or the surrounding topography. The practice of measurement and assessment will continue, and without substantial improvement, so will the crises. Faust and Ziskin's (1988) controversy about the adequacy of psychological assessment and diagnosis as presented by expert witnesses in legal testimony is now moving away from center stage in favor of questions about clinicians and their clients' abilities to reliably distinguish between repressed memories and false one (Loftus, 1993).

Cronbach (1992) concluded a presentation on the history of validation in cognitive ability testing by observing that "there has been progress. We can look forward to more." I believe that significant progress in measurement and assessment is the single most important prerequisite for unification of psychological science and practice.

APPENDIX
10 DATA SETS USED FOR SIMULATING RANDOM RESPONDING

Data Set 1

```
1 5 5 1 1 1 1 4 5 1
5 3 4 4 1 1 1 3 1 1
3 4 2 1 1 1 1 1 5 1
5 1 5 2 1 1 2 1 4 5
1 3 1 1 1 1 1 5 1 1
1 1 3 4 4 1 1 1 5 1
1 3 1 3 4 2 1 1 1 1
1 1 1 5 1 1 2 1 5 1
1 1 4 1 1 1 5 1 4 1
5 1 1 1 1 1 5 1 4 4
5 1 2 3 1 1 1 3 1 1
1 1 1 1 1 1 1 3 1 1
1 1 4 4 5 1 1 3 1 1
1 1 5 1 1 5 1 1 5 4
5 1 1 4 2 1 1 4 2 5
5 1 1 1 1 1 1 1 1 1
1 1 1 1 1 1 1 1 1 1
1 1 1 1 1 1 1 1 1 1
1 1 1 1 1 3 4 4 1 1
1 1 4 1 5 1 1 1 1 1
3 3 3 4 4 1 2 5 2 5
1 2 2 2 5 3 5 2 2 2
3 3 2 2 2 3 4 2 5 5
2 4 5 2 2 2 4 5 2 2
4 2 2 5 2 2 2 5 2 3
2 2 5 3 5 5 2 5 2 4
2 2 2 4 4 4 2 3 3 2
1 1 2 3 2 5 5 2 2 2
3 2 2 2 2 1 2 2 2 5
3 2 4 2 5 5 2 3 2 5
3 3 1 2 2 2 2 2 2 2
2 2 1 3 2 2 2 5 2 2
2 4 2 2 2 2 5 2 5 2
2 3 2 2 2 5 2 1 2 2
1 2 2 4 5 4 4 2 1 1
2 3 1 5 2 2 2 2 3 2
2 4 1 2 2 4 3 2 5 2
2 5 3 3 5 2 2 1 2 4
1 4 2 2 2 2 2 2 2 2
4 2 5 5 2 2 4 1 2 2
1 1 4 5 3 3 4 2 2 3
4 3 2 3 3 3 2 4 2 3
1 2 3 3 3 3 1 3 5 3
3 3 3 3 3 1 1 3 2 5
3 3 2 3 3 1 3 3 3 3
3 1 3 4 5 3 5 5 2 3
```

```
3 2 3 5 3 3 3 3 4 3
2 3 3 3 3 3 1 1 5 3
3 2 5 3 3 3 3 3 3 1
3 2 3 1 2 3 3 3 3 4
3 3 1 3 2 5 5 3 1 2
2 1 5 3 2 3 3 3 3 3
3 3 3 3 1 3 3 1 4 3
3 3 3 4 3 3 1 4 4 3
3 5 3 3 2 3 4 3 4 3
1 3 3 3 5 3 3 3 3 3
3 3 5 5 3 3 3 3 5 3
5 1 5 5 1 3 3 3 3 1
4 1 3 3 3 3 3 3 1 1
2 3 3 3 3 3 5 5 3 3
4 5 4 4 4 4 4 2 1 4
5 1 5 1 2 1 4 4 1 4
2 4 3 2 4 1 4 4 4 4
1 4 2 4 1 4 1 1 4 3
4 4 5 4 2 4 4 5 5 2
5 4 4 4 4 4 4 1 4 4
4 4 4 4 4 4 4 4 4 4
4 4 4 1 4 3 4 4 3
4 5 4 4 2 4 5 4 4 1
2 4 4 4 4 2 4 4 4 4
5 4 2 4 4 4 3 4 2 3
1 4 4 5 4 2 2 4 2 4
1 4 4 1 3 1 4 4 4 4
4 4 4 4 4 4 1 4 2 3
4 5 4 4 4 1 4 4 4 5
4 4 1 2 4 4 4 4 3 4
4 4 4 4 4 4 4 4 5 4
2 4 4 4 4 4 4 1 4 2
4 4 4 5 4 4 4 4 3 4
4 1 3 4 2 4 4 4 5 4
5 5 5 4 5 5 5 5 5 4
4 5 5 5 5 4 5 5 3 5
4 2 5 5 5 2 4 2 5 2
4 4 2 1 3 5 1 5 5 5
5 1 2 2 5 3 5 5 5 1
5 5 5 5 5 5 3 1 3 1
5 5 5 5 5 5 2 5 5 5
5 5 2 1 1 5 3 2 1 5
5 4 5 1 4 5 5 3 1 3
5 5 5 5 3 5 5 3 5 5
5 4 5 4 4 5 5 5 4 2
1 2 1 4 4 3 3 5 5 3
5 3 5 5 4 5 5 5 5 5
5 1 5 3 1 2 5 5 5 5
5 4 2 1 3 5 5 5 5 5
5 5 5 5 5 5 5 1 1 5
5 5 5 1 5 2 5 5 5 5
5 2 4 5 5 5 2 5 4 2
5 5 5 5 4 5 5 5 5 4
5 5 1 5 5 5 3 5 4 5
```

Data Set 2

```
1 4 3 1 1 3 5 3 4 2
1 3 1 3 2 1 1 1 1 1
2 2 5 1 1 2 4 3 1
1 1 2 1 1 1 1 1 5 4
1 1 1 3 1 5 1 4 2 1
1 1 1 1 1 3 1 3 2 1
1 2 1 1 3 3 2 1 1 1
1 1 4 5 1 5 1 1 1 4
1 1 1 1 1 1 1 1 1 4
1 1 1 2 5 5 1 3 1 3
1 1 1 1 1 1 3 5 2 4
1 1 1 5 1 3 1 1 1 1
3 4 1 2 1 5 1 3 1 1
1 5 3 4 1 4 4 1 1 1
4 3 1 1 1 3 1 1 1 1
4 2 4 5 5 1 1 3 5 1
1 2 1 4 1 1 1 1 1 1
3 1 5 3 2 2 3 1 5 4
1 5 4 1 3 2 5 3 1 1
1 1 2 3 1 1 3 1 1 2
5 3 4 3 5 2 2 2 2 2
2 2 2 2 4 2 2 1 1 2
2 2 2 2 2 1 2 2 3 2
2 3 4 2 2 3 2 4 4 4
2 4 2 2 3 2 3 2 2 2
2 2 4 2 1 3 2 2 2 3
3 4 1 2 3 2 1 2 1 2
2 2 2 4 2 5 2 4 2 2
2 3 2 5 1 5 2 3 2 1
2 2 4 2 2 5 2 2 2 2
2 2 2 2 2 2 2 2 3 2
2 3 1 2 2 3 2 2 2 5
2 5 5 2 4 2 3 1 3 2
2 2 2 1 2 2 2 5 2 5
3 2 5 3 2 2 2 2 2 2
5 2 2 2 2 2 1 4 2 5
2 4 5 2 5 2 4 4 2 3
2 2 2 2 2 3 2 2 3 2
3 1 2 2 5 2 2 5 4 2
3 2 5 2 2 4 1 2 2 2
1 3 3 3 3 2 5 2 3 3
2 4 3 4 1 3 3 3 3 5
1 3 3 3 2 3 5 3 5 3
3 3 3 3 5 3 3 3 3 3
2 3 5 3 3 5 3 4 3 5
3 3 3 3 3 5 3 3 1 1
3 4 2 3 2 5 3 3 4 4
5 3 3 3 5 2 2 3 3 3
3 3 3 3 3 4 3 3 3 3
3 4 1 3 3 2 3 2 2 3
2 1 5 3 2 3 3 3 4 3
```

```
3 1 4 1 4 1 3 1 1 1
1 1 1 5 1 1 1 3 3 3
1 1 3 1 1 5 2 3 1 1
4 1 2 5 1 1 1 1 1 5
1 1 4 1 4 3 4 2 1 4
4 1 1 1 1 5 1 5 3 4
1 1 1 3 1 3 1 2 1 1
1 1 1 5 1 1 4 4 1 3
1 1 1 1 1 1 1 1 5 1
1 1 1 2 5 2 5 1 1 1
4 2 3 1 1 3 1 2 5 1
1 1 3 1 4 1 1 1 3 1
1 3 4 2 1 1 2 2 1 2
1 1 1 1 1 1 5 1 1 1
1 4 1 3 1 2 1 1 1 1
4 1 4 1 5 1 5 3 4 1
1 3 1 1 1 1 1 4 5 2
5 3 1 4 1 4 1 3 1 1
1 2 2 5 3 2 2 3 3 3
2 2 3 1 2 5 2 3 2 2
4 1 2 5 2 2 2 2 2 5
1 1 4 2 4 3 4 2 2 4
4 2 2 2 2 2 2 5 3 4
2 2 2 3 2 3 2 3 2 2
1 2 2 5 2 2 4 2 1 3
2 2 2 2 2 1 2 2 5 2
2 1 2 2 5 2 5 1 2 2
4 2 3 2 2 3 1 2 5 2
2 2 3 2 4 2 2 2 3 2
2 3 4 2 2 2 2 2 2 2
2 2 2 2 2 2 5 2 2 2
2 4 2 3 2 2 2 2 1 2
4 1 4 2 5 2 5 3 4 1
2 3 5 2 2 1 2 4 5 2
5 3 2 4 2 4 2 3 2 2
2 2 2 5 2 2 2 2 3 3
3 2 2 3 1 2 5 2 3 2
2 4 1 2 5 2 2 2 2 2
5 1 1 4 3 4 3 4 2 3
4 4 3 3 3 3 3 2 5 3
4 3 3 3 3 3 3 3 3 3
3 1 3 3 5 3 3 4 4 3
3 3 5 3 3 3 3 3 4 3
3 2 1 3 3 3 3 3 3 3
3 3 3 3 5 3 3 2 3 3
3 5 4 3 3 3 3 3 3 1
3 1 3 3 3 4 3 2 3 2
3 3 1 4 3 3 3 3 3 4
3 2 4 3 3 1 5 3 3 3
3 3 4 3 4 3 2 3 3 3
4 5 1 2 3 3 3 4 3 3
3 3 2 2 3 5 3 1 3 3
3 3 3 1 3 3 2 3 3 4
5 3 3 2 3 3 3 5 4 3
```

```
3 2 3 2 2 4 3 2 3 1
4 3 3 2 2 3 3 3 4 2
2 3 3 3 3 3 4 4 1 3
4 5 5 2 4 3 3 3 3 3
5 4 3 3 3 3 3 3 1 3
3 3 1 1 3 3 1 3 3 5
5 3 1 2 3 3 3 3 3 3
1 3 3 3 3 1 3 3 2 5
4 2 3 3 4 2 3 5 4
4 4 3 1 4 4 4 4 4
3 4 4 4 5 1 4 3 3 3
4 3 4 5 4 4 2 4 4 4
3 4 5 4 4 4 5 4 4 4
2 5 1 5 4 3 4 4 4 1
4 2 4 4 1 5 4 4 2 5
4 5 4 4 4 4 4 1 3 4
2 4 4 4 4 4 1 3 4 1
4 4 4 5 2 5 4 4 5 3
3 2 4 4 4 3 4 3 4 4
1 2 4 4 1 5 2 4 1 3
4 4 4 4 4 2 4 3 4 4
4 3 4 4 1 1 4 1 4 4
4 4 5 4 4 4 4 2 2 5
5 4 1 2 3 4 4 1 4 4
4 3 5 1 4 4 4 3 1 4
2 5 1 4 4 3 4 4 1 3
3 4 3 4 1 4 4 4 2 4
4 4 5 4 3 4 4 1 4 3
4 4 3 4 3 5 3 4 4 4
3 5 2 3 5 5 5 5 5 5
5 5 5 5 5 5 5 5 5 5
5 5 5 5 5 5 5 5 5 5
5 5 5 5 5 5 2 5 5 5
3 4 5 2 4 5 5 3 5 5
5 1 5 2 5 2 5 5 4 1
2 1 3 3 5 5 5 5 5 5
1 2 2 5 2 3 5 5 5 5
3 5 5 5 5 5 5 2 1 5
5 5 3 4 5 1 1 5 3 3
1 1 5 2 5 5 5 5 3 5
5 5 5 4 2 3 5 2 3 3
3 3 5 4 5 4 5 5 1 4
4 2 4 5 5 5 2 5 5 5
1 5 5 2 5 3 1 1 4 2
1 5 5 5 5 5 2 5 5 3
5 5 5 2 2 5 2 5 4 2
1 3 5 5 4 5 5 5 5 5
3 5 5 5 5 1 5 5 2 5
5 2 5 3 3 2 5 5 3 5
```

Data Set 3

```
1 4 1 5 1 5 3 4 1 1
1 5 1 1 1 1 4 5 2 5
```

```
3 3 3 4 2 1 3 1 3 3
3 5 2 2 3 3 4 3 1 4
3 3 3 3 3 4 3 2 4 3
3 1 5 3 3 3 3 3 4 3
4 3 4 4 4 4 4 5 5 1
2 2 4 4 3 4 4 4 2 3
4 5 4 1 4 4 3 3 4 4
4 4 3 3 4 4 4 5 4 4
4 4 4 5 4 4 4 4 1 3
4 4 4 2 4 4 5 4 1 4
4 3 5 4 1 4 3 5 2 4
1 4 4 4 2 5 4 4 1 5
3 4 4 4 3 4 4 4 3 5
4 2 4 4 4 3 4 1 4 4
4 4 4 4 3 2 4 4 4 1
4 4 4 3 3 4 4 4 4 3
3 4 4 4 5 4 4 4 4 4
2 5 2 1 3 4 4 4 2 4
4 5 4 1 4 4 3 5 4 1
4 3 2 4 4 4 1 4 4 4
2 5 4 4 1 5 3 4 4 4
3 4 4 5 3 4 4 4 2 4
4 4 3 4 1 4 4 4 4 4
4 3 2 4 4 4 1 5 4 4
3 5 5 5 5 3 3 5 5 4
2 5 5 5 5 3 1 4 5 3
5 5 4 3 1 5 5 5 1 5
2 4 5 5 4 5 5 5 5 3
3 2 5 5 5 3 5 5 5 2
2 5 4 2 5 5 5 1 5 5
5 5 4 5 4 5 4 4 5 5
5 5 3 2 5 5 1 2 5 5
5 5 2 5 2 3 5 5 5 5
3 3 5 5 4 2 5 5 5 5
3 1 4 5 3 5 4 4 3 1
5 5 5 1 5 2 4 5 5 4
5 5 5 5 3 3 1 5 5 5
3 5 5 5 2 2 5 4 2 5
5 5 1 5 5 5 5 4 5 5
2 4 4 5 5 5 5 3 2 5
5 4 5 2 5 5 5 5 2 5
2 3 5 5 5 5 3 3 5 5
4 2 5 5 5 5 3 1 4 5
3 5 4 3 3 1 5 5 5 1
```

Data Set 4

```
3 1 3 1 3 1 1 1 1 1
5 1 1 4 1 1 1 5 3 3
4 1 3 2 1 1 1 1 1 1
3 1 1 1 1 1 1 1 1 4
2 1 1 2 1 1 1 5 4 1
1 1 3 3 1 1 1 1 1 1
3 4 1 2 1 2 1 3 1 4
```

```
1 1 1 1 1 4 1 2 4 1
1 1 5 3 1 1 1 3 4 1
4 3 2 1 1 1 4 5 1 2
1 1 1 4 3 1 1 1 1 2
1 5 1 1 1 1 3 3 1 1
1 3 2 1 1 4 5 1 1 2
1 1 1 5 4 1 1 1 1 4
2 1 1 1 1 1 1 5 2 2
1 3 3 1 1 4 1 1 1 1
1 4 1 2 4 1 1 1 5 3
1 1 1 3 4 1 4 3 1 1
1 1 1 5 5 1 2 2 1 4
3 1 1 1 2 3 1 5 1 1
2 2 3 3 2 2 2 2 3 3
2 2 4 5 2 2 2 2 2 2
5 4 1 3 2 2 2 2 4 2
5 2 1 2 2 3 5 2 1 2
3 2 2 4 1 2 4 2 2 5
2 2 1 5 3 2 2 2 3 4
2 4 3 2 2 2 5 2 2 2
2 3 2 1 4 2 2 2 2 4
3 2 4 2 2 1 5 5 3 2
2 2 2 3 3 2 2 4 5 2
2 2 2 2 5 4 2 3 2
2 2 2 2 4 2 5 2 1 2
2 3 5 2 1 2 3 2 2 4
2 5 4 2 2 5 2 2 1 5
3 2 2 2 3 4 2 5 3 2
2 2 2 2 2 2 2 2 3 2
1 4 2 2 2 2 4 3 2 4
2 2 1 5 3 4 2 2 2 2
3 3 2 5 4 2 2 2 2 2
3 1 4 2 3 2 4 4 3 1
3 5 3 1 3 2 4 3 5 4
3 3 3 3 3 3 1 3 1 3
3 5 3 2 2 3 4 2 3 3
3 1 3 3 3 5 4 3 3 3
4 4 3 3 3 3 3 2 3 5
1 2 3 3 5 3 2 3 2 3
3 3 3 3 3 3 3 3 5 4
2 3 3 3 3 3 1 4 3 3
3 4 3 3 1 3 5 3 1 3
2 4 3 5 4 3 3 3 3 3
3 1 3 1 3 3 5 3 2 2
3 4 2 3 3 3 1 3 3 3
5 4 3 3 3 3 3 5 1 3
3 3 3 2 3 3 4 3 2 3
3 5 3 2 3 2 3 3 3 3
3 3 3 3 3 5 4 2 3 3
3 3 3 1 4 3 3 3 4 3
3 1 3 5 3 1 3 2 4 3
5 4 3 3 3 3 3 3 1 3
1 3 3 5 3 2 3 3 4 2
4 4 4 1 4 1 5 4 4 4
```

```
4 4 4 5 1 4 4 4 3 2
4 4 4 4 2 4 4 5 4 2
4 2 4 4 4 5 4 3 3 4
5 4 2 4 4 4 4 3 1 4
4 3 4 4 3 2 1 4 5 4
1 4 2 4 4 5 4 4 4 4
4 3 3 1 4 1 2 4 5 4
2 3 4 4 2 4 4 4 1 4
1 5 5 4 4 4 4 4 4 1
4 4 4 3 3 4 4 4 4 2
4 4 5 4 2 4 2 4 4 4
1 4 3 3 4 5 4 2 4 4
4 3 4 1 4 4 3 4 4 3
2 4 4 1 4 2 3 4 1 4
4 4 4 4 4 4 3 4 2 1
4 4 4 4 2 4 4 3 2 4
3 4 4 4 5 4 4 1 4 2
3 4 4 4 2 1 2 4 4 4
4 3 4 4 4 2 2 4 5 4
1 5 5 3 3 5 4 1 5 5
5 5 5 5 5 5 5 5 5 5
2 2 5 1 4 5 5 5 5 5
5 2 4 5 1 3 5 3 4 5
1 5 5 5 3 2 5 4 3 4
5 5 5 3 4 5 5 4 5 5
5 5 4 5 1 5 5 5 4 5
5 2 5 4 5 5 5 5 4 2
2 4 5 5 1 5 2 5 5 4
5 2 3 3 5 5 4 2 5 5
5 4 5 1 4 5 3 5 4 3
2 5 5 1 5 2 3 5 1 5
5 5 5 5 5 4 3 5 2 1
5 5 5 5 2 5 4 3 5 5
5 3 5 5 5 5 5 5 1 5
2 3 4 5 5 2 5 5 2 5
5 5 4 3 5 5 5 2 2 5
5 5 1 5 5 3 3 5 4 1
5 5 5 5 5 5 5 5 5 5
5 5 2 2 5 1 4 5 5 5
```

Data Set 5

```
5 5 4 1 4 1 4 4 1 4
2 1 3 1 3 1 1 1 1 1
1 1 1 5 1 1 1 1 3 1
1 4 1 2 5 2 1 3 1 4
1 1 3 2 1 1 1 1 3 2
2 1 1 1 1 4 5 3 4 3
4 1 1 3 1 1 1 1 1 1
4 4 1 1 3 1 1 1 1 1
5 1 3 5 3 5 2 4 2 4
2 4 2 1 4 1 3 1 1 1
1 1 1 1 1 5 1 1 1 1
2 5 4 1 2 5 2 1 3 1
```

```
4 1 1 3 2 1 1 1 1 2
1 1 2 1 1 1 1 4 5 3
4 3 4 1 1 3 1 1 1 1
1 2 1 1 1 1 4 1 4 1
3 1 1 1 1 1 1 1 2 1
1 1 1 1 5 1 1 1 1 2
1 1 1 1 2 1 5 1 1 3
1 4 5 2 5 1 1 2 1 1
2 2 2 1 3 1 2 5 2 5
5 2 2 2 2 2 2 2 3 5
1 5 2 2 2 2 2 1 2 2
2 2 2 4 2 2 5 5 3 2
2 5 2 2 2 2 2 1 2 2
5 4 2 5 3 4 1 4 2 2
2 3 1 4 5 2 5 2 2 4
2 2 2 3 2 2 2 2 2 2
2 1 2 2 4 5 2 1 2 2
1 2 2 2 1 2 2 2 1 3
1 2 5 2 2 2 2 1 2 4
5 3 4 3 4 2 2 3 2 2
2 2 2 2 1 2 2 4 2 4
1 3 1 2 2 2 1 2 2 2
2 2 1 2 2 3 3 2 2 2
2 2 2 2 2 2 5 2 2 3
1 4 5 2 5 1 2 2 2 1
2 2 2 1 3 1 2 5 2 5
5 2 2 2 2 2 2 2 3 5
1 5 2 2 2 2 2 1 2 2
3 3 3 4 3 3 5 5 3 3
3 5 2 3 2 3 3 1 3 3
5 4 3 5 3 4 1 4 2 3
3 3 1 4 5 2 5 3 3 4
3 3 3 3 3 3 3 3 2 3
3 3 5 2 4 5 3 2 3 3
1 2 3 3 1 3 3 3 1 3
1 5 3 3 2 3 3 1 3 4
5 3 4 3 4 3 3 3 3 3
3 3 3 2 1 3 3 4 3 4
1 3 1 3 3 3 1 3 3 2
3 3 1 3 3 3 4 3 3 3
2 3 3 3 3 2 3 5 3 3
3 1 4 5 2 5 3 2 3 3
1 3 3 3 1 3 1 2 5 2
5 5 3 2 3 3 5 3 3 3
3 5 1 5 3 3 3 3 3 1
3 3 3 3 3 4 3 3 5 3
1 3 3 5 2 3 2 3 3 1
3 3 5 4 3 5 3 4 1 4
4 1 4 3 1 4 5 2 5 4
4 4 4 4 4 3 4 4 4 4
2 4 4 5 2 4 5 4 2 4
4 1 2 4 4 1 4 4 4 2
3 4 2 3 2 2 4 4 1 4
4 5 3 4 3 4 4 4 3 4
```

```
4 4 4 4 5 1 4 4 4 4
4 1 3 1 4 4 4 1 4 4
2 4 4 4 4 2 4 4 4 4
2 4 4 4 4 2 4 5 4 4
3 1 4 5 2 4 4 4 2 4
4 1 4 4 4 1 3 1 2 5
2 5 5 4 2 5 1 4 3 1
4 4 4 4 4 4 4 2 4 4
4 4 4 2 4 4 4 1 4 4
4 4 4 4 4 2 4 4 4 1
5 2 4 4 4 4 4 4 4 5
4 2 4 4 4 4 5 5 2 4
4 4 4 3 4 4 4 1 2 4
5 3 4 4 4 3 4 4 4 1
5 2 2 5 5 3 5 5 5 2
5 5 5 5 4 5 5 5 5 4
2 1 5 1 5 5 5 5 2 2
5 3 3 5 1 4 5 5 5 5
5 4 5 2 4 5 5 1 5 3
5 5 5 3 4 5 4 3 2 5
5 5 5 5 1 2 2 5 4 3
5 5 5 2 2 5 5 5 1 5
5 3 3 5 1 5 3 2 5 5
4 5 5 5 5 5 5 5 5 5
4 5 2 5 4 2 1 5 1 5
1 5 2 5 5 5 3 4 5 1
5 5 5 5 5 5 4 5 2 5
5 5 5 1 5 5 4 3 5 5
5 5 1 5 5 5 5 4 2 5
5 5 1 2 2 5 4 4 5 5
5 2 3 5 5 5 1 5 5 3
3 5 5 4 5 1 5 2 5 5
5 4 5 1 2 5 5 5 1 3
5 5 5 2 4 1 5 1 5 3
```

Data Set 6

```
1 1 2 1 1 1 5 1 4 4
1 4 2 5 2 4 1 1 4 1
1 1 3 1 1 1 1 1 3 1
2 1 1 1 1 1 5 1 4 1
1 1 1 1 5 1 1 1 1 3
5 1 1 3 5 1 5 1 1 1
1 1 1 1 1 1 2 1 2 1
1 1 1 1 1 5 1 1 1 1
1 1 1 1 1 1 5 1 4 3
1 4 5 1 1 1 1 1 1 5
1 3 5 3 1 2 2 1 5 1
1 3 1 4 5 2 5 1 2 1
1 1 1 1 1 1 3 1 2 5
1 2 1 1 1 1 4 2 2 1
3 5 1 2 1 1 5 1 4 1
5 4 1 4 1 1 1 1 1 5
1 1 1 1 4 5 4 1 1 1
```

```
1 1 1 4 1 4 1 5 1 5
3 1 1 1 1 1 1 5 1 1
1 1 4 5 1 2 1 1 1 1
2 2 2 2 3 2 2 3 2 3
2 1 1 2 2 2 2 2 5 2
5 2 2 2 2 2 2 2 2 1
2 2 5 3 2 2 2 2 1 2
2 2 2 2 4 2 2 3 3 1
2 2 5 2 2 2 2 2 1 4
2 3 2 2 2 2 2 2 2 2
2 2 2 2 4 1 2 3 2 2
3 3 2 2 2 2 4 2 5 3
2 4 2 4 2 3 2 2 1 2
2 5 2 2 2 3 3 3 2 2
3 2 1 3 5 1 5 2 4 5
2 1 2 4 2 4 3 3 2 2
2 2 2 2 2 2 2 4 1 4
2 3 5 2 2 1 2 2 2 2
5 3 4 1 4 2 2 2 2 2
2 4 5 2 5 2 2 4 2 2
2 3 2 2 2 2 2 5 1 5
2 4 5 2 2 2 2 2 2 1
3 5 1 5 2 2 2 2 3 2
4 1 2 5 2 3 3 1 3 3
1 3 4 3 4 3 4 2 3 4
4 3 3 3 3 5 3 5 3 4
3 3 3 3 3 3 3 2 3 3
3 3 3 4 4 5 4 3 5 3
3 4 5 2 5 3 4 1 3 3
3 3 3 3 3 3 2 3 3 1
3 3 3 1 3 1 2 5 2 4
5 3 2 3 3 2 2 3 3 1
3 3 5 3 4 4 2 4 3 3
3 3 3 3 3 3 3 3 1 3
3 2 3 4 3 5 3 5 3 4
3 3 3 3 3 3 3 3 3 3
2 3 3 5 3 3 4 3 3 3
5 3 5 2 4 2 3 4 3 3
3 2 3 3 1 4 3 2 3 3
2 2 3 3 1 3 3 5 2 3
3 2 3 2 2 3 3 1 3 4
3 3 3 1 3 3 2 3 4 3
5 5 5 1 3 3 2 3 4 3
5 4 5 3 4 1 1 4 1 4
4 4 5 3 5 2 4 2 1 4
4 4 4 4 4 4 4 2 4 4
1 4 2 5 2 5 1 4 2 4
4 2 4 5 2 5 1 4 2 4
4 2 3 2 3 3 2 1 1 4
4 5 1 1 4 4 4 5 5 5
4 4 1 4 4 4 3 4 3 4
4 4 2 2 4 4 4 4 4 4
2 4 1 4 4 4 1 4 4 5
4 4 1 4 4 1 3 1 4 5
```

```
2 5 4 4 4 4 4 4 4 4
4 2 4 4 2 3 2 2 4 4
2 1 1 4 4 2 4 4 1 4
4 4 1 4 5 3 4 3 3 4
4 3 4 4 4 4 2 4 4 4
4 4 3 4 4 1 4 4 5 4
4 1 4 4 2 4 4 4 5 4
4 4 4 5 3 5 2 4 4 4
4 4 4 4 3 4 4 4 4 3
5 2 5 5 1 5 5 5 5 5
5 5 5 1 5 5 5 5 5 5
1 4 1 2 1 3 5 1 5 5
5 5 5 5 5 5 5 2 2 5
2 5 5 5 5 5 5 2 5 5
2 5 5 1 5 5 5 5 5 4
2 1 5 5 2 5 5 1 5 5
5 5 3 5 2 5 5 5 5 2
5 5 5 5 3 1 2 5 3 3
5 5 2 5 5 1 5 5 5 4
5 5 5 2 3 2 2 5 5 1
5 4 5 3 5 4 5 5 5 3
2 5 5 5 1 5 5 5 2 2
5 2 5 5 5 5 5 5 3 5
5 3 5 5 3 5 2 5 5 1
5 2 4 2 4 5 3 1 5 5
5 1 5 5 5 5 4 5 4 5
5 5 2 2 5 5 5 5 2 5
1 4 5 5 5 3 2 1 1 5
2 5 2 5 5 5 2 5 5 2
```

Data Set 7

```
1 4 4 1 3 1 1 1 1 1
1 1 5 1 1 1 1 4 5 2
5 3 1 1 1 2 1 3 1 1
3 1 2 5 1 1 1 3 3 3
1 1 3 1 1 3 5 1 5 2
4 5 1 1 1 1 1 1 5 1
1 4 1 4 3 2 1 1 1 1
2 1 4 1 5 1 5 3 4 1
1 1 3 1 3 1 3 1 1 4
4 5 4 1 5 1 3 1 5 1
4 1 4 1 1 3 5 1 1 1
1 3 3 1 1 3 1 1 3 3
1 1 2 1 1 1 1 1 1 1
3 5 1 5 2 4 5 1 2 1
1 2 2 1 1 1 1 1 5 1
4 4 2 3 2 3 1 1 1 1
1 1 1 1 1 1 1 1 2 1
4 1 5 1 5 3 4 1 1 1
3 1 3 1 3 1 1 1 1 1
5 1 1 4 1 1 1 5 3 5
2 4 2 2 3 3 2 2 2 2
2 1 2 2 2 1 3 1 2 5
```

```
2 5 1 2 2 2 2 2 3 2
2 1 2 2 5 2 4 4 2 4
3 3 2 2 3 2 2 2 2 2
1 2 2 2 2 4 2 5 2 5
3 4 2 2 2 3 2 3 2 3
2 2 2 2 2 5 2 2 5 2
2 2 5 3 5 2 4 2 2 4
2 3 2 2 2 2 1 2 2 3
2 2 2 2 2 2 2 1 2 2
5 2 4 1 2 1 3 5 1 4
2 4 5 2 4 3 3 2 2 3
2 2 2 2 2 1 2 2 2 2
4 2 5 2 2 2 2 1 2 2
5 2 2 1 2 3 5 3 5 2
4 2 2 3 3 2 3 5 2 4
2 2 4 2 3 2 2 2 2 1
2 2 2 2 3 1 2 5 2 1
2 2 5 2 4 1 2 1 3 5
1 5 3 3 3 3 3 1 3 3
3 3 3 3 3 3 3 3 3 3
1 3 3 2 3 4 3 5 3 5
3 4 1 1 3 1 3 3 3 5
3 5 2 4 2 3 3 3 3 3
3 3 3 3 1 4 3 3 4 3
3 3 2 3 3 1 3 3 5 3
4 1 2 5 2 5 1 1 3 5
1 5 1 3 3 2 1 1 3 3
5 1 1 4 3 4 3 4 3 4
1 4 3 3 3 3 3 3 3 3
3 3 3 5 3 3 1 3 3 3
5 3 1 3 3 5 3 5 2 4
3 3 4 3 3 3 3 3 3 3
3 2 3 4 3 3 3 1 3 3
5 3 4 1 2 5 3 5 1 3
2 3 3 2 3 3 3 4 5 3
1 1 3 3 5 1 1 4 3 4
3 4 2 3 3 5 4 3 3 3
3 3 3 3 3 3 3 3 5 3
4 2 4 4 4 5 4 4 4 4
5 3 5 2 4 4 4 4 4 4
4 3 4 4 4 4 2 4 3 4
4 4 1 4 5 4 4 1 2 1
3 5 1 4 2 4 4 2 3 2
2 4 4 1 1 1 4 4 5 1
1 4 4 4 3 4 2 4 4 4
4 4 3 4 4 3 4 4 4 4
4 4 1 4 4 2 4 4 4 5
4 4 4 4 4 2 4 3 4 4
4 4 4 4 4 4 3 4 4 4
4 2 4 3 4 4 4 1 2 5
2 1 2 1 3 5 1 4 2 4
4 2 3 2 2 4 4 1 4 4
5 3 5 4 1 4 4 4 3 4
2 4 4 4 4 4 3 4 4 1
```

```
4 4 5 4 4 1 4 4 2 4
4 4 5 4 4 4 4 4 2 4
4 4 3 4 4 4 3 4 4 3
4 4 4 4 2 4 3 4 4 4
1 2 5 2 5 3 5 4 3 5
1 5 5 5 5 2 3 2 2 5
5 1 5 4 5 3 4 3 4 5
2 5 5 1 5 5 5 1 5 5
4 5 4 1 3 1 5 5 5 1
5 5 5 5 5 4 2 4 5 5
5 2 5 5 5 5 2 5 5 5
5 3 1 4 5 3 3 5 5 2
5 5 1 5 5 5 1 3 1 2
5 2 5 5 5 5 4 2 2 1
3 5 1 5 5 5 5 5 5 1
5 5 5 5 5 4 5 5 3 3
1 5 5 5 2 5 2 5 5 1
5 5 5 4 5 5 3 4 1 4
5 1 5 3 1 4 5 2 5 5
5 4 5 5 5 3 5 5 5 5
2 5 1 5 2 4 5 5 1 5
5 1 2 5 5 1 5 5 5 1
3 1 2 3 5 2 5 5 1 5
4 5 3 4 3 4 5 5 3 5
```

Data Set 8

```
1 1 1 1 1 1 5 3 5 2
4 2 1 3 3 1 1 1 1 1
2 4 2 1 4 1 3 1 2 1
1 1 1 1 5 1 4 1 2 5
2 5 1 1 3 5 1 5 1 1
3 2 1 1 1 1 5 1 1 4
1 4 3 5 3 4 1 4 1 1
3 1 3 1 1 1 1 1 1 5
1 1 1 1 1 1 1 1 1 1
1 3 5 3 5 2 4 1 1 4
1 1 1 3 1 1 1 1 2 2
2 1 1 1 1 1 5 1 4 1
2 5 3 5 1 1 2 1 1 2
1 5 2 4 5 1 1 1 1 1
5 1 1 4 1 4 3 4 2 1
1 5 4 1 1 3 1 3 1 1
1 1 1 1 5 1 1 2 1 1
1 5 1 4 4 1 5 3 5 2
4 1 1 4 1 1 1 3 1 1
1 1 2 1 3 1 1 4 1 1
2 5 2 4 1 2 1 3 5 1
2 2 2 2 2 3 2 2 2 5
2 1 1 2 2 5 1 1 4 2
4 3 4 2 2 4 4 2 2 3
3 3 2 2 2 2 2 2 1 2
2 2 2 2 2 5 2 4 4 2
4 2 2 3 2 4 2 2 4 2
```

```
2 2 3 2 2 2 2 2 3
2 2 4 1 2 5 4 1 2 1
3 5 1 2 2 2 2 2 3 2
2 2 2 1 2 4 5 2 5 1
1 4 2 4 3 4 2 2 4 4
2 2 3 2 2 1 2 2 2 2
2 1 2 2 2 2 2 2 5 2
4 4 2 4 2 2 4 2 3 2
2 4 2 2 2 3 2 2 2 2
2 2 3 2 2 4 1 2 5 2
2 3 2 4 3 5 1 5 2 2
2 2 3 2 2 2 2 1 2 4
5 3 4 3 4 2 2 2 2 1
3 3 5 1 3 3 4 3 4 1
3 1 3 3 3 1 3 3 5 2
4 2 4 3 3 3 2 3 3 3
3 2 3 5 3 3 3 1 2 3
3 3 3 3 2 3 3 1 3 3
3 1 3 1 2 5 2 5 5 3
3 4 2 2 1 3 5 1 5 3
3 3 3 3 1 3 3 3 3 3
4 3 3 3 3 1 3 3 5 2
3 2 3 3 1 3 3 5 4 3
5 3 4 1 3 3 3 1 3 3
1 4 5 2 5 3 3 4 3 3
3 3 3 3 3 3 2 4 3 5
2 4 5 3 1 3 3 1 2 3
3 1 3 3 3 1 3 1 3 3
2 2 3 3 1 3 4 5 3 4
3 4 3 3 3 3 3 3 3 3
5 1 3 3 4 3 4 1 3 1
3 3 3 1 3 3 2 3 3 1
3 3 5 3 3 3 2 3 3 3
4 2 4 5 4 4 3 1 4 5
2 5 1 4 4 1 4 4 4 1
3 1 2 5 2 5 5 4 2 4
4 2 2 4 4 4 5 1 5 4
4 4 4 4 1 4 4 4 4 4
4 4 4 5 5 3 4 1 2 4
2 4 4 1 4 4 5 4 4 5
3 4 1 4 2 4 2 2 4 4
5 2 5 4 4 4 4 4 4 3
4 4 4 4 2 4 4 1 4 4
1 5 4 2 4 4 1 2 4 4
1 4 4 4 1 3 1 2 5 2
5 1 4 4 4 5 3 4 3 4
4 4 3 4 4 4 4 4 2 4
4 3 4 4 1 4 4 3 1 4
4 4 1 4 4 2 4 4 1 4
4 5 4 3 5 3 4 4 4 2
4 5 4 4 3 1 4 5 2 5
1 4 4 4 4 3 2 1 4 4
2 5 2 5 5 4 2 4 4 2
2 5 5 1 5 5 5 5 4 4
```

```
5 1 5 5 5 5 5 4 5 5
5 5 3 4 1 4 2 3 5 5
5 4 5 2 5 3 4 1 4 2
5 2 2 5 5 1 5 5 2 5
4 1 5 5 5 3 5 5 5 5
2 5 5 1 5 4 1 2 1 3
5 1 5 5 1 5 5 5 2 3
1 2 5 2 5 1 5 2 5 5
5 5 1 5 3 4 5 5 3 5
5 5 5 5 2 5 5 3 5 5
1 5 5 5 5 5 4 4 1 5
5 2 5 5 1 5 5 5 5 3
5 3 5 1 4 5 5 5 2 2
5 4 5 2 5 1 4 1 5 3
2 1 1 5 5 2 5 5 5 5
5 5 2 5 5 2 2 5 5 1
5 5 5 5 4 4 2 4 3 3
5 1 5 3 5 5 3 3 5 5
5 4 4 5 5 5 5 5 5 4
```

Data Set 9

```
3 1 3 5 1 1 1 4 1 2
1 1 1 1 1 1 2 1 5 1
1 3 1 4 5 2 5 1 4 4
1 5 1 1 2 1 1 2 3 1
1 2 1 1 5 1 4 1 2 1
4 1 1 1 1 1 3 3 1 1
1 2 2 1 2 1 1 1 1 1
1 5 1 1 1 1 4 1 1 3
5 3 5 1 1 3 1 3 5 1
1 1 1 1 1 1 1 1 1 1
1 1 2 1 5 1 1 3 1 4
5 2 5 1 1 4 1 1 1 4
1 1 2 1 1 2 3 2 2 1
1 5 1 4 1 2 1 3 5 1
1 3 3 1 1 1 2 2 1 2
1 1 1 1 1 1 5 1 1 1
4 1 1 1 3 5 3 5 2 4
2 3 5 1 1 1 1 1 1 1
1 1 5 1 1 2 1 5 1 1
3 1 4 5 2 5 1 1 4 1
2 2 3 2 2 2 5 2 3 2
2 2 2 5 2 4 1 2 1 3
5 1 5 2 2 2 2 2 2 2
2 2 2 2 2 2 2 2 2 2
2 5 2 2 2 2 4 2 4 1
5 3 5 2 4 2 3 5 2 2
1 2 2 2 1 2 2 5 2 2
1 2 5 2 2 3 1 4 5 2
5 2 2 4 2 2 2 3 2 2
2 5 2 2 1 2 2 2 2 2
5 2 4 1 2 1 3 5 1 5
2 2 2 2 2 1 2 2 2 2
```

```
2 2 2 2 2 2 2 2 5 2
2 2 2 4 2 4 1 4 2 2
3 2 4 2 4 5 3 1 2 2
2 1 2 2 5 2 2 1 2 4
5 2 2 2 2 2 2 2 2 2
2 3 2 2 3 5 1 5 2 2
2 3 3 3 5 2 2 2 1 3
5 1 5 2 4 5 2 1 2 2
3 3 5 1 1 4 3 3 3 3
3 3 3 3 1 3 3 2 3 4
3 5 3 5 3 4 3 3 3 3
3 2 3 3 3 3 1 5 4 3
4 2 3 4 3 3 3 3 3 3
3 3 5 3 5 2 4 3 3 2
2 3 3 1 3 4 2 3 3 3
3 1 5 3 1 1 3 3 2 3
3 1 3 3 3 1 3 4 1 3
3 2 2 3 5 5 4 5 3 4
1 3 3 3 3 3 2 3 3 1
3 4 1 4 3 5 3 3 1 3
3 3 1 3 3 5 3 3 1 3
4 5 2 5 3 3 4 3 3 3
3 3 3 3 5 1 5 3 3 3
3 3 3 3 3 3 1 3 5 5
1 5 2 4 5 3 1 3 3 3
3 5 1 1 4 3 4 3 4 2
3 3 3 2 3 4 3 5 3 5
3 4 3 3 3 3 3 3 3 2
4 4 5 4 4 4 2 4 4 4
3 4 4 4 4 4 1 4 4 5
4 4 1 4 2 4 4 4 4 4
4 1 4 4 2 3 4 4 3 1
2 5 4 4 4 3 4 4 4 4
1 4 4 4 1 3 4 2 4 4
2 2 4 2 4 4 4 4 4 4
4 4 1 3 4 4 3 4 2 4
4 1 4 4 1 4 4 5 4 5
1 4 4 4 1 4 4 5 4 4
1 4 4 5 2 5 3 4 4 4
4 4 4 4 4 3 1 2 5 4
4 4 3 3 3 4 4 3 1 4
5 2 3 4 4 2 4 5 4 1
4 4 4 4 5 1 1 4 4 4
3 4 2 4 4 4 4 4 4 5
4 5 3 4 4 4 4 3 4 3
4 3 4 4 1 4 4 5 4 4
4 4 4 3 4 4 4 4 4 1
4 4 5 4 4 1 4 2 5 2
5 2 1 5 4 2 3 5 5 3
1 2 5 5 5 5 3 5 4 5
5 5 5 5 5 1 3 4 2 5
5 2 2 5 2 5 5 5 5 5
5 5 5 5 5 3 5 5 3 5
2 5 5 1 5 4 1 4 5 5
```

```
5 5 3 4 1 5 5 5 5 5
5 1 5 4 5 2 5 3 5 4
5 4 5 3 5 5 2 5 2 5
5 5 5 3 3 3 5 5 3 1
5 5 2 3 5 5 4 1 5 5
1 5 5 5 5 5 1 1 4 5
4 3 4 2 5 4 4 5 5 1
5 5 5 3 4 5 5 5 3 5
3 5 3 5 5 1 5 5 5 5
5 4 2 4 5 5 3 5 5 5
5 5 3 4 5 3 2 1 5 5
5 5 5 3 5 5 5 3 5 5
2 5 5 1 5 5 5 1 3 5
1 5 2 4 5 5 1 5 5 2
```

Data Set 10

```
3 1 3 5 1 1 1 1 1 1
1 1 1 5 1 1 1 1 5 1
1 3 1 4 5 2 5 1 1 4
1 1 1 3 1 1 1 5 1 1
3 2 2 1 1 5 1 4 1 2
1 3 5 1 5 1 1 1 1 1
1 1 2 2 1 2 1 1 1 1
1 1 5 1 1 1 4 1 4 1
4 2 1 3 1 4 2 3 5 1
1 1 1 1 1 1 1 1 5 1
1 1 1 4 5 3 1 4 5 2
5 1 1 4 1 1 1 3 2 1
1 5 1 1 1 1 1 2 1 1
5 1 4 1 2 1 3 5 1 5
1 1 1 1 1 1 1 1 1 2
1 2 1 1 1 1 1 1 5 1
1 1 1 4 1 4 1 4 2 1
2 2 3 1 3 5 1 1 1 1
1 1 1 1 1 5 1 1 1 1
4 5 2 5 4 5 2 5 1 1
4 2 2 2 3 2 2 2 5 2
2 1 2 2 5 2 2 5 2 4
1 2 1 3 5 1 5 2 2 2
2 2 1 2 2 2 2 2 4 2
2 2 2 2 2 2 5 2 2 2
2 4 2 4 1 4 2 2 2 2
2 2 4 5 3 1 2 2 2 1
2 2 5 2 2 1 2 4 5 2
5 3 2 2 2 2 3 2 2 3
5 1 5 2 2 2 3 3 3 2
2 3 1 2 5 5 1 5 2 4
5 2 1 2 2 2 2 5 1 1
4 2 4 3 4 5 2 2 2 2
2 4 2 5 2 5 3 4 2 2
2 3 2 3 2 2 2 2 5 4
2 4 2 2 4 2 3 2 2 2
2 2 1 2 2 5 2 2 1 2
```

```
2 3 2 2 2 2 1 2 4 2
3 2 2 3 1 2 5 2 2 2
3 2 2 2 1 2 2 2 1 3
4 1 3 3 2 2 3 2 3 3
3 3 3 3 3 5 3 3 3 3
3 3 2 3 3 1 3 4 1 4
3 5 3 5 3 4 3 1 3 3
5 3 3 1 3 4 5 2 5 3
3 4 3 4 3 3 3 3 5 5
3 5 3 3 3 3 3 3 3 3
3 1 3 5 2 3 3 3 4 4
5 3 1 3 3 3 3 5 1 1
4 3 4 3 4 2 3 4 4 3
3 1 5 3 5 3 4 3 3 3
3 3 3 3 2 3 3 1 3 3
5 3 3 3 3 4 3 3 3 3
3 3 3 1 3 3 5 3 3 1
3 2 5 2 5 1 3 3 4 2
3 3 3 3 1 2 5 3 3 3
3 3 4 3 3 3 3 3 1 3
4 2 3 3 2 2 3 2 3 3
3 3 3 3 5 3 3 3 3 4
3 3 3 2 3 3 1 3 4 1
4 4 5 4 5 3 4 1 4 3
4 4 4 4 1 4 4 5 2 5
3 4 4 4 4 4 3 4 4 1
4 4 5 3 4 4 3 3 3 4
4 3 1 4 5 2 3 4 4 4
1 2 5 2 4 4 4 5 1 1
4 4 4 3 4 2 4 4 4 4
4 4 4 4 4 2 5 4 4 4
4 4 3 4 3 4 3 4 4 1
4 4 5 4 4 4 4 3 3 4
4 4 4 4 1 4 4 5 4 4
1 4 2 5 2 5 1 4 2 4
4 4 3 4 4 3 1 2 5 4
4 4 3 4 4 4 4 4 3 2
4 4 4 4 4 4 4 2 2 4
2 4 4 4 4 4 4 5 4 4
4 4 4 5 4 2 4 4 1 4
4 1 4 4 5 4 5 3 4 1
4 3 4 4 3 3 4 4 5 2
5 3 4 4 4 4 4 3 4 4
2 5 5 5 5 4 1 5 3 3
5 5 3 1 5 5 2 3 5 5
4 1 2 5 2 5 5 1 5 1
1 4 5 4 3 4 2 5 4 4
5 5 5 5 5 5 2 5 5 1
3 5 5 3 5 3 5 3 5 5
1 5 5 5 5 5 4 5 5 5
5 3 3 4 5 3 2 1 5 5
5 5 5 3 5 5 5 5 1 5
5 5 4 2 5 5 5 5 5 1
5 5 5 1 3 5 1 5 2 4
```

```
5 5 1 5 5 1 2 5 5 1
5 5 5 5 4 4 2 3 2 3
5 5 5 5 5 5 5 5 5 1
5 5 2 5 4 5 5 5 5 3
4 5 5 5 3 5 3 5 2 5
5 1 5 5 5 5 5 4 5 5
5 5 3 5 2 4 2 5 3 3
5 5 2 5 5 1 5 5 5 1
3 1 2 5 2 5 1 5 2 5
```

REFERENCES

Abelson, J. L., & Curtis, G. C. (1989). Cardiac and neuroendocrine responses to exposure therapy in height phobics: Desynchrony within the "physiological response system." *Behaviour Research and Therapy, 27*, 561–567.

Abler, R. M., & Sedlacek, W. E. (1986). *Nonreactive measures in student affairs research* (Research Rep. 5–86). College Park: University of Maryland.

Adams, K. M., & Heaton, R. K. (1987). Computerized neuropsychological assessment: Issues and applications. In J. N. Butcher (Ed.), *Computerized psychological assessment* (pp. 355–365). New York: Basic Books.

Aiken, L. R. (1989). *Assessment of personality.* Boston: Allyn & Bacon.

Aiken, L. S., West, S. G., Sechrest, L., Reno, R. R., Rodiger, H. L., III, Scarr, S., Kazdin, A E., & Sherman, S. J. (1990). Graduate training in statistics, methodology, and measurement in psychology: A survey of PhD programs in North America. *American Psychologist, 45,* 721–734.

Alexander, A. F. O'D. (1962). *The planet Saturn.* New York: Dover.

Alker, H. A. (1978). MMPI. In O. K Buros (Ed.), *Eighth mental measurements yearbook.* Highland Park, NJ: Gryphon Press.

Allport, G. W. (1921). Personality and character. *Psychological Bulletin, 18,* 441–455.

Allport, G. W. (1937). *Personality.* New York: Henry Holt.

Allport, G. W. (1942). *The use of personal documents in psychological science* (Bull. No. 49). New York: Social Science Research Council.

American Psychiatric Association (1987). *Diagnostic and Statistical Manual of Mental Disorders* (3rd rev. ed.). Washington, DC: Author.

American Psychological Association. (1954). Technical recommendations for psychological tests and diagnostic techniques [Supplement]. *Psychological Bulletin, 51* (2, Pt. 2).

American Psychological Association. (1966). *Standards for educational and psychological tests and manuals.* Washington, DC: Author.

American Psychological Association. (1974). *Standards for educational and psychological tests.* Washington, DC: Author.

American Psychological Association. (1985). *Standards for educational and psychological tests.* Washington, DC: Author.

American Psychological Association. (1992). Call for book proposals for test instruments. *APA Monitor, 23,* 15.

Anastasi, A. (1985). Some emerging trends in psychological measurement: A fifty-year perspective. *Applied Psychological Measurement, 9,* 121–138.

Anastasi, A. (1986). Evolving concepts of test validation. *Annual Review of Psychology, 37,* 1–15.

Anastasi, A. (1992). A century of psychological science. *American Psychologist, 47,* 842.

Anderson, R. V. (1987). Computerization of a chemical dependency assessment. *Minnesota Medicine, 70,* 697–699.

Andreassi, J. L. (1980). *Psychophysiology.* New York: Oxford University Press.

Angleitner, A., & Demtroder, A. I. (1988). Acts and dispositions: A reconsideration of the act frequency approach. *European Journal of Personality, 2,* 121–141.

Angleitner, A., John, O. P., & Lohr, F. (1986). It's what you ask and how you ask it: An itemmetric analysis of personality questionnaires. In A. Angleitner & J. S. Wiggins (Eds.), *Personality assessment via questionnaires* (pp. 61–108). New York: Springer-Verlag.

Anisman, H., & Zacharko, R. M. (1992). Depression as a consequence of inadequate neuro-chemical adaptation in response to stressors. *British Journal of Psychiatry, 160,* 36–43.

Arisohn, B., Bruch, M. A., & Heimberg, R. G. (1988). Influence of assessment methods of self-efficacy and outcome expectancy ratings of assertive behavior. *Journal of Counseling Psychology, 35,* 336–341.

Asher, J. J., & Sciarrino, J. A. (1974). Realistic work sample tests: A review. *Personnel Psychology, 27,* 519–553.

Austin, J. T., & Hanisch, K. A. (1990). Occupational attainment as a function of abilities and interests: A longitudinal analysis using Project TALENT data. *Journal of Applied Psychology, 75,* 77–84.

Babor, T. F., Brown, J., & Del Boca, F. K. (1990). Validity of self-reports in applied research on addictive behaviors: Fact or fiction? *Behavioral Assessment, 12,* 5–31.

Babor, T. F., Stephens, R. S., & Marlatt, G. A. (1987). Verbal report methods in clinical research on alcoholism: Response bias and its minimization. *Journal of Studies on Alcohol, 48,* 410–424.

Baerends, G. P. (1972). A model of the functional organization of incubation behavior. In G. P. Bearends & R. H. Drent (Eds.), *The herring gull and its egg. Behaviour Supplement, 17,* 261–310.

Bagby, R. M., Atkinson, L., Dickens, S., & Gavin, D. (1990). Dimensional analysis of the Attributional Style Questionnaire: Attributions of outcomes and events. *Canadian Journal of Behavioural Science, 22,* 140–150.

Bailey, J. M., & Bhagat, R. S. (1987). Meaning and measurement of stressors in the work environment: An evaluation. In S. V. Kasl & C. L. Cooper (Eds.), *Stress and health: Issues in research methodology* (pp. 207–230). New York: Wiley.

Baker, T. B., & Brandon, T. H. (1990). Validity of selfreports in basic research. *Behavioral Assessment, 12,* 33–51.

Bales, J. (1990). Validity of assessment debated in courtrooms. *APA Monitor, 21,* 7.

Bandler, R., & Grinder, J. (1975). *The structure of magic I.* Palo Alto, CA: Science and Behavior Books.

Bandura, A. (1977). Self-efficacy: Toward a unifying theory of behavioral change. *Psychological Review, 84*, 191–215.

Bandura, A. (1986). *Social foundations of thought and action: A social cognitive theory.* Englewood Cliffs, NJ: Prentice-Hall.

Bandura, A. (1991). Human agency: The rhetoric and the reality. *American Psychologist, 46*, 157–162.

Barlow, D. H. (1977). *Behavioral assessment in clinical settings: Developing issues.* In J. D. Cone & R. P. Hawkins (Eds.), *Behavioral assessment* (pp. 283–307). New York: Brunner/Mazel.

Barlow, D. H. (1981). On the relation of clinical research to clinical practice: Current issues, new directions. *Journal of Consulting and Clinical Psychology, 49*, 147–155.

Barlow, D. H., Hayes, S. C., & Nelson, R. O. (1984). *The scientist practitioner.* New York: Pergamon.

Barlow, D. H., & Hersen, M. (1984). *Single case experimental designs* (2nd ed.). New York: Pergamon.

Barlow, D. H., Mavissakalian, M. R., & Schofield, L. D. (1980). Patterns of desynchrony in agoraphobia: A preliminary report. *Behaviour Research and Therapy, 18*, 441–448.

Barrett, T. C., & Tinsley, H. E. A. (1977). Measuring vocational self-concept crystallization. *Journal of Vocational Behavior, 11*, 305–311.

Beaber, R. J., Marston, A., Michelli, J., & Mills, M. J. (1985). A brief test for measuring malingering in schizophrenic individuals. *American Journal of Psychiatry, 142*, 1478–1481.

Beail, N. (Ed.). (1985). *Repertory grid technique and personal constructs.* London: Croom Helm.

Beatty, J., & Wagoner, B. L. (1978). Pupillometric signs of brain activation vary with level of cognitive processing. *Science, 199*, 1216–1218.

Bellack, A. S., & Hersen, M. (1988). Future directions of behavioral assessment. In A. S. Bellack & M. Hersen (Eds.), *Behavioral assessment* (3rd ed., pp. 610–615). New York: Pergamon.

Bem, D. J., & Allen, A. (1974). On predicting some of the people some of the time: The search for crosssituational consistencies in behavior. *Psychological Review, 81*, 506–520.

Benjamin, L. S. (1988). *SASB short form user's manual.* Madison, WI: INTREX Interpersonal Institute.

Bennett, T. (1988). Use of the Halstead-Reitan Neuropsychological Test Battery in the assessment of head injury. *Cognitive Rehabilitation, 6*, 18–25.

Ben-Porath, Y. S., & Waller, N. G. (1992). Five big issues in clinical personality assessment. *Psychological Assessment, 4*, 23–25.

Berg, I. A. (1955). Response bias and personality: The deviation hypothesis. *Journal of Psychology, 40*, 61–72.

Bergin, A. E., & Lambert, M. J. (1978). The evaluation of therapeutic outcome. In S. L. Garfield & A. E. Bergin (Eds.), *Handbook of psychotherapy and behavior change: An empirical analysis* (2nd ed., pp. 139–190). New York: Wiley.

Berk, L. A., & Fekken, G. C. (1990). Person reliability evaluated in the context of vocational interest assessment. *Journal of Vocational Behavior, 37*, 7–16.

Bernreuter, R. G. (1933). Validity of the personality inventory. *Personality Journal, 11*, 383–386.

Berry, D. T. R., Wetter, M. W., Baer, R. A., Larsen, L., Clark, C., & Monroe, K. (1992). MMPI-2 random responding indices: Validation using a self-report methodology. *Psychological Assessment, 4*, 340–345.

Biemer, P. P., Groves, R. M., Lyberg, L. E., Mathiowetz, N. A., & Sudman, S. (1991). *Measurement errors in surveys.* New York: Wiley.

Block, J. (1965). *The challenge of response sets.* New York: Appleton-Century-Crofts.

Block, J. (1977). Advancing the psychology of personality: Paradigmatic shift or improving the quality of research. In D. Magnusson & N. S. Endler (Eds.), *Personality at the crossroads: Current issues in interactional psychology* (pp. 37–64). Hillsdale, NJ: Erlbaum.

Block, J. (1989). Critique of the act frequency approach to personality. *Journal of Personality and Social Psychology, 56*, 234–245.

Bloom, B. S., Hastings, J. T., & Madaus, G. F. (1971). *Handbook on formative and summative evaluation of student learning.* New York: McGraw-Hill.

Blumenthal, T. D., & Cooper, J. A. (1990). Using the Macintosh computer in psychophysiological research: Programs for stimulus presentation, data collection, and response quantification. *Behavior Research Methods, Instruments, & Computers, 22,* 99–104.

Boice, R. (1983). Observational skills. *Psychological Bulletin, 93,* 3–29.

Boorstin, D. J. (1983). *The discoverers.* New York: Random House.

Borgen, F. H., & Seling, M. J. (1978). Expressed and inventoried interests revisited: Perspicacity in the person. *Journal of Counseling Psychology, 25,* 536–543.

Boring, E. G. (1919). Mathematical vs. scientific significance. *Psychological Bulletin, 16,* 335–338.

Boring, E. G. (1920). The logic of the normal law of error in mental measurement. *American Journal of Psychology, 31,* 1–33.

Boring, E. G. (1942). *Sensation and perception in the history of experimental psychology.* New York: Appleton-Century-Crofts.

Boring, E. G. (1950). *A history of experimental psychology.* New York: Appleton-Century-Crofts.

Boring, E. G. (1957). *A history of experimental psychology* (2nd ed.). New York: Appleton-Century-Crofts.

Botvin, E. M., Botvin, G. J., Renick, N. L., Filazzola, A. D., & Allegante, J. D. (1984). Adolescents' self-reports of tobacco, alcohol, and marijuana use: Examining the comparability of video tape, cartoon and verbal bogus-pipeline procedures. *Psychological Reports, 55,* 379–386.

Botwin, M. D. (1991). *Social desirability in act frequency data.* Paper presented at the 99th annual convention of the American Psychological Association, San Francisco.

Botwin, M. D., & Buss, D. M. (1989). Structure of act-report data: Is the five-factor model of personality recaptured? *Journal of Personality and Social Psychology, 56,* 988–1001.

Bower, G. H. (1981). Mood and memory. *American Psychologist, 36,* 129–148.

Bower, G. H., Monteiro, K. P., & Gilligan, S. G. (1978). Emotional mood as a context for learning and recall. *Journal of Verbal Learning and Verbal Behavior, 17,* 573–585.

Bowers, K. S. (1973). Situationism in psychology: An analysis and a critique. *Psychological Review, 80,* 307–336.

Brackwede, D. (1980). The bogus pipeline paradigm: A survey of experimental results to date. *Zeitschrift für Sozialpsychologie, 11,* 50–59. (From *PsycLit* abstract)

Bray, D. W., & Grant, D. L. (1966). The assessment center in the measurement of potential for business management. *Psychological Monographs, 80* (17, Whole No. 625).

Brebner, M. T., & Welford, A. T. (1980). Introduction: An historical background sketch. In A. T. Welford (Ed.), *Reaction times* (pp. 1–24). London: Academic Press.

Brennan, R. L. (1983). *Elements of generalizability theory.* Iowa City, IA: ACT Publications.

Bridge, R. G., Reeder, L. G., Kanouse, D., Kinder, D. R., Nagy, J. T., & Judd, C. M. (1977). Interviewing changes attitudes sometimes. *Public Opinion Quarterly, 41,* 56–64.

Brody, G. H., & Forehand, R. (1986). Maternal perceptions of child maladjustment as a function of the combined influence of child behavior and maternal depression. *Journal of Consulting and Clinical Psychology, 54,* 237–240.

Bulkley, J. A. (1992). The prosecution's use of social science expert testimony in child sexual abuse cases: National trends and recommendations. *Journal of Child Sexual Abuse, 1,* 73–93.

Burisch, M. (1984). Approaches to personality inventory construction. *American Psychologist, 39,* 214–227.

Burke, J. (1978). *Connections.* Boston: Little, Brown.

Burke, P. A., Kraut, R. E., & Dworkin, R. H. (1984). Traits, consistency, and self-schemata: What do our methods measure? *Journal of Personality and Social Psychology, 47,* 568–579.

Buros, O. K. (Ed.) (1970). *Personality tests and reviews: I.* Highland Park, NJ: Gryphon Press.

Buss, D. M., & Craik, K. H. (1983). The act frequency approach to personality. *Personality Review, 90,* 105–126.

Buss, D. M., & Craik, K. H. (1985). Why not measure that trait? Alternative criteria for identifying important dispositions. *Journal of Personality and Social Psychology, 48,* 934–946.

Butcher, J. N. (1987a). *Computerized psychological assessment.* New York: Basic Books.

Butcher, J. N. (1987b). Computerized clinical and personality assessment using the MMPI. In J. N. Butcher (Ed.), *Computerized psychological assessment* (pp. 161–197). New York: Basic Books.

Butcher, J. N. (1990). *MMPI-2 in psychological treatment.* New York: Oxford University Press.

Butterfield, E. C., Nielson, D., Tangen, K. L., & Richardson, M. B. (1985). Theoretically based psychometric measures of inductive reasoning. In S. E. Embretson (Ed.)., *Test design: Developments in psychology and psychometrics* (pp. 77–148). New York: Academic Press.

Cacioppo, J. T., & Tassinary, L. G. (1990). Inferring psychological significance from physiological signals. *American Psychologist, 45,* 16–28.

Calvert, E. J., & Waterfall, R. C. (1982). A comparison of conventional and automated administration of Raven's Standard Progressive Matrices. *International Journal of Man-Machine Studies, 17,* 305–310.

Campbell, D. P. (1971). *Handbook for the strong vocational interest blank.* Stanford, CA: Stanford University Press.

Campbell, D. T. (1950). The indirect assessment of social attitudes. *Psychological Bulletin, 47,* 15–38.

Campbell, D. T., & Fiske, D. W. (1959). Convergent and discriminant validity by the multitrait-multimethod matrix. *Psychological Bulletin, 56,* 81–105.

Canfield, M. L., Walker, W. R., & Brown, L. G. (1991). Contingency interaction analysis in psychotherapy. *Journal of Consulting and Clinical Psychology, 59,* 58–66.

Carbonell, J. L., Moorhead, K. M., & Megargee, E. I. (1984). Predicting prison adjustment with structured personality inventories. *Journal of Consulting and Clinical Psychology, 52,* 280–294.

Carroll, J. B. (1992). Cognitive abilities: The state of the art. *Psychological Science, 3,* 266–270.

Carroll, J. S., Wiener, R. L., Coates, D., Galegher, J., & Alibrio, J. J. (1982). Evaluation, diagnosis, and prediction in parole decision making. *Law and Society Review, 17,* 199–228.

Cattell, R. B. (1946a). *Description and measurement of personality.* New York: World Book.

Cattell, R. B. (1946b). Confirmation and clarification of primary personality factors. *Psychometrika, 12,* 197–220.

Cattell, R. B. (1957). *Personality and motivation structure and measurement.* Yonkers-on-Hudson, NY: World Book.

Cattell, R. B. (1973). *Personality and mood by questionnaire.* San Francisco: Jossey-Bass.

Cattell, R. B., & Scheier, I. H. (1961). *The meaning and measurement of neuroticism.* New York: Ronald Press.

Ceci, S. J. (1991). How much does schooling influence intellectual development and its cognitive components?: A reassessment of the evidence. *Developmental Psychology, 27,* 703–722.

Chaplin, W. F., & Goldberg, L. R. (1984). A failure to replicate the Bem and Allen study of individual differences in cross-situational consistency. *Journal of Personality and Social Psychology, 47,* 1074–1090.

Cheek, J. M. (1982). Aggregation, moderator variables, and the validity of personality tests: A peer-rating study. *Journal of Personality and Social Psychology, 43,* 1254–1269.

Christensen, A., Margolin, G., & Sullaway, M. (1992). Interparental agreement on child behavior problems. *Psychological Assessment, 4,* 419–425.

Clark, D. A. (1988). The validity of measures of cognition: A review of the literature. *Cognitive Therapy and Research, 12,* 1–20.

Clark, D. M., & Teasdale, J. D. (1982). Diurnal variation in clinical depression and accessibility of memories of positive and negative experiences. *Journal of Abnormal Psychology, 91,* 87–95.

Cliff, N. (1992). Abstract measurement theory and the revolution that never happened. *Psycho-*

logical Science, 3, 186–190.

Cohen, F. (1987). Measurement of coping. In S. V. Kasl & C. L. Cooper (Eds.), *Stress and health: Issues in research methodology* (pp. 283–306). New York: Wiley.

Cohen, F. (1991). Measurement of coping. In A. Monat & R. S. Lazarus (Eds.), *Stress and coping: An anthology* (pp. 228–244). New York: Columbia University Press.

Cohen, S., & Edwards, J. R. (1989). Personality characteristics as moderators of the relationship between stress and disorder. In R. W. J. Neufeld (Ed.), *Advances in the investigation of psychological stress* (pp. 235–283). New York: Wiley.

Collins, L. M. (1991). Measurement in longitudinal research. In L. M. Collins & J. L. Horn (Eds.), *Best methods for the analysis of change* (pp. 137–148). Washington, DC: American Psychological Association.

Collins, L. M., & Cliff, N. (1990). Using the longitudinal Guttman simplex as a basis for measuring growth. *Psychological Bulletin, 108*, 128–134.

Cone, J. D. (1988). Psychometric considerations and the multiple models of behavioral assessment. In A. S. Bellack & M. Hersen (Eds.), *Behavioral assessment: A practical handbook* (3rd ed., pp. 42–66). Elmsford, NY: Pergamon.

Cone, J. D. (1991). Foreword. In W. W. Tryon. *Activity measurement in psychology and medicine*. New York: Plenum Press.

Cone, J. D., & Foster, S. L. (1991). Training in measurement: Always the bridesmaid. *American Psychologist, 46*, 653–654.

Connell, J. P., & Thompson, R. (1986). Emotion and social interaction in the strange situation: Consistencies and asymmetric influences in the second year. *Child Development, 57*, 733–745.

Contrada, R. J., & Krantz, D. S. (1987). Measurement bias in health psychology research designs. In S. V. Kasl & C. L. Cooper (Eds.), *Stress and health: Issues in research methodology* (pp. 57–78). New York: Wiley.

Conyne, R. K., & Clack, R. J. (1981). *Environmental assessment and design*. New York: Praeger.

Cook, T., & Campbell, D. (1979). *Quasi-experimentation*. Chicago: Rand McNally.

Coombs, C. H. (1964). *A theory of data*. New York: Wiley.

Coombs, C. H., Dawes, R. M., & Tversky, A. (1970). *Mathematical psychology*. Englewood Cliffs, NJ: Prentice-Hall.

Cooper, W. H. (1981). Ubiquitous halo. *American Psychologist, 90*, 218–244.

Craske, M. G., & Barlow, D. H. (1988). A review of the relationship between panic and avoidance. *Clinical Psychology Review, 8*, 667–685.

Craske, M. G., & Craig, K. D. (1984). Musical performance anxiety: The three-systems model and self-efficacy theory. *Behaviour Research and Therapy, 22*, 267–280.

Craske, M. G., Sanderson, W. C., & Barlow, D. H. (1987). How do desynchronous response systems relate to the treatment of agoraphobia: A follow-up evaluation. *Behaviour Research and Therapy, 25*, 117–122.

Crocker, J. (1981). Judgment of covariation by social perceivers. *Psychological Bulletin, 90*, 272–292.

Crocker, L., & Algina, J. (1986). *Introduction to classical and modern test theory*. New York: Holt, Rinehart & Winston.

Cronbach, L. J. (1946). Response sets and test validity. *Educational and Psychological Measurement, 6*, 475–494.

Cronbach, L. J. (1949). *Essentials of psychological testing*. New York: Harper.

Cronbach, L. J. (1950). Further evidence on response sets and test design. *Educational and Psychological Measurement, 10*, 3–31.

Cronbach, L. J. (1957). The two disciplines of scientific psychology. *American Psychologist, 12*, 671–684.

Cronbach, L. J. (1969). Validation of educational measures. In P. H. DuBois (Ed.), *Proceedings of the Invitational Conference on Testing Problems* (pp. 35–52). Princeton, NJ: Educational Testing Service.

Cronbach, L. J. (1970). *Essentials of psychological testing* (3rd ed.). New York: Harper & Row.

Cronbach, L. J. (1975). Beyond the two disciplines of scientific psychology. *American Psychologist, 30,* 116–127.

Cronbach, L. J. (1984). *Essentials of psychological testing* (4th ed.). New York: Harper & Row.

Cronbach, L. J. (1989). Construct validation after thirty years. In R. L. Linn (Ed.), *Intelligence: Measurement, theory and public policy* (pp. 147–171). Urbana: University of Illinois Press.

Cronbach, L. J. (1991a). Emerging views on methodology. In T. D. Wachs & R. Plomin (Eds.), *Conceptualization and measurement of organism-environment interaction* (pp. 87–104). Washington, DC: American Psychological Association.

Cronbach, L. J. (1991b). Methodological studies—a personal retrospective. In R. E. Snow & D. E. Wiley (Eds.), *Improving inquiry in social science* (pp. 385–400). Hillsdale, NJ: Erlbaum.

Cronbach, L. J. (1992, August). Validation concepts and strategies. In W. J. Camara (Chair), *One hundred years of psychological testing.* Symposium conducted at the convention of the American Psychological Association, Washington, DC.

Cronbach, L. J., & Gleser, G. C. (1965). *Psychological tests and personnel decisions* (2nd ed.). Urbana: University of Illinois Press.

Cronbach, L. J., Gleser, G. C., Nanda, H., & Rajaratnam, N. (1972). *The dependability of behavioral measurements: Theory of generalizability for scores and profiles.* New York: Wiley.

Cronbach, L. J., & Meehl, P. E. (1955). Construct validity in psychological tests. *Psychological Bulletin, 52,* 281–302.

Cronbach, L. J., & Snow, R. E. (1977). *Aptitudes and instructional methods.* New York: Wiley.

Cross, K. P., & Angelo, T. A. (1988). *Classroom assessment techniques.* Ann Arbor, MI: National Center for Research to Improve Postsecondary Teaching and Learning.

Crowne, D., & Marlowe, D. (1964). *The approval motive.* New York: Wiley.

Cutrona, C. E., Russell, D., & Jones, R. (1984). Cross-situational consistency in causal attributions: Does attributional style exist? *Journal of Personality and Social Psychology, 47,* 1043–1058.

Dahlström, W. G. (1969). Recurrent issues in the development of the MMPI. In J. Butcher (Ed.), *MMPI: Research developments and clinical applications* (pp. 1–40). New York: McGraw Hill.

Dahlström, W. G. (1985). The development of psychological testing. In G. A. Kimble & K. Schlesinger (Eds.), *Topics in the history of psychology* (Vol. 2, pp. 63–113). Hillsdale, NJ: Erlbaum.

Dahlström, W. G. (1993). Tests: Small samples, large consequences. *American Psychologist, 48,* 393–399.

Dana, R. H. (1993). *Multicultural assessment perspectives for professional psychology.* Boston: Allyn & Bacon.

Danziger, K. (1990). *Constructing the subject.* Cambridge, England: Cambridge University Press.

Dar, R. (1987). Another look at Meehl, Lakatos, and the scientific practices of psychologists. *American Psychologist, 42,* 145–151.

Darley, J., & Fazio, R. (1980). Expectancy confirmation processes arising in the social interaction sequence. *American Psychologist, 35,* 867–881.

Davis, C., & Cowles, M. (1989). Automated psychological testing: Methods of administration, need for approval, and measures of anxiety. *Educational and Psychological Measurement, 49,* 311–320.

Davison, M. L., Damarin, F., & Drasgow, F. (1986). Psychometrics and graduate education. *American Psychologist, 41,* 584–586.

Dawes, R. M., Faust, D., & Meehl, P. E. (1989). Clinical versus actuarial judgment. *Science, 243,* 1668–1674.

Dawis, R. V. (1987). Scale construction. *Journal of Counseling Psychology, 34,* 481–489.

Dawis, R. V. (1992). The individual differences tradition in counseling psychology. *Journal of Counseling Psychology, 39,* 7–19.

Dawis, R. V., & Lofquist, L. H. (1984). *A psychological theory of work adjustment: An individual-*

differences model and its application. Minneapolis: University of Minnesota Press.

Day, H. D., Marshall, D., Hamilton, B., & Christy, J. (1983). Some cautionary notes regarding the use of aggregated scores as a measure of behavioral stability. *Journal of Research in Personality, 17,* 97–109.

DeAngelis, T. (1992). Illness linked with repressive style of coping. *APA Monitor, 23,* 14–15.

Dickinson, T. L., & Baker, T. A. (1989, August). *Training to improve rating accuracy: A meta-analysis.* Paper presented at the annual convention of the American Psychological Association, New Orleans.

Diener, E., & Larsen, R. J. (1984). Temporal stability and cross-situational consistency of affective, behavioral, and cognitive responses. *Journal of Personality and Social Psychology, 47,* 871–883.

Digman, J. M. (1990). Personality structure: Emergence of the five-factor model. In M. R. Rosenzweig & L. W. Porter (Eds.), *Annual review of psychology* (Vol. 41, (pp. 417–440). Palo Alto, CA: Annual Reviews.

Dohrenwend, B. S., Shrout, P. E., Egri, G., & Mendelsohn, F. S. (1980). Nonspecific psychological distress and other dimensions of psychopathology. *Archives of General Psychiatry, 37,* 1229–1236.

Doleys, D. M., Meredith, R. L., Poire, R., Campbell, L. M., & Cook, M. (1977). Preliminary examination of assessment of assertive behavior in retarded persons. *Psychological Reports, 41,* 855–859.

Domino, G. (1971). Interactive effects of achievement orientation and teaching style on academic achievement. *Journal of Educational Psychology, 62,* 427–431.

Dominowski, R. L. (1989). Comment: Method, theory, and drawing inferences. *American Psychologist, 44,* 1078.

DuBois, P. H. (1970). *A history of psychological testing.* Boston: Allyn & Bacon.

Duff, F. L. (1965). Item subtlety in personality inventory scales. *Journal of Consulting Psychology, 29,* 565–570.

Easterbrook, J. A. (1959). The effect of emotion on cue utilization and the organization of behavior. *Psychological Review, 3,* 183–201.

Eastman, C., & Marzillier, J. (1984). Theoretical and methodological difficulties in Bandura's self-efficacy theory. *Cognitive Therapy and Research, 8,* 213–229.

Edwards, A. (1953). The relationship between the judged desirability of a trait and the probability that the trait will be endorsed. *Journal of Consulting Psychology, 24,* 90–93.

Edwards, A. (1970). *The measurement of personality traits by scales and inventories.* New York: Holt, Rinehart & Winston.

Egan, G. (1990). *The skilled helper* (4th ed). Pacific Grove, CA: Brooks/Cole.

Eifert, G. H., & Wilson, P. H. (1991). The triple response approach to assessment: A conceptual and methodological reappraisal. *Behaviour Research and Therapy, 29,* 283–292.

Elliott, R., Hill, C. E., Stiles, W. B., Friedlander, M. L., Mahrer, A. R., & Margison, F. R. (1987). Primary therapist response modes: Comparison of six rating systems. *Journal of Consulting and Clinical Psychology, 55,* 218–223.

Ellis, B. (1966). *Basic concepts of measurement.* Cambridge, England: Cambridge University Press.

Ellis, B. (1967). Measurement. In P. Edwards (Ed.), *The encyclopedia of philosophy* (Vol. 5, pp. 241–250). New York: Macmillan.

Ellis, H. C., & Ashbrook, P. W. (1979). The "state" of mood and memory research: A selective review. *Journal of Social Behavior and Personality, 4,* 1–21.

Elwood, D. L. (1972a). Test retest reliability and cost analyses of automated and face to face intelligence testing. *International Journal of Man-Machine Studies, 4,* 1–22.

Elwood, D. L. (1972b). Automated WAIS testing correlated with face-to-face WAIS testing: A validity study. *International Journal of Man-Machine Studies, 4,* 129–137.

Elwood, D. L. (1972c). Automated versus face-to-face intelligence testing: Comparison of test-retest reliabilities. *International Journal of Man-Machine Studies, 4,* 363–369.

Elwood, D. L. (1972d). Validity of an automated measure of intelligence in borderline retarded subjects. *American Journal of Mental Deficiency, 77,* 90–94.

Embretson, S. E. (Ed.) (1985). *Test design: Developments in psychology and psychometrics.* New York: Academic Press.

Embretson, S. E. (1992). Computerized adaptive testing: Its potential substantive contributions to psychological research and assessment. *Current Directions in Psychological Science, 1,* 129–131.

Embretson, S. E., Schneider, L. M., & Roth, D. L. (1986). Multiple processing strategies and the construct validity of verbal reasoning tests. *Journal of Educational Measurement, 23,* 13–32.

Endicott, J., & Spitzer, R. L. (1978). A diagnostic interview: The schedule for affective disorders and schizophrenia. *Archives of General Psychiatry, 35,* 837–844.

Endicott, J., Spitzer, R. L., Fleiss, J. L., & Cohen, J. (1976). The Global Assessment Scale: A procedure for measuring overall severity of psychiatric disturbance. *Archives of General Psychiatry, 33,* 766–771.

Epstein, S. (1979). The stability of behavior: I. On predicting most of the people much of the time. *Journal of Personality and Social Psychology, 37,* 1097–1126.

Epstein, S. (1980). The stability of behavior II. Implications for psychological research. *American Psychologist, 35,* 790–806.

Epstein, S. (1981). The stability of behavior: II. Implications for psychological research: Reply to Lieberman. *American Psychologist, 36,* 6966–697.

Epstein, S. (1983). The stability of confusion: A reply to Mischel and Peake. *Psychological Review, 90,* 179–184.

Epstein, S. (1990). Comment on the effects of aggregation across and within occasions on consistency, specificity, and reliability. *Methodika, 4,* 95–100.

Erdman, H. P., Klein, M. H., & Greist, J. H. (1985). Direct patient computer interviewing. *Journal of Consulting and Clinical Psychology, 53,* 760–773.

Ericsson, K. A. (1987). Theoretical implications from protocol analysis on testing and measurement. In R. R. Ronning, J. A. Glover, J. C. Conoley, & J. C. Witt (Eds.), *The influence of cognitive psychology on testing* (pp. 191–226). Hillsdale, NJ: Erlbaum.

Ericsson, K. A., & Simon, H. A. (1984). *Protocol analysis: Verbal reports as data.* Cambridge, MA: MIT Press.

Estes, W. K. (1992). Ability testing. *Psychological Science, 3,* 278.

Evans, I. M. (1986). Response structure and the triple-response-mode concept. In R. O. Nelson & S. C. Hayes (Eds.), *Conceptual foundations of behavioral assessment* (pp. 131–155). New York: Guilford Press.

Evans, I. M., & Voeltz, L. M. (1982). *The selection of intervention priorities in educational programming for severely handicapped preschool children with multiple behavior problems* (Final Report). Behavioral Systems Intervention Project, University of Hawaii, Honolulu. (ERIC Document Reproduction Service No. ED 240 765)

Evans, I. M., Voeltz, L. M., Freedland, K., & Brennan, J. M. (1981, April). *Behavioral interrelationships in the design and evaluation of applied intervention research.* Paper presented at the biennial meeting of the Society for Research in Child Development, Boston.

Evans, I. M., & Wilson, F. E. (1983). Behavioral assessment on decision making: A theoretical analysis. In M. Rosenbaum, C. M. Franks, & Y. Jaffe (Eds.), *Perspectives on behavior therapy in the eighties* (Vol. 9, pp. 35–53). New York: Springer.

Exner, J. E., Jr. (1978). *The Rorschach: A comprehensive system* (Vol. 2). Wiley: New York.

Exner, J. E., Jr. (1986). *The Rorschach: A comprehensive system: Vol. 1. Basic foundations* (2nd ed.). New York: Wiley.

Exner, J. E., Jr. (1987). Computer assistance in Rorschach interpretation. In J. N. Butcher (Ed.), *Computerized psychological assessment* (pp. 218–235). New York: Basic Books.

Eyde, L. D., & Kowal, D. M. (1984). *Ethical and professional concerns regarding computerized test interpretation services and users.* Paper presented at the convention of the American Psychological Association, Toronto, Canada.

Eysenck, H. J. (1947). *Dimensions of personality.* London: Routledge & Kegan Paul.

Fairbanks, C. M. (1992). Labels, literacy, and enabling learning: Glenn's story. *Harvard Educational Review, 62,* 475–493.

Falmagne, J. (1992). Measurement theory and the research psychologist. *Psychological Science, 3,* 88–93.

Fancher, R. E. (1966). Explicit personality theories and accuracy in person perception. *Journal of Personality, 34,* 252–261.

Fancher, R. E. (1967). Accuracy versus validity in person perception. *Journal of Consulting Psychology, 31,* 264–269.

Faust, D., & Ziskin, J. (1988). The expert witness in psychology and psychiatry. *Science, 241,* 31–35.

Fazio, R. H., & Zanna, M. P. (1978). Attitudinal qualities relating to the strength of the attitude-behavior relationship. *Journal of Experimental Social Psychology, 14,* 398–408.

Feldman, K. A. (1971). Using the work of others: Some observations on reviewing and integrating. *Sociology of Education, 44,* 86–102.

Feldman, R. (1968). Response to compatriot and foreigner who seek assistance. *Journal of Personality and Social Psychology, 10,* 202–214.

Fishbein, M., & Ajzen, I. (1974). Attitudes towards objects as predictors of single and multiple behavioral criteria. *Psychological Review, 81,* 59–74.

Fisher, K. M., & Lipson, J. H. (1985). Information processing interpretation of errors in college science learning. *Instructional Science, 14,* 49–74.

Fiske, D. (1949). Consistency of the factorial structures of personality ratings from difference sources. *Journal of Abnormal and Social Psychology, 44,* 329–344.

Fiske, D. (1979). Two worlds of psychological phenomena. *American Psychologist, 34,* 733–740.

Fiske, D. W., & Rice, L. (1955). Intra-individual response variability. *Psychological Bulletin, 52,* 217–250.

Fiske, S., & Taylor, S. (1984). *Social cognition.* New York: Random House.

Fleishman, E. A., & Hempel, W. E., Jr. (1954). Changes in factor structure of a complex psychomotor test as a function of practice. *Psychometrika, 19,* 239–252.

Forbes, R. J., & Dijksterhuis, E. J. (1963). *A history of science and technology* (Vol. 1). Baltimore, MD: Penguin Books.

Forzi, M. (1984). Generalizability and specificity of self-schemata. *Bollettino di Psicologia Applicata, 170,* 3–12. (From *PsycLit* abstract)

Fowler, D. R., Finkelstein, A., Penk, W., Bell, W., & Itzig, B. (1987). An automated problem-rating interview: The DPRI. In J. N. Butcher (Ed.), *Computerized psychological assessment* (pp. 87–107). New York: Basic Books.

Franzen, M. (1989). *Reliability and validation in neuropsychological assessment.* New York: Plenum.

Frederiksen, N. (1962). Factors in in-basket performance. *Psychological Monographs, 76* (22, Whole No. 541).

Frederiksen, N. (1986). Toward a broader conception of human intelligence. *American Psychologist, 41,* 445–452.

Freeman, F. N. (1926). *Mental tests.* New York: Houghton Mifflin.

Freeman, F. S. (1955). *Theory and practice of psychological testing* (rev. ed.). New York: Henry Holt.

Fremer, J. (1992). High stakes testing and gate-keeper uses of assessment. In W. J. Camara (Chair), *One hundred years of psychological testing.* Symposium conducted at the convention of the American Psychological Association, Washington, DC.

Fretz, B. R., & Simon, N. P. (1992). Professional issues in counseling psychology: Continuity, change, and challenge. In S. D. Brown & R. W. Lent (Eds.), *Handbook of counseling psychology* (2nd ed.). New York: Wiley.

Freyd, M. (1925). The statistical viewpoint in vocational selection. *Journal of Applied Psychology, 9,* 349–356.

Friedlander, M. L., Ellis, M. V., Siegel, S. M., Raymond, L., Haase, R. F., & Highlen, P. S. (1988). Generalizing from segments to sessions: Should it be done? *Journal of Counseling*

Psychology, 35, 243–250.

Friedman, E. H., & Sanders, G. G. (1992). Speech timing of mood disorders. *Computers in Human Services, 8,* 121–142.

Fulton, R. T., Larson, A. D., & Worthy, R. C. (1983). The use of microcomputer technology in assessing and training communication skills of young hearing-impaired children. *American Annals of the Deaf, 128,* 570–576.

Funder, D. C., & Colvin, C. R. (1991). Explorations in behavioral consistency: Properties of persons, situations, and behaviors. *Journal of Personality and Social Psychology, 60,* 773–794.

Funk, S. C., & Houston, B. K. (1987). A critical analysis of the Hardiness Scale's validity and utility. *Journal of Personality and Social Psychology, 53,* 572–578.

Fuqua, D. R., Johnson, A. W., Newman, J. L., Anderson, M. W., & Gade, E. M. (1984). Variability across sources of performance ratings. *Journal of Counseling Psychology, 31,* 249–252.

Fuqua, D. R., Newman, J. L., Scott, T. B., & Gade, E. M. (1986). Variability across sources of performance ratings: Further evidence. *Journal of Counseling Psychology, 33,* 353–356.

Gaito, J. (1980). Measurement scales and statistics: Resurgence of an old misconception. *Psychological Bulletin, 87,* 564–567.

Galassi, J. P., Frierson, H. T., Jr., & Sharer, R. (1981). Concurrent versus retrospective assessment in test anxiety research. *Journal of Consulting and Clinical Psychology, 49,* 614–615.

Gantt, W. H. (1953). Principles of nervous breakdown. *Annals of the New York Academy of Sciences, 56,* 143–163.

Gaugler, B. B., Rosenthal, D. B., Thornton, G. C., III, & Bentson, C. (1987). Meta-analysis of assessment center validity. *Journal of Applied Psychology, 72,* 493–511.

Geen, R. G. (1987). Test anxiety and behavioral avoidance. *Journal of Research in Personality, 21,* 481–488.

Gelso, C. J. (1979). Research in counseling: Methodological and professional issues. *Counseling Psychologist, 8,* 7–35.

Gentile, J. R. (1982). Significance of single-subject studies and repeated-measures designs. *Educational Psychology, 17,* 54–60.

Gentile, J. R. (1990). *Educational psychology.* Dubuque, IA: Kendall/Hunt.

George, C. E., Lankford, J. S., & Wilson, S. E. (1990). *The effects of computerized versus paper and pencil administration of measures of negative affect.* Unpublished manuscript, Texas Tech University, Lubbock.

George, M., & Skinner, H. (1990). Innovative use of microcomputers for measuring the accuracy of assessment. In R. West, M. Christie, & J. Weinman (Eds.), *Microcomputers, psychology, and medicine* (pp. 251–266). Chichester, England: Wiley.

Giannetti, R. A. (1987). The GOLPH Psychosocial History: Response-contingent data acquisition and reporting. In J. N. Butcher (Ed.), *Computerized psychological assessment* (pp. 124–144). New York: Basic Books.

Gibbons, R. D., Clark, D. C., Cavanaugh, S. V., & Davis, J. M. (1985). Application of modern psychometric theory in psychiatric research. *Journal of Psychiatric Research, 19,* 43–55.

Glaser, R. (1963). Instructional technology and the measurement of learning outcomes: Some questions. *American Psychologist, 18,* 519–521.

Glaser, R., Lesgold, A., & Lajoie, S. (1987). Toward a cognitive theory for the measurement of achievement. In R. R. Ronning, J. A. Glover, J. C. Conoley, & J. Witt (Eds.), *The influence of cognitive psychology on testing and measurement* (pp. 41–86). Hillsdale, NJ: Erlbaum.

Glass, G. (1986). Testing old, testing new: Schoolboy psychology and the allocation of intellectual resources. In B. S. Plake & J. C. Witt (Eds.), *The future of testing* (pp. 9–27). Hillsdale, NJ: Erlbaum.

Gleick, J. (1987). *Chaos.* New York: Viking.

Gleser, G. C., Green, B. L., & Winget, C. N. (1978). Quantifying interview data on psychic impairment of disaster survivors. *Journal of Nervous and Mental Diseases, 166,* 209–216.

Glutting, J. J, Oakland, T., & McDermott, P. A. (1989). Observing child behavior during testing:

Constructs, validity, and situational generality. *Journal of School Psychology, 27,* 155–164.

Goldberg, L. R. (1965). Diagnostician versus diagnostic signs: The diagnosis of psychosis versus neurosis from the MMPI. *Psychological Monographs, 79*(9, Whole No. 602).

Goldberg, L. R. (1968). Simple models or simple processes? Some research on clinical judgments. *American Psychologist, 23,* 483–496.

Goldberg, L. R. (1970). Man versus model of man: A rationale plus evidence for a method of improving on clinical inferences. *Psychological Bulletin, 73,* 422–433.

Goldberg, L. R. (1972). Parameters of personality inventory construction and utilization: A comparison of prediction strategies and tactics. *Multivariate Behavioral Research Monographs, 7,* 2.

Goldberg, L. R. (1990). An alternative "description of personality": The Big-Five factor structure. *Journal of Personality and Social Psychology, 59,* 1216–1229.

Goldberg, L. R. (1993). The structure of phenotypic personality traits. *American Psychologist, 48,* 26–34.

Golden, C. J. (1987). Computers in neuropsychology. In J. N. Butcher (Ed.), *Computerized psychological assessment* (pp. 161–197). New York: Basic Books.

Golden, C. J., Hammeke, T., & Purisch, A. (1980). *The Luria-Nebraska Battery manual.* Los Angeles: Western Psychological Services.

Golden, C. J., Sawicki, R. F., & Franzen, M. D. (1990). Test construction. In G. Goldstein & M. Hersen (Eds.), *Handbook of psychological assessment,* (2nd ed., pp. 21–40). New York: Pergamon.

Golding, S. L. (1975). Flies in the ointment: Methodological problems in the analysis of the percentage of variance due to persons and situations.*Psychological Bulletin, 82,* 278–288.

Goldman, L. (1990). Qualitative assessment. *Counseling Psychologist, 18,* 205–213.

Goldman, L. (1971). *Using tests in counseling* (2nd ed.). Pacific Palisades, CA: Goodyear.

Goldstein, G. (1990). Comprehensive neuropsychological assessment batteries. In G. Goldstein & M. Hersen (Eds.), *Handbook of psychological assessment* (2nd ed., pp. 197–227). New York: Pergamon.

Goldstein, G., & Hersen, M. (1990). Historical perspectives. In G. Goldstein & M. Hersen (Eds.), *Handbook of psychological assessment* (2nd ed., pp. 3–17). New York: Pergamon.

Golembiewski, R. T. (1989). The alpha, beta, gamma change typology. *Group and Organization Studies, 14,* 150–154.

Golembiewski, R. T., Billingsley, K., & Yeager, S. (1976). Measuring change and persistence in human affairs: Types of change generated by OD designs. *Journal of Applied Behavioral Science, 12,* 133–157.

Goodenough, F. L. (1950). *Mental testing.* New York: Rinehart.

Goodstein, L. (1978). *Consulting with human service systems.* Reading, MA: Addison-Wesley.

Gordon, M., DiNiro, D., Mettelman, B. B., & Tallmadge, J. (1989). Observations of test behavior, quantitative scores, and teacher ratings. *Journal of Psychoeducational Assessment, 7,* 141–147.

Gotlib, I. (1984). Depression and general psychopathology in university students. *Journal of Abnormal Psychology, 93,* 19–30.

Gould, S. J. (1981). *The mismeasure of man.* Norton: New York.

Graham, J. R. (1990). *MMPI-2 Assessing personality and psychopathology.* New York: Oxford University Press.

Gray, J. (1971). *The psychology of fear and stress.* London: Weidenfeld & Nicolson.

Greaner, J. L., & Penner, L. A. (1982). The reliability and validity of Bem and Allen's measure of cross-situational consistency. *Social Behavior and Personality, 10,* 241–244.

Green, C. D. (1992). Is unified positivism the answer to psychology's disunity? *American Psychologist, 47,* 1057–1058.

Gregory, R. J. (1992). *Psychological testing.* Boston: Allyn & Bacon.

Greist, J. H., Klein, M. H., Eischens, R. R., & Faris, J. T. (1979). Running as a treatment for depression. *Comprehensive Psychiatry, 20,* 41–54.

Gronlund, N. E. (1985). *Measurement and evaluation in teaching* (5th ed.). New York: Macmillan.

Gronlund, N. E. (1988). *How to construct achievement tests* (4th ed.). Englewood Cliffs, NJ: Prentice-Hall.

Groth-Marnat, G. (1990). *Handbook of psychological assessment* (2nd ed.). New York: Wiley.

Guarnaccia, V. J., Daniels, L. K., & Sefick, W. J. (1975). Comparison of automated and standard administration of the Purdue Pegboard with mentally retarded adults. *Perceptual & Motor Skills, 40*, 371–374.

Guilford, J. P. (1946). New standards for test evaluation. *Educational and Psychological Measurement, 6*, 427–439.

Guilford, J. P. (1967). *The nature of human intelligence.* New York: McGraw-Hill.

Guion, R. M. (1976). Recruiting, selection, and job placement. In M. D. Dunnette (Ed.), *Handbook of industrial and organizational psychology* (pp. 77–828). Chicago: Rand McNally.

Guion, R. M. (1977). Content validity—The source of my discontent. *Applied Psychological Measurement, 1*, 1–10.

Guion, R. M., & Gottier, R. F. (1965). Validity of personality measures in personnel selection. *Personnel Psychology, 18*, 135–164.

Gulliksen, H. (1950). Intrinsic validity. *American Psychologist, 5*, 511–517.

Guttman, L. (1955). *A personal history of the development of scale analysis.* Unpublished manuscript, Stanford University, Center for Advanced Study in the Behavioral Sciences.

Gynther, M. D., & Green, S. B. (1982). Methodological problems in research with self-report inventories. In P. C. Kendall & J. N. Butcher (Eds.), *Handbook of research methods in clinical psychology* (pp. 355–386). New York: Wiley.

Hall, K. S., Binik, Y., & diTomasso, E. (1985). Concordance between physiological and subjective measures of sexual arousal. *Behaviour Research and Therapy, 23*, 297–303.

Halmi, K. A., Sunday, S., Puglisi, A., & Marchi, P. (1989). Hunger and satiety in anorexia and bulimia nervosa. In L. H. Schneider, S. J. Cooper, & K. A. Halmi (Eds.), *The psychobiology of human eating disorders: Preclinical and clinical perspectives* (pp. 431–445). New York: New York Academy of Sciences.

Hambleton, R. K., & Swaminathan, H. (1985). *Item response theory.* Boston: Kluwer-Nijhoff.

Hambleton, R. K., Swaminathan, H., & Rogers, H. J. (1991). *Fundamentals of item response theory.* Newbury Park, CA: Sage.

Hansen, J. C. (1987). Computer-assisted interpretation of the Strong Interest Inventory. In J. N. Butcher (Ed.), *Computerized psychological assessment* (pp. 292–324). New York: Basic Books.

Harrell, T. H., Honaker, L. M., Hetu, M., & Oberwager, J. (1987). Computerized versus traditional administration of the Multidimensional Aptitude Battery-Verbal Scale: An examination of reliability and validity. *Computers in Human Behavior, 3*, 129–137.

Harrell, T. H., & Lombardo, T. A. (1984). Validation of an automated 16PF administrative procedure. *Journal of Personality Assessment, 48*, 638–642.

Harris, T. O. (1991). Life stress and illness: The question of specificity. *Annals of Behavioral Medicine, 13*, 211–219.

Hartman, D. P. (1984). Assessment strategies. In D. H. Barlow & M. Hersen (Eds.), *Single case experimental designs* (pp. 107–139). New York: Pergamon.

Hathaway, S. (1972). Where have we gone wrong? The mystery of the missing progress. In J. N. Butcher (Ed.), *Objective personality assessment* (pp. 24–44). New York: Academic Press.

Hathaway, S. R., McKinley, J. C., Butcher, J. N., Dahlstrom, W. G., Graham, J. R., Tellegen, A. & Kaemmer, B. (1989). *Minnesota Multiphasic Personality Inventory—2 (MMPI-2): Manual for administration and scoring.* Minneapolis: University of Minnesota Press.

Hayes, S. C., & Nelson, R. O. (1986). Assessing the effects of therapeutic interventions. In R. O. Nelson & S. C. Hayes (Ed.), *Conceptual foundations of behavioral assessment* (pp. 430–460). New York: Guilford.

Hayes, S. C., Nelson, R. O., & Jarrett, R. B. (1987). The treatment utility of assessment. *American Psychologist, 42*, 963–974.

Haymaker, J. C., & Erwin, F. W. (1980). *Investigation of applicant responses and falsification detection procedures for the Military Applicant Profile* (Final Project Report, Work Unit No. DA644520). Alexandria, VA: U. S. Army Research Institute for the Behavioral and Social Sciences.

Heaton, R. K., Grant, I., Anthony, W. Z., & Lehman, R. (1981). A comparison of clinical and automated interpretation of the Halstead-Reitan Battery. *Journal of Clinical Neuropsychology, 3,* 121–141.

Hedges, L. (1987). The meta-analysis of test validity studies: Some new approaches. In H. Wainer & H. Braun (Eds.), *Test validity for the 1990's and beyond* (pp. 191–212). Hillsdale, NJ: Erlbaum.

Hedl, J. J., O'Neil, H. F., & Hansen, D. N. (1973). Affective reactions toward computer-based intelligence testing. *Journal of Consulting & Clinical Psychology, 40,* 217–222.

Hedlund, J. L., Vieweg, B. V., & Cho, D. W. (1984). Mental health computing in the 1980s: II. Clinical applications. *Computers in Human Services, 1,* 1–31.

Heidbreder, E. (1933). *Seven psychologies.* Englewood Cliffs, NJ: Prentice-Hall.

Helfrich, H. (1986). On linguistic variables influencing the understanding of questionnaire items. In A. Angleitner & J. S. Wiggins (Eds.), *Personality assessment via questionnaires* (pp. 178–190). New York: Springer-Verlag.

Helms, J. E. (1992). Why is there no study of cultural equivalence in standardized cognitive ability testing? *American Psychologist, 47,* 1083–1101.

Helzer, J. E. (1983). Standardized interviews in psychiatry. *Psychiatric Developments, 2,* 161–178.

Hembree, R. (1988). Correlates, causes, effects, and treatment of test anxiety. *Review of Educational Research, 5,* 47–77.

Hendrickson, D. E. (1982). The biological basis of intelligence. In H. J. Eysenck (Ed.), *A model for intelligence* (pp. 151–228). New York: Springer-Verlag.

Henson, D. E., Rubin, H. B., & Henson, C. (1979). Analysis of the consistency of objective measures of sexual arousal in women. *Journal of Applied Behavior Analysis, 12,* 710–711.

Heppner, P. P., Kivlighan, D. M., & Wampold, B. E. (1992). *Research design in counseling.* Pacific Grove, CA: Brooks/Cole.

Herman, K. C. (1993). Reassessing predictors of therapist competence. *Journal of Counseling and Development, 72,* 29–32.

Hilgard, E. R. (1987). *Psychology in America.* San Diego: Harcourt Brace Jovanovich.

Hill, C. E. (1978). Development of a counselor verbal response category system. *Journal of Counseling Psychology, 25,* 461–468.

Hill, C. E. (1982). Counseling process researcher: Philosophical and methodological dilemmas. *Counseling Psychologist, 10,* 7–20.

Hill, C. E., Helms, J. E., Tichenor, V., Spiegel, S. B., O'Grady, K. E., & Perry, E. S. (1988). Effects of therapist response modes in brief psychotherapy. *Journal of Counseling Psychology, 32,* 3–22.

Hitti, F. J., Riffer, R. L., & Stuckless, E. R. (1971). *Computer-managed testing: A feasibility study with deaf students.* Unpublished manuscript, Rochester Institute of Technology, Rochester, NY.

Hodgson, R. I., & Rachman, S. J. (1974). Desynchrony in measures of fear. *Behaviour Research and Therapy, 12,* 319–326.

Hogan, J., & Hogan, R. (1989). Noncognitive predictors of performance during explosive ordnance disposal training. *Military Psychology, 1,* 117–133.

Hogan, R., & Nicholson, R. A. (1988). The meaning of personality test scores. *American Psychologist, 43,* 621–626.

Hoijtink, H. (1990). A latent trait model for dichotomous choice data. *Psychometrika, 55,* 641–656.

Holden, C. (1988). Research psychologists break with APA. *Science, 241,* 1036.

Holden, R. R. (1989). Disguise and the structured self-report assessment of psychopathology: II. A clinical replication. *Journal of Clinical Psychology, 45,* 583–586.

Holden, R. R., Fekken, G. C., & Cotton, D. H. (1991). Assessing psychopathology using structured test-item response latencies. *Psychological Assessment, 3,* 111–118.

Holden, R. R., & Jackson, D. N. (1979). Item subtlety and face validity in personality assessment. *Journal of Consulting and Clinical Psychology, 47,* 459–468.

Holden, R. R., & Kroner, D. G. (1992). Relative efficacy of differential response latencies for detecting faking on a self-report measure of psychopathology. *Psychological Assessment, 4,* 170–173.

Holden, R. R., Kroner, D. G., Fekken, G. C., & Popham, S. M. (1992). A model of personality test item response dissimulation. *Journal of Personality and Social Psychology, 63,* 272–279.

Holland, J. L. (1959). A theory of vocational choice. *Journal of Counseling Psychology, 6,* 35–45.

Holland, J. L. (1985). *Making vocational choices: A theory of vocational personalities and work environments* (2nd ed.). Englewood Cliffs, NJ: Prentice-Hall.

Hollingworth, H. L. (1916). *Vocational psychology.* New York: Appleton.

Holt, R. R. (1986). Clinical and statistical prediction: A retrospective and would-be integrative perspective. *Journal of Personality Assessment, 50,* 376–386.

Honaker, L. M. (1988). The equivalency of computerized and conventional MMPI administration: A critical review. *Clinical Psychology Review, 8,* 561–577.

Horst, P. (1941). *The prediction of personal adjustment* (Bull. No. 48). New York: Social Science Research Council.

Horvath, A. O., & Greenberg, L. S. (1989). Development and validation of the Working Alliance Inventory. *Journal of Counseling Psychology, 36,* 223–233.

Hoshmand, L. L. S. (1989). Alternative research paradigms: A review and teaching proposal. *Counseling Psychologist, 17,* 3–80.

Hough, H. G. (1962). Clinical versus statistical prediction in psychology. In L. Postman (Ed.), *Psychology in the making* (pp. 526–584). New York: Knopf.

Hough, L. A., Eaton, N. K., Dunnette, M. D., Kamp, J. D., & McCloy, R. A. (1990). Criterion-related validities of personality constructs and the effect of response distortion on those validities. *Journal of Applied Psychology, 75,* 581–595.

Howard, A. (1983). Work samples and simulations in competency evaluation. *Professional Psychology: Research and Practice, 14,* 780–796.

Howard, G. S. (1981). On validity. *Evaluation Review, 5,* 567–576.

Howard, G. S. (1982). Improving methodology via research on research methods. *Journal of Counseling Psychology, 29,* 318–326.

Howard, G. S., Millham, J., Slaten, S., & O'Donnell, L. (1981). Influence of subject response style effects on retrospective measures. *Applied Psychological Measurement, 5,* 89–100.

Howard, G. S., Ralph, K. M., Gulanick, N. A., Maxwell, S. K., Nance, D. W., & Gerber, S. K. (1979). Internal invalidity in pretest-posttest self-report evaluations and a re-evaluation of retrospective pretests. *Applied Psychological Measurement, 3,* 1–23.

Howell, W. (1992). Field's science deficit will have dire results. *APA Monitor, 23,* 21.

Howell, W. (1993). Listen to academics—the future is talking. *APA Monitor, 24,* 22.

Hser, Y.-I., Anglin, M. D., & Chou, C.-P. (1992). Reliability of retrospective self-report by narcotics addicts. *Psychological Assessment, 4,* 207–213.

Huebner, L. (1979). Redesigning campus environments. In U. Delworth & G. Hanson (Eds.), *New directions for student services* (pp. 1–22). San Francisco: Jossey-Bass.

Humphreys, L. G. (1992). Commentary: What both critics and users of ability tests need to know. *Psychological Science, 3,* 271–274.

Hunt, E. (1987). Science, technology and intelligence. In R. R. Ronning, J. A. Glover, & J. C. Conoley (Eds.), *The influence of cognitive psychology on testing* (pp. 11–40). Hillsdale, NJ: Erlbaum.

Hunter, J. E., & Hunter, R. F. (1984). The validity and utility of alternative predictors of job performance. *Psychological Bulletin, 96,* 72–98.

Isen, A. M., Shalker, T., Clark, M., & Karp, L. (1978). Affect, accessibility of material in memory, and behavior: A cognitive loop? *Journal of Personality and Social Psychology, 36*, 1–12.

Jackson, D. N. (1967). Acquiescence response styles: Problems of identification and control. In I. A. Berg (Ed.), *Response set in personality assessment* (pp. 71–114). Chicago: Aldine.

Jackson, D. N. (1970). A sequential system for personality scale development. In C. Spielberger (Ed.), *Current topics in clinical and community psychology* (Vol. 2). New York: Academic Press.

Jackson, D. N. (1971). The dynamics of structured personality tests. *Psychological Review, 78*, 229–248.

Jackson, D. N. (1975). Multimethod factor analysis: A reformulation. *Multivariate Behavioral Research, 10*, 259–275.

Jackson, D. N. (1992). One hundred years of personality and intelligence testing. In W. J. Camara (Chair), *One hundred years of psychological testing*. Symposium conducted at the convention of the American Psychological Association, Washington, DC.

Jackson, D. N., & Messick, S. (1958). Content and style in personality assessment. *Psychological Bulletin, 55*, 243–252.

Jackson, D. N., & Messick, S. (1961). Acquiescence and desirability as response determinants on the MMPI. *Educational and Psychological Measurement, 21*, 771–792.

Jackson, D. N., & Messick, S. (1962). Response styles on the MMPI: Comparison of clinical and normal samples. *Journal of Abnormal and Social Psychology, 65*, 285–299.

Jackson, D. N., & Messick, S. (1967). Response styles and the assessment of psychopathology. In D. N. Jackson & S. Messick (Eds.), *Problems in human assessment* (pp. 541–558). New York: McGraw-Hill.

Jackson, D. N., & Messick, S. (1969). A distinction between judgments of frequency and of desirability as determinants of response. *Educational and Psychological Measurement, 29*, 273–293.

James, L. R., & White, J. F. (1983). Cross-situational specificity in managers' perceptions of subordinate performance, attributions, and leader behaviors. *Personnel Psychology, 36*, 809–856.

Jensen, A. R. (1982). Reaction time and psychometric g. In H. J. Eysenck (Ed.), *A model for intelligence* (pp. 93–132). New York: Springer-Verlag.

Jensen, A. R. (1992). Commentary: Vehicles of g. *Psychological Science, 3*, 275–278.

Jessor, R., & Hammond, K. R. (1957). Construct validity and the Taylor anxiety scale. *Psychology Bulletin, 54*, 161–170.

Jobe, J. B., & Mingay, D. J. (1991). Cognition and survey measurement: History and overview. *Applied Cognitive Psychology, 5*, 175–192.

Jobe, J. B., White, A. A., Kelley, C. L., Mingay, D. J., Sanchez, M. J., & Loftus, E. F. (1990). Recall strategies and memory for health care visits. *Milbank Quarterly, 68*, 171–189.

John, O. P., Angleitner, A., & Ostendorf, F. (1988). The lexical approach to personality: A historical review of trait taxonomic research. *European Journal of Personality, 2*, 171–205.

Johnson, C. W., Hickson, J. F., Fetter, W. J., & Reichenbach, D. R. (1987). Microcomputer as teacher/researcher in a nontraditional setting. *Computers in Human Behavior, 3*, 61–70.

Joint Commission on Mental Health and Illness. (1961). *Research sources in mental health. In action for mental health*. New York: Basic Books.

Jones, E. E., & Nisbett, R. E. (1971). The actor and the observer: Divergent perceptions of the causes of behavior. In E. E. Jones, D. E. Kanouse, H. H. Kelly, R. E. Nisbett, S. Valins, & B. Weiner (Eds.), *Attribution* (pp. 79–94). Morristown, NJ: General Learning Press.

Jones, E. E., Rock, L., Shaver, K. G., Goethals, G. R., & Ward, L. M. (1968). Pattern of performance and ability attribution: An unexpected primacy effect. *Journal of Personality and Social Psychology, 10*, 317–340.

Jones, E. E., & Sigall, H. (1971). The bogus pipeline: A new paradigm for measuring affect and attitude. *Psychological Bulletin, 76*, 349–364.

Joreskog, K. G. (1974). Analyzing psychological data by structural analysis of covariance matrices. In R. C. Atkinson, D. H. Krantz, R. D. Luce, & P. Suppes (Eds.), *Contemporary developments in mathematical psychology* (Vol. 2, pp. 1–56). San Francisco: Freeman.

Judson, H. F. (1980). *The search for solutions.* New York: Holt, Rinehart &d Winston.

Kagan, J. (1988). The meanings of personality predicates. *American Psychologist, 43,* 614–620.

Kaloupek, D. G., & Levis, D. J. (1983). Issues in the assessment of fear: Response concordance and prediction of avoidance behavior. *Journal of Behavioral Assessment, 5,* 239–260.

Kantor, J. R. (1924). *Principles of psychology* (Vol. 1). Bloomington, IN: Principia Press.

Kaplan, A. (1964). *The conduct of inquiry.* San Francisco: Chandler, 1964.

Kaplan, C., & Owen, A. (1991, August). *Observing behavior during testing: Development of a method for quantifying clinical judgment.* Paper presented at the annual convention of the American Psychological Association, San Francisco.

Karson, S., & O'Dell, J. W. (1987). Computer-based interpretation of the 16PF: The Karson Clinical Report in contemporary practice. In J. N. Butcher (Ed.), *Computerized psychological assessment* (pp. 198–217). New York: Basic Books.

Kazdin, A. E. (1980). *Research design in clinical psychology.* New York: Harper & Row.

Kazdin, A. E. (1985). Selection of target behaviors: The relationship of the treatment focus to clinical dysfunction. *Behavioral Assessment, 7,* 33–48.

Kelly, G. A. (1955). *The psychology of personal constructs* (Vols. 1–2). NY: Norton.

Kendall, P. C., & Buckland, W. R. (1957). *Dictionary of statistical terms.* Edinburgh: Oliver & Boyd.

Kendall, P. C., Hollon, S. D., Beck, A. T., Hammen, C. L., & Ingram, R. E. (1987). Issues and recommendations regarding use of the Beck Depression Inventory. *Cognitive Therapy and Research, 3,* 289–299.

Kenny, D. A., & Kashy, D. A. (1992). Analysis of the multitrait-multimethod matrix by confirmatory factor analysis. *Psychological Bulletin, 112,* 165–172.

Kincey, J., & Benjamin, S. (1984). Desynchrony following the treatment of pain behaviour. *Behaviour Research and Therapy, 22,* 85–86.

King, N. J., Ollendick, T. H., & Gullone, E. (1990). Desensitisation of childhood fears and phobias: Psychophysiological analyses. *Behaviour Change, 7,* 66–75.

Klein, M. H., Greist, J. H., Gurman, A. S., Neimeyer, R. A., Lesser, D. P., Bushnell, N. J., & Smith, R. E. (1985). A comparative outcome study of group psychotherapy vs. exercise treatments for depression. *International Journal of Mental Health, 13,* 148–177.

Kleinmuntz, B. (1967). *Personality measurement: An introduction.* Homewood, IL: Dorsey Press.

Klimoski, R., & Brickner, M. (1987). Why do assessment centers work? The puzzle of assessment center validity. *Personnel Psychology, 40,* 243–260.

Klimoski, R. J., & Strickland, W. J. (1981). *The comparative view of assessment centers.* Unpublished manuscript, Ohio State University, Department of Psychology, Columbus.

Klinger, E. (1987). The interview questionnaire technique: Reliability and validity of a mixed idiographic-nomothetic measure of motivation. In J. N. Butcher & C. D. Spielberger (Eds.), *Advances in personality assessment* (Vol. 6, pp. 31–48). Hillsdale, NJ: Erlbaum.

Koch, W. R., Dodd, B. G., & Fitzpatrick, S. J. (1990). Computerized adaptive measurements of attitudes. *Measurement and Evaluation in Counseling and Development, 23,* 20–30.

Kolb, B., & Whishaw, I. Q. (1990). *Fundamentals of human neuropsychology* (3rd ed.). New York: Freeman.

Korchin, S. J., & Schuldberg, D. (1981). The future of clinical assessment. *American Psychologist, 36,* 1147–1158.

Krantz, D. H., Luce, R. D., Suppes, P., & Tversky, A. (1971). *Foundations of measurement: Vol. I. Additive and polynomial representations.* New York: Academic Press.

Kraut, R. E., & McConahay, J. B. (1973). How being interviewed affects voting: An experiment. *Public Opinion Quarterly, 36,* 398–406.

Krech, D., & Crutchfield, R. (1948). *Theory and problems in social psychology.* New York: McGraw-Hill.

Kryspin, W. J., & Feldhusen, J. T. (1974). *Developing classroom tests.* Minneapolis, MN: Burgess.

Kuhn, T. S. (1970). *The structure of scientific revolutions.* Chicago: University of Chicago Press.

Kunce, C. S. (1980). The Rasch one-parameter logistic model applied to a computerized, tailored administration of Mini-Mult scales (Doctoral dissertation, University of Missouri-Columbia, 1979). *Dissertation Abstracts International, 40,* 5017A.

Lacey, J. I. (1967). Somatic response patterning and stress: Some revisions of activation theory. In M. H. Appley & R. Trumball (Eds.), *Psychological stress* (pp. 14–42). New York: Appleton-Century-Crofts.

Laing, J. (1988). Self-report: Can it be of value as an assessment technique? *Journal of Counseling and Development, 67,* 60–61.

Lambert, N. M. (1991). The crisis in measurement literacy in psychology and education. *Educational Psychologist, 26,* 23–35.

Lambert, M. J., & Hill, C. E. (1994). Assessing psychotherapy outcomes and processes. In A. E. Bergin & S. L. Garfield (Eds.), *Handbook of psychotherapy and behavior change* (4th ed.; pp. 72–13). New York: Wiley.

Lamiell, J. T. (1990). Explanation in the psychology of personality. *Annals of Theoretical Psychology, 6,* 153–192.

Lamiell, J. T. (1991, August 18). *Does quantification in psychological research necessarily entail a positivistic philosophy of science?* Presentation at the convention of the American Psychological Association, San Francisco.

Landy, F. J. (1989). *The psychology of work behavior* (4th ed.). Belmont, CA: Brooks/Cole.

Landy, F. J., & Farr, J. L. (1980). Performance rating. *Psychological Bulletin, 87,* 72–107.

Landy, F. J., & Farr, J. L. (1983). *The measurement of work performance: Methods, theory, and applications.* New York: Academic Press.

Lang, P. J. (1968). Fear reduction and fear behaviour: Problems in treating a construct. In J. M. Shlien (Ed.), *Research in psychotherapy* (Vol. 3, pp. 90–102). Washington, DC: American Psychological Association.

Lang, P. J. (1971). The application of psychophysiological methods to the study of psychotherapy and behavior change. In A. E. Bergin & S. L. Garfield (Eds.), *Handbook of psychotherapy and behavior change* (pp. 75–125). New York: Wiley.

Lanning, K. (1988). Individual differences in scalability: An alternative conception of consistency for personality theory and measurement. *Journal of Personality and Social Psychology, 55,* 142–148.

Lanyon, R. I., & Goodstein, L. D. (1982). *Personality assessment* (2nd ed.). New York: Wiley.

Latham, G., & Wexley, K. (1977). Behavioral observation scales. *Journal of Applied Psychology, 30,* 255–268.

Lautenschlager, G. J., & Atwater, D. C. (1986). *Controlling response distortion on an empirically keyed biodata questionnaire.* Unpublished manuscript.

Lazarus, A. A. (1973). Multimodal behavior therapy: Treating the "basic id." *Journal of Nervous and Mental Disease, 156,* 404–411.

Lazarus, A. A. (1981). *The practice of multi-modal therapy.* New York: McGraw-Hill.

Leitenberg, H., Agras, S., Butz, R., & Wincze, J. (1971). Relationship between heart rate and behavioral change during the treatment of phobias. *Journal of Abnormal Psychology, 78,* 59–68.

Lessler, J., Tourangeau, R., & Salter, W. (1989). *Questionnaire design in the cognitive research laboratory* (Series 6: No. 1). Hyattsville, MD: U.S. Department of Health and Human Services.

Lewin, K. (1935). *A dynamic theory of personality.* New York: McGraw-Hill.

Lewin, K. (1951). *Field theory in social science: Selected theoretical papers.* New York: Harper.

Licht, M. H., Paul, G. L., & Power, C. T. (1986). Standardized direct-multivariate DOC systems for service and research. In G. L. Paul (Ed.), *Assessment in residential treatment settings* (pp. 223–266). Champaign, IL: Research Press.

Lichtenstein, S., & Fischhoff, B. (1977). Do those who know more also know more about how much they know? The calibration of probability judgments. *Organizational Behavior and Human Performance, 20,* 159–183.

Liska, A. E. (Ed.) (1975). *The consistency controversy.* New York: Wiley.

Lloyd, G. G., & Lishman, W. A. (1975). Effect of depression on the speed of recall of pleasant and unpleasant experiences. *Psychological Medicine, 5,* 173–180.

Loevinger, J. (1957). Objective tests as instruments of psychological theory [Monograph Supplement No. 9]. *Psychological Reports, 3,* 635–694. .

Lofquist, L. H., & Dawis, R. V. (1969). *Adjustment to work: A psychological view of man's problems in a work-oriented society.* New York: Appleton-Century-Crofts.

Loftus, E. F. (1993). The reality of repressed memories. *American Psychologist, 48,* 518–537.

Lohman, R. L. (1989). Human intelligence: An introduction to advances in theory and research. *Review of Educational Research, 59,* 333–373.

Lowman, R. L. (1991). *The clinical practice of career assessment: Interests, abilities, and personality.* Washington, DC: American Psychological Association.

Lord, C. G. (1982). Predicting behavioral consistency from an individual's perception of situational similarities. *Journal of Personality and Social Psychology, 42,* 1076–1088.

Lord, F. M. (1952). A theory of test scores. *Psychometric Monograph,* No. 7.

Lord, F. M. (1953a). An application of confidence intervals and of maximum likelihood to the estimation of an examinee's ability. *Psychometrika, 18,* 57–75.

Lord, F. M. (1953b). The relation of test score to the trait underlying the test. *Educational and Psychological Measurement, 13,* 517–548.

Lord, F. M. (1953c). On the statistical treatment of football numbers. *American Psychologist, 8,* 750–751.

Lord, F. M. (1980). *Applications of item response theory to practical testing problems.* Hillsdale, NJ: Erlbaum.

Lord, F. M., & Novick, M. R. (1968). *Statistical theories of mental test scores.* Reading, MA: Addison-Wesley.

Lubin, B., Larsen, R. M., & Matarazzo, J. D. (1984). Patterns of psychological test usage in the United States: 1935–1982. *American Psychologist, 39,* 451454.

Lubinski, D., Tellegen, A., & Butcher, J. N. (1981). The relationship between androgyny and subjective indicators of emotional well-being. *Journal of Personality and Social Psychology, 40,* 722–730.

Luce, R. D., Krantz, D. H., Suppes, P., & Tversky, A. (1990). *Foundations of measurement: Vol. III. Representation, axiomatization, and invariance.* New York: Academic Press.

Luce, R. D., & Tukey, J. W. (1964). Simultaneous conjoint measurement: A new type of fundamental measurement. *Journal of Mathematical Psychology, 1,* 1–27.

Lundberg, G. A. (1926). Case work and the statistical method. *Social Forces, 5,* 61–5.

Lundberg, G. A. (1929). *Social research.* New York: Longmans, Green.

Lynch, W. J. (1985). Neuropsychological testing: Essentials of differential diagnosis. In D. P. Swiercinsky (Ed.), *Testing adults* (pp. 74–88). Kansas City, KS: Test Corporation of America.

MacGregor, D., Lichtenstein, S., & Slovic, P. (1988). Structuring knowledge retrieval: An analysis of decomposed quantitative judgments. *Organizational Behavior and Human Decision Processes, 42,* 303–323.

Macnab, D., & Fitzsimmons, G. W. (1987). A multitraitmultimethod study of work-related needs, values and preferences. *Journal of Vocational Behavior, 30,* 1–15.

Magnusson, D., & Endler, N. S. (1977). *Personality at the crossroads: Current issues in interactional psychology.* Hillsdale, NJ: Erlbaum.

Mahl, G. F. (1987). *Explorations in nonverbal and verbal behavior.* Hillsdale, NJ: Erlbaum.

Maloney, M. P., & Ward, M. P. (1976). *Psychological assessment: A conceptual approach.* New York: Oxford University Press.

Mariotto, M. J., & Licht, M. H. (1986). Ongoing assessment of functioning with DOC systems: Practical and technical issues. In G. L. Paul (Ed.), *Assessment in residential treatment settings* (pp. 191–224). Champaign, IL: Research Press.

Marks, I. M., Marset, P., Boulougouris, J., & Huson, J. (1971). Physiological accompaniments of neutral and phobic imagery. *Psychological Medicine, 1*, 299–307.

Marmar, C. R., Marziali, E., Horowitz, M. J., & Weiss, D. S. (1986). The development of the therapeutic alliance rating system. In L. S. Greenberg & W. M. Pinsof (Eds.), *The psychotherapeutic process: A research handbook* (pp. 367–390). New York: Guilford Press.

Martin, R. A. (1989). Techniques for data acquisition and analysis in field investigations of stress. In R. W. J. Neufeld (Ed.), *Advances in the investigation of psychological stress* (pp. 195–234). New York: Wiley.

Martin, R. P. (1988). *Assessment of personality and behavior problems.* New York: Guilford Press.

Martin, S. L., & Klimoski, R. J. (1990). Use of verbal protocols to trace cognitions associated with self- and supervisor evaluations of performance. *Organizational Behavior and Human Decision Processes, 46*, 135–154.

Maslach, C., & Jackson, S. E. (1981). *Manual for the Maslach Burnout Inventory.* Palo Alto, CA: Consulting Psychologists Press.

Matarrazo, J. D. (1983). The reliability of psychiatric and psychological diagnosis. *Clinical Psychology Review, 3*, 103–145.

Matarazzo, J. D. (1987). There is only one psychology, no specialties, but many applications. *American Psychologist, 42*, 893–903.

Matarazzo, J. D. (1990). Psychological assessment versus psychological testing. *American Psychologist, 45*, 999–1017.

Matarazzo, J. D. (1991). Psychological assessment is reliable and valid: Reply to Ziskin and Faust. *American Psychologist, 46*, 882–884.

Matarazzo, J. D. (1992). Psychological testing and assessment in the 21st century. *American Psychologist, 47*, 1007–1018.

Mavissakalian, M., & Michelson, L. (1982). Patterns of psychophysiological change in the treatment of agoraphobia. *Behaviour Research and Therapy, 20*, 347–356.

Maxwell, J. A. (1992). Understanding and validity in qualitative research. *Harvard Educational Review, 62*, 279–300.

May, T. M., & Scott, K. J. (1989). *Assessment in counseling psychology: Do we practice what we preach?* Paper presented at the convention of American Psychological Association, New Orleans.

Mayer, T. P. (1966). *Self—a measureless sea.* St. Louis, MO: Catholic Hospital Association.

Mayfield, E., Brown, S., & Hamstra, W. (1980). Selection interviews in the life insurance industry: An update of research and practice. *Personnel Psychology, 33*, 225–239.

Mazzeo, J., & Harvey, A. L. (1988). *The equivalence of scores from automated and conventional educational and psychological tests* (College Board Report No. 88-8). New York: College Entrance Examination Board.

McArthur, C. (1956). Clinical versus actuarial prediction. In *Proceedings, 1955 Invitational Conference on Testing Problems* (pp. 99–106). Princeton, NJ: Educational Testing Service.

McArthur, C. (1968). Comment on studies of clinical versus statistical prediction. *Journal of Counseling Psychology, 15*, 172–173.

McArthur, D. L., Schandler, S. L., & Cohen, M. J. (1988). Computers and human psychophysiological research. *Computers in Human Behavior, 4*, 111–124.

McCall, R. J. (1958). Face validity in the D scale of the MMPI. *Journal of Clinical Psychology, 14*, 77–80.

McCall, R. B. (1991). So many interactions, so little evidence. Why? In T. D. Wachs & R. Plomin (Eds.), *Conceptualization and measurement of organism-environment interaction* (pp. 142–161). Washington, DC: American Psychological Association.

McClure, F. D., & Gordon, M. (1984). Performance of disturbed hyperactive and nonhyperactive children on an objective measure of hyperactivity. *Journal of Abnormal Child Psychology, 4*, 561–572.

McCrae, R. R., & Costa, P. T., Jr. (1983). Social desirability scales: More substance than style. *Journal of Consulting and Clinical Psychology, 51*, 882–888.

McCrae, R. R., & Costa, P. T., Jr. (1985). Updating Norman's 'adequate taxonomy': Intelligence and personality dimensions in natural language and in questionnaires. *Journal of Personality and Social Psychology, 49*, 710–721.

McCrae, R. R., & Costa, P. T., Jr. (1987a). Clinical assessment can benefit from recent advances in personality psychology. *American Psychologist, 41*, 1001–1003.

McCrae, R. R., & Costa, P. T., Jr. (1987b). Validation of the five-factor model of personality across instruments and observers. *Journal of Personality and Social Psychology, 52*, 81–90.

McCrae, R. R., & Costa, P. T., Jr. (1989). The structure of interpersonal traits: Wiggins' circumplex and the five-factor model. *Journal of Personality and Social Psychology, 56*, 586–595.

McFall, R. M., & Marston, A. (1970). An experimental investigation of behavior rehearsal in assertive training. *Journal of Abnormal Psychology, 76*, 295–303.

McFall, R. M., & McDonel, E. C. (1986). The continuing search for units of analysis in psychology: Beyond persons, situations, and their interactions. In R. O. Nelson & S. C. Hayes (Eds.), *Conceptual foundations of behavioral assessment* (pp. 201–241). New York: Guilford Press.

McGuire, W. J. (1969). Suspiciousness of experimenter's intent. In R. Rosenthal & R. L. Rosnow (Eds.), *Artifact in behavioral research*. New York: Academic Press.

McIntyre, R. M., Smith, D. E., & Hassett, C. E. (1984). Accuracy of performance ratings as affected by rater training and perceived purpose of rating. *Journal of Applied Psychology, 69*, 147–156.

McLeod, D. R., Hoehn-Saric, R., Zimmerli, W. D., de Souza, E. B., & Oliver, L. K. (1990). Treatment effects of alprazolam and imipramine: Physiological versus subjective changes in patients with generalized anxiety disorder. *Biological Psychiatry, 28*, 849–861.

Means, B., Swan, G. E., Jobe, J. B., Esposito, J. L., & Loftus, E. F. (1989, August). *Recall strategies for estimation of smoking levels in health surveys.* Paper presented at the annual meeting of the American Statistical Association, Washington, DC.

Meara, N. M., Shannon, J. W., & Pepinsky, H. B. (1979). Comparison of the stylistic complexity of the language of counselor and client across three theoretical orientations. *Journal of Counseling Psychology, 26*, 181–189.

Mecklenbrauker, S., & Hager, W. (1984). Effects of mood on memory: Experimental tests of a mood-state-dependent retrieval hypothesis and of a mood-congruity hypothesis. *Psychological Research, 46*, 355–376.

Meehl, P. E. (1954). *Clinical versus statistical prediction: A theoretical analysis and a review of the evidence.* Minneapolis: University of Minnesota Press.

Meehl, P. E. (1957). When shall we use our heads instead of formula? *Journal of Counseling Psychology, 4*, 268–273.

Meehl, P. E. (1959). Some ruminations on the validation of clinical procedures. *Canadian Journal of Psychology, 13*, 102–128.

Meehl, P. E. (1965). Seer over sign: The first good example. *Journal of Experimental Research in Personality, 1*, 27–32.

Meehl, P. E. (1967). Theory testing in psychology and in physics: A methodological paradox. *Science, 34*, 103–115.

Meehl, P. E. (1986). Causes and effects of my disturbing little book. *Journal of Personality Assessment, 50*, 370–375.

Meehl, P. E. (1991). Why summaries of research on psychological theories are often uninterpretable. In R. E. Snow & D. E. Wiley (Eds.), *Improving inquiry in social science* (pp. 13–59). Hillsdale, NJ: Erlbaum.

Meier, S. T. (1984). The construct validity of burnout. *Journal of Occupational Psychology, 57*, 211–219.

Meier, S. T. (1988a). An exploratory study of a computer-assisted alcohol education program. *Computers in Human Services, 3*, 111–121.

Meier, S. T. (1988b). Predicting individual differences in performance on computer-administered tests and tasks: Development of the Computer Aversion Scale. *Computers in Human Behavior, 4*, 175–187.

Meier, S. T. (1991a). Tests of the construct validity of occupational stress measures with college students: Failure to support discriminant validity. *Journal of Counseling Psychology, 38*, 91–97.

Meier, S. T. (1991b). Vocational behavior, 1988–1990: Vocational choice, decision-making, career development interventions, and assessment. *Journal of Vocational Behavior, 39*, 131–181.

Meier, S. T., & Davis, S. R. (1990). Trends in reporting psychometric properties of scales used in counseling psychology research. *Journal of Counseling Psychology, 37*, 113–115.

Meier, S. T., & Davis, S. R. (1993). *The elements of counseling* (2nd ed.). Pacific Grove, CA: Brooks/Cole.

Meier, S. T., & Geiger, S. M. (1986). Implications of computer-based testing and assessment for professional practice and training. *Measurement and Evaluation in Counseling and Development, 19*, 29–34.

Meier, S. T., & Lambert, M. E. (1991). Psychometric properties and correlates of three computer aversion scales. *Behavior Research Methods, Instruments, & Computers, 23*, 9–15.

Meier, S. T., & Wick M. T. (1991). Computer-based unobtrusive measurement: Potential supplements to reactive self-reports. *Professional Psychology: Research and Practice, 22*, 410–412.

Messick, S. (1967). The psychology of acquiescence: An interpretation of research evidence. In I. A. Berg (Ed.), *Response set in personality assessment* (pp. 115–145). Chicago: Aldine.

Messick, S. (1980). Test validity and the ethics of assessment. *American Psychologist, 35*, 1012–1027.

Messick, S. (1989a). Meaning and values in test validation: The science and ethics of assessment. *Educational Researcher, 18*, 5–11.

Messick, S. (1989b). Validity. In R. L. Linn (Ed.), *Educational measurement* (3rd ed., pp. 13–103). Washington, DC: American Council on Education and National Council on Measurement in Education.

Messick, S. (1991). Psychology and methodology of response styles. In R. E. Snow & D. E. Wiley (Eds.), *Improving inquiry in social science* (pp. 161–200). Hillsdale, NJ: Erlbaum.

Meyer, M. (1926). Special reviews. *Psychological Bulletin, 23*, 261–276.

Michelson, L., Mavissakalian, M. R., Marchione, K., Ulrich, R. F., Marchione, N., & Testa, S. (1990). Psychophysiological outcome of cognitive, behavioral and psychophysiologically-based treatments of agoraphobia. *Behaviour Research and Therapy, 28*, 127–139.

Millsap, R. E. (1990). A cautionary note on the detection of method variance in multitrait-multimethod data. *Journal of Applied Psychology, 75*, 350–353.

Millsap, R. E., & Hartog, S. B. (1988). Alpha, beta, and gamma change in evaluation research: A structural equation approach. *Journal of Applied Psychology, 73*, 574–584.

Mineka, S. (1979). The role of fear in theories of avoidance learning, flooding, and extinction. *Psychological Bulletin, 86*, 985–1010.

Miner, G. G., & Miner, J. B. (1979). *Employee selection within the law*. Washington, DC: Bureau of National Affairs.

Mischel, W. (1968). *Personality and assessment*. New York: Wiley.

Mischel, W., & Peake, P. K. (1982). Beyond déjà vu in the search for cross-situational consistency. *Psychological Review, 89*, 730–755.

Mishler, E. G. (1986). *Research interviewing*. London: Harvard University Press.

Moore, D., & Haverkamp, B. E. (1989). Measured increases in male emotional expressiveness following a structured group intervention. *Journal of Counseling and Development, 67*, 513–517.

Moos, R. (1973). Conceptualizations of human environments. *American Psychologist, 28*, 652–665.

Moos, R. (1979a). *Evaluating educational environments*. San Francisco: Jossey-Bass.

Moos, R. (1979b). Improving social settings by social climate measurement and feedback. In R. Munoz, L. Snowden, & J. Kelly (Eds.), *Social and psychological research in community settings* (pp. 145–182). San Francisco: Jossey-Bass.

Moras, K., Di Nardo, P. A., & Barlow, D. H. (1992). Distinguishing anxiety and depression: Reexamination of the reconstructed Hamilton Scales. *Psychological Assessment, 4,* 224–227.

Morrison, R. L. (1988). Structured interviews and rating scales. In A. S. Bellack & M. Hersen (Eds.), *Behavioral assessment* (3rd ed., pp. 252–278). New York: Pergamon.

Mosier, C. I. (1947). A critical examination of the concepts of face validity. *Educational Psychological Measurement, 7,* 191–205.

Moss, P. A. (1992). Shifting conceptions of validity in educational measurement: Implications for performance assessment. *Review of Educational Research, 62,* 229–258.

Motowidlo, S. J., Dunnette, M. D., & Carter, G. W. (1990). An alternative selection procedure: The low-fidelity simulation. *Journal of Applied Psychology, 75,* 640–647.

Mummendey, H. D., & Bolton, H. G. (1981). Modification of social desirability responses when control of truthful responding is anticipated: Bogus-pipeline paradigm. *Zeitschrift für Differentielle und Diagnostische Psychologie, 2,* 151–156. (From *PsycLit* abstract)

Murphy, K. R., & Balzer, W. K. (1981). *Rater errors and rating accuracy.* Presentation at the annual convention of the American Psychological Association, Los Angeles.

Murphy, K. R., & Davidshofer, C. O. (1988). *Psychological testing.* Englewood Cliffs, NJ: Prentice Hall.

Murphy, K. R., Martin, C., & Garcia, M. (1982). Do behavioral observation scales measure observation? *Journal of Applied Psychology, 67,* 562–567.

Murphy, J. T., Hollon, P. W., Zitzewitz, J. M., & Smoot, J. C. (1986). *Physics.* Columbus, OH: Charles E. Merrill.

Murray, H. A. (1938). *Explorations in personality.* New York: Oxford University Press.

National Institute of Mental Health. (1976). *Putting knowledge to use: A distillation of the literature regarding transfer and change.* Rockville, MD: Author.

Naveh-Benjamin, M., McKeachie, W. J., & Lin, Y. (1987). Two types of test-anxious students; Support for an information processing model. *Journal of Educational Psychology, 79,* 131–136.

Nay, W. R. (1979). *Multimethod clinical assessment.* New York: Gardner Press.

Neimeyer, G. J. (1988). Cognitive integration and differentiation in vocational behavior. *Counseling Psychologist, 16,* 440–475.

Neimeyer, G. J. (1989a). Application of repertory grid technique to vocational assessment. *Journal of Counseling and Development, 67,* 585–589.

Neimeyer, G. J. (1989b). Personal construct systems in vocational development and information-processing. *Journal of Career Development, 16,* 83–96.

Neimeyer, G. J., Brown, M. T., Metzler, A. E., Hagans, C., & Tanguy, M. (1989). The impact of sex, sex-role orientation, and construct type on vocational differentiation, integration, and conflict. *Journal of Vocational Behavior, 34,* 236–251.

Neimeyer, G. J., & Neimeyer, R. A. (1993). Defining the boundaries of constructivist assessment. In G. J. Neimeyer (Ed.), *Constructivist assessment* (pp. 1–30). Newbury Park, CA: Sage.

Neimeyer, R. A. (1993). Constructivist approaches to the measurement of meaning. In G. J. Neimeyer (Ed.), *Constructivist assessment* (pp. 58–103). Newbury Park, CA: Sage.

Nelson, B. F. (1991). *Assessing dimensions of cognitive structure: Explanatory factors in the irrational beliefs and maladjustment relationship* (Doctoral dDissertation, SUNY Buffalo, 1989). *Dissertation Abstracts International, 52,* 2309B.

Nelson, L. D., & Cicchetti, D. (1991). Validity of the MMPI Depression scale for outpatients. *Psychological Assessment, 3,* 55–59.

Nelson, R. O. (1977a). Assessment and therapeutic functions of self-monitoring. In M. Hersen, R. M. Eisler, & P. M. Miller (Eds.), *Progress in behavior modification* (Vol. 5, pp. 263–308). New York: Brunner/Mazel.

Nelson, R. O. (1977b). Methodological issues in assessment via self-monitoring. In J. D. Cone

& R. P. Hawkins (Eds.), *Behavioral assessment: New directions in clinical psychology* (pp. 217–254). New York: Brunner/Mazel.

Nelson, R. O., & Hayes, S. C. (1986). The nature of behavioral assessment. In R. O. Nelson & S. C. Hayes (Eds.), *Conceptual foundations of behavioral assessment* (pp. 1–41). New York: Guilford Press.

Nettelbeck, T. (1973). Individual differences in noise and associated perceptual indices of performance. *Perception, 2,* 11–21.

Nettelbeck, T. (1980). Factors affecting reaction time: Mental retardation, brain damage, and other psychopathologies. In A. T. Welford (Ed.), *Reaction times* (pp. 355–402). London: Academic Press.

Neufeld, R. W. J. (1977). *Clinical quantitative methods.* New York: Grune & Stratton.

Nichols, R. C. (1980). Individual differences in intelligence. In J. F. Adams (Ed.), *Understanding adolescence* (4th ed., pp. 164–206). Boston: Allyn & Bacon).

Nisbett, R. E., & Ross, L. (1980). *Human inference: Strategies and shortcomings of social judgment.* Englewood Cliffs, NJ: Prentice-Hall.

Nisbett, R. E., & Wilson, J. D. (1977). The halo effect: Evidence for unconscious alteration of judgments. *Journal of Personality and Social Psychology, 35,* 250–256.

Norman, W. T. (1963). Toward an adequate taxonomy of personality attributes: Replicated factor structure in peer nomination personality ratings. *Journal of Abnormal and Social Psychology, 66,* 574–583.

Norman, W. T. (1969). "To see oursels as ithers see us!": Relations among self-perceptions, peer-perceptions, and expected peer-perceptions of personality attributes. *Multivariate Behavioral Research, 4,* 417–443.

Nunnally, J. C. (1967). *Psychometric theory.* New York: McGraw-Hill.

Oakland, T., & Glutting, J. J. (1990). Examiner observations of children's WISC-R test-related behaviors: Possible socioeconomic status, race, and gender effects. *Psychological Assessment, 2,* 86–90.

Obrist, P. A. (1981). *Cardiovascular psycho-physiology: A perspective.* New York: Plenum.

Office of Strategic Services (OSS) Assessment Staff. (1948). *Assessment of men: Selection of personnel for the Office of Strategic Services.* New York: Rinehart.

Ong, J. (1965). *The opposite-form procedure in inventory construction and research.* New York: Vantage Press.

Osberg, T. M. (1989). Self-report reconsidered: A further look at its advantages as an assessment technique. *Journal of Counseling and Development, 68,* 111–113.

Osberg, T. M., & Shrauger, J. S. (1986). Self-prediction: Exploring the parameters of accuracy. *Journal of Personality and Social Psychology, 51,* 1044–1057.

Osberg, T. M., & Shrauger, J. S. (1990). The role of self-prediction in psychological assessment. In J. N. Butcher & C. D. Spielberger (Eds.), *Advances in personality assessment* (Vol. 8, pp. 97–120). New York: Erlbaum.

Parker, K. C., Hanson, R. K., & Hunsley, J. (1988). MMPI, Rorschach and WAIS: A meta-analytic comparison of reliability, stability, and validity. *Psychological Bulletin, 103,* 367–373.

Parsons, F. (1909). *Choosing a vocation.* Boston: Houghton Mifflin.

Paul, G. L. (1969). Behavior modification research: Design and tactics. In C. M. Franks (Ed.), *Behavior therapy: Appraisal and status* (pp. 29–62). New York: McGraw-Hill.

Paul, G. L. (Ed.) (1986). *Assessment in residential treatment settings.* Champaign, IL: Research Press.

Paul, G. L. (Ed.) (1987a). *The staff-resident interaction chronograph.* Champaign, IL: Research Press.

Paul, G. L. (Ed.). (1987b). *The time-sample behavioral checklist.* Champaign, IL: Research Press.

Paul, G. L., Mariotto, M. J., & Redfield, J. P. (1986a). Assessment purposes, domains, and utility for decision making. In G. L. Paul (Ed.), *Assessment in residential treatment settings* (pp. 1–26). Champaign, IL: Research Press.

Paul, G. L., Mariotto, M. J., & Redfield, J. P. (1986b). Sources and methods for gathering information in formal assessment. In G. L. Paul (Ed.), *Assessment in residential treatment settings* (pp. 27–62). Champaign, IL: Research Press.

Paulhus, D. L. (1991). Measurement and control of response bias. In J. P. Robinson, P. R. Shaver, & L. S. Wrightsman (Eds.), *Measures of personality and social psychological attitudes* (Vol. 1, pp. 17–59). New York: Academic Press.

Paulman, R. G., & Kennelly, J. J. (1984). Test anxiety and ineffective test taking: Different names, same constructs? *Journal of Educational Psychology, 76,* 279–288.

Paunonen, S. V., & Jackson, D. N. (1985). On ad hoc personality scales: A reply to Burisch. *Journal of Research in Personality, 19,* 348–353.

Payne, R. L., & Jones, J. G. (1987). Measurement and methodological issues in social support. In S. V. Kasl & C. L. Cooper (Eds.), *Stress and health: Issues in research methodology* (pp. 167–206). New York: Wiley.

Pervin, L. A. (1984). Idiographic approaches to personality. In N. S. Endler & J. M. Hunt (Eds.), *Personality and the behavioral disorders* (p. 261–282). New York: Wiley.

Peters, J. T., Hammond, K. R., & Summers, D. A. (1984). A note on intuitive vs. analytic thinking. *Organizational Behavior and Human Performance, 12,* 125–131.

Peterson, D. R. (1968). *The clinical study of social behavior.* New York: Appleton-Century-Crofts.

Piotrowski, C., & Keller, J. W. (1984). Psychological testing: Trends in master's level counseling psychology programs. *Teaching of Psychology, 11,* 244–245.

Piotrowski, C., & Keller, J. W. (1989). Psychological testing in outpatient mental health facilities: A national study. *Professional Psychology: Research and Practice, 20,* 423–425.

Piotrowski, C., & Lubin, B. (1990). Assessment practices of health psychologists: Survey of APA Division 38 clinicians. *Professional Psychology Research and Practice, 21,* 99–106.

Platt, J. R. (1977). Strong inference. In H. S. Broudy, R. H. Ennis, & L. I. Krimerman (Eds.), *Philosophy of educational research* (pp. 203–217). New York: Wiley.

Polkinghorne, D. E. (1991). Qualitative procedures for counseling research. In C. E. Watkins, Jr. & L. J. Schneider (Eds.), *Research in counseling.* Hillsdale, NJ: Lawrence Erlbaum.

Popham, S. M., & Holden, R. R. (1990). Assessing MMPI constructs through the measurement of response latencies. *Journal of Personality Assessment, 54,* 469–478.

Popham, W. J. (1978). *Criterion-referenced measurement.* Englewood Cliffs, NJ: Prentice-Hall.

Popham, W. J. (1993). Educational testing in America: What's right, what's wrong? *Educational Measurement: Issues and Practice, 12,* 11–14.

Post, E. M., Burko, M. S., & Gordon, M. (1990). Single-component microcomputer-driven assessment of attention. *Behavior Research Methods, Instruments, & Computers, 22,* 297–301.

Potts, M. (1992, August 16). Virtual reality. *The Washington Post,* 16, H1-H4.

Quarm, D. (1981). Random measurement error as a source of discrepancies between the reports of wives and husbands concerning marital power and task allocation. *Journal of Marriage and the Family, 43,* 521–535.

Rachman, S. (1978). Human fears: A three systems analysis. *Scandinavian Journal of Behaviour Therapy, 7,* 237–245.

Rachman, S., & Hodgson, R. (1974). Synchrony and desynchrony in fear and avoidance. *Behaviour Research and Therapy, 12,* 311–318.

Rasch, G. (1980). *Probabilistic models for some intelligence and attainment tests* (rev. ed.). Chicago: University of Chicago Press.

Reardon, R., & Loughead, T. (1988). A comparison of paper-and-pencil and computer versions of the Self-Directed Search. *Journal of Counseling and Development, 67,* 249–252.

Reckase, M. D. (1990). Scaling techniques. In G. Goldstein & M. Hersen (Eds.), *Handbook of psychological assessment* (2nd ed., pp. 41–58). New York: Pergamon.

Reed, T. E., & Jensen, A. R. (1991). Arm nerve conduction velocity (NCV), brain NCV, reaction time, and intelligence. *Intelligence, 15,* 33–47.

Regan, D. T., & Fazio, R. (1977). On the consistency between attitudes and behavior: Look to the method of attitude formation. *Journal of Experimental Social Psychology, 13,* 28–45.

Reich, J. (1987). Instruments measuring DSM-III and DSM-III-R personality disorders. *Journal of Personality Disorders, 1,* 220–240.

Reise, S. P., & Waller, N. G. (1990). Fitting the 2 parameter model to personality data. *Applied Psychological Measurement, 14,* 45–58.

Reitan, R. M., & Wolfson, D. (1985). *The Halstead-Reitan Neuropsychological Test Battery: Theory and clinical interpretation.* Tucson, AZ: Neuropsychology Press.

Robins, L. N., Helzer, J. E., Croughan, J., & Ratcliff, K. S. (1981). National Institute of Mental Health Diagnostic Interview Schedule: Its history, characteristics, and validity. *Archives of General Psychiatry, 38,* 381–389.

Rogers, R., Bagby, R. M., & Dickens, S. E. (1992). *Test Manual for the Structured Interview of Reported Symptoms (SIRS).* Tampa, FL: Psychological Assessment Resources.

Rosen, L. D., Sears, D. C., & Weil, M. M. (1987). Computerphobia. *Behavior Research Methods, Instruments, and Computers, 19,* 167–179.

Rosenthal, R. (1976). *Experimenter effects in behavioral research* (rev. ed). New York: Halsted Press.

Ross, L. (1977). The intuitive psychologist and his shortcomings: Distortions in the attribution process. In L. Berkowitz (Ed.), *Advances in experimental social psychology* (Vol. 10, pp. 174–221). New York: Academic Press.

Rushton, J. P., Brainerd, C. J., & Pressley, M. (1983). Behavioral development and construct validity: The principle of aggregation. *Psychological Bulletin, 94,* 18–38.

Rushton, J. P., Jackson, D. N., & Paunonen, S. V. (1981). Personality: Nomothetic or idiographic? A response to Kentrick and Stringfield. *Psychological Review, 88,* 582–589.

Ryman, D. H., Naitoh, P., & Englund, C. E. (1984). Minicomputer-administered tasks in the study of effects of sustained work on human performance. *Behavior Research Methods, Instruments, and Computers, 16,* 256–261.

Saal, F. E., Downey, R. G., & Lahey, M. A. (1980). Rating the ratings: Assessing the psychometric quality of rating data. *Psychological Bulletin, 88,* 413–428.

Sackett, P. R., & Dreher, G. F. (1982). Constructs and assessment center dimensions: Some troubling empirical findings. *Journal of Applied Psychology, 67,* 401–410.

Sallis, J. F., & Lichstein, K. L. (1979). The frontal electromyographic adaptation response: A potential source of confounding. *Biofeedback and Self-Regulation, 4,* 337–339.

Salovey, P., Jobe, J. B., Willis, G. B., Sieber, W. J., Turk, D. C., & Smith, A. F. (1989, August). *Response errors and bias in the recall of chronic pain.* Paper presented at the annual meeting of the American Statistical Association, Washington, DC.

Sarason, I. G. (1961). Test anxiety, experimental instructions, and verbal learning. *American Psychologist, 16,* 374.

Sarason, I. G. (1972). Experimental approaches to test anxiety: Attention and the uses of information. In C. D. Spielberger (Ed.), *Anxiety: Current trends in theory and research* (Vol. 2). New York: Academic Press.

Sarbin, T. R. (1942). A contribution to the study of actuarial and individual methods of prediction. *American Journal of Sociology, 48,* 593–602.

Sarbin, T. R. (1986a). Prediction and clinical inference: Forty years later. *Journal of Personality Assessment, 50,* 362–369.

Sarbin, T. R. (1986b). The narrative as a root metaphor for psychology. In T. R. Sarbin (Ed.), *Narrative psychology* (pp. 3–21). New York: Praeger.

Sawyer, J. (1966). Measurement and prediction, clinical and statistical. *Psychological Bulletin, 66,* 178–200.

Schacter, S. (1966). The interaction of cognitive and physiological determinants of emotional state. In C. D. Spielberger (Ed.), *Anxiety and behavior* (pp. 193–224). New York: Academic Press.

Scheidt, D. M., & Meier, S. T. (1994). *Microcomputer assisted assessment of schematic object representations: Content and stability.* Manuscript submitted for publication.

Schmidt, F. L. (1992). What do data really mean? Research findings, meta-analysis, and cumulative knowledge in psychology. *American Psychologist, 47,* 1173–1181.

Schmidt, F. L., & Hunter, J. E. (1977). Development of a general solution to the problem of validity generalization. *Journal of Applied Psychology, 62*, 529–540.

Schmitt, N., Gooding, R. Z., Noe, R. A., & Kirsch, M. (1984). Meta-analyses of validity studies published between 1964 and 1982 and the investigation of study characteristics. *Personnel Psychology, 37*, 407–422.

Schmitt, N., & Stults, D. M. (1986). Methodology review: Analysis of multitrait-multimethod matrices. *Applied Psychological Measurement, 10*, 1–22.

Schneider, D. J. (1973). Implicit personality theory: A review. *Psychological Bulletin, 79*, 294–309.

Schneider, S. M. (1992). Can this marriage be saved? *American Psychologist, 47*, 1055–1057.

Schrader, A. D., & Osburn, H. G. (1977). Biodata faking: Effects of induced subtlety and position specificity. *Personnel Psychology, 30*, 395–404.

Schretlen, D. (1986). *Malingering: Use of a psychological test battery to detect two kinds of simulation.* Ann Arbor, MI: University Microfilms International.

Schroeder, D. H., & Costa, P. T. (1984). Influence of life event stress on physical illness: Substantive effects or methodological flaws. *Journal of Personality and Social Psychology, 46*, 853–863.

Schroeder, H. E., & Rakos, R. F. (1978). Effects of history on the measurement of assertion. *Behavior Therapy, 9*, 965–966.

Schulenberg, J. E., Vondracek, F. W., & Nesselroade, J. R. (1988). Patterns of short-term changes in individuals' work values: P-technique factor analyses of intraindividual variability. *Multivariate Behavioral Research, 23*, 377–395.

Schwab, D. P., & Heneman, H. G. (1969). Relationship between interview structure and inter-interview reliability in an employment situation. *Journal of Applied Psychology, 53*, 214–217.

Schwab, D. P., & Oliver, R. L. (1974). Predicting tenure with biographical data: Exhuming buried evidence. *Personnel Psychology, 27*, 125–128.

Schwenkmezger, P. (1984). Can the consistency postulate of traits be retained through the principle of data aggregation? *Zeitschrift für Differentielle und Diagnostische Psychologie, 5*, 251–272. (From *PsycLit* abstract)

Scott, W. A. (1968). Attitude measurement. In G. Lindzey & E. Aronson (Eds.), *Handbook of social psychology* (pp. 204–273). Reading, MA: Addison-Wesley.

Scriven, M. (1969). Psychology without a paradigm. In L. Breger (Ed.), *Clinical-cognitive psychology: Models and integrations* (pp. 9–24). Englewood Cliffs, NJ: Prentice-Hall.

Seashore, R. H. (1939). Work methods: An often neglected factor underlying individual differences. *Psychological Review, 46*, 475–494.

Sechrest, L. (1963). Incremental validity: A recommendation. *Educational and Psychological Measurement, 23*, 153–158.

Sedlacek, W., Bailey, B., & Stovall, C. (1984). Following directions: An unobtrusive measure of student success. *Journal of College Student Personnel, 25*, 556.

Selye, H. (1956). *The stress of life.* New York: McGraw-Hill.

Shavelson, R. J., Baxter, G. P., & Pine, J. (1991). Performance assessment in science. *Applied Measurement in Education, 4*, 347–362.

Shavelson, R. J., & Webb, N. M. (1991). *Generalizability theory.* Newbury Park, CA: Sage.

Shavelson, R. J., Webb, N. M., & Rowley, G. L. (1989). Generalizability theory. *American Psychologist, 44*, 922–932.

Shedler, J., Mayman, M., & Manis, M. (1993). The *illusion* of mental health. *American Psychologist, 48*, 1117–1131.

Shertzer, B., & Stone, S. C. (1980). *Fundamentals of counseling* (3rd ed.). Boston: Houghton Mifflin.

Shostrum, E. L. (Producer). (1966). *Three approaches to psychotherapy.* Santa Ana, CA: Psychological Films.

Sidman, M. (1960). *Tactics of scientific research.* New York: Basic Books.

Siegman, A. W. (1956). The effect of manifest anxiety on a concept formation task, a nondirected learning task, and on timed and untimed intelligence tests. *Journal of Consulting Psychology, 20*, 176–178.

Silva, F. (1993). *Psychometric foundations and behavioral assessment.* New York: Sage.

Skinner, H. A., & Pakula, A. (1986). Challenge of computers in psychological assessment. *Professional Psychology: Research and Practice, 17*, 44–50.

Smith, M. L., & Glass, G. V. (1977). Meta-analysis of psychotherapy outcome studies. *American Psychologist, 32*, 752–760.

Smith, A. F., Jobe, J. B., & Mingay, D. J. (1991). Retrieval from memory of dietary information. *Applied Cognitive Psychology, 5*, 269–298.

Smith, E. R., & Tyler, R. W. (1942). *Appraising and recording student progress* (Adventure in American Education Series, Vol. 3). New York: Harper.

Smith, G. P., & Burger, G. (1993). *Detection of malingering: A validation study of the SLAM test.* Paper presented at the annual convention of the American Psychological Association, Toronto, Canada.

Smith, T. W., Pope, M. K., Rhodewalt, F., & Poulton, J. (1989). Optimism, neuroticism, coping, and symptom reports: An alternate intepretation of the life orientation test. *Journal of Personality and Social Psychology, 56*, 640–648.

Snow, R. E. (1991). Aptitude-treatment interaction as a framework for research on individual differences in psychotherapy. *Journal of Consulting and Clinical Psychology, 59*, 205–216.

Snow, R. E., & Lohman, D. F. (1984). Toward a theory of cognitive aptitude for learning from instruction. *Journal of Educational Psychology, 76*, 347–376.

Snow, R. E., & Wiley, D. E. (1991). Straight thinking. In R. E. Snow & D. E. Wiley (Eds.), *Improving inquiry in social science* (pp. 1–12). Hillsdale, NJ: Erlbaum.

Snyder, M. L., Stephan, W. G., & Rosenfield, D. (1978). Attributional egotism. In J. H. Harvey, W. Ickes, & R. F. Kidd (Eds.), *New directions in attribution research* (Vol. 2, pp. 91–120). Hillsdale, NJ: Erlbaum.

Sokal, M. M. (Ed.) (1987). *Psychological testing and American Society 1890–1930.* New Brunswick, NJ: Rutgers University Press.

Spearman, C. (1904). "General intelligence," objectively determined and measured. *American Journal of Psychology, 15*, 201–293.

Spearman, C. (1910). Correlation calculated from faulty data. *British Journal of Psychology, 3*, 271–295.

Spielberger, C. D. (1991). *State-Trait Anger Expression Inventory.* Odessa, FL: Psychological Assessment Resources.

Spielberger, C. D., Gorsuch, R. L., & Lushene, R. (1970). *Manual for the State-Trait Anxiety Inventory: STAI.* Palo Alto, CA: Consulting Psychologists Press.

Sprangers, M., & Hoogstraten, J. (1987). Response-style effects, response-shift bias, and a bogus-pipeline. *Psychological Reports, 61*, 579–585.

Sprangers, M., & Hoogstraten, J. (1988). Response-style effects, response-shift bias, and a bogus-pipeline: A replication. *Psychological Reports, 62*, 11–16.

Staats, A. W. (1981). Paradigmatic behaviorism, unified theory, unified theory construction methods, and the Zeitgeist of separatism. *American Psychologist, 36*, 239–256.

Staats, A. W. (1983). *Psychology's crisis of disunity: Philosophy and method for a unified science.* New York: Praeger.

Staats, A. W. (1988, August 12). *Personality as basic behavioral processes: A critical bridging theory.* Invited address, American Psychological Association Convention, Atlanta, GA.

Stagner, R. (1984). Trait psychology. In N. S. Endler & J. M. Hunt (Eds.), *Personality and the behavioral disorders* (2nd ed., Vol. 1, pp. 3–28). New York: Wiley.

Stark, A. (1981). *Reconceptualizing a clinical construct.* Unpublished master's thesis, University of Hawaii, Honolulu.

Stattin, H. (1984). Developmental trends in the appraisal of anxiety-provoking situations. *Journal of Personality, 52*, 46–57.

Staw, B. M., & Ross, J. (1985). Stability in the midst of change: A dispositional approach to job attitudes. *Journal of Applied Psychology, 70,* 469–480.

Steele, F. (1973). *Physical settings and organization development.* Reading, MA: Addison-Wesley.

Stein, S. J. (1987). Computer-assisted diagnosis for children and adolescents. In J. N. Butcher (Ed.), *Computerized psychological assessment* (pp. 145–158). New York: Basic Books.

Steinweg, D. A. (1993). *The influence of naturally occurring, non-pathological fluctuations of mood on recall* (Doctoral dissertation, SUNY Buffalo, 1991). *Dissertation Abstracts International, 53,* 4969B.

Stern, M. J., & Cleary, P. (1982). The national exercise and heart disease project: Long-term psychosocial outcome. *Archives of Internal Medicine, 142,* 1093–1097.

Stern, R. M., Ray, W. J., & Davis, C. M. (1980). *Psychophysiological recording.* New York: Oxford University Press.

Sternberg, R. J. (1977). *Intelligence, information processing, and analogical reasoning: The componential analysis of human abilities.* Hillsdale, NJ: Erlbaum.

Sternberg, R. J. (1984). A contextualist view of the nature of intelligence. *International Journal of Psychology, 19,* 307–334.

Sternberg, R. J. (1988). Applying cognitive theory to the testing and teaching of intelligence. *Applied Cognitive Psychology, 2,* 231–255.

Stevens, S. S. (1951). Mathematics, measurement and psychophysics. In S. S. Stevens (Ed.), *Handbook of experimental psychology* (pp. 1–41). New York: Wiley.

Stone, E. F. (1978). *Research methods in organizational behavior.* Santa Monica, CA: Goodyear.

Stone, E. F., Stone, D. L., & Gueutal, H. G. (1990). Influence of cognitive ability on responses to questionnaire measures: Measurement precision and missing response problems. *Journal of Applied Psychology, 75,* 418–427.

Strong, E. K., Jr. (1943). *Vocational interests of men and women.* Stanford, CA: Stanford University Press.

Sudman, S., & Bradburn, N. (1982). *Asking questions: A practical guide to questionnaire design.* San Francisco: Jossey-Bass.

Super, D. E. (1957). *Psychology of careers.* Harper: New York.

Suppes, P., Krantz, D. H., Luce, R. D., & Tversky, A. (1989). *Foundations of measurement: Vol. II. Geometrical, threshold, and probabilistic representations.* New York: Academic Press.

Surwillo, W. W. (1986). *Psychophysiology.* Springfield, IL: Charles C. Thomas.

Swanson, J. L., & Hansen, J. C. (1988). Stability of vocational interests on 4-year, 8-year, and 12-year intervals. *Journal of Vocational Behavior, 33,* 185–202.

Swezey, R. W. (1981). *Individual performance assessment: An approach to criterion-referenced test development.* Reston, VA: Reston Publishing.

Taft, R. (1955). The ability to judge people. *Psychological Bulletin, 52,* 1–23.

Tanaka-Matsumi, J., & Kameoka, V. (1986). Reliabilities and concurrent validities of popular self-report measures of depression, anxiety, and social desirability. *Journal of Consulting and Clinical Psychology, 54,* 328–333.

Tellegen, A. (1985). Structures of mood and personality and their relevance to assessing anxiety, with an emphasis on self-report. In A. H. Tuma & J. D. Master (Eds.), *Anxiety and the anxiety disorders* (pp. 681–706). Hillsdale, NJ: Erlbaum.

Tellegen, A. (1988). The analysis of consistency in personality assessment. *Journal of Personality, 56,* 621–663.

Tenopyr, M. L. (1992). Court decisions and psychological assessment. In W. J. Camara (Chair), *One hundred years of psychological testing.* Symposium conducted at the convention of the American Psychological Association, Washington, DC.

Tenopyr, M. L. (1993). Construct validation needs in vocational behavior theories. *Journal of Vocational Behavior, 43,* 84–89.

Terman, L. M., & Merrill, M. A. (1937). *Measuring intelligence.* Boston: Houghton Mifflin.

Terman, L. M., & Miles, C. C. (1936). *Sex and personality.* New York: McGraw-Hill.

Tetrick, L. E. (1989). An exploratory investigation of response latency in computerized administrations of the Marlowe-Crowne Social Desirability Scale. *Personality and Individual Differences, 10*, 1281–1287.

Thissen, D., & Steinberg, L. (1988). Data analysis using item response theory. *Psychological Bulletin, 104*, 385–395.

Thomas, G. (1990). The making of COBRS 2.0: The competency-oriented behavior rating system for children and youth services. *Computers in Human Services, 6*, 149–168.

Thorndike, E. L. (1920). A constant error in psychological ratings. *Journal of Applied Psychology, 4*, 25–29.

Thorndike, R. L. (1949). *Personnel selection*. Wiley: New York.

Thorndike, R. L. (1969). *Helping teachers use tests* (A series of special reports, No. 1). National Council on Measurement in Education.

Thorndike, R. L., & Hagen, E. (1961). *Measurement and evaluation in psychology and education* (2nd ed.). New York: Wiley.

Thurstone, L. L. (1938). *Primary mental abilities*. Chicago: University of Chicago Press.

Tichenor, V., & Hill, C. E. (1989). A comparison of six measures of working alliance. *Psychotherapy, 26*, 195–199.

Tinsley, D. J., & Irelan, T. M. (1989). Instruments used in college students affairs research: An analysis of the measurement base of a young profession. *Journal of College Student Development, 30*, 440–447.

Tinsley, H. E. A., Bowman, S. L., & York, D. C. (1989). Career Decision Scale, My Vocational Situation, Vocational Rating Scale, and Decisional Rating Scale: Do they measure the same constructs? *Journal of Counseling Psychology, 36*, 115–120.

Tobler, N. (1986). Meta-analysis of 143 adolescent drug prevention programs: Quantitative outcome results of program participants compared to a control or comparison group. *Journal of Drug Issues, 16*, 537–567.

Torgerson, W. S. (1958). *Theory and methods of scaling*. New York: Wiley.

Townsend, J. T., & Ashby, F. G. (1984). Measurement scales and statistics: The misconception misconceived. *Psychological Bulletin, 96*, 394–401.

Trapnell, P. D., & Wiggins, J. S. (1990). Extension of the Interpersonal Adjective Scales to include the Big Five dimensions of personality. *Journal of Personality and Social Psychology, 59*, 781–790.

Trent, T. T., Atwater, D. C., & Abrahams, N. M. (1986). Biographical screening of military applicants: Experimental assessment of item response distortion. In G. E. Lee (Ed.), *Proceedings of the Tenth Annual Symposium of Psychology in the Department of Defense* (pp. 96–100). Colorado Springs: U. S. Air Force Academy, Department of Behavioral Sciences and Leadership.

Tryon, W. W. (ed.). (1991). *Activity measurement in psychology and medicine*. New York: Plenum.

Tukey, J. W. (1950). Discussion: Symposium on statistics for the clinician. *Journal of Clinical Psychology, 6*, 61–74.

Tupes, E., C., & Christal, R. E. (1961). *Recurrent personality factors based on trait ratings* (ASD-TR-6197). Lackland Air Force Base, TX: Aeronautical Systems Division, Personnel Laboratory.

Tversky, A., & Kahneman, D. (1974). Judgment under uncertainty: Heuristics and biases. *Science, 185*, 1124–1131.

Ursic, M. L., & Helgeson, J. G. (1989). Variability in survey questionnaire completion strategies: A protocol analysis. *Journal of the Market Research Society, 31*, 225–240.

Vansickle, T. R., Kimmel, C., & Kapes, J. T. (1989). Test-retest equivalency of the computer-based and paper-pencil versions of the Strong Campbell Interest Inventory. *Measurement and Evaluation in Counseling and Development, 22*, 88–83.

VanZandt, C. E. (1990). Professionalism: A matter of personal initiative. *Journal of Counseling and Development, 68*, 243–245.

Velten, E. (1968). A laboratory task for induction of mood states. *Behaviour Research and Therapy, 6*, 473–482.

Venkatraman, N., & Grant, J. H. (1986). Construct measurement in organizational strategy research: A critique and proposal. *Academy of Management Review, 11*, 71–87.

Vernon, P. E. (1964). *Personality assessment.* London: Methuen.

Vernon, P. E. (1934). The attitude of the subject in personality testing. *Journal of Applied Psychology, 18*, 165–177.

Vernon, P. E. (1964). *Personality assessment.* London: Methuen.

Violato, C., & Travis, L. D. (1988). An application of generalizability theory to the consistency-specificity problem: The transsituational consistency of behavioral persistence. *Journal of Psychology, 122*, 389–407.

Viteles, M. S. (1925). The clinical viewpoint in vocational psychology. *Journal of Applied Psychology, 9*, 131–138.

Wachtel, P. (1973). Psychodynamics, behavior therapy, and the implacable experimenter: An inquiry into the consistency of personality. *Journal of Abnormal Psychology, 82*, 321–334.

Wainer, H. (1993). Measurement problems. *Journal of Educational Measurement, 30*, 1–21.

Waller, N. G., & Reise, S. P. (1989). Computerized adaptive personality assessment: An illustration with the Absorption Scale. *Journal of Personality and Social Psychology, 57*, 1051–1058.

Walsh, W. B. (1973). *Theories of person-environment interaction: Implications for the college student.* Iowa City, IA: American College Testing Program.

Walsh, W. B., & Betz, N. E. (1985). *Tests and assessment.* Englewood Cliffs, NJ: Prentice-Hall.

Waters, L. K. (1965). A note on the "fakability" of forced-choice scales. *Personnel Psychology, 18*, 187–191.

Watson, D. (1988). The vicissitudes of mood measurement: Effects of varying descriptors, time frames, and response formats on measures of positive and negative affect. *Journal of Personality and Social Psychology, 55*, 128–141.

Watson, D., & Kendall, P. C. (1989). Understanding anxiety and depression: Their relation to negative and positive affective states. In P. C. Kendall & D. Watson (Eds.), *Anxiety and depression: Distinctive and overlapping features* (pp. 3–26). New York: Academic Press.

Watson, D., & Pennebaker, J. W. (1989). Health complaints, stress and distress: Exploring the central role of negative affectivity. *Psychological Review, 96*, 234–254.

Webb, E., Campbell, D., Schwartz, R., Sechrest, L., & Grove, J. (1981). *Nonreactive measures in the social sciences.* Boston: Houghton Mifflin.

Wedding, D. (1983). Clinical and statistical prediction in neuropsychology. *Clinical Neuropsychology, 5*, 49–55.

Wedding, D., & Faust, D. (1989). Clinical judgment and decision making in neuropsychology. *Archives of Clinical Neuropsychology, 4*, 233–265.

Weiner, B. (1985). Human motivation. New York: Springer-Verlag.

Weiss, D. J. (1983). *New horizons in testing: Latent trait test theory and computerized adaptive testing.* San Diego: Academic Press.

Welford, A. T. (Ed.). (1980a). *Reaction times.* London: Academic Press.

Welford, A. T. (1980b). Relationships between reaction time and fatigue, stress age and sex. In A. T. Welford (Ed.), *Reaction times* (pp. 321–354). London: Academic Press.

Wernimont, P. F., & Campbell, J. P. (1968). Signs, samples and criteria. *Journal of Applied Psychology, 52*, 372–376.

West, S. G., & Graziano, W. G. (1989). Long-term stability and change in personality: An introduction. *Journal of Personality, 57*, 175–194.

Wetter, M., Baer, R., Berry, D., Smith, G., & Larsen, L. (1992). Sensitivity of MMPI-2 validity scales to random responding and malingering. *Psychological Assessment, 4*, 369–374.

Wiener, D. N. (1948). Subtle and obvious keys for the Minnesota Multiphasic Personality Inventory. *Journal of Consulting Psychology, 12*, 164–170.

Wiesner, W. H., & Cronshaw, S. F. (1988). A meta-analytic investigation of the impact of interview format and degree of structure on the validity of the employment interview. *Journal of Occupational Psychology, 61*, 275–290.

Wiggins, J. S. (1973). *Personality and prediction: Principles of personality assessment.* Reading, MA:

Addison-Wesley.

Wiggins, J. S. (1979). A psychological taxonomy of trait descriptive terms: The interpersonal domain. *Journal of Personality and Social Psychology, 37,* 395–412.

Wiggins, J. S. (1982). Circumplex models of interpersonal behavior in clinical psychology. In P. S. Kendall & J. N. Butcher (Eds.), *Handbook of research methods in clinical psychology* (pp. 183–221). New York: Wiley.

Wiggins, J. S., & Pincus, A. L. (1989). Conceptions of personality disorders and dimensions of personality. *Psychological Assessment, 1,* 305–316.

Wilder, J. (1957). The law of initial values in neurology and psychiatry. *Journal of Nervous and Mental Disease, 125,* 73–86.

Wilder, J. (1967). *Stimulus and response: The law of initial value.* Bristol: J. Wright.

Wiley, D. (1991). Test validity and invalidity reconsidered. In R. E. Snow & D. E. Wiley (Eds.), *Improving inquiry in social science* (pp. 75–108). Hillsdale, NJ: Erlbaum.

Willis, G. B., Royston, P., & Bercini, D. (1991). The use of verbal report methods in the development and testing of survey questionnaires. *Applied Cognitive Psychology, 5,* 251–267.

Winne, P. H., Marx, R. W., & Taylor, T. D. (1977). A multitrait-multimethod study of three self-concept inventories. *Child Development, 48,* 393–901.

Wissler, C. (1901). The correlation of mental and physical tests. *Psychological Review Monograph, 3* (No. 6).

Wolf, T. H. (1973). *Alfred Binet.* Chicago: University of Chicago Press.

Wong, F. Y., McCreary, D. R., & Duffy, K. G. (1990). A further validation of the Bem Sex Role Inventory: A multitrait-multimethod study. *Sex Roles, 22,* 249–259.

Wormith, J. S., & Goldstone, C. S. (1984). The clinical and statistical prediction of recidivism. *Criminal Justice and Behavior, 11,* 3–34.

Worthen, B. R., Borg, W. R., & White, K. R. (1993). *Measurement and evaluation in the schools.* New York: Longman.

Wright, B. D., & Stone, M. H. (1979). *Best test design.* Chicago: Mesa Press.

Wright, P. M., Lichtenfels, P. A., & Pursell, E. D. (1989). The structured interview: Additional studies and a meta-analysis. *Journal of Occupational Psychology, 62,* 191–199.

Wylie, R. C. (1974). *The self-concept: A review of methodological considerations and measuring instruments* (rev. ed., Vol. 1). Lincoln: University of Nebraska Press.

Wylie, R. C. (1979). *The self-concept: Theory and research on selected topics* (Vol. 2). Lincoln: University of Nebraska Press.

Wylie, R. C. (1989). *Measures of self-concept.* Lincoln: University of Nebraska Press.

Yalom, I. (1985). *The theory and practice of group psychotherapy* (2nd ed.). New York: Basic Books.

Yorke, M. (1989). The intolerable wrestle: Words, numbers, and meanings. *International Journal of Personal Construct Psychology, 2,* 65–76.

Zigler, E., & Glick, M. (1988). Is paranoid schizophrenia really camouflaged depression? *American Psychologist, 43,* 284–290.

Zimmer, J. M., & Cowles, K. H. (1972). Content analysis using FORTRAN: Applied to interviews conducted by C. Rogers, F. Perls, and A. Ellis. *Journal of Counseling Psychology, 19,* 161–166.

Ziskin, J., & Faust, D. (1991). Reply to Matarazzo. *American Psychologist, 46,* 881–882.

Zuckerman, M., Koestner, R., DeBoy, Garcia, T., Maresca, B. C., & Sartoris, J. M. (1988). To predict some of the people some of the time: A reexamination of the moderator variable approach in personality theory. *Journal of Personality and Social Psychology, 54,* 1006–1019.

Zurawski, R. M., & Smith, T. W. (1987). Assessing irrational beliefs and emotional distress: Evidence and implications of limited discriminant validity. *Journal of Counseling Psychology, 34,* 224–227.

AUTHOR INDEX

Abelson, J. L., 63
Abler, R. M., 50
Abrahams, N. M., 54
Adams, K. M., 167
Agras, S., 63
Aiken, L. R., 15
Aiken, L. S., 21
Ajzen, I., 141
Allegante, J. D., 194
Alexander, A. F. O'D., 26, 27
Algina, J., 144
Alibrio, J. J., 81
Alker, H. A., 136
Allen, A., 107, 110
Allport, G. W., 29, 36, 78, 81, 148, 163
American Psychiatric Association, 118
American Psychological Association, 42, 114, 130
Anastasi, A., 39, 97, 115, 136

Anderson, M. W., 80
Anderson, R. V., 166
Andreassi, J. L., 66
Angelo, T. A., 210, 211
Angleitner, A., 134, 155
Anglin, M. D., 53
Anisman, H., 126
Anthony, W. Z., 167
Appley, M. H., 258
Arisohn, B., 205
Aronson, E., 267
Ashbrook, P. W., 195
Ashby, F. G., 149
Asher, J. J., 163
Atkinson, L., 106
Atkinson, R. C., 256
Atwater, D. C., 54
Austin, J. T., 138

Babor, T. F., 18, 22, 42, 44, 63, 194

Baer, R., 52
Baer, R. A., 51
Baerends, G. P., 212
Bagby, R. M., 52, 106
Bailey, B., 50
Bailey, J. M., 196
Baker, T. A., 77
Baker, T. B., 155
Bales, J., 108
Balzer, W. K., 157
Bandler, R., 207
Bandura, A., 100, 106, 108, 165, 190
Barlow, D. H., 2, 53, 63, 64, 67, 125, 181, 212
Barrett, T. C., 95
Baxter, G. P., 164
Beaber, R. J., 52
Beail, N., 159
Beatty, J., 208
Beck, A. T., 18
Bell, W., 167

SUBJECT INDEX

ISBN 0-12-488440-7

90065